THE DNA OF CONSTITUTIONAL JUSTICE IN LATIN AMERICA

In recent times there has been a dramatic change in the nature and scope of constitutional justice systems in the Global South. New or reformed constitutions have proliferated, protecting social, economic, and political rights. While constitutional courts in Latin America have traditionally had limited power and have mostly acted to preserve the status quo, they are now evolving into a functioning part of contemporary politics and a central component of a dynamic system of constitutional justice. This book lays bare the political roots of this transformation, outlining a new way to understand judicial design and the very purpose of constitutional justice. Authors Daniel M. Brinks and Abby Blass use both case studies and quantitative data drawn from nineteen Latin American countries over forty years to reveal the ideas behind the new systems of constitutional justice. They show how constitutional designers entrust their hopes and fears to dynamic constitutional governance systems, expecting to empower their successors to direct the development of constitutional meaning over time.

Daniel M. Brinks is Associate Professor in the Government Department and Law School at the University of Texas at Austin. He is also a senior researcher with the Christian Michelsen Institute.

Abby Blass is a PhD candidate in Government at the University of Texas at Austin.

D1564362

COMPARATIVE CONSTITUTIONAL LAW AND POLICY

Series Editors
Tom Ginsburg
University of Chicago

Zachary Elkins
University of Texas at Austin

Ran Hirschl
University of Toronto

Comparative constitutional law is an intellectually vibrant field that encompasses an increasingly broad array of approaches and methodologies. This series collects analytically innovative and empirically grounded work from scholars of comparative constitutionalism across academic disciplines. Books in the series include theoretically informed studies of single constitutional jurisdictions, comparative studies of constitutional law and institutions, and edited collections of original essays that respond to challenging theoretical and empirical questions in the field.

Books in the Series

The DNA of Constitutional Justice in Latin America: Politics, Governance, and Judicial Design Daniel M. Brinks and Abby Blass

The Adventures of the Constituent Power: Beyond Revolutions? Andrew Arato

Constitutions, Religion and Politics in Asia: Indonesia, Malaysia and Sri Lanka Dian A. H. Shah

Canada in the World: Comparative Perspectives on the Canadian Constitution edited by Richard Albert and David R. Cameron

Courts and Democracies in Asia Po Jen Yap

Proportionality: New Frontiers, New Challenges edited by Vicki C. Jackson and Mark Tushnet

Constituents Before Assembly: Participation, Deliberation, and Representation in the Crafting of New Constitutions Todd A. Eisenstadt, A. Carl LeVan, and Tofigh Maboudi

Assessing Constitutional Performance edited by Tom Ginsburg and Aziz Huq

Buddhism, Politics and the Limits of Law: The Pyrrhic Constitutionalism of Sri Lanka Benjamin Schonthal

Engaging with Social Rights: Procedure, Participation and Democracy in South Africa's Second Wave Brian Ray

Constitutional Courts as Mediators: Armed Conflict, Civil–Military Relations, and the Rule of Law in Latin America Julio Ríos-Figueroa

Perils of Judicial Self-Government in Transitional Societies David Kosař

Making We the People: Democratic Constitutional Founding in Postwar Japan and South Korea Chaihark Hahm and Sung Ho Kim

The DNA of Constitutional Justice in Latin America

POLITICS, GOVERNANCE, AND JUDICIAL DESIGN

DANIEL M. BRINKS

University of Texas at Austin

ABBY BLASS

University of Texas at Austin

CAMBRIDGE
UNIVERSITY PRESS

CAMBRIDGE
UNIVERSITY PRESS

University Printing House, Cambridge CB2 8BS, United Kingdom

One Liberty Plaza, 20th Floor, New York, NY 10006, USA

477 Williamstown Road, Port Melbourne, VIC 3207, Australia

314-321, 3rd Floor, Plot 3, Splendor Forum, Jasola District Centre, New Delhi - 110025, India

79 Anson Road, #06-04/06, Singapore 079906

Cambridge University Press is part of the University of Cambridge.

It furthers the University's mission by disseminating knowledge in the pursuit of
education, learning and research at the highest international levels of excellence.

www.cambridge.org
Information on this title: www.cambridge.org/9781316630914
DOI: 10.1017/9781316823538

© Daniel M. Brinks and Abby Blass 2018

First published 2018
First paperback edition 2019

A catalogue record for this publication is available from the British Library

Library of Congress Cataloging in Publication data
NAMES: Brinks, Daniel M., 1961- author. | Blass, Abby, author.
TITLE: The DNA of constitutional justice in Latin America : politics,
    governance, and judicial design / Daniel M. Brinks, Abby Blass.
DESCRIPTION: Cambridge [UK] ; New York, NY : Cambridge University Press,
    2018. | Series: Comparative constitutional law and policy | Includes
    bibliographical references and index.
IDENTIFIERS: LCCN 2017059344 | ISBN 9781107178366 (hardback)
SUBJECTS: LCSH: Constitutional courts—Latin America. | Constitutional
    law—Latin America. | Political questions and judicial power—Latin
    America. | Judicial process—Latin America. | Justice, Administration
    of—Latin America.
CLASSIFICATION: LCC KG501 .B75 2018 | DDC 342.8—dc23 LC record
    available at https://lccn.loc.gov/2017059344

ISBN 978-1-107-17836-6 Hardback
ISBN 978-1-316-63091-4 Paperback

Contents

Figures

Tables

Acknowledgments

This project started many years ago, as an article-length project on the apparent diffusion of new models of courts throughout Latin America. A paper Dan Brinks was writing for the annual meeting of the American Political Science Association dovetailed with a paper Abby Blass was writing for a graduate seminar, and the project evolved through conversations between the two authors after that. Both Abby and Dan had other projects to attend to, so the collaboration moved slowly, but they both felt it was intellectually productive. In the early stages in particular, each of the authors contributed important elements and carried out a mutual back and forth that makes it difficult to separate each author's contributions to the initial conceptualization and measurement exercises. Similarly, the book's basic argument evolved out of conversations between the authors, with each pushing the other to clarify and specify the argument further. We collaborated fully while conceiving and writing the pieces we called "Conceptualization" (now an article in the *International Journal of Constitutional Law*, and largely contained in Chapter 2 and the Appendix) and "Determinants" (the theory and quantitative analysis that underpins Chapters 3 and 4). These two papers contain the core intellectual contribution of the book, and our joint work on these two pieces is the principal, though not the only, reason Abby is credited as a coauthor.

As the concept for the book-length project coalesced, however, it became clear that Abby would have to devote herself to writing her dissertation and that Dan was better suited to handling much of the remaining empirical work that needed to be done. As a result, Dan carried out the fieldwork and additional research for Chapters 5–7, traveling to Guatemala, Argentina, and Bolivia on multiple occasions and talking to people across the region. When it came time to craft the final manuscript, Dan also took the lead, writing the introductory chapter, integrating the papers on conceptualization and determinants into the first three chapters and working out the concluding chapter. All the chapters, however, benefited greatly from conversations between the two coauthors at different times, and from Abby's input and reactions to the manuscript.

We are grateful to the *International Journal of Constitutional Law* for allowing us to incorporate portions of our article into this manuscript (found at: Brinks, Daniel M. and Blass, Abby. 2017. "Rethinking Judicial Empowerment: The new Foundations of Constitutional Justice." *International Journal of Constitutional Law* 15 (2):296–331).

Given the lengthy history of the project, we are deeply indebted to many people – too numerous to mention individually – who provided substantive feedback in the course of presentations before faculty and students at Emory University; the University of Pittsburgh; the New York University Law School's Colloquium on Law, Economics, and Politics; the University of North Carolina at Chapel Hill; the University of Michigan's Weiser Center for Emerging Democracies; Harvard's Weatherhead Center for International Affairs; Harvard Law School's Institute for Global Law and Policy; the Chilean and the Uruguayan Political Science Associations; Northwestern University's Equality, Development, and Globalization Studies program; the Centre for Law and Social Transformation at the Christian Michelsen Institute and the University of Bergen; the Center for Latin American and Caribbean Studies in the Watson Institute for Public and International Affairs of Brown University; Columbia University; Universidad de los Andes in Bogotá, Colombia; Universidad de Palermo in Buenos Aires; Universidad Diego Portales in Santiago, Chile; Georgetown University; and multiple presentations at annual meetings of the American Political Science Association, the Latin American Studies Association, and the Law and Society Association.

Special thanks are due to Paola Bergallo for doing so much to facilitate Dan's fieldwork in Argentina. Special thanks also to our colleagues at the University of Texas at Austin – Henry Dietz, Zachary Elkins, Kenneth Greene, Wendy Hunter, Raúl Madrid, and Kurt Weyland – for providing extensive and opportune feedback on both conceptualization and determinants. Diana Kapiszewski and Matthew Ingram both also provided extensive comments specifically on the conceptualization and measurement elements of this book. Karina Carpintero, Vicky de Negri, Holly Heinrich, Nathalia Sandoval and Kyle Shen all provided excellent research assistance.

Dan would like to thank his family – Sandra, Derek, Aaron, and Liam – for putting up with the extended absences, and to acknowledge what a pleasure it was to work with Abby on all aspects of this project. Abby would like to thank her family: Timothy, for his wisdom and companionship, and Adeline and Alden, for the delight and joy they bring to each day. She also wishes to thank Dan, an unusually thoughtful and generous mentor, for his guidance and support throughout this project. His ability to cut to the heart of an argument and his endless willingness to debate concepts and methods are parts of what make him an exceptional teacher and colleague, and it has been a privilege to share in the journey of bringing this project to life.

1

Constitutional Justice in the Americas
at the Turn of the Millennium

At the end of the twentieth and the beginning of the twenty-first century, constitutions and constitutional courts have become much more central to the politics of the Global South, in some instances transforming the very nature and practice of democracy. A scant few of the constitutional justice systems in the Global South have followed a classical Anglo-European model, in which they guarantee the basic framework for political competition and public decision-making and protect a limited set of negative rights. Many more systems of constitutional justice in the Global South, however, have been designed to play much more expansive roles, for good or ill. Some have the potential to become hotly contested spaces within which to pursue competing visions of the basic purposes of the state and the common good. Groups disadvantaged in ordinary politics can use these systems as an alternative political space in which to protect their basic interests and secure affirmative goals, such as the expansion of public health care or access to education, protection of the environment, and the like. Still other systems are designed to be powerful tools that the Ruling Coalition – the set of actors who are empowered to make binding decisions in ordinary politics, and who are typically the product of the most recent elections – can use to dismantle the existing normative order and build a new one. These systems can serve to quash dissent more than to incorporate it. The role of constitutional justice has fundamentally changed in most countries of the Global South over the last several decades.

It is not just that the context has changed; the increasing centrality of constitutional rights and constitutional courts in politics is based in part on the considerable expansion, over the last forty or fifty years, of the constitutional provisions that define the sphere of constitutional justice. A cursory review of the texts reveals the extent to which constitution makers have added to the list of rights included in constitutions and made these rights available for judicial enforcement, thus expanding the subjects of constitutional concern. Moreover, they have created new constitutional courts and tinkered with existing high courts, often with the avowed goal of providing stronger judicial enforcement of rights in areas that used to be firmly considered the province of the legislature or the market. Housing, education, health care, the environment, and social provision are only a few of the issues that have come under the aegis of constitutional courts in recent decades. Constitution writers appear to have consciously crafted these newly ambitious systems of constitutional justice,[1] transforming the relationship between the constitution and ordinary politics in the process.

We can trace the roles that various courts have adopted back to their constitutional DNA. Thus, for example, the Venezuelan 1999 Constitution carries in it the seeds of its constitutional court's complicity with the ruling party in dismantling the existing normative framework and suppressing the opposition. Colombia's 1991 constitution sets the foundation for that Constitutional Court's pervasive influence on the politics of social provision. And Pinochet's constitution in Chile successfully crafted a court that was impervious to ordinary politics even after the transition to democracy, and was committed to protecting a conservative project.

This transformation of constitutional justice, ultimately setting the stage for the varied roles that constitutional courts have adopted, has run far ahead of scholars' attempts to grapple with the phenomenon. Our existing conceptual and theoretical tools struggle to describe and compare, let alone explain and evaluate, these changes in global constitutionalism. The normative work on the new constitutionalism of the Global South, which ranges from questioning whether constitutions ought to concern themselves with the social and economic rights that have achieved such prominence, to celebration and hope that mechanisms are emerging for the effective enforcement of long-neglected rights and claims, is often based on unrealistic assumptions about how the system works. The empirical work, in turn, more often focuses on the causes and effects of greater judicial protagonism than on the constitutional texts that contain the DNA of the new constitutionalism of the Global South. We feel there has been insufficient attention to developing conceptual tools adequate to the systematic study of constitutional systems that appear designed to play such varied and important roles in a country's politics. Moreover, we feel that we need to better understand the politics behind the design of the various systems.

In this book, therefore, we turn to a foundational question that has not been fully explored to date. We offer a unifying political account of the origins of the different models of constitutional justice that have emerged in Latin America since the 1970s. We want to know why designers choose to construct different systems of constitutional justice. Some opt for autonomous models that have a relatively limited scope of authority; others craft more ambitious models that appear poised

---

[1]   We refer throughout to systems of constitutional justice – that is, the full package of structural and substantive provisions that define the constitutional court, its attributes, and the panoply of rights it can enforce – rather than to constitutional courts alone. A focus on one aspect or another of the system – say particular rights, or a particular court structure – misses the ways in which these various aspects are designed to work together to produce constitutional justice.

to reshape the politics of nearly every issue in a country, whether at the behest of a quasi-revolutionary Ruling Coalition, or in response to the push and pull of a more inclusive constitutional politics.

More specifically, we will show that the systems of constitutional justice in the region vary significantly in terms of their autonomy from the Ruling Coalition. Moreover, constitutional justice systems vary substantially in terms of the scope of their authority. Some are entrusted with full authority to decide some of the most crucial political questions of the day, on behalf of anyone who might apply, while others have a much more limited agenda, or are encumbered by provisions that sharply restrict applicants' access to the court, or are hamstrung by a lack of decisive capacity and authority. It is the combination of these dimensions – authority and autonomy – that determines the role of the constitutional justice system in the politics of a country. Our goal is to explain both why some systems have more autonomy than others, and why some systems seem to have constitutionalized vast swaths of policy that, in other systems, are matters for ordinary politics.

The project is empirical and focused on constitutional texts, but in the course of providing an account of the political origins of these new constitutional justice systems, we challenge some of the basic assumptions that underlie both normative and empirical explorations of the new constitutionalization of politics. In particular, we reconceptualize and unpack the notion of judicial independence, which we label autonomy. Moreover, we show how, at least in the imagination of constitutional designers, systems of constitutional justice are simultaneously political spaces and sites of contestation that follow a very distinct constitutional logic. As a consequence, courts are at once creatures of a country's contemporary politics and (potentially) distinct political actors within the political system.

The explanations that have been offered for why particular constitutions read the way they do vary considerably. Some scholars believe that countries draw from international sources in designing their constitutions. In this view, constitutions are produced largely through copying specific foreign (or previous domestic) models, or are written to express global ideological trends like liberalism or, more recently, neoliberalism. Others believe that constitutions reflect domestic ideological views, and find constitutions to be akin to party manifestos, or a relatively straightforward byproduct of increasing democratization. Still others have suggested that particular constitutional features, such as judicial review or the allocation of powers across the executive and legislature, respond to the power dynamics of the moment of design. We find ourselves mainly in this last camp, with some important differences driven by our acknowledgment that courts are doing much more than our theories have traditionally assumed, and that they are more influenced by contemporary politics than those same theories have assumed.

Our argument emphasizes the joint roles of ideology and the distribution of power in the constituent assembly, in producing constitutional justice systems with greater or lesser authority, and more or less autonomy, as we preview in the next section. The driving motivation for designers of systems of constitutional justice is to craft political spaces that will reflect their interests, serve their purposes, and secure a role for their successors in governing in the future. Which issues designers place in that space depends both on their ideological goals and on whether they expect that they will need constitutional help if they are to influence ordinary politics in the future. Similarly, designers will craft more pluralistic and inclusive mechanisms to govern the system of constitutional justice, to the extent they are themselves a more pluralistic and inclusive coalition. The international influences, in our view, are at best secondary, and cannot explain why particular countries choose the models they do, even though they provide a ready source of alternative models. Designers certainly look abroad, but they pick and choose among available options to suit their governance goals.

1.1. RECENT TRENDS IN THE DESIGN OF CONSTITUTIONAL JUSTICE SYSTEMS

In its system of constitutional justice, a country's foundational text often specifies the ends of government that are required, permissible, or forbidden, and establishes a framework within which to pursue those ends. Some – perhaps most – of the policy choices involved in governing are consigned to the sphere of ordinary politics. These choices are entrusted to the current Ruling Coalition with very little constitutional supervision or constraint. The decision to use a more or less progressive or regressive taxing system, or to raise the minimum wage, for instance, is understood as a matter for ordinary politics. Other choices are explicitly subjected to constitutional oversight and thus consigned to the sphere of constitutional politics – such as the procedures that must be followed before searching someone's home or imprisoning a criminal suspect. Abstract discussions of constitutionalism sometimes sound as if the distinctions between matters for constitutional justice and matters for ordinary politics are universally true for all constitutions. The traditional prescription, for instance, was that constitutions should always be short and focus on structures and procedures, not substantive rights. But different constitutions have more or less ambitious constitutional justice projects, and many constitutions of the Global South have, over the last half century, both opted for a more expansive sphere of constitutional justice and placed constitutional courts at the center of the framework for pursuing that justice.

A simple Venn diagram helps visualize the change in the constitutional texts of the region. As seen in Figure 1.1a,[2] we can depict three distinct sets of issues as subsets

---

[2]   Figure 1.1 is inspired by Larry Sager's (2004) similar depiction of the normative relationship between adjudicated justice (the inner circle), constitutional essentials (the middle circle), and the full scope of political justice (the outer circle). His point is that not all issues of political justice need to be the subject of constitutional concern and that not all subjects of constitutional concern need to be finally decided by a court. In our case, Figure 1.1 is not a normative argument, but simply a positivistic description of the ambition of different constitutional texts, and how much they purport to subject to constitutional adjudication.

(a)   (b)

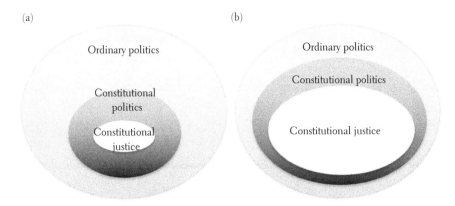

FIGURE 1.1. Constitutional justice in (a) classic and (b) new Global South constitutionalism

of each other: the possible ends of government as pursued in ordinary politics; the constitutionally favored ends of government, which are supported by constitutional arguments but lack judicial enforcement; and the sphere of constitutional justice, in which there is the potential for judicial intervention to protect constitutional principles. In ordinary politics, the Ruling Coalition can pursue all the possible ends of government that are neither required nor forbidden by the constitution, without much allusion to constitutional principles. But some ends are constitutionally favored, without being subject to enforcement in a system of constitutional justice. These constitutionally inflected issues are included in the middle sphere, the sphere of constitutional politics. The innermost sphere is reserved for those issues that are expressly placed under judicial supervision. The nested sets signal that issues do not disappear from ordinary politics simply because they have been constitutionalized. Rather, they are subject to multiple decision-makers and decision-making structures, as well as to the standards and principles of constitutional justice.

The conventional image is that at least until the second half of the last century, Latin America's constitutions, and perhaps those of most other countries of the Global South outside the Communist Bloc, followed a classic, liberal, separation of powers model, with a more negative-rights, procedural vision of constitutional justice, as depicted in Figure 1.1a.

Meanwhile, the literature on the new constitutionalism of the Global South suggests that – on average, around the globe – countries are dramatically expanding the sphere of constitutional justice, to produce the high-justiciability, social rights-oriented, constitutionalism of the Global South represented in Figure 1.1b (Bonilla Maldonado 2013; Brinks et al. 2015).

But this linear narrative is only partially true, especially if the implication is that it simply responds to global trends. In the first place, the more historical analysis of our case studies shows that Latin America's early social constitutionalism was characterized by an expanded sphere of constitutional politics, while the sphere of constitutional justice was both severely restricted and undermined by the lack of autonomy. So Latin America, at least, experimented with an intermediate model that boasted an expanded sphere of constitutional politics. The sphere of constitutional politics contracted, where it did, in response to the wave of coups and Right-wing dictatorships that swept the region in the middle of the last century. Secondly, although by the end of the last century and beginning of this one we do find a vastly expanded sphere of constitutional justice, there is still considerable variation in the scope of constitutional justice across countries. Just as importantly, this variation in the scope of constitutional justice is coupled with varying degrees of autonomy. Finally, we can show that these models are not simply the product of a global fashion, but rather can be traced back to power dynamics and particular political projects at constitutional moments.

At least as early as 1917, the Mexican Constitution inaugurated a concern for social constitutionalism that sought to expand the sphere of constitutional politics beyond civil and political rights to include economic and social rights, such as labor rights and the right to land. Many of the region's constitutions followed its lead, as Gargarella (2013) has chronicled. But most of these experiments in social constitutionalism ended quickly, often in brutal military regimes, and by the 1970s the original experiments had been replaced by more restrictive documents. The last four or five decades, therefore, truly do mark an expansion of the constitutional ends of government. If we measure by what is in the text, many countries of the Global South have settled on a much more inclusive set of constitutionally favored ends than they had before – and certainly more so than most constitutions in the Global North (see, e.g., Brinks and Forbath 2011, 2014; Bilchitz 2013; Brinks et al. 2015). The 1988 Brazilian Constitution, for example, was initially much criticized for its excessive regulation of ordinary politics, and subsequent constitutions have not become shorter or less detailed.

More to the point for our project, in the last four decades or so, many constitutions have also expanded the sphere of constitutional justice. They have explicitly subjected more of those constitutionally favored ends to oversight by constitutional courts (and by other institutions that are not the subject of this book, including ombuds organizations and prosecutors with ample constitutional agendas),[3] turning them justiciable to one degree or another. If there is one thing that is truly new about the new constitutionalism of the Global South it is this concern with the institutional framework for making claims under the new, more robust bills of rights. In other words, not only are we more likely now to find constitutions that establish a larger sphere of constitutional politics, but

---

[3]   Political scientists noticed these new mechanisms of horizontal accountability long before they began paying attention to courts (Mainwaring and Welna 2003; O'Donnell 2003).

we are also more likely to find constitutions that expand the sphere of constitutional justice (see, e.g., Brinks et al. 2015).

As the concentric circles suggest, expanding the spheres of constitutional concern implies layering a new set of constraints on an increasingly large subset of our politics.[4] The effect is not so much to remove the issues from politics but to – at most – narrow the range of possible policy choices and outcomes that are available to the Ruling Coalition by subjecting them to constitutional arguments and procedures. In the middle sphere, constitution-makers are presumably counting on the persuasive and mobilization effects of declaring constitutional goals, but ultimately entrusting the Ruling Coalition to pursue these ends. This was, by and large, the strategy followed by Latin America's original social constitutionalism. Mexico 1917, Argentina 1949, Bolivia 1938, and Guatemala 1956[5] all pursue social constitutionalism, but do not significantly empower the judiciary to enforce all constitutional ends. The doctrine of the social function of property, for instance, which is an important component of this social constitutionalism, was understood to empower the Ruling Coalition, not the courts, to redistribute land. Indeed, opponents feared that it shrank the sphere of constitutional justice, weakening the ability of courts to protect property rights.

By the 1980s and 1990s, however, Latin American designers were no longer willing to entrust the Ruling Coalition with these goals. They were all too aware of the critique that mere words on paper were insufficient to motivate the Ruling Coalition, and they focused on strengthening the mechanisms that might turn parchment into action. They turned, therefore, to expanding the sphere of constitutional justice: constitutional courts and other legal actors became important players in the long-term governance of the issues included in the innermost circle. Our evidence shows, moreover, that neither were Latin American constitution makers prepared to trust in a mechanistic model of adjudication, in which it is sufficient to write down the goals and trust to the discipline of law to keep judges to those goals. They paid close attention to the mechanisms that tie these systems of constitutional justice to their political context, and our theories should do the same if our goal is to present a realistic and empirically sustainable account of the political calculations that lead to the creation of these more ambitious systems of constitutional justice, in all their variety.

---

[4] Gauri and Brinks (2008: 4), for example, define the "legalization of politics" as "the extent to which courts and lawyers . . . become relevant actors, and the language and categories of law and rights become relevant concepts, in the design and implementation of public policy." They go on to say (p. 5), "courts more often add a relevant actor and relevant considerations than seize decision making power from other actors."

[5] For convenience, we use *countryname year* to identify constitutional texts and amendments – thus, Mexico 1917 is Mexico's 1917 Constitution, and Argentina 1994 is Argentina's 1853 Constitution as modified by the 1994 amendments.

1.2. CONSTITUTIONAL GOVERNANCE THEORY IN A NUTSHELL

Why, then, did these apparently new models emerge now? Although there are recognizable trends, the new constitutions are not converging as much as this narrative might suggest. It seems clear, therefore, that constitution-makers were often trying to accomplish very disparate ends with their new systems of constitutional justice. Critics of expanded constitutionalism tend to assume that drafters were uniformly surrendering flexibility in governing to unaccountable judges, withdrawing these issues from politics to put them in an apolitical legal realm. Others have argued that they were, in a relatively unsophisticated, or at least apolitical, way merely following global fads or technocratic prescriptions, whether neoliberal or social-democratic. Even the very brief overview we have given so far of the region's constitutional history, however, suggests that this process was the result of a great deal of struggle between the Left and the Right, motivated by competing ideologies and based on different economic theories.

Our argument, therefore, focuses on the ways in which the politics of the constitutional moment – whether in writing a new constitution or amending an existing one – bring these ideologies into constitutional texts. Using qualitative and quantitative data, we show that constitutional designers did not imagine that they would succeed in locking issues away from politics, in an apolitical sphere ruled by lawyers and judges, disciplined by principles and juridical logic alone. Instead, they sought to build dynamic systems of constitutional governance that would evolve the full meaning and concrete implications of the principles they were laying down, in response to more or less broad coalitions of actors who would have influence in the sphere of constitutional justice. This coalition – the set of actors whose consent is required to exercise control over the system of constitutional justice – is what we call the Constitutional Governance Coalition.

Our argument has several distinct components. First, we argue that designers understand constitutional justice to respond, in very consequential ways, to contemporary politics, rather than exclusively to the founding moment or the foundational text. They understand, for the most part, the indeterminate and evolving nature of constitutional meaning. As a result, designers are not designing systems that are meant to mechanically enforce a set of commitments cast in stone at the constitutional moment. They are, rather, designing systems that they understand will actively govern the sphere of constitutional justice into the future. They build in levers of control, through mechanisms of appointment and removal, through term limits and reappointment clauses, through standing provisions and decision rules. Their goal, whether they ultimately succeed or not, is to extend their influence into the future by giving their successors in interest a role in controlling the system of constitutional justice long after the constituent moment is past.

For this reason, the power relations and ideological struggles of the founding moment translate directly into power relations in the post-constituent sphere of constitutional justice. Different systems empower very different coalitions of control. Sometimes – when the expected Ruling Coalition dominates the constitution-making process – the Constitutional Governance Coalition is indistinct from the Ruling Coalition, and the courts are set up primarily to advance and legitimize the interests of the government. At other times – when the expected Ruling Coalition is a relatively minor partner in the design process – the system responds to a broadly inclusive or minoritarian oppositional coalition of control, and is established mostly to check the Ruling Coalition, should it seek to shift from the status quo on matters subject to constitutional justice. The system of constitutional justice is not unaccountable; it is simply accountable to a coalition that is conceptually (if not always empirically) distinct from the Ruling Coalition.

Second, we argue that constitutional designers are primarily interested in governing to advance their political goals, unconstrained and through ordinary politics whenever possible, and through constitutional justice otherwise. We often imagine that constitutions are somewhat like manifestos, an opportunity to declare all those things that are most important to the designers or that are on some international list of "must-have" provisions. But if we are right thus far, then constitutional justice defines those issues on which the Ruling Coalition must share governance with a Constitutional Governance Coalition. And, for that reason, we should expect a self-confident Ruling Coalition to be reluctant to put everything that it most highly values into that sphere. Indeed, what we find, despite the length of many recent constitutions, is that designers, by and large, put into the sphere of constitutional justice only those issues that cannot be entrusted to the Ruling Coalition because of the country's recent history and expected post-constituent politics. As a result, when the expected Ruling Coalition dominates the design coalition, it exposes less of its agenda to the scrutiny of the future Constitutional Governance Coalition, retaining more of it for ordinary politics and its own unconstrained choices and strategies – the innermost sphere shrinks, even if the middle sphere might remain quite expansive.

Concretely, this means designers will place into the spheres of constitutional justice not necessarily those elements of their political agenda on which there is full consensus, but rather those issues that they feel they cannot entrust to the sole authority of the Ruling Coalition. A strong Left party, for example, can pursue a more statist agenda without resorting to constitutional justice. But a weak Left party that finds leverage in the constitutional moment can put most of its agenda into the constitution in order to pursue it later through the less majoritarian mechanisms of the constitutional justice system. A less statist Right party, on the other hand, does not have much to constitutionalize beyond property and personal autonomy rights, so it may not seek to expand the sphere of constitutional justice, regardless of its leverage at the constitutional moment.

Constitutions, at least insofar as their systems of constitutional justice are concerned, then, should be read not as manifestos, but rather as lists of the hopes and fears of designers that cannot be entrusted to the hazards of ordinary politics.

It is undoubtedly true that constitutions express values (Galligan and Versteeg 2013: 8–18), but designers are far more likely to include those values and to translate them into structures that affect power if they feel they are threatened. We do not completely disagree that constitutions can be read as mission statements (King 2013a), but, from our reading of the evidence, the key provisions of constitutional justice are not so much statements of what the government is going to do or not do, as they are statements of what the government will most likely need extra prodding, supervision, or help to do or not do. Broad and bold declarations in preambles may contribute to the scope of constitutional politics, but the sphere of constitutional justice reflects the threatened and uncertain goals of the constituents, not (necessarily) their most basic principles. The growth in constitutional justice issues, then, is primarily attributable to the increasing pluralism of the design coalitions, and not to global fashions.

The combination of these design choices – more or less supermajoritarian coalitions of constitutional governance that contribute to the autonomy of the system, and more or less expansive spheres of constitutional justice that contribute to the scope of its authority – configures the new systems of constitutional justice that have emerged in Latin America and elsewhere in the Global South. Perhaps most basically, our research shows that these choices are the result of relatively well-considered decisions in response to domestic political conditions. To account for the origins of the operational elements of the constitution, we cannot look to the logic of global fads, institutional inertia, blind faith in rights, or bombastic declarations of political identity. Those motivations tell us much less about the way constitutions are written than does the logic of self-interested pursuit of power in service of ideological goals and interest protection. It is this logic of constitutional governance that dominates the design of the new systems of constitutional justice emerging in the Global South.

Two recent books on Latin American constitutionalism cover similar empirical material, but are actually quite distinct. Negretto (2013) has explored in great detail the way that Latin American constitutions structure the space of ordinary politics. His theoretical approach is similar to ours, focusing on struggles over the distributive effects of constitutional arrangements, but the dependent variable is very different. He explores how decision-making is organized in the largest of the three circles and why countries differ in this regard, while we look at the innermost circle. Gargarella (2013), meanwhile, explores the different conceptions of constitutionally favored ends that are present in Latin American constitutionalism, and how the middle circle has been expanding. His focus is on the ideas that construct both the middle and inner circles, but the "engine room" provisions he addresses – primarily those provisions that define the balance of power between executives and legislatures – remain mostly in the realm of ordinary politics. Our focus, on the other hand, is on how the politics of constitutional design structures the innermost circle – the sphere of constitutional justice – in the constitutions of Latin America since the mid-1970s.

While Gargarella finds, contra to Negretto (2013), that designers have neglected the engine room of ordinary politics, our analysis shows they put a great deal of care into the engine room of systems of constitutional justice.

We build on earlier work on the appearance of judicial review in constitutions around the world (Ginsburg 2003; Hirschl 2004; Ginsburg and Versteeg 2013) in several ways. First, our dependent variable – the system of constitutional justice – is more detailed and systematic, paying attention to the specifics of the mechanisms of control, as well as to the substantive content of constitutional justice (cf. Pozas-Loyo and Rios-Figueroa 2010). We cover more countries than the more detailed, qualitative explorations (see, e.g., Ginsburg 2003; Hirschl 2004), and we explore variation that goes well beyond dichotomous measures of the appearance of judicial review (e.g., Ginsburg and Versteeg 2013). By paying more attention to exactly how the systems of constitutional justice are structured, and reconceptualizing judicial power, we can present a more detailed and realistic description of the variation that we seek to explain.

Second, our theoretical argument incorporates and explains both of these dimensions, rather than working along a single dimension of either more authority or more autonomy. Our theory is decidedly realist and strategic: it takes seriously legal realist critiques of law and strategic accounts of how courts and constitutional interpretation are influenced by contemporaneous politics. The theory also assumes rational and self-interested actors who pursue twin goals – the exercise of power and ideological ends – strategically, although it does not require prescience or great sophistication on the part of constitutional designers. Our key theoretical premises – that designers want to constitutionally protect the values and interests they find threatened by ordinary politics, and that they will want some say in structuring and governing the institution that will protect these interests and values – are well within the grasp of any constitutional assembly member. While we do not believe this is the only logic at play, as we will make clear later on, we do believe this strategic, realist approach can give us the most insight into the configuration of the new systems of constitutional justice in Latin America, and possibly the Global South more generally. We take to heart Galligan and Versteeg's (2013: 22) observation that "the potential of strategic realism is unrealized because of an absence of empirical research deploying that perspective and identifying the causal connections between power plays by elites and the content of constitutions," and seek to partly remedy it here.

1.3. CONSTITUTIONAL FERMENT IN 19 LATIN AMERICAN COUNTRIES, 1975–2009

The empirical focus of the book is on the systems of constitutional justice that have emerged in Latin America from 1975 to 2009, although we will use our case studies to trace the constitutional arrangements in those countries all the way back to independence. We do so to provide historical context and to show that the same logic of governance seems to animate constitutional design over the long run. We track 19 countries in Latin America and the Caribbean, not including Cuba or the non-Iberoamerican countries.[6] For much of the analysis we use an original multidimensional measure of judicial autonomy and authority to score all constitutional events (all new constitutions and all constitutional amendments) in Latin America from 1975 to 2009.[7] We test our constitutional governance theory on Latin American courts in this period for methodological and substantive reasons. There is considerable institutional variation on all these dimensions in the courts of the region during the period, and it captures crucial political and legal changes that are representative of such movements across the world. In the 1970s, nearly all of Latin America was under authoritarian rule. Since then, the region has become nearly uniformly democratic (Mainwaring et al. 2001). Moreover, the change to greater judicial relevance is widely acknowledged to have taken place over this same time period (Tate and Vallinder 1995a; Stone Sweet 1999; Shapiro and Stone Sweet 2002; Sieder et al. 2005; Hirschl 2008; Couso et al. 2010).

Finally, Latin America is one of the areas with the most active constitutional experimentation in the world (Elkins et al. 2009). During this period, on average the countries in our sample reformed their constitutions ten times, for a total of 188 amendment events, each of which could result in many changes to the constitution. All but five of the countries adopted new constitutions and seven of them adopted more than one new constitution in these thirty-five years. Brazil and Mexico have amended their constitutions most often, twenty-eight and thirty times, respectively. Haiti has made no amendments, but has had three different constitutions in that period, as has Ecuador. Not all these changes affect judicial design, of course, but as we will see in the analysis below, these changes had a significant impact on the design of judicial institutions in the region. All this constitutional change produced 215 unique documents and, of those, seventy-five unique courts in our dataset (if we count only constitutional reforms that changed the court's score; a few reforms changed some court features without affecting the score).

Taking this period for analysis has several important methodological advantages. We can examine what happens to constitutional justice over the course of the entire third wave of democratization (Huntington 1991), evaluating an amazingly diverse range of constitutional models that were instituted within a relatively limited time period. In addition, we can compare authoritarian to a variety of transitional and post-transition institutions. Thus, this region and time period should capture the

---

[6] The countries are Argentina, Bolivia, Brazil, Chile, Colombia, Costa Rica, Dominican Republic, Ecuador, El Salvador, Guatemala, Haiti, Honduras, Mexico, Nicaragua, Panama, Paraguay, Peru, Uruguay, and Venezuela.

[7] To produce the quantitative scores on each system of justice, we employed research assistants to code the constitutional texts in their original language and then checked their coding ourselves against the text of the constitutions in question. The full dataset, reporting annual scores for all the courts in Latin America on all dimensions, is available online as both a Stata dataset and an Excel spreadsheet.

major changes in constitutional justice observable over the last few decades and permit us to test whether our multidimensional framework illuminates that variation and uncovers patterns that existing measures miss. While a longer time period might offer interesting comparisons to a less globalized time, by focusing primarily on a relatively shorter period we can carry out a closer examination of the fine morphology of courts and do more informed coding, as well as bring to bear more detailed knowledge of domestic political conditions.

Moreover, although a larger N helps with statistical analyses, we do not feel that a much longer time period would necessarily help in uncovering the intentions of designers in crafting constitutional courts. Our argument (and others) about the origins of judicial review is ultimately about what constitution makers want to accomplish with their courts and how to achieve it. It is unrealistic to expect nineteenth-century designers to think about courts and their behavior in exactly the same way as twentieth and twenty-first-century designers. In effect, we find that a similar logic influenced the design in our cases going all the way back to independence, but the repertoire of rights and mechanisms of control that were readily available at the time were different and more limited than today. It becomes increasingly difficult to make accurate comparative evaluations of the connections between power politics, ideology, and constitutional justice when one is comparing 2009 to 1789, Scandinavia to Honduras, even when designers are facing the same problem and using a similar logic.

Limiting the cases to Latin America over the last four decades thus allows us to test for differences within what is likely to be a relatively homogeneous set of constitutional texts, sharing a constitutional tradition and many of the same thinkers, with a consistent coding of similar features. At the same time, we do feel that the general logic of constitutional governance we lay out here is likely to be applicable to the developing world in modern times, and perhaps more broadly in the developed world as well. We develop this last point anecdotally, by reference to various constitutions around the world. We hope others will take up the challenge to extend our analysis to other regions and periods of history.

We supplement the quantitative comparative regional analysis by looking in more detail at three cases that exemplify the new constitutional moments and models in the region. Guatemala 1985 is a Cold War document, drafted under the influence of neoliberal thought at the tail end of a civil conflict. The need to bring a violent insurgency to an end led a relatively diverse but Right-leaning design coalition to increase the scope of constitutional justice beyond what we might have expected from its ideology alone. In addition, the designers' distrust of the executive and the presence of minoritarian parties led them to craft a Constitutional Governance Coalition that largely excluded the executive, in favor of minoritarian interests and unelected civil society members.

Argentina 1994, the most important set of amendments to Argentina's nineteenth-century constitution, is a post-democratization document, crafted by a Center-Left design coalition that included key players from the semipermanent opposition in Argentine politics. It increases the scope of constitutional justice far beyond Argentina's historical pattern and locates control over the system in a coalition that depends on the cooperation of elected minoritarian interests. This case tells a quite straightforward story of a diverse and inclusive design coalition establishing a diverse and inclusive governance coalition for an ambitious constitutional justice system.

Finally, Bolivia 2009 is an example of the new constitutionalism of Latin America. It demonstrates that the same power politics patterns continue, despite claims of an entirely new approach to democracy. The Ruling Coalition, frustrated by supermajoritarian design rules in the Assembly, first took steps to exclude the opposition, using its dominance of the Assembly to draft an initial document that was very favorable to its interests. When it was forced to include the opposition in the approval process, the document was tempered, shaping a more inclusive constitutional justice system. In Bolivia, we again see the power dynamics of the constitutional moment conditioning the effects of ideology on the resulting system of constitutional justice. In this case our argument is supported by within-case variation, first showing the effects of a process dominated by the Ruling Coalition and then of a more inclusive setting on the same document.

Methodologically, then, we proceed from identifying broad patterns in observational, cross-sectional time series data using quantitative analyses, to qualitative analyses of single-country historical patterns, to more direct evidence of the intentions of the designers at a particular constitutional moment. What we are trying to do in this book is uncover something that is not directly observable: the primary motivations of the designers in crafting systems of constitutional justice. We begin with a quantitative analysis to see if the patterns in the data are consistent with the kinds of motivations we have proposed as the dominant logic of institutional design for systems of constitutional justice. We find that our observations are more consistent with the governance logic that we feel is a more apt description of what designers are trying to accomplish than with other accounts that have been proposed so far. But, of course, these are just correlations. Moreover, this analysis is dependent on the quantitative measures we have designed and collected, which might not be perfectly accurate across space and time.

Thus, in the qualitative chapters, we do two things to bolster the evidence for our argument. First, we use qualitative description to "score" each system on all three dimensions of our dependent variable – ex ante and ex post autonomy and scope of authority – and on the key independent variables. This exercise shows that the same basic patterns we find in the aggregate hold for individual instances of constitution-making, going all the way back to independence, so that our findings are not a pure artifact of the time period we have chosen for analysis. We can also confirm that the results are not artifacts of how we have scored our dependent variables or constructed our independent ones. Then, because our argument is about the motives and intentions of the designers themselves, we go deeply into the debates surrounding the three key constitutional moments we have chosen for in depth examination. In the key section of each case study chapter, we closely analyze the words of the constituents themselves to see if they acknowledge the motives we attribute to them. From the debates we extract the various logics that underlie the design choices, showing that designers justify their choices and demands in precisely the terms we have proposed underlie the governance logic of constitutional justice.

1.4. CONTRIBUTIONS

We believe our book makes three important contributions to the literature on comparative constitutionalism. The first is conceptual. We offer a multidimensional framework that is more suitable for describing and comparing the new systems of constitutional justice that are emerging. This framework depends in part on a reconceptualization of what we mean by judicial independence, one that examines more carefully the relationship between constitutional courts and different actors within the political systems in which they are embedded. It includes a consideration not only of the scope of the new system, but also of the mechanisms that tie it to its political context – ex ante mechanisms that allow a certain coalition of actors to control the ideology of justices, through judicial appointments for example; and ex post mechanisms that allow for accountability and course corrections through the removal of justices and the restructuring of courts and their jurisdiction.

The second principal contribution is empirical and descriptive, both quantitative and qualitative. We use our conceptual framework to produce a score on three dimensions (ex ante autonomy, ex post autonomy, and authority) for all the systems that have appeared in Latin America since 1975, when democracy was at its lowest point in the region, through the present, when the region is nearly fully democratic. We then describe and compare all the systems of the region in terms of these three dimensions. In addition, we use the same conceptual framework to qualitatively evaluate the changes that have taken place in several countries of the region. We offer in-depth case studies of Guatemala, Argentina, and Bolivia, but also briefly describe changes in numerous other countries as needed to advance our argument. We are not aware of any similarly comprehensive, systematic comparison of the systems of constitutional justice in Latin America, or any other region for that matter.

Our third contribution is theoretical. Many of the theories that explain the content of new constitutions ignore the domestic power politics of constitutional design – they expect designers to simply use the constitution to proclaim their key identifying principles, or to copy foreign models, or to follow the advice of experts without paying much attention to the implications of the new arrangements for distributional and power politics. More political-strategic theories for the origins of judicial review do not fully account for the myriad new functions that constitutional courts have assumed and do not fully take on board the implications of what we know about the influence of politics on courts after the founding moment. We offer an account of the creation of these new systems of constitutional justice that can explain their appearance in countries with a variety of different power structures, that relies on a more realistic vision of how courts and law operate, and that specifies with more care the ways in which the new courts will be tied into post-constituent politics.

We propose and defend what we call the constitutional governance model of judicial empowerment. Our evidence shows that Originating Coalitions, in designing constitutions, seek to craft spheres of constitutional justice that will include those issues they feel will be threatened or ignored by the expected Ruling Coalition. The sphere, for that reason, shrinks regardless of ideology and past history when the constitution's designers are more monolithic and tied to the future Ruling Coalitions. In contrast, the sphere of constitutional justice expands as the Originating Coalition becomes more diverse and its members are individually less assured that they will be able to pursue their goals and protect their interests unconstrained. This is especially true if the members of the Originating Coalition have a more state-oriented agenda, as the Left typically does.

Moreover, we will show that designers do not entrust this agenda to unaccountable courts, with a legalistic, formalistic trust in the power of law as a discipline to tie constitutional meaning to their original goals. Contrary to Alter's (2008) suggestion, designers are not limited to the choice between crafting pure agents of the government or handing off power to "trustee" institutions. Rather, they take some care to craft, insofar as they can, an institutional framework for what we call a Constitutional Governance Coalition – the set of actors whose approval is needed to exercise the mechanisms that select, discipline, and shape judges, courts, and constitutional justice. That Constitutional Governance Coalition will exercise more or less indirect influence over the principal mechanism for evolving constitutional meaning in accordance with their goals – the constitutional court. In this model, the court is indeed an agent, but of the Constitutional Governance Coalition rather than the Ruling Coalition.

In short, we answer a series of questions that are fundamental to understanding the emerging constitutionalism of the Global South, taking Latin America as the primary empirical referent. We identify the political origins and characteristics of the new constitutional justice models that arise in Latin America over the last four decades. Specifically, we show that constituent assemblies dominated by hegemonic parties of the Right and the Left lead to systems of constitutional justice that are limited in scope and are closely tied to the Ruling Coalition. More pluralistic but Right-leaning coalitions design systems that are more autonomous but are limited to a narrow set of negative rights and market protections. When the Left is strong within a pluralistic coalition, on the other hand, we find systems with considerable autonomy that promote a more comprehensive vision of social welfare. Pluralistic design coalitions lead to systems that provide a platform for a dynamic and pluralistic politics of constitutional meaning; they create a more contestatory, participatory space for constitutional justice. Originating moments controlled by a single party tend to produce systems designed simply to advance and legitimize the dominant political project; these systems are primarily meant to transmit and enforce monolithic visions of constitutional justice.

1.5. LOOKING AHEAD

Chapter 2 explores the variation we seek to explain. We begin by presenting our reconceptualization of judicial authority and autonomy, and translate these concepts into measureable indicators of the institutional authority and autonomy of a system of constitutional justice. We then use these indicators to show the changes that have taken place in Latin America over the last forty years or so. The measure shows an increase in authority and a general increase in autonomy, but it also shows that some systems locate control more in the legislature, others in more in the executive, and still others in a more inclusive coalition that includes either legislative minorities or actors external to electoral politics. Finally, we compare what the measure tells us about the various systems of constitutional justice to what we know from accounts in the literature of their operation, as a measure of convergent validity. This chapter also includes a methodological discussion of how we approached the construction of our institutional index.

Chapter 3 presents our theory of the design of courts as mechanisms of constitutional governance. We first unify the literature on the origins of strongly empowered constitutional courts with the power of judicial review, exploring the single logic that underlies the credible commitment, hegemonic preservation, and insurance accounts. We call this the logic of constitutional governance, to recognize the fact that constitutional justice remains a means by which to govern, rather than simply a mechanism for constraining governance. We then expand the discussion of our constitutional governance theory, building on the contributions of earlier accounts and extending them to produce a more complete explanation for the full range of emerging systems of constitutional justice. From the general theory, we derive two principles of design that we believe should be at work if designers are guided by the logic of constitutional governance. The first principle is that the ideology of the Originating Coalition determines the scope of constitutional justice, *conditional* on how dominant the Ruling Coalition is within the Originating Coalition – that is, conditional on whether it is likely to believe it will be able to advance its goals in the realm of ordinary politics. The second is that the Constitutional Governance Coalition will reflect the composition of the Originating Coalition in an attempt to project the latter's influence into the post-constituent period. We also discuss possible alternative logics that might be at play in the process of design and drafting, and conclude by discussing some of the implications of this new theory of the origins of constitutional justice systems.

In Chapter 4, we derive concrete testable hypotheses that follow from the two principles of design presented in Chapter 3 and develop empirical models to test these hypotheses. We use regression analysis to evaluate patterns in the design of constitutional systems in Latin America since 1975 and test whether they are consistent with the logic of constitutional governance or with the alternative existing explanations we identify. Using a series of graphs, we demonstrate the impact that different configurations of power, ideologies, and political histories have on the resulting systems of constitutional justice. We find that the observed patterns in the data are largely consistent with the logic of constitutional governance, and hard to explain otherwise. We find some evidence that designers also pay some attention to global trends in deciding on the proper scope of constitutional justice, but not in regard to designing the mechanisms of control. We show evidence of learning from changing patterns in the apparent preferences of designers with similar ideological orientations. The chapter concludes with a discussion of illustrative cases and the implications of the analysis for how we think about constitutional justice.

The next three chapters turn to a qualitative in-depth analysis of the constitutional processes that led to new constitutions in Guatemala (1985), Argentina (1994), and Bolivia (2009). The cases are chosen for their variation on the main variables at issue. They have different power configurations, different ideologies, and different histories, and also took place in different decades. We use within- and across-case variation and causal process observations to show how the logic of constitutional governance was at work in each of the constituent assemblies, producing different outcomes on the various dimensions of their systems of constitutional justice. The analysis begins with a historical analysis of the evolution of the systems of constitutional justice in each case, and describes the configuration of power leading up to the constituent process and shaping the process itself. The core of each chapter is a close analysis of the debates among constituent assembly members regarding the nature and logic of constitutional governance, the constituents' goals, and what they intended to accomplish with the system of constitutional governance they were designing.

In the conclusion (Chapter 8), we return to the various broad themes that we identified in this introduction and in the conclusion to each of the chapters, outlining the lessons learned in the course of the analysis, and the questions that are left open for future research.

2

Judicial Power and the Design of Constitutional Justice

Many have noted the increasing visibility of courts in the political arena, and research on the "judicialization of politics" has grown as a consequence. But until now, we have struggled to find the proper conceptual tools to describe and compare the courts at the center of this phenomenon. In this chapter, therefore, we offer a set of conceptual tools to structure a brief history of the changes to the systems of constitutional justice that emerged in Latin America from 1975 to 2009. To give a full picture of the infrastructure for constitutional justice in these countries, we evaluate the full system of constitutional justice, that is, the complex of rights, mechanisms to enforce rights, and constitutional judicial structures in each country. As noted in Chapter 1, we distinguish this system, which defines the sphere of constitutional justice, from the sphere of constitutional politics, which is inflected with constitutional import but not subject to the scrutiny of a constitutional court, and from the sphere of ordinary politics, in which the Ruling Coalition (RC) has free rein to govern without substantive constitutional constraints. In essence, the sphere of constitutional justice is that subset of political (in)activity that is, at least in principle, subjected to the standards of constitutional rights and the scrutiny of a constitutional court. For reasons that will become apparent, a satisfying analysis of constitutional courts must consider the entire system of constitutional justice, and not just one of its dimensions.

Once we move away from a one-dimensional world in which the only variable of interest is "judicial independence," a series of politically relevant changes and choices springs into view. Drawing on concepts from principal-agent theory, we identify two primary dimensions of judicial empowerment: autonomy (essentially, the nature and identity of a court's control coalition) and authority (more specifically, the scope of a court's authority). A court with more autonomy and more authority is likely to be a more consequential court. As we will see, Latin America has evolved away from a single model in which constitutional justice is relatively marginal to the great political debates of the day toward three new models that vary depending on the ambition of the constitutional project and the inclusiveness of the Coalition of Constitutional Governance. While most systems have increased significantly in the scope of their authority, they vary quite substantially in the extent to which they incorporate – and thus may be willing to protect – a variety of interests. The four models represent simplified ideal types that usefully highlight broad differences in the nature and extent of a court and a constitution's likely political influence, thus defining the sphere of constitutional justice and the coalition that will govern within it.

2.1. UNDERSTANDING AND MEASURING JUDICIAL POWER

To describe the world well, we must begin with proper conceptualization and measurement. As a result, we first clarify some of the conceptual confusion, ultimately mirrored in extant empirical measures, around the notion of judicial power. There is near-consensus among scholars that courts globally are creating new political dynamics that cannot be ignored (Kapiszewski et al. 2013). Ever more powerful courts have begun to protect a broadening array of human rights (Gauri and Brinks 2008), promote political stability (Cross 2001), and contribute to social order and economic development (Weingast 2008). The labels used for judicial empowerment range from the relatively tame "judicialization of politics" (Tate and Vallinder 1995b) to the more alarming "juristocracy" (Hirschl 2004). We have theories of the origin of judicial review (Ginsburg 2003; Hirschl 2004), theories of the social bases of judicialization (Epp 1998; Gauri and Brinks 2008), theories of judicial behavior (Epstein and Knight 1998; Segal and Spaeth 2002), and theories of compliance (Carrubba 2009; Staton 2010). However, compared to the literature for the other two apex institutions – the presidency (see, e.g., Mainwaring and Shugart 1997; Cheibub 2007) and the legislature (a body of literature too vast to recount here) – the comparative, systematic institutional analysis of courts is scant. Add to this a dizzying array of definitions and measures for judicial power and judicial independence, and it is easy to understand Ginsburg's observation that today, despite a wealth of terminology and empirical examples, we do not yet have agreement on the concept or measurement of judicial power (Ginsburg 2003: 94), much less a settled notion of the relevant dimensions and measures with which to anchor a truly comparative analysis of judicial institutions worldwide (Ríos Figueroa and Staton 2014).

We believe the confusion in measurement largely responds to a misconception hidden in prevailing notions of "independence," however this term may be defined. It is banal to say that constitutional courts, like courts generally, but more so, are political institutions in the sense that they affect and are affected by politics. But definitions of independence and judicial power appear to try to deny this essential fact – they define independence as, essentially, the absence of politics, and power as the ability to produce results without relying on other (political) actors. As Dahl (1957: 279) noted long ago, we are "not quite willing to accept the fact that [the Court] *is* a political institution and not quite capable of denying it; so that frequently we take both positions at once." Taking seriously the nature of courts as political institutions means acknowledging that courts of all stripes rest on a socio-political coalition that is, in part, a function of their institutional design. Courts are never independent if by that we mean that they are fully insulated from their social and political context; and they are never powerful if by that we mean that they can produce results without the cooperation of outside social or political actors.

A court's sociopolitical coalition has elements of control and elements of mutual support. A court's coalition of control is the set of actors that can operate the mechanisms of appointment and removal that can recast the court's jurisdiction and attributes, and that can therefore in one way or another affect the identity, the incentives, and the authority of the judges who populate the institution. The court's support coalition is the group of social and political actors who can come to the court's defense in the event of an attack or lack of compliance. The court's design will influence who is willing to come to the court's defense. Those with access to the court, whose rights the court can and does protect, are more likely to do so. Some courts are more strategic than others in constructing that coalition of support, reaching out to different interests in the expectation that those interests will then come to the court's defense when needed (see, e.g., Moustafa 2003 for a description of how the court builds that coalition through its support of human rights NGOs and other groups in Egypt). Staton (2010), for example, describes how a court's decisions in this respect are fundamental to maintaining compliance.

The basic implication of this is that courts are more likely to be politically consequential if their sociopolitical coalition is not identical to the RC – the set of actors who make binding decisions in ordinary politics. From a purely institutional perspective, in order to function as consequential actors in a dynamic political environment, courts (or, more precisely, the judges who sit on them) must be capable of (1) developing and (2) expressing preferences that are substantially distinct (autonomous, in our parlance) from those of a single dominant outside actor. This outside actor is typically the RC or, in many countries, the executive. Moreover, (3) they must have a broad scope of authority, authorizing them to rule on claims regarding the most important issues of the day, on behalf of anyone affected by a public decision. Of these qualities, the first two are a function of judicial autonomy, while the third is quite distinctly about the capacity to intervene effectively in important disputes. Identifying and measuring a court's (institutional) autonomy and authority is a matter of specifying and measuring the ways in which a court's design tends to produce a sociopolitical coalition that is more inclusive than, or at least not identical to, the RC.

The more inclusive the control coalition, the less likely it is to be controlled by the RC; the more broad and inclusive a court's scope of authority, the more likely the court is to intervene on behalf of different actors and to have a support coalition that can impose costs on the RC. In sum, what scholars conventionally identify as "powerful," or "independent," or "impartial," or – our preferred term – "consequential" courts, are those courts that (a) respond to a Constitutional Governance Coalition that is not coterminous with the RC, and (b) are charged with resolving a broad range of disputes, on behalf of a wide range of actors, with the tools they need to act decisively and to broad effect, and actually do so, with the aid of a broad coalition of support.

It should be evident, then, that neither our measures of autonomy and power, nor our theory for the origin of consequential courts, must depend on law being fully separate from politics, or on constitutions that have clear, unambiguous meanings. Our argument – properly – does not depend on courts becoming apolitical guardians with the capacity on their own to prevent powerful actors from crossing clearly marked boundaries. At the same time, our theory does not, as some theories of judicial behavior do, assume there is no difference between the politics of constitutional meaning and ordinary politics. In fact, our view of courts accounts for the institutional bases of that difference, showing how the successors to the originating constitutional coalition might participate in governing the sphere of constitutional justice long after the founding moment is past and how those successors are sometimes practically identical to and sometimes quite distinct from the RC.

Clearly, the politics of the great conflicts that wracked Latin America around the middle of the last century exceeded what passes through the courtrooms and constituent assemblies of the region today. And yet by the end of that century, in many countries, most of those concerns had come to be inscribed in the language of constitutional justice. Redistribution, land reform, and property rights protection; the reach of the welfare state and social provision; public education and health care; indigenous autonomy and central state authority: all these issues can now be contested within the system of constitutional justice. Once we look beyond the courts' independence to also consider the set of rights and interests that have been placed in their care, we can begin to appreciate the role they may play in the politics of a country. Moreover, we believe it is possible to read, from the intersection of a court's formal autonomy and authority, the model of constitutional justice the drafters intended to develop. If realized in practice, these models have profound implications for the varieties of constitutional democracy that are emerging in the region. Opening up the analysis to more than just a single dimension allows us to see patterns that go to the very heart of the newly emerging constitutional and democratic models of Latin America, patterns that are flattened and obscured if we either disregard the new constitutional courts or limit their analysis to a single dimension.

2.2. DISAGGREGATING JUDICIAL POWER

If the more helpful "background concept" of judicial power is not independence but the combination of autonomy and authority, how do we move from this relatively abstract discussion to a "systematized concept" (Seawright and Collier 2014: 114)?

We present each dimension in more detail in the Methodological Appendix. Here we begin with the broad background concept that underlies each dimension, then outline the theory that guides our selection of the specific institutions that operationalize each concept.

2.2.1. *Autonomy*

The traditional variable to describe judiciaries, independence, has considerable affinity with what we call autonomy. But independence is very often limited to a judge's freedom to decide according to his or her own sense of what the law requires: "Judicial independence is a complex and contested concept, but at its core, it involves the ability and willingness of courts to decide cases in light of the law without undue regard to the views of other government actors" (Staton and Moore 2011: 559). That is, it is usually understood to mean a judge's ability to rule sincerely, without fear of undue punishment or hope of undue reward, though just exactly what constitutes "undue" regard is usually left undefined. This and similar definitions implicitly imagine judges as the classic "servants of the law" of the civil law world. Judges are expected to faithfully apply the law to any disputes that arise over time so long as they are protected from external pressures. At best, when law is seen as more indeterminate, judges must be protected from outside influences so they may simply "discover," in a Dworkinian sense, what the law "is," given the principles embedded in that original pact, and perhaps their own political morality (Dworkin 1986; Stone Sweet 1999).

If autonomy is, as Staton and Moore (2011: 559) put it, a court's capacity to carry out a "sincere evaluation of the legal questions presented to it, irrespective of external pressures," then institutional measures of "independence" should look for arrangements that insulate judges from external (political, economic, or social) pressures, so that they can decide purely according to the law. In this view, the empirical ideal-typical independent court is completely autarchic, and it depends for any normative appeal on at least two relatively implausible assumptions. First, this conception of independence assumes that law is an autonomous discipline that can be insulated from politics. And second, it assumes that law is either the source of mostly attractive principles that drive adjudication toward increasingly just outcomes in a Dworkinian model (Dworkin 1986, 1999), or at minimum, in a more originalist model, the depository of what were at one time democratically taken decisions, the specific meaning and application of which can be worked out in a fairly straightforward manner by a technocratic judge (see, e.g., Scalia and Garner 2012).

But judicial autonomy in the sense of complete isolation from external pressures is empirically nonexistent and, in a democracy, normatively suspect; and law as a purely autonomous discipline is just as unlikely. Indeed, we will argue, beginning in Chapter 3, that in the real world constitutional courts are the central components of a constitutional justice system that allows successors to a constitutional Originating

Coalition (OC) to continue participating in governance, through the mechanisms and tools of constitutional politics.[1] As we will see, OCs use judicial design to give the Coalition's successors an ongoing role, through the tools and principles of constitutional politics, in developing constitutional meaning around issues that are considered too important or too threatened to be left to ordinary postconstitutional politics. Courts, through mechanisms of appointment and retention, and a host of other mechanisms, depend on and are answerable to a control coalition that may be more or less distinct from the RC. The ideal-typical goal for autonomy as we understand it is not isolation, but responsiveness to a plural and inclusive control coalition that cannot easily be captured by a single outside interest or faction.

An approach that relies not on the absence of control, but on the absence of *unilateral* control, is consistent with classic views of judicial impartiality without depending on some extra-political standard of impartiality. As Holmes (2003: 50) notes, in real politics "the balance of many partialities is the closest we can come to impartiality." Similarly, Madison (Hamilton et al. 1961: 323–4), in Federalist 51, calls not for the creation of "an interest independent of the majority," but rather for a government that is responsive to "so many parts, interests and classes of citizens" that oppression of any one part by a tyrannical majority becomes unlikely. In the same way, courts subject to multiple overlapping influences are less likely to be biased in favor of (or against) any one partisan faction and less likely to fear punishment by any one faction. Eugenio Zaffaroni, one of the key participants in Argentina's 1994 Constituent Assembly, and later a Supreme Court Justice, made this point very clearly in debating mechanisms of judicial appointment: "You cannot secure impartiality by putting someone above what is human. If someone thinks he is above human frailty, more than a candidate for judge he is a candidate for therapy. In a democracy, impartiality is secured through a guarantee of institutional pluralism."[2] Our definition and measure of autonomy captures that notion of institutional pluralism and seeks to identify the degree of interest pluralism built into a system's DNA.

Importantly, this definition does not unrealistically require courts to be completely unmoored from their political and social surroundings, but still speaks to the normative ideal that courts exist to serve as neutral, impartial third parties to resolve disputes (Shapiro 1981; Stone Sweet 1999). The more judges are free from dependence on or control by any single individual, institution, or interest, the more likely they are to be impartial, especially in disputes involving that interest. This is, essentially, the goal that independence is typically expected to advance.

---

[1] The point can easily be extended to ordinary courts, but here we are concerned with constitutional courts, and limit our analysis to those courts with the power of judicial review, in their capacity as specifically constitutional courts.

[2] Statements made in the course of debates in the 1994 Argentine Constituent Assembly. Transcripts of Debates, Vol. 4, p. 3254 (copy on file with authors).

We split our autonomy variable into two subdimensions, each with deep theoretical roots. These two dimensions address the two basic concerns of principals who decide to empower an agent to whom they delegate power: ex ante controls seek to minimize the risk of adverse selection (i.e., the principal's desire to select a like-minded agent in order to reduce uncertainty over delegating discretionary authority), while ex post controls seek to address moral hazard, once the agent is appointed (i.e., by maintaining a means of influence over an agent in the event of substantial or sustained disagreement). Not by chance, the same two dimensions capture the two dominant strands in the classic judicial behavior literature: ex ante controls offer ways to select judges with particular political attitudes and preferences, in line with the expectations of the attitudinal model (cf. Dahl 1957; Graber 1993; Segal and Spaeth 2002), while ex post controls seek to induce strategic behavior on the part of judges, to reduce the agency costs of delegating power to courts (cf. Epstein and Knight 1998).

For both conceptual and theoretical reasons, it is important to distinguish ex ante from ex post mechanisms of control. Intuitively and normatively both seem important, and theoretically each works very differently. Perhaps most importantly, as a purely empirical matter, when control over appointments is concentrated, it tends to be concentrated in the executive. In contrast, when control over removals and the other features of courts is concentrated, it tends to be concentrated in the legislature. And the two measures do not covary, at least in our data. Clearly there is no reason, *a priori*, to believe designers will always prefer both or neither in equal measure. Moreover, existing theories of judicial behavior disagree on the extent to which each of these is effective. Defining and measuring them separately allows us to explore the divergent preferences of different designers and, eventually, to determine the consequences of choosing one over the other of these mechanisms of judicial control.

The literature abounds with references to each of these control mechanisms. As Whittington observes in connection with the US Supreme Court, "most routinely, the political appointments process creates regular opportunities for elected officials to bring the Court into line with political preferences" (Whittington 2005: 583). Rosenberg similarly notes, "the appointment process, of course, limits judicial independence ... Clearly, changing court personnel can bring court decisions into line with prevailing political opinion" (Rosenberg 1991). The more rationalist literature, on the other hand, emphasizes features of judicial design that expose judges once they are seated and regardless of their sincere preferences, to more or less pressure from political actors: "In the case of judicial selection and retention institutions, the greater the accountability established in the institution, the higher the opportunity costs for judges to act sincerely and thus the more extensive strategic behavior will be" (Epstein et al. 2002: 195, citations omitted). In the one case, the court is held close to the preferences of the dominant actor by the shared, sincere preferences of the agent; in the other, the court is held close by the threat of sanction or the promise of reward. Discriminating between institutions that affect the ideology of appointed judges versus their strategic response to constraints in their political environment will eventually allow us to test competing hypotheses about the factors that shape judicial behavior. Indeed, in a recent quantitative test, Melton and Ginsburg (2014) find that only a combination of ex ante and ex post protections has any influence on the resulting perception of judicial independence.

Formal autonomy, then, is the extent to which a court is designed to be free from control by an identifiable faction or interest outside the court, both *before* the judges are seated, through the formal process of *appointment* (what we will call ex ante autonomy), and *after* the judges have been seated, by formal means of punishing or rewarding judges (what we will call ex post autonomy). Every system of constitutional justice responds to a set of controls exercised by a particular coalition of control. The difference is that some of these coalitions are more plural and diverse, while others are more closely identified with the RC or with a particular social, economic, or political faction. An autonomous court is one that responds to a pluralistic multiplicity of interests, not one that is unmoored from its social and political context.

So which institutional arrangements should be seen as increasing ex ante or ex post autonomy? Specifically in regard to ex ante autonomy, the intervention of more actors in appointments should lead to broadly consensual justices with more mainstream preferences and strong technical qualifications. The presence of multiple veto players in the appointment process should tend to narrow and center the range of possible outcomes, eliminating unqualified, out-of-the-mainstream or transparently biased candidates, and leaving only those who fit broadly shared definitions of what it means to be an acceptable justice with acceptable preferences. In contrast, justices appointed by executive decree, for example, are more likely to faithfully reflect the executive's preferences and to be unconditional allies, and thus to articulate views that are less distinct from those of the executive. In general terms, our score for ex ante autonomy is a function of the number of actors involved in the nomination and confirmation process, plus a bonus if the process requires a supermajoritarian consensus, includes collective actors, or includes extra-political actors, like a professional nominating committee.[3]

Similarly, in the case of ex post control, the presence of more veto players who must coordinate in order to punish or reward judges makes it harder to affect a judge's incentive structure, allowing the judge to express his or her sincere preferences. Judges subject to broadly consensual mechanisms of ex post control may not

[3]   We only increase the score for participation of an outside actor if that actor has a function other than simply nominating justices. If, for example, a nomination committee is simply comprised of presidential nominees selected for that purpose (as in Venezuela), then we consider it to be merely an administrative device to communicate executive preferences. On the other hand, if a majority on the committee is made up of civil society actors who have other functions, like law school deans or the head of the national bar association (as in Guatemala), then we consider that it adds another actor to the process.

be entirely free to "reflect their preferences in their decisions without facing retaliation measures" (Iaryczower et al. 2002: 699), but at least retaliation will have to be based on a broad consensus that they have exceeded the proper bounds of conduct for a judge and the cooperation of multiple actors.[4] In our scoring, a justice who is subject to removal on the sole decision of the president is less autonomous than one who can only be removed after separate positive votes by each chamber of the legislature. And if the legislature must act by a two-thirds vote, we increase the score again. More veto players in the removal process equals more ex post autonomy.

Thoroughly evaluating who can bring pressure to bear on sitting justices, however, requires us to consider several factors in addition to formal removal processes. The first, of course, is the length of judicial tenure. Life terms (or at least very long ones) are frequently considered necessary for judicial autonomy because they free judges from the need to curry favor with outside actors, especially the current RC. Appointment for life conditional only on good behavior, Hamilton famously wrote, "is the best expedient that can be devised in any government to secure a steady, upright and impartial administration of the laws" (Federalist No. 78). Since we are coding institutional features according to the expectations of judicial designers, and since the conventional wisdom is that longer terms are conducive to autonomy, we code term length as positive for ex post autonomy. Short, non-renewable terms moderately decrease ex post autonomy scores (because they may create incentives to please powerful people in order to secure post-term jobs). Short terms *with* reappointment, meanwhile, are coded as most substantially decreasing autonomy, because they encourage judges to curry favor with the politicians who could reappoint them. By the same logic, we code an early mandatory retirement age as negative, as judges looking forward to a second career are more likely to favor powerful outside actors who might be future employers.

Finally, we consider a number of ways – legal and extralegal – in which political actors have historically sought to pressure judges into rendering favorable decisions. Court packing, jurisdiction stripping, and monetary pressures on the court and the judges are common and well-known schemes. As a result, some constitutional designers have made it more difficult to generate these pressures, with constitutional provisions fixing the number of judges to reduce the threat of court-packing schemes, salary protections to shield judges from monetary pressures, and so on. Where these controls are left to ordinary law or the discretion of other actors, they are more open to manipulation by the RC. We increase the score for ex post autonomy for each one of these parameters that is constitutionally protected. The Methodological Appendix summarizes all these indicators and their effect on the final score.

---

[4] Note that this is very nearly the opposite of the logic suggested by Epstein et al. (2002), who essentially assume that any single actor involved in the removal process can punish or reward, thus increasing the constraints on judges' ex post autonomy.

2.2.2. *Authority*

Still, the most autonomous and unaccountable court in the world will not be an influential political force if it is beyond the reach of most actors or lacks the tools to act decisively on a wide range of issues. Constitutional courts have in their charge a set of issues – a sphere of constitutional justice – that may be more or less expansive. The authority dimension measures a court's ability to intervene efficiently and decisively in a broad range of politically significant disputes on behalf of a broad range of actors. Moreover, courts may be more or less open to claims coming from different kinds of actors – including political elites, whether in the majority or the opposition, or ordinary citizens. Constitutional courts that can only receive complaints from majoritarian actors who are members of the other two branches (as, for example, the French *Conseil Constitutionnel* when it was first created) are expressly designed simply to resolve interbranch disputes among members of the RC. Courts with more generous access provisions give standing to outsiders who might be inclined to challenge the decisions of that RC. Some courts are prevented from easily issuing broadly binding rulings by supermajority decision requirements or by limiting the effect of their decision to the case at hand, while others can easily issue broadly binding, universally applicable decisions. The more comprehensive the sphere of constitutional justice, and the more accessible and decisive a court is, the greater its scope of authority.

In design terms, this requires us to evaluate judicial features in three domains: a court's formal toolkit, its accessibility, and its decisive capacity. The first includes all the elements that define the scope of the court's jurisdiction – the nature and number of rights it is charged with enforcing, as well as any ancillary powers it might have beyond deciding cases, such as impeaching presidents or supervising elections. The second relates to the nature and number of actors that are empowered to bring cases before the court, and the ease with which they can do so. Some constitutional courts are limited to hearing complaints brought by elected officials, others are more generally accessible, while still others have expedited procedures and lowered barriers. This generally captures what has been labeled access to justice, at least for constitutional claims. The final component relates first to the effect of a court's decision – essentially whether the court is empowered to make decisions with generally binding effects, or whether its decisions are binding only on the parties before the court; whether it can invalidate a law for unconstitutionality or is limited to refusing to apply the law in a particular case. In this domain, we also evaluate whether the court is hamstrung by a supermajority decision rule for findings of unconstitutionality, requiring a sometimes paralyzingly high degree of consensus to find a law or action unconstitutional.

In sum, a court's scope of authority (authority for short) refers to the nature and scope of a court's potential sphere of action: its formal capacity to intervene efficiently and decisively in a broad range of politically significant disputes on behalf of a broad range of actors. The Methodological Appendix provides additional detail on scoring this dimension.

The example of the Ecuadorean Tribunal of Constitutional Guarantees, as defined in the 1978 Constitution of that country, illustrates the need to unpack the different dimensions. This court was composed of justices representing diverse sectors of the state and society, including representatives of workers, chambers of commerce, the courts, the legislature, and the executive, giving it substantial autonomy from, say, the executive. An exclusive focus on independence might lead to the conclusion that its actual, de facto weakness was unrelated to its institutional design. But this would ignore some additional institutional features. The court was required to submit its declarations of unconstitutionality for final approval to the legislature, thus limiting its authority. Moreover, the 1995 amendments to the Ecuadorean Constitution limited access to the court to a few select actors, not including the opposition: the President, the Legislature (upon a vote by the majority of its members), the Supreme Court (again, on a majority vote), provincial or municipal councils in limited instances, the Defensor del Pueblo (a legislatively appointed ombudsman), or a thousand citizens working together (if their petition is approved by the ombudsman). Questions of access and the Court's ability to issue binding decisions are crucial to understanding its weak role in politics.

A full account of judicial power, in short, must offer insight into each of these dimensions of judicial functioning; and an adequate analysis of formal empowerment must similarly include the mechanisms that affect each of these three requirements for truly consequential courts. Others have made some suggestions in this direction, at times identifying these two dimensions as important, but they have mixed behavioral and institutional features (Brinks 2011), simplified each dimension and then ultimately aggregated the measures (Ríos Figueroa 2011) or used simplified versions of these dimensions (Melton and Ginsburg 2014). These are valuable contributions, but the measure presented in this paper moves beyond them: we ground our indicators in a more explicit theory that informs the concepts of autonomy and authority, and we offer a more nuanced and complete set of indicators to operationalize each concept.

There are, of course, other institutional measures of judicial independence, and Appendix A, section 4, explores in more detail the empirical relationship between our measures and extant quantitative measures of independence. Keith (2002), for example, simply sums certain formal features of a nation's constitution, giving a court additional points for each of seven distinct constitutional provisions, including formal guarantees of tenure, judicial finality, protection of jurisdictional scope, and the presence of military courts. Note that some of these features affect what we call authority, while others affect autonomy. Ríos-Figueroa (2011) defines independence and power dimensions but collapses them into a single aggregate measure. Others, like Cingranelli and Richards (2010), mix formal institutions and behavioral criteria. But no existing institutional measure uses what we know about the wellsprings of judicial behavior to create comprehensive measures for both judicial autonomy and authority, paying careful attention to how the various features within and across dimensions interact with each other and treating each separately to permit scholars to test whether and how each dimension shapes judicial behavior.

2.2.3. *Interacting Autonomy and Authority*

For courts to be consequential, then, they need both autonomy and authority. Although elements of authority and ex ante and ex post autonomy are sometimes aggregated into one-dimensional measures of judicial independence (Ríos Figueroa and Staton 2014), there are good conceptual and empirical reasons to treat these characteristics as distinct dimensions of formal empowerment. A court with great autonomy but little authority can offer a perspective that is distinct from the political players in its environment, but its potential sphere of influence will remain limited. Likewise, a court with high authority but little autonomy is well equipped to shape politics and policy, but is unlikely to speak with a different voice than its legislative and executive counterparts. Neither will be as consequential as an autonomous and authoritative court, but it matters where the weakness lies, and we should not lump these very different courts into one intermediate category.

Each of these models is likely to carry out a very different political function in postconstitutional politics and to shape very different sorts of constitutional democracies. Highly efficient courts with a broad scope of authority but no autonomy may be powerful instruments of repression and legitimation, as authoritarian courts frequently are. Conversely, highly autonomous courts may remain completely irrelevant if any of the following features limit their authority: they can hear only mundane and inconsequential disputes; they are precluded from issuing broadly binding rulings on the key issues of the day; they are paralyzed by supermajority decision rules; or they can be accessed only by a few select actors. Such courts are fully compatible with the arbitrary exercise of power. Latin America's experiences with impartial but relatively marginal courts (for example, in Chile or Uruguay), or activist but politically compromised courts (in Nicaragua or Venezuela), as well as with the presence of active and impartial courts (in Colombia or Costa Rica) calls attention to the interplay between the two dimensions. In this section, we take these two dimensions of formal judicial power and show how they interact to create a typology of four models of constitutional justice, illuminating the key constitutional transformations in Latin America in recent decades.

Interacting the autonomy and authority dimensions produces four distinct models of constitutional justice, as depicted in Table 2.1. Each of the four models represents a different approach to the relationship between (constitutional) law and (ordinary) politics, giving constitutional courts[5] and constitutional law a greater or lesser role in structuring social disputes and public policymaking, and granting the court greater or lesser autonomy from the RC in interpreting and applying the constitutional form a country has chosen.

---

[5] We use this label to refer to the apex court, regardless of its formal designation as a supreme court, a special constitutional chamber, or otherwise, so long as it has the power to interpret and apply the constitution.

TABLE 2.1. Models of constitutional justice

	Low autonomy	High autonomy
Broad authority	**Court Is Regime Ally**: constitutional justice channels majoritarian politics, reinforces RC goals	**Court Is Major Policy Player**: contested versions of thick constitutional justice permeate politics
Narrow authority	**Court Is Sidelined**: constitutional justice largely irrelevant to politics; intervenes only to legitimize	**Court Is Procedural Arbiter**: courts allow contestation, but are limited to protecting market and political processes

A very brief historical overview of the region suggests these categories are descriptive of constitutional projects – and as a measure of convergent validity, we will see how well these projects line up with our coding of the actual documents in the following section.

2.3. UNEVEN GROWTH OF JUDICIAL POWER IN LATIN AMERICA

We answer two questions in this section. First, does the general trajectory match the conventional view of linear, if uneven, empowerment and growth in independence, as well as a gradual convergence on a version of a Western constitutional model, or is it better described by a multidimensional approach? And second, can we locate the various systems of constitutional justice in this matrix in a way that resonates with what we know of these courts by simply looking at the features that affect their autonomy and authority?

2.3.1. *Using the Quantitative Measure to Describe the Region*

Coding all the constitutional designs of the region with a systematic, quantitative, fully comparable measure, allows us to evaluate the developments in systems of constitutional justice in Latin America since the 1970s. Our choice of 1975 as a starting point obscures much of the prior struggle over the expansion of constitutional politics, since most of the advances toward social constitutionalism had been rolled back by dictatorships and Right-wing reactions by that time (as we will see in Chapter 5, in the discussions of Guatemala and Chile; and Chapter 6, in the discussion of Juan Perón's constitution in Argentina, among other places). However, as noted in Chapter 1, most of that movement had been an expansion and contraction in the intermediate sphere of constitutional politics, rather than in what we have called the sphere of constitutional justice. Thus, this chapter describes the full range of variation in the scope and autonomy of constitutional justice in the region, starting at its lowest point (in modern times) and ending at its highest point to date.

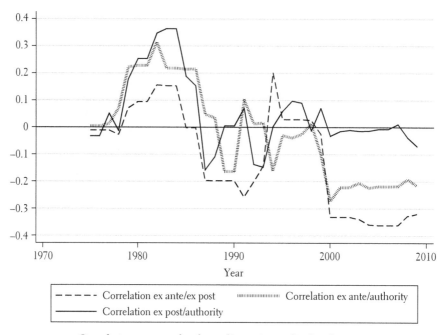

FIGURE 2.1. Correlation among the three dimensions of judicial power, 1975–2009

As a preliminary matter, the way in which the dimensions relate to each other offers support for a multidimensional framework. If we simply look at their averages over the whole period, the two dimensions are only modestly (or even negatively) associated.[6] But this weak association hides important changes in the choices designers made over the course of the last thirty-five years. Figure 2.1 shows the changing correlations among the three dimensions over time: through 1985, all three measures show increasingly high positive correlations – as designers increased (decreased) a court's authority, they also increased (decreased) the court's autonomy. Moreover, as they limited the executive's control over appointments, they simultaneously limited the legislature's control over the judges' fate once in office. During this period, designers were increasingly reluctant to give a court too much power without also enhancing its autonomy.

The next decade shows considerable experimentation, perhaps as designers began to see the effects of newly empowered courts in other countries and attempted to find the right balance between the three components of judicial power. This decade

---

[6] The correlation between ex ante and ex post autonomy is −0.06 and not significant; that between ex ante and authority is 0.25 ($p = 0.001$); and that between ex post and authority is 0.21 ($p = 0.002$). This analysis is done using the unique document as the case. We could do the same analysis for all country years (correlations are similar but slightly lower and equally significant), or only for unique courts (correlations are similar but slightly higher, with lower levels of significance given a smaller number of observations).

shows the highest annual rate of change to court structures and the greatest variability in correlations. The relationship between ex ante and ex post autonomy becomes negative, then briefly positive; the relationship between authority and each dimension of autonomy oscillates in a narrow range around zero.

The final decade of our period shows a very different, much more consistent pattern. Increases in one dimension of autonomy were offset by decreases in the other, producing a negative correlation that stabilizes at roughly 0.35 (and is significant beyond 0.01, if we isolate the last decade). Increases (decreases) in authority were accompanied by decreases (increases) in ex ante autonomy, suggesting that designers made tradeoffs across dimensions rather than across-the-board cuts or increases to judicial power, producing a negative correlation. On the other hand, ex post autonomy shows no relationship with authority at all – as we will see in a moment, this is because in the final period designers settled into three distinct patterns of constitutionalism, with different mixes of authority and autonomy, rather than converging around a single model.

The correlations, however, do not tell us much about the direction of the dominant trends in judicial design – whether the movement was toward greater or lesser authority or autonomy. Figure 2.2 traces the changes in the regional mean for each dimension of formal court design. Whereas the conventional account of judicial empowerment suggests (with very few exceptions) a slow but inexorable movement toward greater formal independence for judges, this figure reveals a more complicated story and provides further support for a measure that disaggregates the two components of autonomy, rather than collapsing everything into "independence."[7]

Figure 2.2 shows (a) an expansion of judicial authority, coupled with (b) increased ex ante autonomy (that is, increased pluralism in the appointments process), but with (c) a much more modest (average) increase in the insulation of judges once on the bench. As we will see, the small average increase does not indicate a lack of change. Rather, it is reflective of the increasing diversity in design on this dimension. In other words, compared to thirty-five years ago, courts in Latin America on average have a broader mandate. Judges are the product of more inclusive, less partisan appointments, but may still remain subject to some political control once seated.

What does this mean for the dominant logic of judicial design in Latin America? Given what we know about ex post and ex ante mechanisms of control, the picture describes an interesting shift in the mode and locus of political control over courts in the region. The more the number of actors in the appointment process is restricted, the more the process typically becomes dominated by the executive. Ex post control, on the other hand, is usually exercised by the legislature, through impeachments, court-packing schemes, and various other "court-curbing"

---

[7]   To produce Figure 2.2 we mean-centered the values of the three variables by subtracting the 1975 regional mean for each one; any movement up or down in the demeaned variables thus reflects changes from the 1975 regional mean.

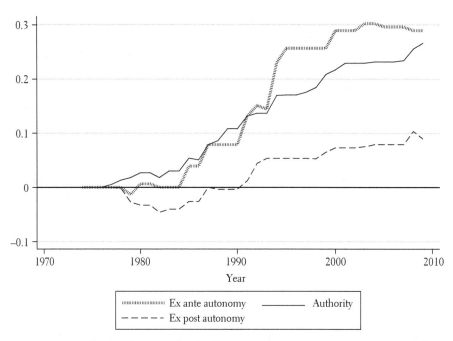

FIGURE 2.2. Regional average levels of ex ante autonomy, ex post autonomy, and
authority in Latin America, 1975–2009

behaviors (see, e.g., Rosenberg 1992 for a description of these devices in the US
context). The executive typically plays no direct role in ex post controls, although it
may occasionally have the power to initiate disciplinary proceedings, as in Mexico.

When autonomy is low, both ex ante and ex post control should tend to produce
largely majoritarian judiciaries, aligned with the RC and unlikely to significantly
challenge its preferences over constitutional meaning. But there are differences
between the two. Ex ante control is typically exercised in more dominant fashion
by a unitary actor, the executive. Ex post control, on the other hand, must be chan-
neled through a legislature. The legislature may or may not be a rubber stamp for
the executive, depending on the configuration of power in a country at any given
time, but it is a more cumbersome, collective, indirect mode of control. Thus, low
ex ante autonomy indicates a court controlled by the executive, while low ex post
autonomy indicates a court accountable to a legislature, acting by simple majority.

The scatterplot of courts in 1975 and 2009 in Figure 2.3 shows this temporal shift
in the locus of political control quite dramatically. For purely illustrative purposes,
we divide the plot into quadrants defined by the overall means on each dimension.
Except for Uruguay's – generally acknowledged to be one of the few truly autonomous courts in the region prior to the 1970s – all the courts in the upper-right
quadrant, which have high autonomy both ex ante and ex post, are 2009 courts, and
all the courts in the lower-left quadrant are from 1975. With only two exceptions,
all the courts in the lower-right quadrant – which deny the executive unilateral

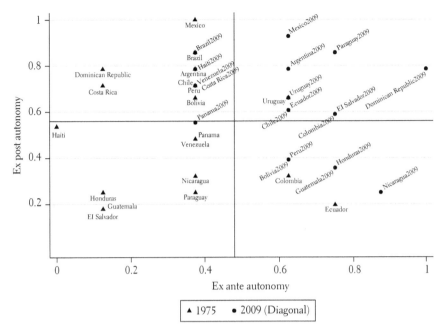

FIGURE 2.3. Political control of courts in Latin America, 1975 and 2009

appointment control, but make sitting judges more accountable to the legislature –
are also from 2009. The upper-left quadrant is mixed, but twice as many early courts
as late ones give the executive more control over appointments and then insulate the
resulting judges from pressure.

As suggested by the regional mean, the pattern shows a fairly uniform increase in
ex ante autonomy, limiting the power of executives over the courts. As courts were
given increasing rights to enforce, more tools to intervene in policy disputes, and
more decisiveness, constitution-makers also pluralized and diversified the appointments process. Less uniformly, they also protected sitting judges from political
pressure: five different courts experienced a decline in ex post autonomy over this
period, compared to only one for which ex ante autonomy declined. By the end of
the period, then, the dominant approach had limited the executive's control over
appointments, while showing a great deal more diversity in the degree to which
courts are insulated from control by the legislature. The changes appear to express
a uniform preference for pluralizing the mechanism for choosing who sits on the
bench (and therefore what judicial preferences are present) while simultaneously
maintaining, at least formally, some degree of promajoritarian ability to discipline
or remove judges once they are seated.

In Section 2.2.3 however, we identified four conceptually distinct models of constitutional justice, based on the levels of autonomy and authority designers choose
to give their constitutional courts. Figure 2.3 simply shows that by 2009, *if* autonomy
is low, it is more likely to be so because judges are exposed to pressures once on the

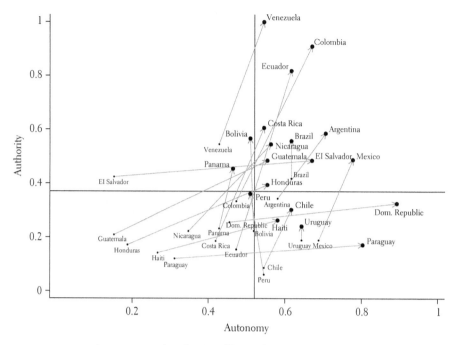

FIGURE 2.4. Autonomy and authority of Latin American courts, 1975 and 2009

bench, rather than because appointments are susceptible to capture. Figure 2.4, on the other hand, is arranged to match the conceptual space described in Table 2.1 and shows whether our measure maps onto the models we identified in Section 2(c). Again using the means on each dimension – admittedly an arbitrary cutoff point – we divide the scatterplot into quadrants that correspond to the categories (high and low autonomy, narrow and broad authority) in Table 2.1.[8] We then plot the locations of all the countries of Latin America on our measures of authority and autonomy (using the mean of ex ante and ex post autonomy) at the beginning and end of the period of analysis – 1975 and 2009. Notably, all the courts varied their institutional design, at least by a small amount; just as notably, all the courts moved in the direction of greater autonomy, greater authority, or both.

2.3.2. *Qualitative Overview of Regional Trends*

How well does this quantitative evaluation match up with a more qualitative description of the same regional trends? In the mid-1970s, the starting point of our analysis, courts and constitutional justice were largely irrelevant to the politics of

---

[8]   As with Figure 2.3, the quadrants are defined by the means for authority and autonomy of all the distinct documents of the region for this period.

the day. While many of the region's high courts served to resolve private disputes, constitutional justice was a different matter: the great distributive and political conflicts that shook the region took place outside the purview of constitutional justice. The Right trusted the military more than constitutional courts to protect its property rights, while the Left often took to the jungles and the mountains to fight for its goals rather than working through constitutional means. Repression was largely extralegal, with some variation (Pereira 2005), and executives routinely violated constitutional strictures. Constitutional courts were not serious checks on the power of even democratically elected regimes. In our terms, they had neither great autonomy nor a great scope of authority.

The impulse toward social constitutionalism embodied in the more radical third strand of the region's constitutional politics might have led to a greater scope of authority and thus to more consequential courts (see Gargarella 2010, 2013 for a discussion of conservative, liberal, and radical ideologies in Latin American constitutionalism). But the most important attempts to establish early social constitutionalism did not rely greatly on constitutional courts and constitutional justice to advance those ends. To take just one example, albeit the most important and enduring one, Mexico 1917 depended on the RC to develop and implement its social mandate. In early social constitutionalism, social goals were entrusted to the RC.

Moreover, by the 1970s most of the attempts at social constitutionalism had been rolled back by the successive tides of repression that swept the region in the second half of the century. Mexico 1917, of course, is still in place. But most of the constitutions that followed in its footsteps were short-lived even by Latin American standards. In Brazil, Getúlio Vargas's 1934 constitution was replaced first by his very own "Estado Novo" constitution of 1937, and then by a quite different constitution in 1940. Similarly, in Argentina, Juan Perón's 1949 constitution was replaced by the old 1863 constitution a mere six years later, while Guatemala's "revolutionary" social constitution of 1945 was replaced by an anticommunist document in 1956, after the coup that brought down Jacobo Arbenz. Juan Bosch's 1963 social constitution in the Dominican Republic did not last out the year. All these regimes – admittedly of varying democratic credentials – ended in military coups and a turn away from social constitutionalism; Bosch's and Arbenz's ended with the open intervention and assistance of the United States.

The early literature on Latin American constitutionalism and judicial politics reflects this reality. Some suggested that courts not only had long been ineffective as checks on power but were likely to continue that way for strong cultural and traditional reasons (Merryman 1985; Rosenn 1987). Others presented the constitutions themselves as instruments of their own demise, because they contained excessively generous regimes of exception (Loveman 1993). As Gargarella (2013: 85) describes the constitutional model that prevailed at the starting point for our analysis, for most of the twentieth century constitutional regimes in Latin America fit the lower left cell of Table 2.1: they "were characterized by their exclusionary legal systems, the concentration of powers in the Executive, limited political rights, and the extreme use of the State's coercive powers" and not by the importance of their courts or their constitutional guarantees.

In the 1980s, more or less contemporaneously with the transition to democracy, a market-oriented constitutional model began to take hold that depended on more consequential courts, albeit with a restricted scope of authority. This model was picked up and pushed forward by second-generation neoliberal reforms, which included strengthening the courts in order to protect property rights and stimulate economic growth. International actors poured vast amounts of money into the region, seeking to create a particular model of courts. Courts were supposed to be insulated from the rough and tumble of democratic politics (including by adopting something like a merit selection process for lower court judges), but were largely limited to protecting property rights and commercial predictability, along with some classic liberal negative freedoms (Domingo and Sieder 2001; Salas 2001; Sarles 2001; Rodríguez Garavito 2010). This neoliberal model can be described as depending on courts with high autonomy but low authority and therefore fits quite well in the lower-right quadrant.

To varying degrees, Chile 1980 and Guatemala 1985 are examples of this model. Both courts and constitutions were conceived in the midst of the Cold War struggle, under the tutelage of pro-market reformers on the Right with the nearly complete exclusion of the Left, although, as we will see in Chapter 3, the Center-Left and the lurking threat of the armed Left played an important role in tempering the Guatemalan model. The amendments that transformed the Dominican Republic's constitution in 1994 belong to the same class, although they came later. If our coding is right, these and the other constitutions that fall in this quadrant should epitomize the Procedural Arbiter model, defined in Table 2.1, with high levels of autonomy but a restricted sphere of constitutional justice. They should have a mostly negative rights agenda, designed to protect propertied interests and the basic civil liberties that provide a foundation for democracy, but have little influence in broader social and economic conflicts, at best creating the space for the market and ordinary extraconstitutional politics to do that work. Chapter 5 is dedicated to these constitutional systems.

Competing with this model is a set of constitutional projects that define a broader, more positive constitutional agenda. The designers of this set of constitutions imagined a thicker version of constitutional justice, motivated often by disillusion with the results of neoliberal reform and a quest to democratize societies by promoting social and economic inclusion (Brinks and Forbath 2014). Using our two-dimensional analysis, they still relied on autonomous constitutional courts, but gave the courts far greater responsibilities, including, in the Latin American cases, a long list of social and economic rights, strong mechanisms for claiming individual and collective rights, and more generous provisions for access. The courts they designed – located in the upper-right corner of Table 2.1 – appear destined to be major policy players.

In this model, constitutional courts become spaces where great distributional conflicts can play out using the language of expansive constitutional justice (Bonilla Maldonado 2013), but are open to competing interpretations of that language. In the most extreme cases – such as Colombia or Costa Rica – the justices themselves defined influential visions of democratic constitutionalism, defending or expanding the welfare state and extending the benefits of social and economic rights to previously excluded groups. In all these cases, however, constitutional courts became one of several spaces where competing visions of constitutional justice could be articulated and debated. Whereas second-generation constitutions contained a very thin notion of constitutional justice, these new social covenants constitutionalized many erstwhile private interactions and much social and economic state policy, without withdrawing their concern for classic liberal rights (Brinks and Forbath 2014). Brazil's 1988 and Colombia's 1991 documents are typical social rights constitutions. Later on, Argentina 1994 would join this group, as we will see in Chapter 6.

By the late 1990s the pendulum had swung away from the classic liberal model. Beginning in Venezuela, but continuing in Ecuador in 2007 and Bolivia in 2009 (and with a nearly successful attempt in the same direction in Argentina under Cristina Fernández's administration), constituent assemblies embodying "Bolivarian socialism" appeared in the region. Their constitutional models made no secret of their disdain for old-fashioned liberal representative democracy and expressly advocated for law and courts as instruments of social transformation in the service of the Bolivarian project (Brinks 2012; Couso 2013). Courts that aim to meet these requirements must have a broad agenda, somewhat like the social democratic courts. But if they are to advance the correct agenda, and not impose too many constraints on these quasirevolutionary governments, they must also be closely tied to the preferences of the executive and dominant party. Chapter 7 explores this quadrant of Table 2.1, with a full case study of the politics that produced Bolivia's 2009 constitution and a more abbreviated overview of the creation of Venezuela's 1991 constitution.

The crucial distinction between the two models along the top row of Table 2.1 is that, without autonomy, there is no room for competing visions of constitutional justice. In the models with Major Policy Player courts, constitutional justice becomes the space where distinct visions of the country's fundamental commitments can be debated and contested. Expansive language of constitutional justice is deployed by groups with alternative visions of how the constitutional text should inform the politics of particular issues. By contrast, when the courts are Regime Allies, the specific content of constitutional justice is dictated by the preferences of the dominant RC, and the courts are closely tied to that faction so that they endorse and promote those preferences. Regime Allies become not spaces for contesting visions of constitutional justice, but tools to impose and legitimize the particular vision defined by whoever is in power. Rather than entertaining competing accounts of constitutional justice, they suppress them.

These four models of constitutional justice are not unique to Latin America – we believe they can be used, *mutatis mutandis*, to map global postwar trends in judicial empowerment. But given the ferment of constitutional change in the region, they occurred on a somewhat abbreviated timescale in Latin America during the last wave of democratization. Crucially for our purposes, this abbreviated and very broad-brush qualitative description of developments in Latin America suggests that the changes in the quantitative measure match up reasonably well with what we know of broad regional trends. What happens when we drill down a little deeper into individual countries? Does the design of their systems of constitutional justice track with these ideas about the role of law in politics? Moreover (although recall that our project is meant to understand the politics of institutional design, not institutional functioning) as a suggestive indication of how much these formal models might ultimately track with behavioral measures, can we see some correspondence between qualitative descriptions of their role in politics and our formal, purely institutional measure of judicial autonomy and authority?

2.3.3. *Individual Countries*

The arrows in Figure 2.4 run from the location of the court in 1975 to its location in 2009. The location of individual courts at the beginning and end of our period of analysis, as shown in that figure, tracks reasonably well with what we know about the origins and behavior of courts in Latin America. As suggested above, the majority of constitutions in place in 1975 established courts designed to sit on the sidelines. These courts had little autonomy – as seen in Figure 2.3, executives largely dominated appointments – and very little authority. Guatemala, Honduras, Haiti, and Paraguay, deep in dictatorship, are good examples of courts that failed to constrain politics in any significant way, and they score among the lowest on both dimensions of our measure. Even Costa Rica, which was by then a long-standing democracy with a reputation for the rule of law, had a court that was completely dormant until the 1990 reform, which moved it out of the lower left quadrant and produced the court we see by 2009 (Wilson et al. 2004). By the end of the period, only Peru's court remained in this category, and even this court is close to the boundaries on both dimensions.

In the lower-right quadrant, we expect to see traditional Procedural Arbiter courts: those that are designed to be autonomous enough to police and protect basic market rules and procedural political guarantees but that lack the broad scope of authority needed to reshape the political landscape across multiple substantive domains. As expected, the Pinochet-designed Chilean Constitutional Court, even with the limited changes that took place after redemocratization and moved it left and up, is squarely in this quadrant, as is the Uruguayan Supreme Court, which has barely changed since its original design in 1952. Uruguay's court has, as many have noted, a high degree of autonomy, but it has never been a significant player in the politics of that country, except to guarantee compliance with the basic rules of the game (Skaar 2011); the Chilean court has the same reputation (Hilbink 2003, 2012). The Dominican Republic's high court has, by all accounts, improved in its autonomy since the 1970s, but it remains a court with little influence. Paraguay's court, defined in 1992 under a transitional military government, in a constitution that was meant to provide a foundation for the return to civilian rule, is deep in this quadrant. This court has intervened in politics recently, including by becoming deeply involved in presidential politics, but it has not become a protagonist in disputes beyond the basic rules of the game on impeachment or property rights.

Similarly, we expected the courts contemplated in Guatemala's 1985 constitution and El Salvador's 1992 reforms to be relatively low in authority but high in autonomy, in line with the neoliberal model. Like Paraguay's constitution, they were crafted under right-wing military rule as part of a transition to civilian government. As we will see in much more detail in Chapter 5, Guatemala's constitutional convention included a range of political forces, but everyone to the left of the Christian Democratic Party was still in exile. The Salvadoran court was reformed a year before the signing of the peace agreements. Both have similar levels of authority, slightly above the overall mean for the entire period. They fall in a line, with Panama and Mexico, below recognizably more social-democratic constitutions like Brazil 1988, Argentina 1994, and Costa Rica 1991. Indeed, all the countries that were (at least until recently) dominated by Right-wing parties since the transition to democracy – El Salvador, Guatemala, Honduras, and Paraguay – ended up with courts that were below the 2009 mean for authority (0.503).

Notably, the upper-right quadrant – Major Policy Player courts, in our terms – includes effectively no courts from the 1975 period (Brazil's pre-1988 Supreme Court is just barely above the mean on authority). According to our conceptual map, these are courts with a broad social democratic agenda, designed to be important spaces for policy contestation. Enabled by their relative insulation from political pressure, their accessibility, and a broad toolkit to exert their influence across many domains, they occasionally acted against the interests of dominant political actors. By 2009, this quadrant included the courts of Colombia (1991), Costa Rica (1990), Argentina (1994), and Brazil (1988), which by all accounts have become significant players in the major policy disputes of each country. Colombia, widely recognized as the country with the most active and consequential court in the entire region, has the court with the highest degree of authority among this group. Nicaragua, the one Central American country where the Left won the violent struggles of the 1980s, and which has had a consistently strong Leftist party, is within this quadrant as well. Its autonomy from Sandinista politics – even when the Sandinistas were out of power – has been called into question, but it has been an advocate of social policies on several occasions.

Mexico's trajectory illustrates the difference between the establishment of what we call constitutional politics and constitutional justice. The Mexican

Constitution, long recognized as one of the first to incorporate social and economic rights, was nevertheless low in authority, as its court was hamstrung by a series of procedural and decision rules that impeded its action (Pou Giménez 2012). By 2011, however, a series of constitutional reforms – while far from dramatically empowering the court – brought Mexico's constitutional justice mechanisms more into line with its social constitutionalist impulses. On the one hand, the 2011 reforms "do not substantially alter amparo procedural designs that shelter 'points of obstruction' which are particularly damaging if one is interested in widening access to justice, in creating a dialogue between courts, citizens and political branches on the meaning of the constitution . . ." (Pou Giménez 2012: 5). On the other hand, these reforms did include the ability to strike down a law in the abstract for unconstitutionality and added indigenous rights, stronger nondiscrimination provisions, and so on. As a result, the Mexican court moved up slightly in authority, while preserving a design that seemed intended to insulate it from the political realm.[9]

Finally, in the northwest quadrant we expect courts that behave as Regime Allies, meaning that these courts will have comparatively broad authority but only limited autonomy from majoritarian political actors. Far from passive rubberstamps to a regime, these courts are equipped with a broad agenda, open access, and decisive rule-making authority, making them a valuable means to project and extend power while harnessing the relative legitimacy of judges and the rule of law. The Bolivarian courts – Venezuela, Ecuador, and Bolivia – roughly meet our expectations for courts designed on this twenty-first century socialist model. All three are ranked among the top-five courts in terms of levels of authority, with Venezuela and Ecuador scoring particularly high. They are also, broadly speaking, low in formal autonomy – especially for the period in which they were created – although not as low as we had expected. Venezuela and Bolivia are, respectively, right above and right below the overall mean for autonomy. We will explore the reasons for this in greater detail in Chapter 7. Ecuador breaks the pattern somewhat. Although the Ecuadorean court's autonomy is quite low for the period in which it was designed, and among the lowest in this quadrant, it shows levels of formal autonomy that are not all that different from the courts defined in more social democratic countries.

In practice, of course, all three of these courts have been even less autonomous than their design would suggest. In the case of Venezuela, the courts have been extensively manipulated in extralegal, extraconstitutional ways, and have become powerful tools of repression and social and political control (Pérez Perdomo 2003; Inter-American Commission on Human Rights 2009; Brinks 2012; Weyland 2013).

---

[9]   Of course, Mexico was dominated by a hegemonic party that responded quite directly to the President for many years, so the Executive had considerable authority in spite of its formal weakness. By the same token, institutional protections had limited consequence in a context in which one party dominated the Executive, the national legislature, and all state legislatures.

In Ecuador and Bolivia, the country's high courts have also become identified with the ruling regime, and have served a similar purpose (Weyland 2013). They legitimize and give constitutional blessing to the major social and economic transformations proposed by the regime, and help eliminate legal and political obstacles to their realization. All these courts, in short, have acted in the way suggested by our formal measure, but extraconstitutional factors have pushed them even further into the northwest quadrant than their mere design would suggest.

In sum, the data demonstrate clear variation in the levels of authority and autonomy designed into the newly reformed courts of Latin America. The systematic variation in institutional design contradicts the notion of a clear-cut, region-wide (if still incomplete) movement toward a liberal constitutionalist, rights-based model of democratic politics achieved through the creation of powerful and autonomous courts. Just as strongly, it contradicts any simplistic account of design diffusion and emulation. Rather, it shows considerable variation that appears to respond to domestic circumstances and domestic politics. In matters of institutional design, at least, constitution drafters built into their courts different mechanisms of political control that are more or less inclusive, and gave their courts more or less authority to intervene in the weightiest matters of the day.

Our historical exercise, as necessarily superficial as it was, highlights the utility of our new, three-dimensional measure of judicial power for understanding constitutional change in Latin America over the last thirty-five years. It is unrealistic, of course, to expect perfect congruence between the dominant political project and formal constitutional provisions, or between the latter and judicial behavior years later. The discussion so far has focused only on ideology, and our basic finding is that the power dynamics of the constitutional moment can matter far more to the politics of constitution-making and constitutional change than ideology. But even this first approximation suggests that our new variables capture important aspects of the relationship between a country's politics, constitutional design, and postconstituent judicial and constitutional reality. None of the one-dimensional measures that have dominated the literature so far can capture the full range of this relationship and the interesting variation exhibited by the actual courts of Latin America over the last thirty-five years.

2.4. CORRELATION OR CAUSATION: DO FORMAL INSTITUTIONS MATTER?

This focus on the texts that form the DNA of constitutional justice often triggers the objection that it presents a misleading or at least incomplete picture of reality. Many have argued that judicial institutions in Latin America, as with many institutions in much of the developing world, are weak, and thus that institutional arrangements may be poor or even blatantly misleading indicators of the sort of court a country might have. If formal institutional arrangements are "nonsense," then a project that seeks to explain the political origins of different institutional designs is "nonsense on stilts," to paraphrase Jeremy Bentham's comment on natural rights. Why should we care about the political origins of institutional design, if it is not clear that institutional design matters? And why should designers themselves care, if they assume the institutions will not work as designed? The association between design and outcomes laid out above is quite impressionistic and general, so before moving on from this discussion of our institutional measure, it may be worth justifying at somewhat greater length the focus on institutional arrangements.

It is true that the decades-long investment in formal judicial reforms in the region produced decidedly mixed results. As we have very briefly seen, some high courts in the region – most notably in Colombia, Costa Rica, Brazil, and Argentina – have emerged as pioneering forces at the very center of policy debates in their countries, while others (e.g., in Peru or Haiti) have remained largely on the political sidelines, unwilling or unable to contribute meaningfully to the politics of the day. Most fall somewhere in between: in Ecuador and Bolivia, for example, the country's high courts have most recently exercised a "majoritarian" political influence by legitimizing the regime's major social and economic policies and helping to eliminate legal and political obstacles to their realization, while their counterparts in Chile and Uruguay have acquired reputations for impartiality without activism, remaining on the sidelines of most political disputes and challenging regime interests only occasionally.

Such variation has prompted some, including those who advocated judicial reforms, to conclude that rule change has failed to produce real change in a region long plagued by strong executives and weak formal institutions (Hammergren 1998; Pásara 2012). Others have pointed to noninstitutional explanations for such unevenness, including an entrenched conservative legal/political culture among judges, or an unwillingness to upset the status quo in the face of opposition from executives or legislatures with the ability to pressure judges or undermine their decisions (Rosenn 1987; Larkins 1998). While these factors undoubtedly shape a court's willingness and ability to affect politics, we feel existing measures of judicial empowerment substantially underestimate the importance of judicial institutions' DNA for two main reasons. In the first place, they do not capture the multidimensional structure of formal empowerment, as we have laid out here in some detail. In the second place, and relatedly, they overlook components of judicial design that may appear subtle but are critical for exercising judicial power. Although we feel we make substantial progress in this book, we agree with Julio Ríos-Figueroa and Jeff Staton (2014: 128) when they say, "it is not yet clear that we have identified well the rules (or sets of rules) that produce the incentives we hope to measure." Thus, before we dismiss *de jure* explanations for judicial behavior altogether we must take a closer look at what exactly a court's formal institutional design can show us about the kind of political influence it was designed to exercise.

We readily concede that judicial power is not simply a function of institutional design, just as executive or legislative power is not purely a function of institutional design and an organism's destiny is not purely a function of its DNA. The literature that addresses the sources of *de facto* judicial power tends to emphasize one or more of three sets of contextual variables. First, the distribution of preferences and power in a court's political environment is thought to influence the degree to which a court must behave strategically or will challenge powerful interests (Epstein and Knight 1998; Epstein et al. 2001; Bill Chavez 2004a, b). Second, scholars point to societal variables, such as mobilization efforts by nongovernmental actors like NGOs and legal organizations (Epp 1998, 2009; Gauri and Brinks 2008), or the lay public through mass public opinion (Gibson et al. 1998; Vanberg 2001; Staton 2004, 2010), to explain why courts become key actors in certain policy arenas. Third, many have argued that judges' ideological orientations and policy preferences influence their willingness to take advantage of the tools they are equipped with and the strategic openings afforded by their political environments, particularly in cases where the law is indeterminate or conflicting (Hilbink 2012). Thus the literature suggests that whether and how courts use their formal power is contingent upon several contextual variables that are beyond the scope of the present analysis.

At the same time, close examination of the foregoing explanations for *de facto* judicial power suggests that they are not independent from institutional design; formal institutions mediate the influence of the contextual variables, in a sort of "nature *and* nurture" story of institutional performance. In the US context, the dominant theories of judicial behavior rely on a (sometimes unacknowledged) role for institutional features. It is in part institutional design that allows judges to follow their own political preferences; as Segal and Spaeth (2002: 349) acknowledge, "the federal judiciary was designed to be independent, so we should not be surprised that it in fact is." Of course, the strategic theories explicitly incorporate the institutional context into their accounts; it is in part the design of the particular institution that determines whose preferences judges have to take into consideration (Epstein and Knight 1998: 17–18). This suggests that institutional accounts are always at least part of the story behind observed differences in judicial behavior.

The accounts of particular courts typically include some consideration of institutional factors. Informal institutions that make tenure less secure can magnify the ability of other political actors to punish defiant justices, for example, thus making them more or less sensitive to their political environment (Helmke 2005). The extent to which social actors are granted standing to assert constitutional claims, and the nature of the claims that can be made, informs the extent to which social groups will see the court as an ally and mobilize to protect it (Gauri and Brinks 2008; Wilson 2009). Appointment mechanisms crucially condition the extent to which judicial preferences can be controlled by dominant political actors (Dahl 1957). It is the judiciary's institutional design that allows a conservative formalistic culture to flourish and persist in Chile (Hilbink 2003, 2007). Recent quantitative analyses suggest that certain institutional features matter to judicial performance (Melton and Ginsburg 2014). In short, empirical accounts of how courts behave in particular cases often rely on institutional features without attempting a systematic comparative classification of those features. Although we ourselves have not fully tested, in a systematic way, the effect that our measure might have on judicial behavior, it is clear that we have good reason to think that it or something like it might matter.

This is not to say that formal design in constitutional texts is the only or even the most important thing about courts. Informal institutions may sometimes be crucial in filling out the institutional analysis. Political, historical, and even cultural contextual factors may ultimately explain a great deal of the most interesting variation in actual judicial behavior. Our own view is that the behavioral outcomes of formal institutions are a conditional function of their social and political contexts; similar institutions can produce different outcomes and different institutional solutions can lead to the same outcome, although in relatively predictable ways (Locke and Thelen 1995; Brinks 2008: 256–9). Therefore, a unified framework for describing courts over time and across countries is an indispensable addition to our toolkit and essential if we hope to understand the motivations that drive constitutional designers and the origins of judicial design.

Whether constitutional designers in the end get the courts they thought they designed is a separate question. There is bound to be a great deal of slippage between the hopes of the drafters and the way the institution works in practice. But if our institutional measure captures the way designers think design works, then it will work to test the political conditions that lead them to design courts with varying (expected) degrees of autonomy and authority. Our in-depth analysis of the arguments deployed in the course of constitutional conventions in Chapters 5 through 7 satisfies us that, in fact, we have captured what these designers were thinking – sometimes intuitively and implicitly – about the courts they were creating.

Every scholar who has used an institutional measure or studied a formal institution – especially those who work on the Global South – has heard the critique that formal institutions actually do not matter, or matter less than informal institutions, or less than some other variable alleged to actually fully explain the outcome. Many who study constitutions have expressed similar skepticism about the value of constitutional texts in Latin America in particular. Javier Couso, a Latin American constitutionalist himself, repeats the refrain that "Latin America has had many constitutions, but very little constitutionalism" (Couso 2011: 1519 citing Brian Loveman; see also King 2013b). If for no other reason than to prove this skeptical claim true, we need good institutional analyses. Many of the institutional measures we have seen may in fact not explain anything, but only because they are bad measures. In light of all the political energy expended in writing constitutions around the world, it behooves us as researchers to take seriously the challenge of showing both the political origins of these texts and the extent to which, if at all, institutions matter in different contexts. Both of these tasks require systematic, well-constructed, formal institutional measures. In this book, we offer such a measure. Moreover, we use it to classify and describe the different models of constitutional justice that have emerged in the region over the last four decades, and we explore the political origins of these models. We leave for later work the task of understanding when and to what extent the models' effects actually match up to their designers' expectations.

2.5. CONCLUSION

Despite growing attention to the causes and consequences of judicial empowerment and the judicialization of politics, there is no consensus on the concept or the measure of judicial power. In this chapter we have presented and defended an original and comprehensive conceptual framework that includes two dimensions: autonomy and authority. We used this coding to show the empirical patterns that have arisen in Latin America over the last four decades. First, high and low levels of autonomy and authority interact to produce four qualitatively different models of constitutional justice, reflecting differences in the goals of political actors in the design of their courts. Second, we applied the framework to the formal institutional changes to courts in Latin America over thirty-five years, yielding a detailed and dynamic survey of judicial design in the region. The multidimensional framework and measure reveal several important insights not captured by other measures of judicial empowerment.

Although the conventional narrative is one of linear empowerment – albeit with cross-national variation – we expect different models to emerge, as a function of tradeoffs among dimensions, rather than straightforward increases in formal autonomy and authority. Our empirical results bear out that expectation. By the end of the period, designers were unwilling to grant courts greater authority without securing some control over their autonomy, and vice versa. And while they made appointments less easy to control, they often compensated by making judges accountable ex post. The application of our framework to Latin American courts suggests that institutional designers in the region understood the tradeoff between judicial autonomy and accountability and chose different ways to resolve the tension by emphasizing either ex ante or ex post controls over judicial autonomy – or, at times, both. Specifically, compared to historic patterns, the chosen resolution appears to have shifted influence over the judiciary from the executive to the legislature. This result is congruent with Negretto's (2013) finding that presidential power, especially in the area of appointments, has declined in Latin American constitutionalism.

Qualitative descriptions of the region's trends and individual courts support our multidimensional conceptual framework and measurement strategy. Purely additive or one-dimensional measures do not capture this complexity and miss much of the interesting diversity in recent changes to constitutional justice in Latin America and elsewhere. The conventional, somewhat teleological, narrative of eventual approximation to the liberal model of Anglo-European constitutionalism – and especially to US-style minimal-procedural constitutionalism – does not fit the empirical reality of emerging constitutional models. Not one, but at least three distinct models of constitutional justice have emerged in Latin America, likely with important implications for the nature of democracy. Like Uprimny (2011), we show the appearance of new models of constitutionalism that define new goals for constitutional justice. But our analysis suggests that the ability to contest and debate the implications of these new goals is importantly constrained by the levels of autonomy accorded to constitutional courts. One implication of this is that the constitutional justice systems of the new multinational, multicultural constitutions are vulnerable to capture from the moment of their design. It is worth recalling O'Donnell's (1996) admonition that we should not simply assume Latin America is partway along some path toward the advanced industrial world's model of democracy, but rather should take care to observe the distinct patterns that are being institutionalized in the developing world.

3

Constitutional Governance and the Politics of Judicial Design

There is a disjuncture between our theories about the origin of strong courts with the power of judicial review and the work that courts are actually doing in most countries. The diversity in the design of systems of constitutional justice is matched by the diversity in the roles these systems play in different countries. As many scholars have noted, courts today play a role in shaping healthcare policy, moderating political conflict, defining the boundaries of citizenship, and deciding some of the most contentious issues of the day – including everything from the outcome of particular elections to the very nature of national identity. These interventions are not always positive and they are not always in defiance of powerful political actors, but they are often very consequential for the politics and policies of a country. In this chapter, we offer a theory for the origin of these new systems of constitutional justice that can account for both the scope of their authority and the degree of their autonomy from the Ruling Coalition (RC).

The new broad-spectrum relevance of constitutional justice seems especially true in Latin America, where the literature on courts and law transitioned quickly and nearly seamlessly from jeremiads on the perpetual weakness of courts in the region to sometimes celebratory and sometimes critical reflections on the increasing judicialization of politics. The region's high courts have granted to or withheld from presidents the right to run for reelection. They have tackled the toughest environmental challenges in their countries. They have taken on or (mostly) made room for extractivist developmental models in the face of indigenous opposition, they have endorsed or stalled privatization schemes and the marketization of public health, and they have upheld or (mostly) struck down amnesty schemes for former dictators and their henchmen. In short, constitutional courts are now, in many – though clearly not all – countries, deeply enmeshed in the politics of some of the most contentious and intractable public policy debates in the region. They have become deeply consequential political actors, whether acting to challenge or carry out the Ruling Coalition's political project.

And yet our theories for the origin of these newly powerful courts fail to take into account both the reach and the political limitations of these institutions. Existing theories typically conceptualize constitutional courts as checks on political power, seeking to explain why otherwise unfettered politicians might create mechanisms that will limit their freedom of action in postconstituent politics. The answer typically has to do with the aggregate, intertemporal benefit of precommitting to a set of fixed principles, with constitutional courts modeled as a (or the) mechanism to prevent defections from an original pact. But this simplified model, though quite fertile thus far in guiding our research, needs to be complicated to match the more complex roles that courts have assumed, and the more nuanced outcomes we see in the texts. Courts do both less and more than what the models assume.

On the one hand, these theories implicitly assume that constitutional courts are expected to fulfill more modest roles, perhaps limited to guaranteeing the fairness of political competition, or at most, to enforcing a clear agreement on, say, property rights with a predictable, if not a settled, meaning. On the other, the theories downplay the implications of the considerable body of literature showing that courts remain creatures of politics long after their creation. Finally, their basic assumptions defy what we know about the indeterminacy of constitutional texts, the importance of ongoing judicial (and extrajudicial) interpretations in giving meaning to those texts, and the role of contemporaneous politics in shaping both courts and interpretations. Our goal is to propose and defend a theory of the origin and configuration of constitutional courts that is more congruent with the way courts and constitutional law actually operate, and that offers more promise in explaining how the various countries of the region ended up with the courts they have.

3.1. PUTTING EXISTING THEORIES ON THE SAME PLANE

In all the stylized stories explaining the appearance of strong courts with the power of judicial review, there are two decision-making moments with potentially different decision-making coalitions. Constitutions are drafted, under special rules of decision, by elite actors usually representing identifiable social interests, such as a political party, a politicized ethnic group, ideology, or a material interest. At the constitution-making moment, then, the Originating Coalition (OC) consists of the set of actors whose agreement is required in order to produce a binding initial pact – either a constitution or a constitutional amendment. The power of judicial review is conventionally seen as a (or the) mechanism to enforce constitutional precommitments against the wishes of a later Ruling Coalition (RC), by which we mean the set of actors whose agreement is required to produce a publicly binding decision in ordinary postconstituent politics (cf. Elster 2000). The dominant theories thus all assume that courts are more or less willing and able to enforce the OC's initial agreement against the possible defection of a subsequent RC, and assign courts a largely negative, boundary-policing role in postconstitutional politics.

 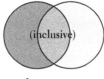 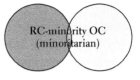

Credible commitment   Insurance   Hegemonic preservation

FIGURE 3.1. Relationship of the Originating Coalition to the Ruling Coalition in existing theories of the creation of judicial review

Although often imagined as the same (unitary) actor, conceptually the OC and the RC are two distinct sets of actors, and membership in these two sets can range from near identity to no overlap at all. Most often, as a function of procedures that set a higher bar for constitutional creation and amendment than for ordinary legislation, the OC is more inclusive, perhaps a supermajoritarian coalition.[1] The RC, meanwhile, typically has less inclusive, more purely majoritarian, rules for decision-making, although the rules for ordinary governing may also vary in their inclusiveness (Lijphart 2012). In these cases, and especially for amendments as opposed to new constitutions, the OC is often a superset of the expected RC. Other times, a single very strong party may dominate the constitutional process, even under democracy, and expect to govern thereafter, so that the OC closely represents the RC. In fact, in countries with hegemonic governing parties, the OC could even be a subset of the RC. Alternatively, the OC could be limited to a narrow set of actors selected by an outgoing regime to craft the constitution. In these cases, the OC might exclude the expected RC altogether, or assign it a minimal role. See Figure 3.1 for a graphic depiction of the relationship between the OC and RC in different contexts.

We can find examples of judicial review under all three of these conditions. Brazil 1988[2] was written by a broadly inclusive OC. In that case, a transitional civilian regime oversaw the election of a constituent assembly under proportional representation rules. This election produced a fragmented, broadly pluralistic body that included representatives of all the interests that could plausibly make up future RCs. In contrast, President Chávez's party controlled more than 95 percent of the seats in the constituent assembly that wrote Venezuela 1999; and that party continued to govern, as it had planned all along, under the new constitution. Similarly, Egypt 1979 is a case in which the OC expected to actually be the RC – Mubarak had no intention of stepping down when he amended the constitution to establish judicial review and a strong court (Moustafa 2003). In both of these cases, the

---

[1]   To be clear, by supermajoritarian we simply mean that it requires the agreement of a broader coalition of elites than would be required for ordinary political decision-making. Whether or not the OC actually represents more than a majority of people or interests in society is a different question.

[2]   For efficiency, we use the convention *country year* to refer to new constitutional texts or amendments. In this example, "Brazil 1988" refers to the constitution produced by Brazil's 1988 constituent assembly.

RC dominated the OC, even though one constitutional moment happened under dictatorship and the other under democracy. In contrast, in Chile 1980, Turkey 1961, and Egypt 2013 an authoritarian regime handpicked a set of drafters to write a constitution that would reflect the preferences of the regime, purposely excluding important, possibly majoritarian interests but including a set of (minority) interests that were not expected to be part of the RC. All three constitutions were written against a return to democracy when popular majorities might be hostile to the values enshrined in the respective constitutions; all three consequently provide for strong judicial review mechanisms with a great deal of autonomy from the RC.

Although the literature does not discuss the differences in these terms, it is this varying relationship between the OC and the expected RC that distinguishes the various theories explaining the appearance of judicial review. Each has a different basic assumption about the relationship of the OC to the expected future RC, and thus imputes a different purpose for the constitutional court. In the credible commitment story (Ferejohn and Sager 2003; Moustafa 2003), a relatively unconstrained sovereign (the current and future RC) acting as the OC unilaterally sets up a court and a constitution that will bind its future lawmaking self, in order to induce a third party to enter a relationship of some sort – a purely economic game between a ruler and outside investors in Moustafa (2003), or a more broadly socioeconomic pact in North and Weingast's (1989) account. In the insurance theory, a more balanced and inclusive OC made up of several elite groups (each of which expects to alternate control of the RC) seeks to constrain temporary future majorities to the terms of their initial agreement in order to protect the mechanisms for alternation in power (Ginsburg 2003; Finkel 2005). In Hirschl's hegemonic preservation story, a currently dominant narrow OC – comprised of threatened economic, political, and judicial elites – sets up a court to protect a set of constitutionally entrenched interests against the predations of a future, more democratic RC in which they will have, at best, a marginal role (see Beard 1913 on the US Constitution; also Hirschl 2004; Belge 2006).

Figure 3.1 organizes the existing theories of the creation of judicial review, arranging them on a continuum from RC-dominant to RC-minority. We label RC-dominant Originating Coalitions "majoritarian" because the OC excludes all interests beyond the expected RC, and RC-minority OCs "minoritarian" because the OC includes minoritarian social interests often to the exclusion of the RC. We label the intermediate model "inclusive," because it includes both majority and minority interests.

In each case, according to all these accounts, the court's role is to prevent the winning bargain at the constitutional moment from being undone in ordinary politics. Each of these theories gives us some insight into the motivations for establishing judicial review, and the insurance theory (Ginsburg 2003; Ginsburg and Versteeg 2013) in particular yields impressive predictions for the importance of political fragmentation in leading to judicial review, yet it is important to push the theory further.

One initial dissatisfaction with existing theories is observational: each theory implicitly or explicitly suggests that we should not see courts with judicial review at other points along the continuum, and yet we do. As discussed above, each of these accounts plausibly describes the creation of particular constitutional courts around the world. At minimum, then, we might like to see something like a unifying theory that tells us something about the characteristics of the resulting systems of constitutional justice, based on the nature of the OC that creates them. Secondly, we often see constitutional courts doing much more than (or something altogether different from) constraining a current government to the relatively fixed terms of an initial agreement. Every day, courts address situations never even considered by the OC on the basis of rights and meanings that are – at best and in the most generous interpretation – implicit in the constitutional text. On the one hand, courts often pursue goals that were not part of the original constitutional discussions, and on the other, they just as often legitimize as limit the decisions of the RC. What courts actually do does not line up very well with what the theories assume they are designed to do.

In addition, and perhaps most importantly, the theories appear to ask too much of courts, given what we know about the politics of judicial behavior. All three theories rest on the basic assumption that a court created by the OC at time t will be able to significantly constrain the RC to the foundational agreement at $t + n$, long after the OC has dissolved. But the literature on judicial behavior and the nature of judicial power unanimously calls into question a court's ability to be consistently and importantly countermajoritarian over even the medium term. Once past the inaugural moment, courts are always in one way or another subject to postconstitutional politics. Through appointments, the manipulation of judicial incentives, lawmaking, noncompliance, and the need for popular support, courts remain tethered to a greater or lesser degree to contemporary, rather than foundational, politics (Dahl 1957; Epstein and Knight 1998; Vanberg 2001; Staton 2004; Rosenberg 2008). Just as fatal to this basic assumption is the nature of constitutional law. On the most important issues, constitutions are open-ended, polysemous texts, unsuited to establishing clear boundaries and hard constraints. Without more assurance of their future meaning, the broad, open-ended statements of principle that occupy large portions of constitutional text do not seem calculated to do much to allay uncertainty and fear. And, most basically still, in the final analysis, the very structure and existence of the court is subject to renegotiation: a sufficiently strong, sufficiently importuned RC can often simply create a new court by constituting a new OC.

The implausibility of courts as standalone mechanisms to enforce preexisting agreements against a determined RC is exacerbated at both ends of the continuum. At the Credible Commitment end, the RC is essentially identical to the OC, and there are no veto players to protect the court, which is in consequence fully endogenous to the RC/OC. Thus, a credible commitment theory needs a story about collective action or social enforcement (e.g., Weingast 1997; Carrubba 2009), or there is nothing to keep the RC from simply redrawing the terms of the constitutional pact, as it ultimately did in Egypt (Moustafa 2003). For theories of hegemonic preservation, which sit at the opposite, strongly minoritarian, end of the continuum, the problem is even more pointed – the court is tasked with enforcing an agreement in which the RC had no part, for the express purpose of limiting the ambitions of the RC, on behalf of a group that is no longer part of the dominant lawmaking coalition or even plausibly part of a new constitutional coalition. There is nothing in the theory to keep the RC from constituting itself as a new OC and crafting a pact and a court more to its liking – as the Morsi government did in 2012, before it was brought down. And yet, in Turkey, for reasons that are not explicitly addressed by existing theories, just such a strongly countermajoritarian arrangement appears to have lasted for decades (cf. Belge 2006), until the recent collapse of that constitutional settlement. Our theories of judicial creation need to be more explicit about what happens after the moment of creation to make that possible.

In the middle range, where we find the insurance theory, the problem is less acute. In the more inclusive cases, we find two plausible, but ultimately unsatisfying, ways in which the courts might be protected from the RC. One account of postconstituent politics is that each of the members of the OC who achieves RC status has an incentive to respect the court while in power, in exchange for the court's protection when out of power in the future. But self-restraint in hopes of a future payoff is not a particularly powerful motive for compliance. Current majorities should have a high future discount rate, especially since constitutional transgressions (like cheating at elections or restraining freedom of expression) can make it more likely they will retain RC status indefinitely, thus rendering the court's protection unnecessary. The temptation to violate the constitutional pact is exacerbated by the fact that every future RC will have the same powerful incentive to violate the pact. The alternative account is that the other members of the OC, or the general population, retain sufficient power in postconstitutional politics to protect the court and generate compliance when the court calls out a violation. The minoritarian members of the OC or an offended populace could, for instance, impose political costs on the RC for any transgressions of the original pact.

But even this modest claim can only be operative in particular circumstances, primarily when the court is less necessary. When the RC is very strongly majoritarian, it should be difficult for the opposition to impose political costs for a transgression against the constitution made precisely on behalf of that majority. This is especially true when the transgression affects the core interests of the government and the opposition, such as the ability to retain power (Epstein et al. 2001), or important goals, such as those that touch on constitutional issues. When the RC is weaker or the issues less important, the other members of the OC should be equally able to veto or punish a serious transgression without the help of the "weakest branch." They can resist in ordinary politics or wait for the next election to reverse the transgression. The fact that, presumably, the RC responds more immediately and directly to majoritarian elements in the population means they are less likely to pay a price for doing precisely what the majority has elected them to do.

In the end, we are left with Whittington's (2005: 583) observation: "For 'judicial activism' . . . to be sustained over time, the courts must operate in a favorable political environment." A satisfactory theory of judicial creation cannot be based on the idea that constitutional designers – in many cases experienced and influential political operatives – have romantic and implausible notions of how courts work. What is missing from the story, then, is an acknowledgment that the constitutional pact is not a black and white document, and judicial interpretation is more than simply preserving and enforcing the meaning of an original agreement. Also missing is an account that endogenizes the conditions under which a court might be able and willing to constrain the RC, or alternatively, serve to legitimize the RC's decisions. We need a theory of consequential courts that is not blind to the politics of judicial behavior. In the next section, we elaborate a theory of constitutional justice that takes into account both the diversity of what courts actually do in practice and the ways in which contemporaneous politics affect them.

3.2. A UNIFYING THEORY: COURTS AS MECHANISMS OF CONSTITUTIONAL GOVERNANCE

What are the political origins of these different models of constitutional justice? Can we uncover a single logic underlying the very disparate systems of constitutional justice that appear in global constitutionalism in recent decades? In Chapter 4, we will exploit the multidimensional comparative measure to uncover the correlates of the various models, but first we need to take a closer look at, and complicate, our existing theories of the origins of judicial review.

As previewed above, rather than being imagined as a hard constraint to prevent transgressions from a foundational agreement that can be read from a text with a settled meaning, we argue judicial review primarily serves an ongoing dynamic governance function for issues of constitutional significance – what we will call constitutional governance. And we expect that the logic of institutional design will be consistent with the logic of constitutional governance. Elkins et al. (2009, ch. 4, 106–9) note that constitutions are incomplete contracts subject to renegotiation. As they do, we also conceive of judicial review as one way to elaborate on the meaning of that contract in response to changing conditions, but we explicitly theorize the way in which the Originating Coalition establishes the sphere of constitutional governance and builds in mechanisms of control and accountability to ensure – as far as it can – that this sphere remains linked to its principles and interests.

First, from Hirschl's (2004) theory of hegemonic preservation, we take the more general point that constitutions define a space of constitutional politics for issues of exceptional importance to the OC that appear to be threatened by the expected RC. Within the sphere of constitutional justice, the governing coalition's discretion is limited and directed to particular ends, under the supervision of a new set of actors and institutions. In many cases, especially if the constitution is largely reflective of the RC's values, we might imagine that this constitutional oversight will not be a significant constraint, and therefore that there is little cost to a dominant actor in constitutionalizing all of its values. But once we move away from a notion of (constitutional) law as something fairly determinate and predictable, it is easy to see that any decisions within this space can be challenged. And while some constitutional terms may be quite specific (as procedural provisions tend to be) many of the crucial provisions are both substantive and exceptionally open ended.

Rights, in particular, enshrine broad constitutional principles without necessarily constraining outcomes in a way that can be predicted ex ante. For example, Sanford Levinson (2012) notes that the US Constitution can be seen as including a "Constitution of Settlement" and a "Constitution of Conversation" – terms that mark two ends of a continuum to be sure, but still a useful distinction for thinking about how the overall system is constituted.[3] A Constitution of Conversation is clearly unsuited to the task of demarcating uncrossable boundaries, but it is exactly the tool needed to define a sphere of constitutional justice that may be governed using the special procedures and language of constitutional politics. As we noted in Chapter 1, the broader the scope of constitutional justice, the greater the number of issues for which the RC must share governance with a (potentially) broader set of actors and institutions. The decision to put a particular issue within the sphere of constitutional justice is not cost-free, so we should expect constituents to constitutionalize only the issues and policies they believe may be threatened in postconstituent politics.

Second, and for related reasons, constitution writers should understand the constitutional court(s) as a crucial (though certainly not the only) political space where the meaning of the constitutional text will be developed (Stone Sweet 1999). Because the task is dynamic and evolving, with meanings that are not settled in advance and courts that remain subject to contemporary politics, these courts should not be imagined as apolitical actors simply transferring and applying normative commitments from a historical OC to the current RC. Rather, designers should (implicitly or explicitly) understand constitutional justice systems (and their courts) as ongoing political spaces in their own right, subject to contestation and control. In contrast to Stone Sweet's (1999) model, which gives judges and interpretation near complete autonomy in the process of evolving constitutional meaning, a reasonably sophisticated OC will build in ways to influence the court even after the constitutional moment is past.

---

[3]   According to Levinson, the "Constitution of Settlement" consists of the provisions of the US Constitution, such as the January 20 date of the presidential inauguration, which are not subject to constitutional debate and varied interpretation. In contrast, the "Constitution of Conversation" consists of those constitutional provisions that are the subject of debate and differing interpretations in courtrooms, law schools, and other institutions of legal thought.

In order to accomplish this goal, the design of constitutional courts must define a third coalition – what we call a Constitutional Governance Coalition, or CGC – to operate the mechanisms that mediate between the court and politics. We define the CGC as the coalition of actors whose agreement is required to exercise the mechanisms of judicial control – appointments, retention, removal, court packing, and the rest – and who have access to the court for protection of their substantive interests. Members of the CGC, by definition, will be able to raise constitutional questions and challenge legislative outcomes and executive actions on the issues that are of crucial importance to the OC. These issues should include both (a) questions of access to power, the primary concern of the insurance theory and (b) substantive goals, the primary concern of the hegemonic preservation theory. Its members will be able to continue to influence the court through the very mechanisms of judicial control that create problems for existing theories of the creation of judicial review. These mechanisms will allow members of the CGC to participate in governing in the sphere of constitutional justice, via the principles and mechanisms of constitutional justice. Not coincidentally, the CGC can also become the court's support constituency when it needs protection or compliance muscle.

The CGC will be generically reflective of the OC, but a product of postconstituent politics, replacing the original players with their successors in interest, or with new players who occupy the same political spaces. For example, a court designed by a group of actors who expect to be in opposition will make room in the CGC for the opposition, while a court designed by a dominant RC will restrict constitutional governance to the RC, crafting courts with limited autonomy. When the constituent process is dominated by actors who distrust the executive but expect to occupy the legislature, they will reduce the role of the executive in the CGC and expand that of the legislature. When they have reason to feel they might be external to electoral politics altogether, they will constitute a CGC with a strong role for unelected actors, especially those whom they feel might be sympathetic to their views. The power dynamics of the OC should be clearly visible in the resulting CGC.

3.3. PRINCIPLES OF DESIGN FOR CONSTITUTIONAL GOVERNANCE

With this in mind, the constitutional governance theory leads directly to two basic principles of design – one for the scope of constitutional justice and another for the degree of autonomy. Recall that the sphere of constitutional justice is defined by a court's scope of authority: essentially, the court's formal capacity to intervene decisively in a broad range of politically significant disputes on behalf of a broad range of actors. The mechanisms of judicial control and accountability central to the construction of the CGC are the institutional features that define a court's formal ex ante and ex post autonomy. These formal institutions mediate between political actors and the court, both before the judges are seated, through the formal process of appointment, and after the judges have been seated, by formal means of punishing or rewarding judges. By specifying who can exercise control over the court, these two dimensions define the CGC.

We turn first to the genesis of a system's scope of authority. The first implication of our model is that the scope of constitutional justice should largely reflect the consensus of the OC – including particularistic concessions to individual veto players in the OC and logrolling compromises – *over any issues that cannot be entrusted to the RC*. Of course, the ideology of the originating constitutional coalition should matter since it determines the potential set of preferences that are available to be constitutionalized. But we expect the OC to select and constitutionalize only those issues it does not expect the future RC to govern according to its preferences. The more the expected future RC looks like the OC, the fewer issues need to be constitutionalized. A threatened Left, for instance, in a constitutional governance model, will work harder to constitutionalize its preferences than a powerful one. Thus, we have Principle 1.

> Principle 1:   The ideology of the OC determines the scope of constitutional justice, <u>conditional</u> on the extent to which the RC dominates the OC. A more dominant RC will constitutionalize less of its project, and vice versa.

There is an obvious alternative hypothesis. If the "expressive" function of law – that is, the way law articulates a particular normative vision – dominates constitutional design, ideology should translate directly into the constitutional text. Thus, for example, a more expansive state project by a dominant member of the OC should produce a constitution that demands a more expansive role for the state. In an "expressive law" model, the more the OC is dominated by, say, a Left party, the more the constitution should reflect the preferences of the Left.

This first principle has to do with what interests an OC might seek to protect through constitutionalism and judicial review. However, as our stylized constitutional governance narrative above suggests, designers should recognize that legal texts and professionalism alone are not enough to ensure that the constitutional court will continue to advance the interests of the OC well into an unpredictable future. Thus, the OC should seek to retain some influence over the court through the CGC's use of ex ante and ex post controls, rather than aiming to craft an autarchic court that is beyond anyone's control. This brings us to Principle 2.

> Principle 2:   The CGC will reflect the composition of the OC. A minoritarian OC will constitute a minoritarian CGC, a balanced OC will constitute an inclusive CGC, and a majoritarian OC will constitute a majoritarian CGC.

Here the most immediate contrary expectation is one based on a naïve formalistic model of constitutional adjudication. We have proposed that the OC will typically be sophisticated enough to attend to the construction of a suitable CGC. But a naïvely legalist constituent coalition that is not dominated by the future RC will seek to insulate its creation from politics altogether, rather than crafting a governance coalition that looks like itself. In this alternative model, the OC trusts its threatened values to the discipline and logic of the law, rather than to a politics of constitutional governance through the use of ex ante and ex post mechanisms of control.

We do not have strong expectations regarding whether the OC will give the CGC more ex ante or more ex post tools to exercise control. Our overall theory is more directly addressed to ex ante controls, which orient future judicial outcomes in a general direction according to broad ideological perspectives, rather than offering a chance to micromanage the court or craft particular outcomes in particular cases. They allow the controllers to imbue the court with a particular ideology and philosophy of judging (by appointing sincere judicial allies), without necessarily engaging in actions that are seen as harmful to conventional notions of judicial independence (e.g., removing a particular judge or an entire court). In this sense, ex ante controls are more congruent with the image we have presented of a CGC exercising positive, if probabilistic, controls over an evolving system of constitutional justice that captures their deepest fears and convictions, without undermining that system through visible manipulation and interference.

Ex post controls can help reverse, and maybe prevent, undesired outcomes – either through the threat of punishment or through removal of the offending judges and eventually the reversal of their decisions – but they are less likely to produce a court willingly embarked on a common constitutional project. As a result, we should expect that levels of ex post autonomy might respond to relatively different political dynamics than ex ante autonomy. If it is true that the CGC has the ability to set the general direction the court will take, it may make sense for the RC to have more control over ex post controls – an emergency brake, should the court become a runaway train. However, as we do not have a strong expectation in this regard, we will assume for now that the OC sees these two mechanisms of control as either fungible or jointly necessary and will seek to occupy both. After the empirical analysis, we will speculate about the meaning of some of the differences we find in the politics of the two mechanisms of control.

There is a third, very general expectation that we can derive from our theory. The constitutional governance theory depends on our sense that constitutional democracies enshrine dual systems of governance, one for ordinary politics and one for constitutional justice issues, each with its own governing coalition. If we are wrong altogether about the connection between the OC and CGC, it may be that an observation made long ago by Martin Shapiro contains more truth. Shapiro (1981: 34) once noted, "No regime is likely to allow significant political power to be wielded by an isolated judicial corps free of political restraints."[4] While this observation is

---

[4] In fairness, Martin Shapiro was speaking in the context of the origins of the common law, in which the sovereign constituted the courts *and* expected to govern. For these situations, where the RC dominates

essentially what underlies our claim that there will be a CGC, without more it assumes that governance is unitary and responsive to the RC (the "regime"), rather than being dual: responsive to the CGC for constitutional matters and the RC for ordinary politics. If governance is unitary, as Shapiro assumes, rather than dual, as we argue, we should expect that, all else equal, courts with more authority will be subject to greater controls (i.e., less autonomy). But if governance is split, as we contend, then a court with more authority (to attend to the concerns of a more pluralistic CGC, as seen above) will have more autonomy from the RC (i.e., will be governed by a more pluralistic CGC).

In all this we are speaking, of course, of the designers' goals. It is worth repeating at this point that what we expect is for designers to have the intent to preserve a role for their successors in interest in the CGC, and that this intent will be reflected in the DNA of constitutional justice. Whether or not they succeed in controlling the CGC years later, given what actually happens in post-constituent politics, is another matter altogether. We predict that OCs will seek to protect their threatened interests from a hostile RC, not that they will succeed in doing so, or, for that matter, that they will need to do so.

3.4. ALTERNATIVE LOGICS

We proposed a constitutional governance model of judicial design in which the dominance of the expected RC within the OC is decisive. We also argued that the logic of constitutional governance implies the conditional importance of ideology and a history of violence. Perhaps the most straightforward alternative expectations are simply the converse of the constitutional governance theory, as already laid out above. The first, for authority, derives from the expressive value of law. If the expressive logic dominates over the logic of governance, then ideology should have an unconditional effect. The second, for autonomy, is based on a formalist model of law, and would expect efforts to insulate the court from all influences, rather than an attempt to subject the court to a CGC that reflects the OC. The final one, for autonomy, is derived from Shapiro's observations that no "regime" would grant a powerful court significant autonomy. If governance is unitary rather than split between ordinary and constitutional politics, there should be an unconditional inverse relationship between authority and autonomy. At the most general level, then, these constitute the null hypotheses for our analyses.

We will show in Chapter 4 and in the case studies that follow that, in fact, the logic of constitutional governance dominates the design decisions at the constitutional moment. But that does not mean that no other logics are at play. The members of constituent assemblies are a heterogeneous group with varying degrees of

---

the OC, we too would expect unitary governance, with a CGC that is also dominated by the RC, although we would expect courts with less authority.

sophistication and different ideas of how law should and does work. Moreover, the process of constitution-making is a messy one, and there are bound to be competing imperatives at work, to say nothing of competing goals and competing notions of how to achieve even shared goals. Gary Jacobsohn (2010) has noted the prevalence of "constitutional disharmonies" in constitutions around the world, and we fully expect that these disharmonies respond, at least in part, to very different conceptions of how constitutional justice works, and not just competing views of what it should contain. Our argument is that the logic of constitutional governance dominates the design of systems of constitutional justice, not that it is the only logic at work in the drafting of constitutions. Next, we present some alternative logics that are not directly contrary to ours, but could be complementary and also at work in the constitutional moment.

Perhaps the most fundamental objection we must overcome in making our case is the idea that constitutional designers rarely spend enough time thinking about constitutional justice to even introduce a systematic politics into its design. Relatedly, our entire account could be seen as resting on a relatively sophisticated legal realist understanding of how courts and law work within a political system. One could object that Latin American constituents are more likely to hold a naïve legalist view of law and courts, and thus that they should simply seek to follow formalist civil law traditions in the design of their institutions. Either way, constituents would be more likely to borrow technocratic solutions from other constitutions than to seriously tailor the system to their own circumstances.

We disagree, of course. In our view, our argument rests on a fairly intuitive sense on the part of constituents that, if a particular institution is going to adjudicate matters that are important to them, they should take steps to ensure they have a voice in choosing (ex ante) and monitoring (ex post) the decision-makers within that institution. But if constituents are uninterested or unsophisticated, or if a truly naïve model of adjudication dominates the thinking of constitution makers in the region, it is possible that we would see decisions that are oblivious to the power politics of constitutional governance. In that case, we should not expect the constitutional governance logic to explain very much at all.

3.4.1. *Diffusion of Regional and Period Models*

Elkins et al. (2009) find that constitutional design generally is most importantly influenced by the previous constitutional model, the time period, and the region. We restrict the analysis to a single region, usually understood as having a relatively unified constitutional tradition; to a relatively short period (and we further control for the passage of time); and we control for country-specific autocorrelation. Given the Elkins et al. findings, if designers are slavishly following common models, then there should be very little remaining variation to explain, and what remains should be quite idiosyncratic. To the extent that we find any results at all for our variables, we can conclude that the logic of constitutional governance is a sufficiently power-ful motivator to overcome these cultural/ideational inertias.

Another possible alternative source of systematic variation is diffusion, whether within the region, or from external, perhaps more prestigious, models, such as the Spanish or German model. As we will see in Chapters 5–7, a glance at the tran-scripts of constitutional debates in the region makes it evident that designers were keenly aware of different foreign models, and often sought to emulate them. Given the importance of constitutional governance as we have described it, however, we would expect the OC to pick and choose from among international models, and to tweak the chosen ones even further, to suit its governance needs. Diffusion, in the constitutional governance model, serves as a drafting toolkit from which to draw provisions that best suit an OC's purposes (see Frankenberg 2013, ch. 1, for an evocative description of this process). It is not our principal goal here to test for the importance of diffusion in the design of systems of constitutional justice, but in order to ensure that our findings are not artifacts of global changes, we will control for global trends that might be affecting all the countries.

3.4.2. *Learning*

We believe there is quite clear evidence of learning at work. Although our first round of testing confirmed key expectations for ex ante and ex post autonomy, there are indications in the data and the literature that we should be looking for slightly differ-ent patterns in the two dimensions. First, our results for ex post autonomy, as we will see in Chapter 4, are considerably weaker than those for ex ante autonomy. Second, the correlation between the two autonomy subdimensions changes, as we saw in Chapter 2, about midway through the period. Moreover, Sandra Botero (2017) has argued that the Right in particular changed its views on highly autonomous courts halfway through this period. The very courts neoliberal reformers thought would be essential to a market economy ended up embracing a variety of progressive, redis-tributive projects, leading to a backlash against courts from the Right. As a result, in addition to our basic findings for ex post autonomy, we also test for evidence of learning – we will check to see whether the Right changed its preferences on auton-omy at some point during the period of this study.

Of course, this is not really a different logic, but rather a source of variation in designers' preferences within the logic of constitutional governance. The Right initially adopted the second generation Washington Consensus gospel that more autonomous courts were good for development in the context of a relatively unre-strained market model. But by the end of the 1990s, it was clear that highly auton-omous courts with a broad scope of authority, especially in places like Costa Rica and Colombia, were interfering with attempts to roll back the welfare state and introduce market reforms. It was the Right, then, that led the call in the early 2000s for curbing courts' autonomy. In Brazil, for example, Cardoso's government pushed for many years, and finally secured with the help of Lula's continuity-oriented government, a series of reforms meant to enhance what they called "external control" of the judiciary (Brinks 2005; Nunes 2010b).

3.4.3. *Regime-Specific Logics (Legitimacy)*

Yet others have made the argument that dictatorships prefer weak (i.e., low authority) but independent (i.e., high autonomy) courts, in order to secure some legitimacy for their regime. Our expectation, in contrast, is that authoritarian regimes (like any other OC) are more likely to seek to control the courts as spaces for continued governance, rather than entrust the mechanisms of control to an alternative coalition, simply to score some legitimacy points. Existing explanations for judicial empowerment tend to assume that democratization is the main impetus behind the appearance of courts that are more autonomous and more powerful. In fact, we expect that the logic of constitutional governance, and the dominance of the expected RC in designing the system of constitutional justice, will have a continuous effect on autonomy and authority, regardless of the nature of the regime. While authoritarian regimes designing their own constitutions are more likely to dominate the OC, it is that feature and its effect on constitutional governance that will make the difference, and not some desire for legitimacy.

Indeed, if anything, we do not believe that the preferences of authoritarian regimes will be that much different from those of democratic systems with a similar distribution of power between the RC and the rest of the OC. Recall the five functions that Shapiro (1981), and Ginsburg and Moustafa (2008) attribute to authoritarian courts, in addition to the basic dispute resolution function: "(1) establish social control and sideline political opponents, (2) bolster a regime's claim to 'legal' legitimacy, (3) strengthen administrative compliance within the state's own bureaucratic machinery and solve coordination problems among competing factions within the regime, (4) facilitate trade and investment, and (5) implement controversial policies so as to allow political distance from core elements of the regime" (Ginsburg and Moustafa 2008). All of these functions have been equally important to authoritarian and democratic governments in Latin America since the 1970s.

Our argument throughout the book is based on a basic insight: that courts – real courts – can provide many benefits to a regime or sociopolitical coalition, including facilitating social control, monitoring bureaucratic behavior, legitimizing regime decisions, and the like, with comparatively fewer costs and lower risks than other mechanisms (Shapiro 1981; Moustafa 2003; Hirschl 2004; Ginsburg and Moustafa 2008). But to be "real courts," even an autocrat's courts must be endowed with non-trivial measures of authority and autonomy. In fact, both the potential benefit and the potential agency costs of courts to an autocrat or any RC are directly related to the levels of authority and autonomy with which they are endowed. Thus we expect that, rather than avoiding courts altogether or crafting exceptionally weak courts that cannot provide any benefits, strategic dictators will rely to a greater or lesser degree on courts that have some degree of autonomy and authority – much to the same degree as any other designer with the same monolithic characteristics.

3.5. CONCLUSION

As the logic of constitutional governance would predict, the terms that define the CGC and its mechanisms of control tend to be settled, in Levinson's (2012) terms, while the substantive terms establishing the guidelines for ruling within the sphere of constitutional justice are much more like parameters for a conversation. Together, they define a system of constitutional governance that can give certain actors the assurance that they will have a continuing role in that conversation, without having to settle at the constitutional moment all the issues that will come up in post-constitutional politics. The system is dynamic without being radically indeterminate. Law in the form of otherwise very indeterminate statements of rights matters insofar as it defines the basic subjects of concern, and the basic goals or principles that adjudication should seek to maximize. It does not determine the outcomes, but it determines the subject and the tenor of the conversation that will take place in the realm of constitutional justice. Importantly, it serves to subject certain issues to a CGC that has the potential, depending on the design of the system, to be more inclusive than the RC.

This goes some way toward addressing the possible democratic deficit of constitutions. King (2013a: 95) has no other solution to the problem of the "inescapable conservatism" of constitutions than to recommend more ease of amendment, that is, to "reconsider the tradition of strong entrenchment of constitutions." But if we are right, then constitutionalism is not (necessarily) unrepresentative or conservative. So long as the system of constitutional justice responds to a broader, more inclusive coalition, rather than a narrow but countermajoritarian one, and so long as the basic principles entrenched are susceptible to progressive as well as conservative interpretations, it can be a dynamic system for evolving constitutional meaning in line with secular movements in a country's understanding of constitutional justice. And it can do so without becoming a mere reflection of ordinary politics.

In short, in our account, judicial review and the constitutional text define a coalition that shares in governing within the sphere of constitutional justice, is a product of evolving political dynamics, and could be identical to neither the OC nor the current RC. The court, as a product and agent of the CGC, evolves and protects interpretations of the text that are probabilistically in harmony with the interests and values of the CGC. Rather than serving as a hard constraint to enforce pre-set boundaries, the court's role is to participate in constitutional governance, and to signal when certain actors are exceeding the bounds of acceptable constitutional politics, so that the remaining members of the CGC can respond accordingly. So long as the CGC continues to be strong relative to the RC, the court is not orphaned at the time of compliance, and is protected from a rewriting of the foundational agreement. Indeed, because the RC is usually a member of the CGC and (depending on institutional design and the political context) often the dominant one, the court will frequently be working to legitimize and enforce the decisions of the RC, rather than protecting countermajoritarian interests. Absent a fundamental shift in the power structure of the society, the constitutional governance scheme should be sustainable.

Note that, by this account, we would not expect constitutional justice to serve the interests of true outsiders – those who are outside the CGC – except serendipitously. We can and should expect constitutional justice to protect the goals chosen by the CGC, even on behalf of those members of the CGC who are minoritarian or in the opposition in respect to the RC. Some values, of course, have more or less universal application, and in the interests of consistency if nothing else, courts may extend their benefits to even the most marginal of outsiders. Moreover, to preserve their "courtness" and thus serve the function they are meant to perform, courts must act as courts, with all this implies, and therefore may be compelled to extend protection to similarly situated true outsiders to the CGC.[5] But we should not expect that to be their main task, and we should not expect them to be especially good at it or especially solicitous in that regard. Moreover, we should not expect courts to protect true outsiders whose interests or values are at odds with those that the CGC chose to protect. When we say that it is the courts' task to protect the interests of minorities, therefore, we should be more specific. It is the courts' task to protect the interests of the members of the CGC, especially when they are minorities in ordinary politics, but it is also the courts' task to legitimize the decisions of the RC when they advance the constitutional goals to which the CGC adheres.

---

[5] Shapiro (2001: 275–6) uses the colorful image of a "junkyard dog" to make this point: anyone who wishes to secure the benefits of a guard dog must expect to be bitten from time to time. To serve its useful legitimizing, rule making, and dispute resolution functions, a court must pose some risk, or it is no better than a simple committee setup to carry out a task.

4

Identifying the Political Origins of Constitutional Justice through Quantitative Analysis

We take two separate approaches to testing our constitutional governance theory. In Chapters 5–7, we will look in detail at the features of Originating Coalitions (OCs) in different countries, and at the debates in three different constituent processes. In each chapter, we also look more summarily at other cases of constitution-making, using both within-country historical comparisons and cross-country comparisons. Those chapters provide direct qualitative evidence of the logic of constitutional governance at work. In this chapter, in contrast, we deploy our quantitative measure of authority and autonomy and use regression analysis to see if the broad patterns we see taking place across the region are broadly consistent with our conjecture that this logic is dominant in the design of systems of constitutional justice. From the broad principles of design detailed in Chapter 3, we first derive concrete, testable, empirical implications specific to the region and the era that is the subject of our analysis. In order to test these hypotheses, we generate a new independent variable measuring the dominance of the expected Ruling Coalition (RC), and a variable that might approximate the dominant ideological orientation of the RC at the time of constitutional change.

The patterns we find in the data are consistent with our argument. In terms of authority, we find that a dominant RC has a tendency to constitutionalize less of its project, while a threatened one constitutionalizes more of it. Specifically, the Left, which has an expansive view of constitutional justice in this period, produces more ambitious spheres of constitutional justice when it is less assured that it will govern ordinary politics in the postconstitutional moment. The Right, which has a more restricted proposal for constitutional justice, prefers a Procedural Arbiter model, regardless of its dominance within the OC. A history of violence raises the stakes for both Left and Right but pushes them in opposite directions. A threatened Left, in a country with a history of violence, increases the authority of its constitutional courts. A threatened Right, in a similar context, pushes for a less robust system of constitutional justice – perhaps (though this is speculation) to avoid prosecution for rights violations.

In terms of autonomy, the Left and Right behave more or less the same way with the important exceptions we explore in this chapter. When they expect to dominate postconstitutional politics, both ends of the political spectrum seek to tie the Constitutional Governance Coalition (CGC) to the RC. When they cannot be confident that they will secure the RC, they expand the CGC to include minoritarian actors. When they cannot trust representative politics, they seek to expand it even further to civil society actors through the use of devices such as nominating commissions and the like.

4.1. FROM THEORY TO HYPOTHESES TO OPERATIONALIZATION

We begin with the principles of design we derived from our constitutional governance theory. The basic intuition is that the system of constitutional justice will be charged with those things the OC feels are important and threatened. A less secure OC, one less confident that it will be able to govern unconstrained, will put more of its constitutional project into the sphere of constitutional justice and will strengthen the mechanisms for protecting those issues. In other words, it will create systems with a greater scope of authority, if indeed it has an ideological project that requires the state to intervene on many issues. Moreover, the OC will seek to ensure that the gears and levers of the constitutional justice system remain subject to the influence of its successors after the constitutional moment is past. Thus, an OC in which the expected RC is less dominant will craft a CGC in which the RC is less dominant, and vice versa. Each of these principles leads to concrete observable implications that may be more or less specific to the Latin American context.

We test for the effect of the nature of the design coalition using a variable we constructed for each constitutional moment. We look at coalitions that produced both amendments and new constitutions in Latin America since 1975, and the constitutions that enter the sample in 1975. The variable is a function of the proportion of votes of the OC that are controlled by the ruling party, defined as the party of the current executive. Mathematically, the variable is equal to the difference between (a) the percentage of votes needed for approval of the constitutional text or amendment (typically, either a majority or two-thirds), which is what we have defined as the OC, and (b) the percentage of votes in the relevant body held by the currently ruling party.[1] We represent this visually in Figure 4.1: the variable measures the difference between the overlapping and the darker shaded portions in Figure 4.1 (which follows Figure 3.1). The variable also allows the RC to significantly exceed

---

[1] This variable is more complex to construct than might appear at first sight. When a series of decision instances (e.g., the House and Senate) have to approve a text, we take the maximum shortfall of the ruling party in any one of those instances. When the text has to be approved by a referendum, we assume the ruling party "controls" the percentage of presidential votes it earned in the most recent election. When the text is produced by an authoritarian regime (e.g., a decree of the ruling *junta*), we assume the regime controls 100 percent of the OC.

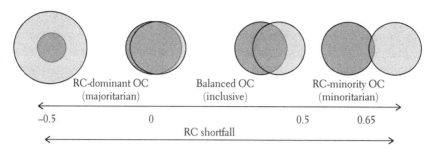

FIGURE 4.1. Relationship of the OC to the RC in the constitutional moment as measured by RC shortfall variable

the minimum OC if it controls more than the requisite percentage of the seats in the constituent body (as it did in Venezuela in 1998, with 95 percent of the seats).

To retain a positive sign for the coefficients, we refer to this variable as the "RC short-fall" (rather than as its opposite, RC dominance). The RC shortfall increases as we move from left to right in Figure 4.1. At the left end, where we depict an RC-dominant OC, we have negative values for the RC shortfall. At the right end, an RC-minority constituent assembly produces large positive values. The smaller the percentage of seats this party holds in the constituent body – whether it is a legislative assembly making amendments or a constituent assembly writing a new constitution – the less confidence we consider that this party (or any other) can have that they will rule unconstrained in the future. Our data offer substantial variation for this variable. In our sample the RC shortfall runs nearly the full logical range, from −0.5 (for dictators who write their own constitutions) or −0.45 (for Venezuela, where the constitutional assembly was dominated by one party with 95 percent of the seats and decided by a simple majority), at one end, to 0.65 at the other. The latter reflects the one instance (Ecuador 1997) in which the ruling party had a mere 2 percent of the seats in the Assembly, and the Assembly had a two-thirds majority decision rule. A description of this, and other key variables, is given in Table 4.1, found at the end of this chapter.

The focus on the currently ruling party as a stand-in for the expected RC is, in most cases, justified, even if in some instances the variable may not measure what we want. At the right end of the spectrum, it is highly unlikely that a government that calls for an assembly or constitutional amendment, and only holds a minority of the seats in that process, would expect to be hegemonic in the future. At the far left end, it is a bit more complicated. Without going deep into the particulars of each process, it may be impossible to distinguish between an assembly that is dominated by a government writing a constitution or amendment against the moment when it loses control, and one that is dominated by a government that is doing so in order to consolidate its power and continue governing. On average, we feel the latter – which is what we want to measure – is more likely in the Latin American context. Assemblies like the most recent Venezuelan or Ecuadorean ones are clear examples of this pattern and produce very low values on our RC shortfall variable. Moreover, amendments passed by legislative bodies are both more frequent and more likely to follow this pattern.

The one ambiguous case that comes to mind is the Chilean 1980 Constitution. In that case, Pinochet controlled the writing process and expected to govern for a long time. However, in some ways he was writing against the possibility that elections might bring a different party to power. In this case, as we will see in Chapter 5, the constitution was specifically designed to be an aid in governing for Pinochet and his Right-wing sociopolitical coalition and a constraint on any others who might come to power. In any event, the result of the plebiscite that was required to approve this constitution reflects this ambivalence, producing results in the mid-range for the variable. The values suggest uncertainty rather than either an expectation of hegemony or a certainty of loss. We feel that, on the whole, this variable adequately tests our theory any time the constitutional designers interpret the strength of the currently ruling party as a rough predictor of the strength of any future ruling party. So long as party system fragmentation is not expected to change dramatically, the variable should reflect generalized expectations of whether there will be dominant ruling parties or weak ones after the constitutional moment is past.

4.1.1. *First Principle: The Ruling Coalition and the Scope of Authority*

Principle 1: The ideology of the Originating Coalition determines the scope of constitutional justice, conditional on the dominance of the Ruling Coalition within the Originating Coalition.

If the logic of constitutional governance dominates design, then the subset of preferences that gains constitutional protection should be more extensive (a) when the RC is weaker within the OC and (b) to the extent the members of the OC have a more extensive state-based project than the likely RC. This is because, when a coalition that fully expects to govern in the postconstitutional moment controls the design, we expect it to restrict the space of constitutional justice in order to give itself free rein in governing the entire space of ordinary politics. On the other hand, when the expected RC is a small subset of the OC, we should expect a longer list of issues to be subjected to constitutional justice and a stronger court to push back against the RC. As the OC adds more and more players who are not assured of holding the dominant role in ordinary politics, on average, more and more issues are likely to make it onto the agenda for constitutional justice.

The first concrete hypothesis therefore is this:

H1: When the expected ruling party represents a smaller percentage of the constituent assembly, the court should have more authority. Conversely, when the expected ruling party dominates the assembly, the court should have less authority.

But ideology clearly matters. Not all OCs, regardless of the power dynamics within them and whether or not they expect to govern, want the same thing. Ideology provides the subject matter for these preferences. In Latin America, the great divide in modern constitutional politics is largely a Left–Right divide (Rodríguez Garavito 2010; Gargarella 2013), rather than, for instance, a secular–religious or center–periphery divide. The Left should prefer more state interventionism and a greater welfare state. This could be reflected in the inclusion of social and economic rights to ensure that its redistributive commitments are accorded some priority when it is not in power. If the OC reaches out to indigenous groups, as the Left has recently done in Latin America, it should also include cultural rights in the sphere of constitutional justice. To the extent that it relies on a more popular base, the OC will seek to ease access to justice. All these elements, in our coding, contribute to a greater scope of authority. The Right, on the other hand, is concerned primarily with protecting property rights, views social and economic rights and international human rights with suspicion, and is not overly concerned with populist mechanisms to access constitutional courts, all of which should contribute to systems with more limited authority. The Left, in short, should have a more robust constitutional governance agenda than the Right.

If our constitutional governance model – rather than an expressive model – of constitution-making is correct, the Left should constitutionalize more of this agenda when its expectation of ruling is weak. In contrast, the Right, not interested in an expansive state project, has little to constitutionalize in any event. So long as some basic rights are protected, the Right is content to let the market allocate outcomes whether or not it is in power, so it should create relatively lean, thin systems of constitutional justice, regardless of whether or not it dominates the constitutional coalition. This leads to our second concrete hypothesis, and the crucial test of our theory, at least on this dimension of design:

> H2:   The effect of ideology on the scope of authority is conditional on the expected dominance of the ruling party within the OC. The Left should craft more expansive constitutional courts, particularly when it is weaker. The Right, on the other hand, should always prefer a court with less authority, regardless of its dominance.

To test for this conditional effect, we use an interaction term between a measure of ideology and the RC shortfall variable. We measure the ideology of the RC using a modification of an index of the structural reforms associated with neoliberalism (Escaith and Paunovic 2004). Our variable measures each country's distance from the regional mean on that measure of neoliberal policies. The unmodified measure did not work for our purposes, as all countries in Latin America show a secular trend upward in the structural reform index for the period under study. Even the Left eventually abandoned the high levels of statism and protectionism that characterized the region in the 1970s, although it always stayed on the more statist side. Thus, to adjust for the time-variant meaning of the variable, we use each country's difference from the annual regional mean, identifying countries that are to the Right or the Left in the region for a given year (the range is −0.23 to 0.26; the mean is approximately zero, as expected). The modified measure reflects conventional understandings of which countries were to the right or left of the others at particular times, at least in terms of actual economic policy.

The measure is not directly a measure of ideology, but is a good proxy for the revealed preferences of the RC as a whole. The RC, nearly by definition, controls policy, and thus current policy should reveal approximately that coalition's preferences, whether it is the product of a single hegemonic party, or of a broad coalition of parties that join to produce a majority. We use this variable for two reasons. First, we use the variable because it better expresses the consensus of the RC, which is what we want to measure, rather than merely the views of the first party in that coalition. Second, we use it because it is available for more countries and more years, and is more reliably measured, than most measures of party ideology.

In addition to ideology, history shapes a people's preferences in constitution writing, and nothing has marked recent political history in Latin America more than violence. This history of political violence offers an additional opportunity to test for the logic of constitutional governance. In Latin America, the violence was more often than not directed at the Left, precisely in order to keep the Left out of governing. Thus, a weak Left should prefer more authority generally, as described above, but its preferences should be all the more strong when there is a history of violence, for additional protection and to expand the space within which it might have influence, even if it is in the minority. By construction, a court's scope of authority goes up when a constitution incorporates international human rights treaties, something a threatened Left might want in order to put the content and enforcement of rights beyond the reach of domestic majorities. We have already argued that the Right should generally prefer a less ambitious scope of constitutional justice, albeit one that protects certain basic negative rights. But a weak Right that was complicit in prior repression and now feels threatened by a future RC may prefer even weaker constitutional justice, if for no other reason than to avoid prosecution for past human rights violations.

H3: The effect of past violence on judicial authority is conditional on who writes the constitution. The more violence in the recent past, the less authority for courts crafted by a threatened Right, but the more authority for courts crafted by a threatened Left.

The dominant Right and Left should be essentially unaffected by a history of violence, since they do not need the constitutional sphere to pursue their goals or protect their interests.

To test this hypothesis, we use a three-way interaction between a measure of the country's recent history of violence,[2] our measure of ideology, and the RC shortfall.

4.1.2. *Second Principle: The Originating Coalition and the Constitutional Governance Coalition*

Principle 2:   the Constitutional Governance Coalition will reflect the composition of the Originating Coalition.

When it comes to autonomy, in contrast to what we expect for the scope of authority, the logic of constitutional governance leads to the same prediction for OCs of all ideological stripes. It may well be that the Right and the Left have differing commitments to judicial autonomy. Indeed, we test for this too and find that at the beginning of the period the Right did prefer slightly more autonomy, regardless of its position in the OC. However, from a strict governance perspective, we expect a dominant RC to reserve for itself a dominant role in the CGC, regardless of political sign. Whether through ex ante or ex post mechanisms of control, power relations within the coalition crafted to exercise judicial control should reflect power relations within the OC. Concretely, in our autonomy coding, more autonomy represents a CGC that increasingly exceeds the RC, so we should observe progressively more judicial autonomy as we move from an RC-dominant OC to an RC-minority one (that is, as we move left to right in Figure 4.1). We test this using the RC-shortfall variable. If the logic of ex ante control is similar to that of ex post control, the results should be positive and significant for both dimensions.

H4:   When the expected ruling party represents a smaller share of the constituent assembly, the court should have more ex ante autonomy and more ex post autonomy.

Moreover, and in contrast to what Shapiro might have predicted, if governance is split between ordinary politics and constitutional politics, as we propose, then more autonomy should follow upon more authority. As more issues are entrusted to constitutional justice by a more inclusive OC, more social actors should be included in the CGC, leading to higher scores on our autonomy variables. We agree with Shapiro's basic intuition: that actors empowering a court will want to retain some degree of control over the institution. But once we allow for a distinction between the RC and the CGC, we can resolve the tension between the desire to craft a more powerful *and* autonomous judiciary and the reluctance to surrender governance

---

[2]   We use a three-year running average of the Banks weighted conflict indicator of domestic violence for three years prior to the observation in question (range 0–13,000; mean 1,474). Alternative measures of violence, including a simple dummy for the presence of guerrilla activities, produce very similar results.

to an unsupervised court. The OC actually retains control over the court, but by constituting a more diverse CGC that is distinct from the RC, it can do so without compromising judicial autonomy. Thus, our fifth hypothesis:

H5: Courts with more authority will have more ex ante autonomy and more ex post autonomy.

As with a court's scope of authority, a history of violence may matter independently in the case of autonomy for reasons fully consistent with a Constitutional Governance model. Even a CGC that does not include the Left may have to offer a role in constitutional governance to armed groups that are laying down their arms, if for no other reason than to bring the conflict to an end. In such cases, we might see the CGC expanded beyond what we would expect from looking at the composition of the OC alone. The UN-sponsored peace negotiations and judicial reform projects in El Salvador and Guatemala can be read this way. This is a straightforward expectation from a triadic model of courts (Shapiro 1981; Stone Sweet 1999): if the erstwhile guerrillas are to be one of the members of the dyad of constitutional adjudication, then they will want some say in constituting the triadic dispute resolver. Or, to put this in terms of our model, armed groups might be persuaded to put down their weapons in exchange for the chance to participate in constitutional governance, which would raise the scores on ex ante or ex post autonomy, or both. This leads to the sixth hypothesis:

H6: More violence in the recent past will produce courts with greater ex ante autonomy and ex post autonomy.

4.2. ALTERNATIVE EXPLANATIONS

As noted in Chapter 3, we do not expect that the logic of constitutional governance will exhaust the reasoning of constitutional designers. Different features could be included for many different reasons, and the members of a constituent assembly may value different rationales instead of, or in addition to, the logic of constitutional governance – more expressive values, perhaps, or cultural and historical continuity, to name just two prominent examples. It is important, therefore, to control for these other logics to ensure we are actually telling the most important parts of the story of constitutional justice in contemporary Latin America. In this section, we explain how we test for the principal alternative logics that might explain the patterns we observe.

4.2.1. *Testing for Learning*

A change over time in the sign and impact of the key variables would suggest learning and a change in the logic of design. This is not so much an alternative as a complement to the constitutional governance logic – designers might change their preferences over time, as they experiment with, and see the results of, governing with an enhanced sphere of constitutional justice. The initial set of judicial reforms in our sample came after decades of judicial impotence in protecting mostly the Left, but occasionally the Right, from the excesses of the RC. They also happened in the midst of the neoliberal moment, when the conventional wisdom was that more judicial autonomy is always better for the market. The most visible courts in Latin America – Colombia, Costa Rica, Brazil, and occasionally others – distinguished themselves beginning in the late 1990s by protecting economic and social rights and resisting attempts to roll back the welfare state (Gauri and Brinks 2008; Rodríguez Garavito and Rodríguez Franco 2010; Brinks and Forbath 2011, 2014; Yamin and Gloppen 2011). We might expect the Left to be heartened and the Right to be disappointed by this pattern of behavior; as a result, we might expect the Right to be much more ambivalent about judicial autonomy after the 1990s.

Second-generation amendments to judicial structures suggest that attempts to constrain this behavior focused on ex post accountability (although they were not always initiated by the Right). Amendments to the Brazilian Constitution in 2004 – first pushed for ten years by the centrist coalition led by Fernando Henrique Cardoso, then realized when the recently elected Workers' Party joined in – were aimed at increasing the "*controle externo do judiciário*" and focused on ex post controls at all levels of the judiciary (Brinks 2005). A recent set of proposed amendments to the Colombian Constitution, labeled "Reform to Balance the Branches," also includes a variety of proposals to limit ex post autonomy. In a recent paper, Sandra Botero (2017) makes a similar argument for a change of heart by the Right.

Concretely, then, we might expect that ex post autonomy initially responds to the RC shortfall in the same way as ex ante autonomy, but then should reverse signs when the OC tilts to the Right, as designers on the Right become more wary of unaccountable courts. Hypothesis 7, then, is meant to test whether the Right learned a negative lesson in institutional design from the behavior of progressive activist courts in Latin America. If progressive activist courts scared the Right but pleased the Left, the Left's preferences should not change.

> H7: In the early period, Right and Left should behave essentially the same (a greater RC shortfall should lead to more ex post autonomy, regardless of ideology) but in the late period, the Right should prefer less ex post autonomy. The Left's preferences should remain essentially unchanged from the beginning to the end of the period.

To carry out the test, we simply interacted the RC shortfall variable with our Left/Right variable and a dummy for the first half of the time period. We test for learning on both dimensions of autonomy, although the focus on "accountability" suggests the emphasis is on ex post autonomy of already sitting justices.

4.2.2. *Testing for Diffusion*

We do not explicitly test for the diffusion of particular models. We ran some preliminary tests to see whether contemporaneous amendments tend to reflect similar goals, and whether more geographically proximate countries tend to adopt similar arrangements, and did not find any patterns at all. It is possible that more in-depth testing might uncover more complex patterns, but the sample is somewhat limited both geographically and temporally to serve this purpose adequately. Since it is not our goal to explore the diffusion of judicial models per se, and since it seems unlikely that true diffusion patterns might be highly correlated with the variables we are interested in testing, thus distorting our findings, we limit ourselves to a very basic test for the influence of external models: a simple time counter reflecting the year of the observation. If the year variable retains significance even after we control for all the domestic variables, this is evidence that countries are following global (or regional) trends. If the domestic variables retain significance, it supports our theory that, regardless of global trends, designers are following the logic of constitutional governance in response to domestic politics when they engage in judicial design. We will look at the logic of diffusion in more detail in the in-depth case studies that follow.

4.2.3. *Testing for Authoritarian Preferences*

As noted in Chapter 3, it is possible that democracies and dictatorships prefer very different judicial institutions. Our own intuition is that, to the extent democracies and dictatorships differ, it is the logic of constitutional governance that drives that difference. That is, to the extent authoritarian regimes tend to design different systems of constitutional justice, this is a function of the same power dynamics that affect design in democracies. The difference is simply that, in all authoritarian regimes (and only a few democracies), the RC tends to dominate the OC. Once we control for this, a simple dummy for regime type should essentially be insignificant. We test for this using data from Mainwaring et al.'s (2001, 2007) classification of Latin American countries into democratic, semidemocratic, and authoritarian.

Finally, we include a control for per capita Gross Domestic Product to account for research (e.g., Acemoglu et al. 2001) suggesting that wealthier countries can afford stronger institutions.

4.3. RESULTS

For each of the three dimensions (ex ante autonomy, ex post autonomy, and authority), we test essentially the same variables, and we add interaction terms only when we have a theoretical reason (as noted above) to believe that one or more of the variables will have a conditional effect.[3] As mentioned earlier, we test our predictions on a time-series, cross-sectional data set with country-year observations, so we use Prais–Winsten regression, with panel-corrected standard errors, and we control for within-panel autocorrelation. Our estimator assumes the disturbances are heteroskedastic within panels and contemporaneously correlated across panels. After testing for, and finding, the presence of autocorrelation, we further correct for panel-specific autocorrelation. The requisite Stata .do file is available online, along with a replication data set.[4] For each dimension, we begin with a simple model that includes only our key variables of interest – the RC shortfall and the ideology of the RC. We then run the full model, including interactions when appropriate and all controls. The full results of all the models are given in Table 4.3, at the end of this chapter. Table 4.2 also shows the correlations among the various key variables we use in the analysis.

We run the complete models on the full sample of country-years, for all Latin American countries, from 1975 to 2009. As shown in Table 4.3, we also run the baseline model on only those country-years in which a reform to the courts results in a score change on any of our three dimensions. The latter strategy may seem more appropriate, as it only tests the theory on actual instances of court reform. But we feel it is problematic for two reasons: it excludes from the sample all those instances in which the RC was satisfied with the existing arrangements and decided not to push for a change. Also, it excludes all those cases in which the RC wanted to change and was prevented from doing so by the CGC. Both instances, and the latter in particular, are integral to our theoretical model. As seen in Table 4.3, with the sole exception of ex post autonomy, we find essentially the same results in any event for either the full sample or the subsample, giving us confidence that our results are not due to a few idiosyncratic cases that do not change over time for reasons exogenous to our model. In the text, we discuss only the marginal effects of key variables as necessary to advance the discussion. We first discuss the results for each dimension separately, in the order of the hypotheses, and then show the distinct courts that are produced by distinct political configurations.

4.3.1. *The Courts' Scope of Authority*

Our first and most basic claim – that a court's scope of authority is a function of the relative dominance of the ruling party within the OC (H1) – is strongly supported. Our RC-shortfall variable is positive and significant in all the models, whether interacted with ideology or by itself. But the true test of our theory lies in our expectation that this variable will condition the impact of ideology. We find clear support for our expectation that the Left will constitutionalize more of its project when it is less

---

[3]   We run the models on Stata using the XTPCSE command.
[4]   The .do files and replication data are available on our website at http://liberalarts.utexas.edu// government/faculty/dmb629#replication-data.

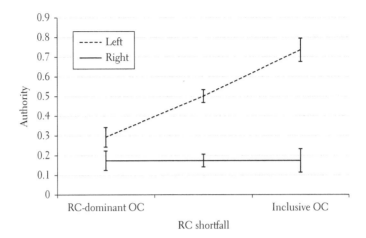

FIGURE 4.2. Effect of ideology and RC-dominance on authority in cases of court reform only (Model II)

All marginal predictions are produced using the Stata command "margins," which produces predicted scores of the dependent variable for specified values of the variables of interest, while maintaining the scores on all other variables at their actual values. The whiskers on the lines denote the 95 percent confidence interval of the marginal estimate.

assured of ruling unimpeded while the Right will unconditionally prefer a thinner constitutional project.[5] In the simplest model, the interaction term offers evidence of both (a) a logic of expressive effects and (b) a conditional effect springing from a logic of constitutional governance. The Left always prefers more authority than the Right, but packs more into the sphere of constitutional justice as its dominance of the OC decreases. By contrast, the Right prefers thinner constitutionalism, independent of its dominance within the OC, exactly as we predicted.

The "whiskers" on the lines denote the 95 percent confidence interval. The lack of an overlap even when the Left is dominant suggests a significant, independent effect of ideology on judicial design – what we called the expressive logic of constitutions – in addition to the conditional effect. This is, as noted, the baseline model. We now turn to the full model, to see if both the independent and conditional effects of RC-dominance hold up.

When we run the three-way interaction on the full sample, to test for the effect of a history of violence on the conditional preferences of the Right and Left, respectively (H3), we find even stronger support for our constitutional governance model, while some of the evidence of an expressive logic disappears. The weak Left always prefers more constitutional authority than the dominant Left or the Right, but now the difference between the weak Left and the weak Right is not statistically significant. And the weak Left prefers increasingly more authority in countries with a

---

[5] This is true whether we use the full sample, or only use those cases that actually changed the judiciary (the latter, which has more dramatic results, is depicted in Figure 4.2).

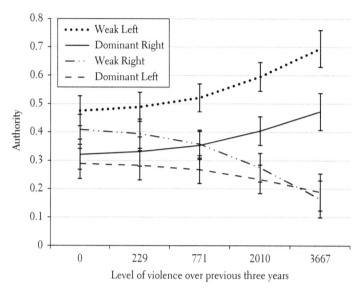

FIGURE 4.3. Effect of historical violence on the preferences of the Right and Left for more or less authority (Model III)

greater history of violence. The strong Left, on the other hand, prefers less authority than the weak Left or the weak Right (and roughly the same as the strong Right), and is essentially unaffected by the history of violence. (The slope is slightly downward but the confidence intervals at high levels of violence overlap with those at low levels of violence.) The weak Right prefers slightly stronger courts than the strong Right (although the difference is not statistically significant), but its preferences slope sharply and significantly downward as historical levels of violence increase.

The results confirm the governance logic shown in Figure 4.2. Moreover, they suggest that the expressive intent indicated by the baseline model may not be sustainable when a peaceful history lowers the stakes, increasing confidence in ordinary politics and reducing the perceived need for constitutional justice. In contrast to the findings in Figure 4.2, at low levels of violence, the Dominant Left and Right are nearly identical, showing stronger support for a pure logic of governance rather than expression. Moreover, as predicted, and consistent with Figure 4.2, so long as it need not worry about human rights prosecutions, the Right prefers thin constitutions, whether it is weak or strong. However, Figure 4.3 shows that, when there is a history of violence the weak Right prefers significantly less authority than the strong Right. Further in keeping with a governance logic, the weak Left prefers significantly more authority than a dominant RC of the Left or Right. In the end, whether we use the full sample or a more limited one, a simple model or a fully specified one with three-way interaction effects, the results are all strongly consistent with our constitutional governance theory.

Other logics are also apparently at work. In an unpredicted result, the strong Right has an increasing preference for stronger courts as historical violence increases. Our theoretical model does not predict this, but we speculate that this could be the result of a logic of credible commitment. As in El Salvador perhaps, a strong Right in a transition to democracy might create a stronger court to reassure the opposition in cases in which there has been a high level of violence against that opposition. But as our critique of the credible commitment logic anticipates, we find that it does not really provide credible commitment once we look at the design more closely. When we put all three dimensions together (as in Figure 4.7), we find that these courts are likely to have low levels of autonomy. Thus the RC offers substantive promises through its constitutional design, but then counts on its political dominance and an easily controlled CGC to keep the court from harming its interests.

The results show that the scope of constitutional justice grows, on average, over time, even when we account for the domestic variables we think drive the politics of constitutional governance. This may or may not be measuring the effect of diffusion, of course, but it is evidence that some broad trends affect design in an important way. All else equal, moving from 1975 to 2009 adds approximately 0.25 – one-quarter of the full range of the scale – to the courts' scope of authority, even after we control for all the other factors. This is not a trivial effect, and reflects a general global trend to include more rights, more international human rights treaties, and more mechanisms for enforcing rights in constitutions, regardless of considerations of ideology and governance.

In addition, we tested the insurance theory of judicial creation using a variable that has been used to measure political uncertainty – the difference in seat share between the largest and second-largest party. The effect of this variable is weaker than the effect of our RC shortfall variable and, most importantly, rather than peaking when the two parties are at parity producing the most uncertainty, the court's authority peaks when the difference between parties is approximately 35 percent of the seats. This result is more consistent with a logic of constitutional governance, in which greater pluralism at the constitutional moment monotonically produces greater pluralism in the CGC, than with a logic of uncertainty. Given that our theory correctly predicts interactive effects that are unanticipated by the insurance theory, and that the key measure of uncertainty performs worse than our shortfall variable, we conclude that there is more evidence for a constitutional governance logic than for a pure insurance logic, at least when it comes to a court's scope of authority. In fairness, it should be noted that the insurance theory does not really address the content of constitutional justice.

As we expected, alternative hypotheses regarding the effect of authoritarian regimes and wealth are not supported by the data. Once we control for the size of the expected RC, the variable for authoritarian regimes is not significant. It is not true for these data, then, that authoritarian regimes have different preferences than electoral regimes with a similar concentration of power in one faction. As we will see, this holds true for all three dimensions of judicial design. What matters in both democracy and dictatorship is the size of the RC – which, to be sure, will be dominant in most authoritarian regimes. Wealth is marginally significant in this model, but its effects are substantively unimportant. All else equal, moving from the tenth percentile to the 90th percentile in GDP adds only 0.05 on the 0–1 scale.

4.3.2. *Ex Ante Autonomy*

It does not appear, as the literature on judicial reform might have suggested, that the Right has a significantly stronger ideological preference for (ex ante) judicial autonomy than the Left, independently of its governance position. If it were true that the Right unconditionally prefers more judicial autonomy while the Left's preferences are conditional on its weakness, we would find the mirror image of what we found for authority – the effect of RC dominance would be significant for the Left, but the Right would always prefer more autonomy, whether it dominates the OC or not. In other words, the graph plotting the effect of RC-shortfall should show a significant positive slope for the Left, but a flat and *higher* line for the Right.

In fact, the Left–Right variable is a barely significant correlate of ex ante autonomy, and when we look at the marginal predictions from the full model, with the interaction term, it becomes clear that the crucial variable is the RC shortfall, as predicted by the constitutional governance model of judicial design (H4). As shown in Figure 4.4, the slope is barely steeper for the Left (hence the significant coefficient), but once we calculate the effect of the shortfall, the difference between the Left and the Right is not significant at any level of RC dominance. Meanwhile, the relative size of the RC within the OC produces a significant and substantively important effect on ex ante autonomy, regardless of ideological orientation. A more inclusive OC tends to set up a more inclusive CGC to match, regardless of ideology.

Contrary to our expectations (H6), a history of violence is not, on average, a significant predictor of greater ex ante autonomy. This is true both by itself, and conditional on the presence of a weak Left/weak Right. We tested for an interactive effect, like that for authority (not reported), but found no significance. It appears that a history of violence does not meaningfully influence preferences for more judicial autonomy. As with authority, wealth and the passage of time are marginally significant. Contrary to expectations, GDP has a negative, statistically significant effect on ex ante autonomy, but is still substantively superficial, taking only 0.06 from the average ex ante score, as we move from the tenth to the ninetieth income percentile.[6]

---

[6]   Given the counterintuitive result, the marginal level of significance, and the trivial substantive effect, we suspect that this is simply a quirk of the data and the sample. The results for other variables and the overall fit are not substantially affected by the inclusion or exclusion of this variable from the model.

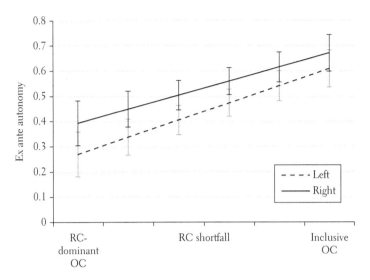

FIGURE 4.4. Effect of ideology and RC shortfall on ex ante autonomy (Model VI)

The effect of time is as expected: it is positive and highly significant, but less important than for authority. Keeping all other variables at their actual values, the move from 1975 to 2009 implies an increase from 0.42 to 0.56 (that is, from just below to just above the overall mean for the entire period). While not trivial, the effect of time, which captures global trends, is dwarfed by the effect of the RC's dominance of the OC. Taken together, these results show patterns in the data that are strongly consistent with the logic of constitutional governance, and far less consistent with other rationales – such as ideology and emulation – that might lead designers to craft strong courts. In contrast to what we find for authority, then, the trend toward greater autonomy we described in Chapter 2 is almost entirely a function of a decline in the likelihood that a single actor will dominate processes of constitutional change in the region. Designers, in other words, are content to follow global trends in constitutional and human rights law but, in a nod to the importance of structural provisions, they will tailor control over the mechanism for interpreting and applying that law to the desires of the OC.

In order to isolate the effect of electoral uncertainty, the key element in the insurance model, we also tested for a nonlinear effect of RC-dominance by including a squared term. By one measure, uncertainty should be low at both ends of RC-dominance, and highest at the center. For example, Ginsburg (2003: 29) suggests the level of judicial power should peak when the parties in the constitutional assembly are at parity, which would produce a score of roughly 0 in our shortfall variable in a two-party system, and scores slightly above 0 in a multiparty system. If uncertainty were driving judicial authority, the line should be flat and low until about 0 and then begin rising more sharply until it comes down again when the RC is a small minority of the OC. Although the squared term is significant, the results do not resemble that pattern. The slope rises continuously across all values of RC shortfall, flattening somewhat after the peak of uncertainty. Moreover, it rises more quickly at the very beginning, rather than staying low. A cubic spline does not add any explanatory power.

We also tested for the effects on autonomy of the difference in seats between the first and second party, the variable typically used to test the insurance model. As when we tested for its impact on authority, the difference in seats variable also performs less well than the RC-shortfall variable. Using the difference and the square of the difference, we find a slightly curvilinear relationship between the difference variable and ex ante autonomy, as the insurance theory would predict, but the effect is very attenuated – the predicted value of ex ante autonomy rises by about 0.05, then drops again by about 0.15. Since there is a close relationship (a correlation of −0.78) between this variable and our RC shortfall variable that could explain that attenuated relationship, and since our variable performs better, it seems clear that the patterns in the data more closely resemble what we would expect from a governance theory – a linear relationship arising from inclusion of additional actors and interests – than what we expect from insurance – a curvilinear relationship peaking at the height of uncertainty.

4.3.3. *Ex Post Autonomy*

Does ex post autonomy also respond to a logic of constitutional governance? If so, how, if at all, is it different than ex ante autonomy? Our results show remarkable similarities, given how different the actual variables are and how different the logics of their operation are. The RC shortfall is statistically significant (H4), although substantively less important for ex post autonomy. In contrast to ex ante autonomy, we do find the ideological effect predicted in the literature for the Right – a practically flat slope[7] and higher values throughout than those for the Left. The difference between Right and Left loses statistical significance only once the Left RC becomes less dominant and begins to prefer more autonomy (Figure 4.5). As with ex ante autonomy, violence is also not significant, contrary to our expectations (H6).

Earlier we noted that Shapiro (1981) would expect a trade-off between authority and autonomy: the more authority a court has, the more it threatens the RC, and thus the more pressure there should be for control. We expect the opposite (H5). In the end, the data support our expectation, not Shapiro's: the patterns in the data are consistent with an intent by OCs to create more powerful courts that are simultaneously more autonomous from the RC. Within the logic of constitutional governance, this does not mean those courts become unaccountable substitute rulers. Rather, on

---

[7] While the slope is slightly negative for the Right, the difference between the beginning and the end points is not significant. For all practical purposes, then, the slope is flat.

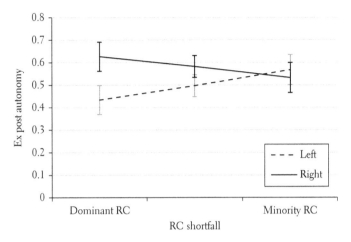

FIGURE 4.5. Effect of ideology and RC shortfall on ex post autonomy (Model IX)

average and *ceteris paribus*, when the OC decides to entrust the courts with a wide scope of authority, it also decides to spread control over those courts across a wider CGC. Thus, we observe a positive and significant relationship between authority and both autonomy dimensions, even after we control for the dominance of the RC. The relationship holds for both ex ante and ex post autonomy, though the effect is about twice as great for ex ante autonomy. Judicial design is more consistent with the dual-governance logic of constitutional governance than with a straightforward analysis of the interests of a unitary ruler.

However, we were puzzled by some of these results for ex post autonomy and, in particular, by some important differences with ex ante autonomy. The substantive effect of the RC shortfall is one quarter of what it was for ex ante autonomy, causing the variable to lose significance when we use the more limited sample (years of judicial reform). And why should the Right prefer less (albeit not significantly less) autonomous courts when it is in a *weaker* position? These differences prompted us to explore a learning hypothesis, suggested, as noted in our theoretical discussion, by anecdotal evidence and some of the qualitative literature. It may be that the Latin American Right became disenchanted with activist courts that seemed to be pushing redistributive agendas and interfering with attempts to scale back the state. To test this theory, we created a three-way interaction with a variable marking the first half of the period, to see if the Right and Left changed their conditional preferences for ex post autonomy over the time period in question. The results of Model X are presented in Table 4.4, at the end of this chapter.

The results are striking. Throughout the entire period, the Left behaves as predicted by our Constitutional Governance model – it broadens the coalition of control as it becomes less dominant. The two lines overlap perfectly. The Right, on the other hand, changes dramatically. Early on, it is driven more by ideology

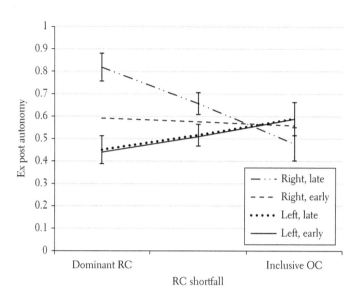

FIGURE 4.6. Impact of ideology and RC shortfall on ex post autonomy, early and late
in the period

than by the logic of constitutional governance. Contrary to our expectations, the
line is perfectly flat, showing a preference for more autonomy at the beginning of
the period that was insensitive to the size of the RC in the OC. In the second half
of the period, however, the Right behaves in a dramatically different way – now,
the more the OC exceeds the RC, the *less* ex post autonomy the Right is willing
to grant the courts. In this new model, the slopes are more dramatic, and the
substantive effect is more important.

Given these findings, we returned to the models for ex ante autonomy and authority, and tested for a similar learning process, but found that, in those cases, the
passage of time did not significantly alter the conditional preferences of the Left
and Right. In other words, for authority and ex ante autonomy, the effect of time
is linear, suggesting a global trend toward expanding the sphere of constitutional
justice and more autonomous judiciaries, with no change in the basic orientation
of designers' preferences. Without the interaction term, in contrast, the change in
preferences for the Right, late in the period, washes out much of the conditional
effect of ideology on ex post autonomy.

4.3.4. *Combining the Three Dimensions*

Finally, we consider all three dimensions together, conditioned on the ideology of
the dominant party, to explore how the composition of an OC affects the overall
design of a court. The most important finding is the effect of the relative strength

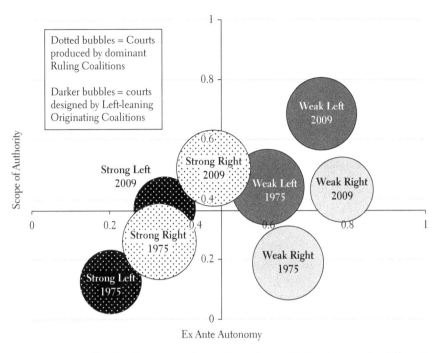

FIGURE 4.7. Predicted values on three dimensions of judicial power for different
Originating Constitutional coalitions (Models III, VI, and X)

of the RC within the Originating Constitutional Coalition (Figure 4.7). We use
marginal predictions for all three dimensions to construct a bubble graph depicting various idealized courts for the range of values on our key variables. The *y*-axis
represents the courts' scope of authority – courts higher in the graph have greater
authority. The *x*-axis reflects ex ante autonomy – as courts move from left to right,
the coalition needed to appoint justices to the courts becomes broader and more
inclusive, producing courts with more ex ante autonomy. The size of the bubbles
denotes the courts' ex post autonomy – the bigger bubbles denote courts that are
more insulated from pressures from the RC. The axes intersect at the overall mean
for each variable. We map courts at their values in 1975 and in 2009 to show the
changes over the entire period.

The dotted bubbles denote courts produced by RC-dominant constitutional coalitions, which we depicted at the left in Figure 4.1, while the solid bubbles represent
courts designed by more diverse, RC-minority coalitions. As expected, we find the
former all to the left in Figure 4.6, indicating that RC-dominant coalitions design
appointments to be more easily subjected to the control of the RC in postconstitutional politics. The difference with RC-minority coalitions is clear: broad and inclusive OCs tend to craft broad and inclusive CGCs (appearing well to the right of the
mean), at least for ex ante autonomy.

The conditional effect of ideology on authority creates a more complicated pattern, again confirming the basic intuitions of the governance model. The Left, as expected, places more into the sphere of constitutional governance as its expectations of dominating ordinary politics decline. Indeed, the differences between the strong and the weak Left are the most dramatic in the graph. The Right, meanwhile, prefers courts with less authority, almost without regard to its eventual likelihood of governing unimpeded. As a result, the darker bubbles for the Left are higher than the contemporaneous lighter bubbles for the Right when the RC is weak (on the right side of the graph), and the opposite when it is strong (on the left side of the graph). Although we do not show it here, the difference in scope of authority between the weak Left and the weak Right is sharpened when there is a history of violence – the weak Left moves up and the weak Right moves down.

Earlier, we noted a somewhat unexpected result: the Right allows for a more expansive sphere of constitutional justice when it has a clear expectation of governing. The 3D graph may well explain this result: first, the difference is not that important, in substantive terms; and second, in those cases, the Right retains relatively tight majoritarian control over appointments (as expected), and insulates those judges from external pressures by the legislature, thus giving the executive more control over constitutional interpretation and limiting the role of the more populist legislature. The sphere is more expansive, but it is also under tighter control by the executive.

The results for ex post autonomy are also instructive. The strong Right prefers executive-dominated appointments (i.e., low ex ante autonomy) that are insulated from the legislature (i.e., high ex post autonomy), perhaps because the Right distrusts the more populist legislature. The model is remarkably similar to that of many central banks. The strong Left designs executive-dominated courts that are also exposed to pressures from the legislature (low on both autonomy dimensions) perhaps because the Left feels it is more likely to have allies in the legislature. In contrast, when they are both weak it is the Left that seeks to ensure a broader ex post control coalition, and thus more autonomy for the courts, while the Right continues to prefer more accountable courts, especially late in the period.

There is plenty of variation that is not explained by a strict logic of constitutional governance. The simple passage of time makes it increasingly difficult for designers to craft the spare constitutions – and hence courts with extremely limited authority – that were in style decades earlier. Similarly, it is no longer permissible to have courts that are pure agents of the executive – one can hardly imagine a modern constituent assembly giving the executive the power to unilaterally appoint justices, as was the case in Haiti 1975 or Guatemala 1983. However, it is surprising that any one logic of design has as much explanatory power as what we find here. As Elkins et al. (2009) show, institutional legacies are hard to overturn, constitutional bargaining is messy and collaborative, and we should expect idiosyncratic considerations – all the way down to the particular personal experiences and ambitions of the constituents – to affect the ultimate design. In spite of all this, the patterns in the data show that designers have an intuitive sense that courts are creatures of politics and paramount actors in producing evolving constitutional meaning and that they try to structure control over the mechanisms of constitutional justice accordingly.

4.4. ILLUSTRATIVE CASES

Some illustrative cases, and the more detailed case studies that follow, support these quantitative findings. On all three dimensions, the early weak Right looks much like Guatemala 1985, and matches well on our independent variables, as we will see in Chapter 5. The OC in that country was fragmented, but generally leaned to the Right, and pursued an early neoliberal economic model attenuated by the need to grant concessions to a militant Left. It created a court with highly fragmented appointment mechanisms, subject to ex post controls and with fairly limited authority. As we will see in Chapter 5, the model slightly underpredicts the level of authority granted the court, both because it comes on the heels of a prior court that had dramatically less authority and because the Assembly granted more authority in response to generalized concerns about the violence that had tormented the country up to that point. In particular, the sharp break with the past leads to an underprediction, since the model expects a high degree of serial correlation. Chile 1980 is a more pure expression of the Right's affinity for what we call a Procedural Arbiter. In that case, as will see in more detail, Pinochet meant to create a framework that would protect a market-based development model, whether he or someone else was in charge. The resulting system of constitutional justice has high levels of autonomy and very low levels of authority, exactly as the model predicts.

The quintessential example of a Major Policy Player court (as defined in Table 2.1) in the service of social democratic constitutionalism is Colombia. In that case, the RC at the time of the constituent assembly was actually further to the right than our measure shows, as the neoliberal reforms it was to pursue had not yet been approved. But the measure adequately describes, as it is meant to, the general center-left tilt in the constituent assembly, which was strongly influenced by the M-19 (a demobilizing guerrilla force), and had relatively weak participation by the RC. Colombia was ahead of its time – pursuing in 1991 a model that looks more like a 2009 court. In all other respects, however, it matches both dependent and independent variables with our model, producing a court that is very nearly identical on all three dimensions to the late, weak Left courts shown in Figure 4.7, especially once we add the influence of a history of violence.

Finally, the model predictions for the late, strong Left look – as we would expect – like a blend of Bolivia's and Ecuador's latest constitutions. These systems of constitutional justice were designed by constituent assemblies dominated by the Left, under RCs that expected to continue ruling. In fact, in these two countries and in Venezuela 1999, the new constitution is expressly promoted as a way to establish a new model of democracy under the guidance of the recently victorious ruling party. Under these conditions, the model predicts exactly what we see here. Despite a general expectation that these constitutions would be manifestos proclaiming the goals of the new RC, with the exception of Venezuela they do not include spheres of constitutional justice that are quite as expansive as these goals would suggest. This is consistent with the logic of constitutional governance, as it leaves the RC somewhat freer to pursue those goals unconstrained by a broader CGC.

Only Venezuela, the first of the three to seek a new "Bolivarian" constitutional model, seems to have created a system of constitutional justice commensurate with its stated revolutionary ambitions. This system was designed before any of the new Major Policy Player courts could reveal their true potential, so it is possible that the designers did not expect the court to be much of a constraint on the RC – as, indeed, it has not been. Given its low levels of autonomy, the court has become a very effective tool for dismantling the existing normative order at the behest, initially, of the RC, and now (as of 2018) at the instance of the Executive, as we discuss in more detail in Chapter 7. The very low levels of autonomy designed into this court suggest that it resembles our fourth model – Regime Ally courts that are expressly meant to be instruments for a dramatic, normative reordering in line with the dominant political project.

4.5. IMPLICATIONS

These empirical results have important implications for both normative and empirical theories of constitutionalism. One that we return to in the final chapter is that it becomes more difficult to defend an originalist view of constitutional interpretation if, in fact, the OC is designing a system for ongoing dynamic constitutional governance, as our findings show, rather than seeking to protect an immutable original pact. Another is that normative, substantive commitments play a part in constitutional design but are strongly conditioned by the logic of constitutional governance – the Left (or the Right) does not forget its normative commitments when it dominates the OC, but it only needs to constitutionalize those commitments when it cannot be assured a free hand in pursuing its goals in postconstitutional politics. Constitutional justice systems should be read not to express the deepest commitments of their framers, but rather should be seen to reflect the deepest commitments that appear to be vulnerable in ordinary, postconstitutional politics. Constitutions are catalogs of hopes and fears, not statements of certainty or manifestos.

Finally, this model suggests at least one way in which law is political without being identical to what we have called ordinary politics. Constitutional meaning responds to the particular constituencies, mechanisms, and principles of constitutional politics, which are no less political for being distinct from the ordinary politics of everyday policymaking. The models and arguments found in Negretto's (2013) recent work relate to the construction of the space for ordinary politics – partisan contestation, presidential permanence, and the allocation of power between executives and legislatures. Our own findings demonstrate that the politics of structuring the space for contestation over constitutional meaning relates to similar, but not identical, incentives. Here, the concerns are not only about balancing power across branches, but also about including minorities, favoring the interests of some groups over others, and constructing coalitions of inclusion to advance some goals that may not be fully considered by the RC.

TABLE 4.1. Key variable descriptive statistics

Variable	Description	Obs	Mean	Std. Dev.	Min	Max
Ex ante autonomy	Authors' construction	665	0.48	0.25	0	1
Ex post autonomy	Authors' construction	665	0.56	0.24	0	1
Scope of authority	Authors' construction	665	0.37	0.19	0.04	1
RC maximum shortfall	Difference between ruling party's seat share and share needed for a binding decision (authors' construction)	663	0.05	0.30	−0.5	0.67
Relative Right	Distance from that year's regional mean on neo-liberal reforms (based on Escaith and Paunovic 2004 and subsequent updates)	665	0.00	0.07	−0.23	0.26
Party1–Party2	1st party seat share minus 2nd party seat share (authors' construction, multiple sources)	663	0.43	0.37	0	1
Past violence	Three-year running average of Domestic Violence (Banks)	665	1,474	1,910	0	12,083
Authoritarian regime	Mainwaring, Brinks, and Pérez-Liñán coding	665	0.26	0.432	0	1
GDP per capita	Penn World Tables	665	2,896	2,002	191	9,894

TABLE 4.2. Correlations among key variables – coefficient and significance levels

	Ex ante autonomy	Ex post autonomy	Scope of authority	RC maximum shortfall	Relative Right	Party1–Party2	Past violence	Authoritarian regime
Ex post autonomy	0.07							
	0.55							
Scope of authority	**0.27**	0.20						
	0.02	0.09						
RC maximum shortfall	**0.57**	0.10	**0.35**					
	0.00	0.07	0.00					
Relative Right	0.07	0.21	−0.17	**0.27**				
	0.57	0.07	0.13	0.00				
Party1–Party2	**−0.41**	**0.08**	**−0.14**	**−0.79**	**−0.38**			
	0.00	0.05	0.00	0.00	0.00			
Past violence	0.71	−0.04	0.19	−0.02	**−0.11**	0.07		
	0.55	0.73	0.11	0.83	0.00	0.07		
Authoritarian regime	**−0.40**	−0.12	**−0.51**	**−0.60**	0.05	**0.41**	−0.07	
	0.00	0.30	0.00	0.00	0.17	0.00	0.52	
GDP per capita	**0.08**	**0.61**	**0.51**	0.25	**0.22**	**−0.14**	0.07	**−0.26**
	0.04	0.00	0.05	0.33	0.00	0.00	0.55	0.03

TABLE 4.3. Model results

Variables	Baseline I Authority	Baseline new courts II Authority	Full model III Authority	Baseline IV Ex ante	Baseline new courts V Ex ante	Full model VI Ex ante	Baseline VII Ex post	Baseline new courts VIII Ex post	Full model IX Ex post
Authority						0.399*** (0.00)			0.204*** (0.00)
Violence			4.06E−06* (0.09)			2.70E−07 (0.92)			−6.80E−07 (0.76)
Relative Right	−0.185** (0.04)	−0.670** (0.02)	−0.0105 (0.90)	0.0613 (0.46)	0.0630 (0.88)	0.155* (0.05)	0.146** (0.05)	0.810** (0.05)	0.187** (0.02)
Violence × relative Right			−2.89E−05 (0.269)						
RC shortfall	0.252*** (0.00)	0.207*** (0.00)	0.115*** (0.00)	0.418*** (0.00)	0.431*** (0.00)	0.337*** (0.00)	0.0770*** (0.00)	0.0663 (0.51)	0.0407** (0.03)
Violence × RC shortfall			9.20E−06 (0.12)						
Relative Right × RC shortfall	−0.150 (0.53)	−1.033 (0.20)	−0.0949 (0.59)			−0.305 (0.20)			−0.416*** (0.01)

	(1)	(2)	(3)	(4)	(5)	(6)	(7)	(8)	(9)
Violence × relative Right × RC shortfall			−3.30E−04*** (0.00)						
Authoritarian			0.004 (0.68)			0.001 (0.41)			0.006 (0.59)
GDP p/c			1.24E−05*** (0.00)			−1.52E−05** (0.01)			3.58E−05*** (0.00)
Year			0.007*** (0.00)			0.004*** (0.01)			−0.0008 (0.42)
Constant	0.354*** (0.00)	0.355*** (0.00)	−14.17*** (0.00)	0.478*** (0.00)	0.457*** (0.00)	−7.638*** (0.01)	0.577*** (0.00)	0.548*** (0.00)	2.036 (0.33)
N	663	71	663	663	71	663	663	71	663
R-squared	0.177	0.180	0.396	0.344	0.317	0.507	0.516	0.049	0.445

Coefficient *** $p < 0.01$, ** $p < 0.05$, * $p < 0.1$ $(p > z)$.

TABLE 4.4. Full model – learning

Model X	
Dependent variable: ex post autonomy	
Authority	0.19***
	(0.000)
Past violence	−1.17E−06
	(0.636)
Relative Right	0.32***
	(0.007)
Max shortfall	−0.04
	(0.14)
Relative Right × max shortfall	−0.87**
	(0.19)
Relative Right × max shortfall × early	0.51
	(0.173)
Early × max shortfall	0.11***
	(0.001)
Relative Right × early	−0.18
	(0.126)
Early	−0.04***
	(0.000)
Authoritarian	8.51E−03
	(0.449)
GDP p/c	3.05E−05***
	(0.000)
Year	−1.44E−03
	(0.157)
Constant	3.28
	(0.104)
R^2	0.43
N	663

Coefficient ***$p > 0.01$, **$p > 0.05$ ($p > z$).

5

Guatemala (1985)

Building Constitutional Justice in the Shadow of Civil War

What has been the cause of our tyranny? Hasn't it been the superstructure, the superpower, the superagility of the State in relation to the individual, to the people?

> Rep. Luis Alfonso López, Constituent Assembly Member,
> Guatemala 1984, in debates about how to begin the constitutional
> text (Transcript of Debates in the Commission
> of the Thirty, Vol. I, Session 4, p. 8).

Guatemala's 1985 constitution was founded more on fear than hope. By the time of the Assembly, in 1984, Guatemala had been living through about twenty-five years of a bloody internal conflict that had produced victims of state violence from the Right and the Left. The violence and instability persuaded the current military regime that a new constitution was needed as a foundation for a return to democracy. Although it drew upon a long-standing history of social constitutionalism in the country, the resulting constitution defines a system of constitutional justice that represents a dramatic departure from Guatemala's historical experience, with far higher levels of ex ante autonomy and moderately high levels of authority. The changes in ex post autonomy are also noticeable but less dramatic, leaving ex post control squarely in the hands of the Congress, but giving opposition parties some veto power in that process. As a result, Guatemala returned to democracy with a significantly more expansive sphere of constitutional justice, albeit one that is quite limited compared to later models in the region, and with a Constitutional Governance Coalition (CGC) that largely excluded whoever might occupy the presidential palace at any given moment, but included the legal profession and a supermajoritarian congressional component.

In this chapter, we chronicle how the dynamics of the constituent assembly, the ideologies present within the Originating Coalition (OC), and recent political history led the designers to this result. The assembly was relatively inclusive, with a plurality of interests but exclusion of the Left, and was marked by a strong fear on both the Right and the Left of the abuses of state power. This motivated the constituents to strengthen the authority of constitutional justice, but not to dramatically expand its scope, focusing primarily on personal integrity and negative rights. Although the bulk of the constituents expected to be part of a future legislature, they had less confidence in their ability to control the state's security apparatus. Moreover, a history of military takeovers and fraud led them to distrust the executive as well. As a result, they located control over appointments in a broad coalition of actors outside the executive, including unelected actors, crafting a judiciary with remarkable ex ante autonomy. But their experience with abuses of power by those who occupied the state for too long, and their expectation that they would be in the legislature after the transition, led them to restrict ex post autonomy, locating ex post control squarely in the legislature. The result was a court with very short renewable terms and other features that rendered the justices quite vulnerable to the legislature.

5.1. THE HISTORY OF GUATEMALA'S CONSTITUTIONAL JUSTICE SYSTEM

Guatemala's constitutional history began in 1825, when the country was part of the Central American Federation, with a classically conservative document. The first constitution established a system of constitutional justice that was exceptionally weak and tied to the Ruling Coalition (RC). While Guatemala would soon move to a more secularist, liberal constitution, this model of constitutional justice would be more or less sustained for the next 120 years. Justices in this period were to be chosen through indirect elections by the same electors who selected the members of the other two branches (Guatemala 1825, Art. 199). Their terms expired after four years, although they could be reelected, so that as much as half the Supreme Court could potentially be renewed every two years at every general election (Art. 199). Especially given that the election was in the hands of electors, rather than the general public, the system virtually guaranteed that the court's control coalition would faithfully reflect current majorities.[1] The text said nothing about removals, perhaps because the terms were so brief.

The scope of authority of this system was also exceedingly narrow, and favors the interests of dominant elites. The constitution includes a relatively brief list of core rights – equality before the law, protection of the home from searches, right to property, right to travel, and freedom of thought and expression are there (Arts. 20–34) – but there is no mechanism to protect these rights. The text does not mention habeas corpus, or any mechanism for the redress of rights violations akin to what would later be called the *amparo*, and there is no mention of powers of judicial review.[2] It also

---

[1]   Although indirect elections for judges may seem like an odd arrangement, Mexico's early nineteenth-century constitutions also provided for the indirect election of the members of all three branches (see, e.g., Mexico 1857). A comparison of nineteenth-century and early twentieth-century constitutions suggests that Guatemala was heavily influenced by trends present in its northern neighbor, at least early in its history.
[2]   The *amparo*, like the Colombian *tutela*, is an expedited procedure for redress in the event of a rights violation (Brewer-Carías 2005). Although it is subject to different restrictions in different countries,

establishes Catholicism as the state religion and forbids the public exercise of any other faith. It coexisted with labor conditions for indigenous people that approached slavery, or at least serfdom. At least in regard to the essential terms of its system of constitutional justice, this document was basically re-enacted in 1851, some years after the Central American Federation fell apart.

In 1879, an anticlerical reaction led to a new constitution declaring the separation of church and state. The new constitution, sometimes referred to as marking the beginning of the liberal period, established some of the tools for an expansion of the sphere of constitutional justice, but this sphere remained very limited, especially in terms of its autonomy. Article 34 of Guatemala 1879 established the right to habeas corpus, but otherwise retained a very limited set of rights, and remained silent on the power of judicial review. Justices still served only four years by constitutional mandate, and nearly everything else about the judiciary, including its method of selection, was placed in the realm of ordinary politics by a brief provision that said all other features of the judiciary would be regulated by law. This arrangement endured until an important set of amendments in 1921 introduced a version of social constitutionalism and greater autonomy.

For approximately the first 100 years, from 1825 to 1921, regardless of whether it reflected a conservative or a liberal approach (for a discussion of these constitutional ideologies, see Gargarella 2013), Guatemala's system of constitutional justice was notable for its narrow scope and near complete identification with the RC. Indeed, it appears to have been designed primarily to carry out and legitimize the wishes of that coalition, with few mechanisms or substantive principles with which to challenge government decisions or state actors. It is, in short, much more an aid to the exercise of power than a restraint on power.

Only in 1921 did a series of amendments to this constitution provide the first significant expansion of the scope of constitutional justice. Under the influence of Mexico's famous 1917 social constitution, Guatemala also adopted an extensive set of labor rights – the right to just remuneration, to strike, to social security, and to a safe working environment. At the same time, the further regulation of labor was expressly required to be by statute, thus placing key aspects of labor rights into the sphere of ordinary politics. Rights to social provision were also expanded. The press received new protection to criticize public officials. For the first time, a Guatemalan constitution expressly established jurisdictional mechanisms beyond habeas corpus petitions for the protection of individual freedom and physical integrity. The amendments constitutionalized the amparo, which could be filed by anyone who felt his or her constitutional rights were being violated. Moreover, in Article 93(c), the courts secured the ability to exercise diffuse control of constitutionality in concrete cases. Thus, courts at all levels could decide not to apply laws they believed violated the

---

it generally shares two features: it is meant to provide a mechanism to bring rights violations to the attention of the courts, and it is an emergency, expedited procedure.

constitution, although they were explicitly told that their decisions would have only *inter partes* effects.[3] The 1921 document also adds state ownership of most natural resources, requires the state to make provision for social security and pensions, and generally expresses a more ambitiously state-centric constitutional project.

This more muscular and extensive system of constitutional justice was, however, brought under even closer congressional control. Article 93 regulated the mode of selecting and removing justices. Under the new system, the President of the Supreme Court would be elected in a direct popular vote rather than selected by electors, making that figure a majoritarian one, though not one dependent on the other branches. The Legislature would name all the other justices of that court and all appellate judges directly by a simple majority. The Supreme Court, in turn, would name all the trial judges. As before, judges served for only four years and could be reelected. The Court remained a creature of ordinary politics.

With many details of the court's conformation still left to an ordinary law, plus short terms and reelection, this institutional arrangement both ensured a close affinity between the justices and the RC, and left the justices exposed to constant pressures to conform. The CGC, in short, was squarely within the RC. Although (as we will also see in early Bolivian constitutions) the institutional arrangement did not contemplate formal direct participation by the Executive, the debates leading up to the 1985 Constitution make it clear that the president was understood to informally control appointments through his control of Congress.

In any event, this expansion of constitutional justice was rendered nearly meaningless by a succession of Right-wing military regimes that lasted until 1944 when the next major constitutional innovation took place. Guatemala 1945, known as the Revolutionary Constitution (Maldonado Aguirre 1984), is a remarkable document in light of Guatemala's political history. Coming at the end of the dictatorship of General Ubico, it strongly reinforced the trend toward social rights constitutionalism that began in 1921. The new constitution included a set of labor provisions that largely paralleled Art. 123 of Mexico 1917. The document provided that "the laws that regulate relations between capital and labor, shall take account of the economic and social circumstances of the country . . . With respect to agricultural workers [who had to that point been held under serf-like conditions], the State shall take into account their conditions and needs" (Art. 58). The constitution again required the RC to take the lead in labor regulation, but imposed many more basic

---

[3] One key element in strengthening courts in Latin America has been the move from decisions that only bind the parties to the case – decisions with *inter partes* effects – to decisions that bind everyone – decisions with *erga omnes* effects. Abstract challenges to a statute, of course, always produce *erga omnes* effects, when successful. Similarly, the US Supreme Court's decisions have *erga omnes* effects, but only by virtue of binding precedent. Recent constitutions in Latin America have begun to specify that constitutional decisions are binding on all public authorities. Under the old model, at least in theory, the constitutionality of a particular action or statute would have to be relitigated by every affected person.

requirements, such as a decent minimum salary; maximum work hours; paid vacations; equal pay without regard to age, race, sex, or nationality; the rights to unionize and to strike; and special protections for women workers, such as paid maternity leave and nursing breaks during the workday. Natural resources remained under state ownership, and there were restrictions on their alienation and on the length of exploitation contracts. Indeed, Art. 88 required the state to "orient the national economy to the benefit of the people, in order to secure for each individual an existence that is dignified and productive for the collectivity."

The constitution's social provisions go well beyond regulating the relationship between the state and citizens. In a move that would deeply mark the debates around Guatemala 1985 some forty years later, the constitution relativized the protection of private property by stating that private property must fulfill a social function or be at risk of extinguishment. Latifundia were forbidden, and the state was required to dismantle them and redistribute the land. Collective forms of land ownership such as the *ejido* and collective title for "recognized communities" were explicitly recognized. Article 83 contemplated, though did not require, legislation for the economic, social, and cultural benefit of indigenous groups that took into account their traditions and customs. In short, much like efforts in Ecuador and Bolivia half a century later, the new constitution aimed to dismantle existing inequalities built on wealth and ethnicity, envisioning the more or less wholesale transformation of the relationship between citizens – one that had been, in Guatemala as much as anywhere in Latin America, marked by profound inequalities.

Nor did this constitution neglect the enforcement mechanisms for all these rights. Article 50 strengthened judicial review, declaring null and void any law that might impinge on the rights declared in the constitution. Article 51 reinforced the amparo action, albeit still limiting it to *inter partes* effects. Article 170 maintained the 1921 provision giving all courts the right to declare the inapplicability of any law violating the constitution but eliminating the explicit restriction to *inter partes* effects. Moreover, Art. 170 added that whenever a law was declared unconstitutional, the decision should be directed to Congress or the corresponding Ministries and published in the Official Register in an apparent attempt to give the decision some effect beyond that particular case, though it did not specify what effects this might have. A special "Amparo Tribunal" was established to hear cases alleging a violation of constitutional rights. In short, the realm of constitutional justice had expanded considerably, through the inclusion of substantive rights and the strengthening of judicial mechanisms through which to claim those rights.

At the same time, the reforms did nothing to expand the CGC beyond contemporary legislative majorities. Many constitutional mandates were still the province of ordinary politics, rather than providing a platform for challenging the RC. The pro-redistribution property rights provisions do this implicitly, weakening individual rights protections and giving the RC the capacity, but not the obligation, to redistribute. The indigenous provisions are a more explicit example of this expansion of

constitutional politics with full deference to the RC, since the constitution empowered, but did not require, the government to advance indigenous rights. The same
is true for labor rights. At best many of the new constitutional commitments were
entrusted to the space we labeled constitutional politics, rather than placed within
the sphere of constitutional justice.

More fundamentally, even judicially enforceable constitutional mandates were
to be given substance by courts that came directly out of the RC, reflecting what we
called the Regime Ally model in Chapter 3. Simple majorities in Congress named
and could remove the Supreme Court justices (and the court's President) as well as
all appellate judges. The Supreme Court, in turn, named (and disciplined) all lower
court judges. Even the fact that rulings of unconstitutionality were sent back to the
legislature would raise the stakes for judges and allow Congress to respond as it saw
fit. The Amparo Tribunal, charged with redressing individual rights violations, was
unregulated in the constitution and organized in an ordinary law. Constitutional
justice went from responding to elections (indirect in the nineteenth century, then
direct after 1921) to being a creature of congressional majorities. Notably, and contrary to general descriptions of the region for this period, the executive had very
little formal control over Guatemala's courts, but the courts were clearly a creature
of legislative majorities. The perception is that the executive controlled the court
by controlling the legislature. As many 1985 constituent assembly members clearly
recalled, constitutional justice was a device for the RC to pursue its goals, rather
than one in which to contest competing visions of justice.

In our quantitative assessment of the political roots of judicial autonomy and scope
of authority, we highlighted the importance of an inclusive and diverse OC. As our
theory predicts, the closely held system of constitutional justice in Guatemala 1944
was produced by a monolithic OC dominated by a faction that was having a banner
year in Guatemalan politics: "The third election decreed by the junta, that for a constitutional assembly, was also devoid of violence, and also went to the 'Arevalistas,' who
captured fifty of the sixty-five seats. They had swept all three political contests: legislative, constitutional assembly, and the presidency" (Leonard 1984: 85). Also in keeping
with our theory, the Left-revolutionary Arevalistas, given their control over both the
RC and the OC, wrote a constitution with a very permissive statist agenda framed as
constitutional politics, but a relatively restricted sphere of constitutional justice.

Guatemala's mid-century turn to the Left was cut short less than a decade later by
the US-supported coup against the next elected president, Jacobo Arbenz, in 1954,
on suspicions that Arbenz was a communist. This coup led immediately to a new constituent assembly, and, eighteen months later, to a new constitution, drafted entirely
by what Maldonado calls the Liberationist coalition (Maldonado Aguirre 1984).
Perhaps because this coalition was in a strong position, as our findings in Chapter 4
for the strong Right predict, Guatemala 1956 does not appear at first glance to be
a full return to the spare constitutionalism of the pre-1921 charters, even though
it was born out of a Right-wing military dictatorship. However, it is clear that its

overriding concern was with pushing back communism. Thus, Art. 23 guaranteed the right to form and operate political parties governed by democratic principles, but declared that it was "forbidden to organize or operate any entity that promotes a communist ideology or any other totalitarian system." Article 54 enshrined freedom of association, but then said, "It is forbidden, however, to organize or operate groups that act in accordance with or in subordination to international entities that promote the communist ideology or any other totalitarian system." And, should there be any doubt regarding the preferred economic model, Art. 40, in contrast to Art. 58 of Guatemala 1945, instructed the State to "stimulate *private initiative* for all the ends of social assistance and improvement, and provide the most ample support for its development" (emphasis added).

At the same time, at the formal level at least, this shift from (relatively) far Left to far Right produced only a moderate reduction in the content of constitutional justice. The labor rights secured in Guatemala 1945 survived, as did most of the other social rights, although with important differences. Guatemala 1956, for example, expressly forbade unions from engaging in any political activity. Private property was guaranteed without qualifications, losing the requirement that it must fulfill a social function. The prohibition on latifundia disappeared. But social guarantees, like a right to education and health care, persisted. In short, Guatemala 1956 moderated, but did not eliminate, the social impulses found in Guatemala 1945, even though it is quite clearly a Cold War constitution.

On individual rights, the constitution appeared quite strong. It continued to provide a cause of action for violations of the constitution, with an entire chapter for amparo. A finding in an amparo proceeding that a norm violated someone's constitutional rights would immediately suspend the norm. The new text, however, prefaced the provisions on amparo with the clarification that its essential function was to sustain "individual guarantees," an explicit reference to the immediately preceding chapter by that title (Arts. 40–78), which contains only classic civil and political rights, rather than social rights. Economic, social, and cultural rights are contained in other chapters, and therefore do not fall under the protection of the amparo. This restriction can be read as an attempt to narrow constitutional justice to individual rights, especially since in the previous constitution the amparo explicitly protected all "rights and guarantees."

Interestingly, as we would expect from an RC-dominant OC, the new constitution did nothing to shift the locus of control away from the legislature, which continued to name and remove justices by simple majority. The modest reduction in the scope of authority may reflect the fact that neither side trusted the State, and that the Right did not see social rights as much of a threat, since it had strong control of the RC. This would be especially clear since, as detailed above, their effectiveness seemed largely to be entrusted to the government rather than the courts.

A new constitution in 1965, the result of yet another coup, deepened the anti-communist bent of Guatemala 1956, outlawing any parties or entities that, because of their "doctrinal tendencies," might threaten "the bases of Guatemala's demo-cratic organization" (Art. 27). The coup's, and therefore the new charter's, main concern was not so much the idea that the country was drifting too far Left or Right, but rather a dissatisfaction with the conduct and results of ordinary politics. As a result, it sought to foster a more stable, two-party system through high thresholds for registering new parties and cleaner elections through an Electoral Council.

Because it was not the product of a significant change in the structure of power or dominant ideology, Guatemala 1965 did not significantly modify the content of the country's constitutional justice system. The few changes that were made are more in the nature of emphasis than direction: they continue the gradual retreat from the high-water mark of social constitutionalism established in 1945. Social protections were weakened slightly, but the basic rights arrangement persists. A telling passage can be found in the disparate treatment of the right to work. Although both constitutions noted that work is both a right and a duty, the first four words in old Art. 111 (1956) are, "Work is a right." The first five words in new Art. 112 (1965) are "Work is a social obligation."

Beyond these differences in emphasis, however, the 1965 Constitution was most notable for creating a new institutional structure for rights enforcement. Recall that, until this time, constitutional review had been exercised in a decentralized fashion by all trial courts, with appeals following the same course whether or not they involved a constitutional issue. After 1965, trial courts retained only the abil-ity to refuse to apply a law in a particular case if they judged the outcome would be unconstitutional. Binding constitutional decisions became the province of the Constitutional Court. For the first time in Guatemala's history, the constitution defined a centralized constitutional court with the capacity to invalidate laws it con-sidered unconstitutional. Indeed, with the exception of a short-lived Tribunal of Constitutional Guarantees in Ecuador (1945–7), which was in any event a purely advisory body, this is the first standalone constitutional court in Latin America.[4]

However, closer examination suggests that the new court was meant more to make visible and centralize control over constitutional adjudication, and to check its free exercise, than to provide a more autonomous, effective forum. In the first place, the new court was designed to respond very closely to the RC. The justices of the Court of Constitutionality were seconded from existing courts – the President and four magistrates from the Supreme Court sat on it, plus seven additional members chosen at random from judges on the courts of appeals and the administrative court. These judges, as always, were chosen by a simple majority of the Congress. Their ex post autonomy was slightly increased – although they continued to serve for a mere four years and they could still be removed by the Congress, their impeachment now required a vote by two-thirds of the legislature, rather than a simple majority.

---

[4] For details on the Ecuadorean Tribunal of Constitutional Guarantees, see Title 14 of the 1945 Constitution of Ecuador. For an explicit statement that the legislature is the sole authority on the constitutionality of laws, see Art. 165 of the same constitution.

Given how short their tenures were, however, impeachment was more likely to address grave misconduct than ideological inconsistency. In short, the power to declare laws unconstitutional moved from trial courts to a single, central court that was kept on a very short leash by Congress, revealing the deep ambivalence the designers felt about the power of judicial review.

Perhaps as importantly, the new court was quite limited in its reach and decisive capacity. Access was not very open, although it was not as restrictive as in some of its contemporaries: claims of unconstitutionality could be filed directly with the court by the Council of State, the Bar Association, and the President (through the Prosecutors), or by any persons directly affected by the law, so long as they could find ten practicing lawyers to sign the petition. The court also heard the final appeal in cases that involved claims of unconstitutionality. But the Court could only declare the unconstitutionality of a law by a vote of eight of its twelve members (Art. 263).[5]

The odds that the court would find many of Congress's laws objectionable are strikingly low: a full two-thirds of a court named by a majority vote in the Congress, for a mere four years at a time, would have to agree that the Congress had done something unconstitutional. The two-thirds majority requirement, in particular, essentially guaranteed that only laws that were well outside the current majority's preferences had any chance at all of being stricken. There was little or no chance that the court could act as a significant alternative voice for any position not at the center of the RC. Indeed, members of the 1985 Constituent Assembly later remarked that the 1965 court's constitutional powers went largely unexercised.[6] Centralized, specialized oversight of lower court constitutionality decisions simply allowed for closer supervision of the diffuse control of constitutionality. This reform, then, brought the production of constitutional meaning closer still to the RC, and limited the decisive authority of constitutional justice, even as it preserved some of the breadth of the sphere of constitutional justice that was established in 1921 and 1945.

Guatemala 1965 was the last formal constitution before Guatemala 1985, the main focus of our analysis. There is, however, one more important constitutional event that shaped the historical context for the 1985 constituent assembly. As Guatemala's internal conflict intensified, repression and violence became pervasive, elections continued to be fraudulent and fragile, and elected presidents rarely ended their terms. In 1982, General Efraín Ríos Montt took power in a coup and unleashed a three-year campaign of terror that decimated guerrilla groups, even as it exposed Guatemala to increasingly harsh international condemnation.

---

5   However, the court could temporarily suspend a law if its constitutional defects were "notorious" and it would cause irreparable harm.

6   One of the members of the Drafting Commission that produced the constitutional draft in 1985, known as the Commission of the Thirty, noted that, while the 1965 Constitution introduced the action of unconstitutionality, and while all judges even before that time had the ability to recognize the supremacy of the constitutional text, in reality "they never used those faculties." Transcripts of Debates in the Commission of the Thirty, Volume IV, Session 89, p. 72.

When he took power, Ríos Montt enacted a legal decree,[7] with the look and feel of a constitutional document, entitled "Basic Governing Statute" (Estatuto Fundamental de Gobierno). The Basic Governing Statute replaced Guatemala 1965 and destroyed any pretense of a separate, autonomous realm of constitutional justice. The Statute borrowed much of the language of the previous constitution, simply leaving out inconvenient provisions. It eliminated the Amparo Court and the Court of Constitutionality (as well as the Electoral Court). It severely restricted habeas corpus, and declared that an amparo action could not lie against any security measure taken by the junta. It made no mention of freedom of the press or the right to counsel, and eliminated many social rights guarantees, including the right to health. It formally retained certain core civil rights, such as freedom of speech and the right to property, even as it eviscerated all the mechanisms for rights enforcement. And it explicitly stated that all rights and individual guarantees were subordinated to any security measures the ruling Junta might dictate. From 1982 to 1985, the sphere of constitutional justice was as constrained as one can imagine it to be, while still being presented in constitutional language.

Moreover, the regime set itself up as the CGC. Among the "executive functions" of the governing military junta, Guatemala 1982 included the power "to make the following appointments: the President of the Judicial Branch and Supreme Court of Justice, the Justices of the Supreme Court, and the judges of the other collegiate courts [i.e., all appellate courts and various other specialized high courts]. The Governing Military Junta shall appoint the judges of the other collegiate courts, preferably [but apparently not necessarily] from a list proposed by the Supreme Court of Justice" (Art. 26). To ensure absolute control, this article went on to say, "In all cases covered by the foregoing subsections we shall observe the principle that whoever appoints may also remove." All the judges, in short, were appointed by and served at the pleasure of the military regime.

This was the existing normative framework, and the constitutional history of the country, at the time Ríos Montt was removed by what remains the last successful coup in Guatemala's political history. The new military regime called for elections to the constituent assembly that would craft Guatemala 1985, the constitution that remains in place to this day. We can make the historical trajectory of Guatemalan constitutionalism clear using our measures of autonomy and authority to graphically represent the various constitutional arrangements along these two dimensions. While during its entire history Guatemalan constitutional justice has been primarily an instrument of the RC, as indicated by its low levels of autonomy, Left–Right struggles have, by turns, significantly expanded and contracted the scope of its constitutional justice system. Since 1921, a perennially threatened Left has worked harder to enshrine its constitutional preferences, while the more self-confident Right has

---

7 Decreto Ley Número 24-82, Estatuto Fundamental de Gobierno.

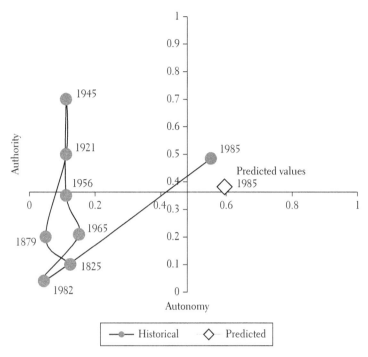

FIGURE 5.1. Autonomy and authority in Guatemala's constitutions

rarely (except in moments of purely arbitrary military rule) felt the need to strip all those commitments from the text.

Upon leaving the nineteenth century behind, the struggle for social justice constitutionalism pushed the measure of authority ever higher, until its peak in 1945. Although this was not undone from one day to the next, each successive document after that eroded the scope of constitutional justice. Finally, in 1982, the Ríos Montt regime essentially emptied constitutional justice of any content, so that the regime could rule without constraints.

However, a mere three years later there was a dramatic change. As defined in Guatemala 1985, the CGC significantly exceeded the RC for the first time in Guatemala's history, and the scope of constitutional justice rose to levels mirroring the first efforts to import standards of social justice into the constitutional sphere. As much of an outlier as this arrangement appears to be in relation to Guatemala's constitutional history, it is very much in line with the empirical model we presented in Chapters 3 and 4, as shown by the predicted value in Figure 5.1.[8]

---

[8] To generate the predicted value, we used the "margins" command in Stata to generate marginal predictions for all three dimensions, setting all the right-hand variables at their actual values for Guatemala 1985.

In the next section, we briefly describe the key elements of the new system of constitutional justice established in 1985, and then turn to the primary focus of this chapter – understanding in full detail the historical, ideological, and political factors that explain its scope and autonomy.

5.2. KEY FEATURES OF THE 1985 SYSTEM OF CONSTITUTIONAL JUSTICE

The members of the 1985 Assembly took the task of crafting a system of constitutional justice quite seriously.[9] They did not spend a lot of time debating the technical aspects of the courts and constitutional protection mechanisms they were creating in the plenary sessions, but this was primarily because the basic structure was worked out in a separate committee that secured the support of the key blocks of the Assembly. Only three official drafting committees produced text for the Plenary to debate and approve: the Commission on the Electoral Law, which needed to set the bases for the upcoming election; the Commission on Amparo, Habeas Corpus and Constitutionality (Comisión de Amparo, Exhibición Personal y Constitucionalidad); and the Commission of the Thirty (the C30), which produced the overall text of the Constitution. The C30 was composed of the key representatives of all the parties present in the Assembly, and was the core decision-maker within the Assembly. It had a rotating presidency, representing the three largest partisan blocs in the Assembly. Alejandro Maldonado Aguirre was the president of the Commission on Constitutionality, which had twelve members, also representing the various political forces.

The C30 generally wrote the drafts of most of the provisions for the General Assembly to vote on, sometimes modifying proposals received from subcommittees, and sometimes working from scratch. At the same time, it considered the Commission on Amparo as its equal, so that the draft of the provisions produced by the latter was briefly debated and transmitted directly to the Plenary Assembly with little modification.[10] Transcripts of the debates of the Commission on Amparo are not available, but in a recent "History of the Court of Constitutionality," compiled by the Court's staff, the work of the Commission on Amparo is described in

---

[9] Most of the following discussion is based on the transcripts of the debates in the Plenary Sessions of the Constituent Assembly, and in the sessions of the Commission of the Thirty, which was charged with producing the actual text on the basis of contributions by subcommittees, for later debate and approval in the Plenary. The transcripts are organized into two series, one for the Plenary Sessions and one for the Commission of the Thirty, in volumes that aggregate individual sessions. For convenience, the references will be labeled in the text as follows: PS (for Plenary Session) or C30 (for the Committee of the Thirty); followed by the volume number in parentheses, since the sessions are numbered consecutively, regardless of the volume; and then by the session number and the page number, separated by a colon. For example, "C30 (I)22:25–6," is a reference to the transcripts of the debates of the Commission of the Thirty, Volume I, Session 22, pages 25 to 26.

[10] See the discussion in the Commission of the Thirty, at C30 (IV) 100:14.

some detail.[11] Gabriel Larios Ochaíta, one of the members of this Commission, also prepared a brief summary of the Commission's work while he was President of the Court of Constitutionality.[12] In preparing its draft, the Commission reviewed Guatemala's constitutional history and invited the public to two forums for comments and input. The Bar Association also conducted two forums of its own and collaborated with the commission in preparing a draft.

The new system of constitutional justice, established in 1985, was marked by the transformation of a subordinate, part-time Court of Constitutionality into a standalone, permanent court, with its own mechanisms of appointment. These mechanisms gave it a great deal of ex ante autonomy from the RC. The court was staffed with five justices, each designated by a different actor: the Supreme Court, the Congress, the President with his Cabinet, the Superior Council of the University of San Carlos de Guatemala, and the Assembly of the Bar Association. Three of the five appointments came from outside the structure of partisan competition and majoritarian representation that configures ordinary politics.

The Supreme Court, one of the three ostensibly apolitical actors in the coalition of ex ante control was, however, fairly closely tied to the Congress, albeit with an important role for certain actors who were outside electoral politics. All appointments to the Supreme Court were subject to final approval from the Congress, but the nominations came from a variety of sources. From 1985 to 1993, four justices were chosen by Congress, at will, while the other five were selected by Congress from a list of thirty nominees proposed by a Nominating Commission. The Commission was composed of the law school deans, the Bar Association, and one representative of the Judicial Association, chosen by the Supreme Court.[13] We would expect such a court to represent a variety of interests, both internal to the partisan structure of the Congress and coming from the legal profession, if for no other reason than because the number of nominees to be appointed would lend itself to logrolling and compromise. This is all the more true in that, as the key court designer himself acknowledged, Guatemala has never had a dominant party that could control congressional majorities, so partisan compromise is typically required

---

[11] "Historia de la Corte de Constitucionalidad," 2011, unpublished manuscript compiled by Georgina de Muralles, available on request from the authors. Produced by the Court of Constitutionality of Guatemala.

[12] "Ley de Amparo, Exhibición Personal y de Constitucionalidad y Exposición de Motivos," 1994, unpublished manuscript compiled by Gabriel Larios Ochaíta, available on request from the authors. Produced by the Court of Constitutionality of Guatemala.

[13] In 1993, an amendment expanded the seats on the Supreme Court to thirteen, and required the Congress to choose all members, rather than five out of nine, from a list of nominees proposed by the Nominating Commission. The threshold for nomination in the Commission was increased to 2/3. The same amendment reduced the terms of Supreme Court justices to five years from six. In other words, and in line with the quantitative findings on the shifting preferences of the Right, the 1993 amendments increased the Supreme Court's ex ante autonomy but slightly reduced its ex post autonomy.

even for purely majoritarian decisions.[14] At the same time, the fact that nominees are approved by a simple majority tends to tie the Supreme Court more closely than the Court of Constitutionality to the congressional component of the RC, in spite of having a truly outsider nominating committee.

The 1985 constituents balanced out this high level of ex ante autonomy for the Court of Constitutionality with very low levels of ex post autonomy. The magistrates of the Court of Constitutionality serve only five years – one year longer than the legislature and the president, but one of the shortest terms for any court in Latin America in recent times – and can be reappointed. This gives the coalition of ex ante control the ability to fairly quickly produce a course correction through the appointment of a new set of justices if the current court is straying from its prefer-ences, or to stay the course if the justices are meeting their needs. Congress also has the right to initiate and approve, by a two-thirds vote, impeachment proceedings against the judges of the Court of Constitutionality (as it does for all high-ranking officials in Guatemala, from the President, to the Attorney General, to the Supreme Court). Focused emergency control, therefore, in the sense of midterm corrections through impeachment of individual members, centers in the Congress, but requires a somewhat more inclusive coalition, drawn from the parties with congressional representation. At the same time, given the members' very short terms in office it is unlikely that impeachment will ever be needed.

Congress emerges as the dominant actor in both the ex ante and ex post coalitions of control, but with an important role (especially in ex ante control) for the legal profession, which can propose more than half the nominees for the Supreme Court, and can directly appoint two of the five members of the Court of Constitutionality. The Congressional sector of the RC has a strong (but not overwhelming) role in the CGC, and the Executive virtually no role at all. The two members coming from the legal profession can serve a sort of swing vote role, joining with either a representative of the Congress, the Supreme Court (itself an attenuated creature of the Congress, as noted above), or the President, to forge a majority on the Court. The result is a court that, in general, should have a voice that is at least potentially distinct from the RC, and represents a diversity of preferences.

As to the scope of authority of the Court of Constitutionality, the 1985 system is remarkably open and relatively muscular. Access is not difficult. For concrete judicial review, all judges have the obligation to evaluate the constitutionality of any statute at issue in a particular case, either on their own initiative or on petition of the parties. Individuals who feel their rights have been violated can also file an amparo with any court at any time ("all days and hours are working hours," the law says), and the court has to give these cases precedence over any other pending cases. Amparos filed against higher ranking officials, who might be too threatening to a local judge,

---

[14] Author interview Alejandro Maldonado Aguirre, Guatemala City, July 23, 2014.

must be filed with higher-ranking courts – either the courts of appeal, the Supreme Court, or the Court of Constitutionality. If someone files a case in the wrong court, it is that court's obligation to ascertain which court actually has jurisdiction and to transfer the case. Rather than a passive, formalistic approach, once the case is filed, the trial court is required to act on its own initiative, whether the parties are active or not, to correct any formal errors in the filing. It is obligated to do whatever is needed to ensure prompt and effective adjudication of the substantive claim. Appeals from decisions impugning the constitutionality of a statute, or in any amparo case, are taken to the Court of Constitutionality.

In addition, the Court of Constitutionality has original jurisdiction in abstract cases. As well as the Bar Association, the Solicitor General ("Procurador General"), and the Solicitor for Human Rights ("Procurador de Derechos Humanos"), any person who can get three lawyers to sign the brief can file an abstract challenge to any law. In the case of abstract challenges, of course, a decision of unconstitutionality has the effect of nullifying the law. It may well be that this is what was intended for concrete cases as well (in contrast to what had been the practice before and to the practice in many countries). But this is left implicit in the actual constitutional text rather than stated clearly. As a result, from the text alone, at least, it is somewhat ambiguous as to whether any law that is found to be unconstitutional in a concrete case is considered to be null, thus giving the court's decision full *erga omnes* effects, or merely inapplicable to the actual parties in the case.

Recall that there are three elements in our conceptualization of the scope of authority of a system of constitutional justice: ease of access, the ability to make broadly binding decisions, and the ambit of a court's jurisdiction. Although the Guatemala 1985 system's decisive authority is, as noted, quite muscular, and access to it is quite unrestricted, it suffers slightly in comparison to others in two ways. First, it does not occupy some of the spaces that other courts do. A military court carves out some of its jurisdiction, and it lacks ancillary powers, such as the ability to oversee elections or the impeachment of the president. Second, it has a slightly restricted roster of rights to enforce.

On the third element, the constitution protects the full panoply of individual civil and political rights. On this account, it has a fully empowered court. As we will see, it is quite clear that the constituent assembly meant to provide individuals the fullest measure of protection from state actors in the classic areas of civil liberties and political guarantees. The list of social and economic rights, though not as extensive as the protections for civil and political liberties, is still substantial and includes standard social and economic rights that have become obligatory in Latin American constitutionalism – health, education, labor rights like a limited work day, and some limited cultural rights. But some of these rights are expressed in negative – rather than positive – terms. The right to work, for instance, is expressly set forth as the right to freely choose an occupation, rather than a more robust right to work, with a concomitant obligation on the part of the state to ensure an adequate supply of opportunities. In general, the system is above the mean – and slightly higher than our model predicts – in authority, but below some of the courts in the region that emerged in following years, which scored considerably higher on this dimension.

5.3. THE EMERGENCE OF A ROBUST AND AUTONOMOUS SYSTEM IN GUATEMALA

In this first qualitative chapter, it is worth recalling the key arguments we developed to explain the scope and autonomy of the system of constitutional justice that emerges from a constituent process. Our first claim was that a court's scope of authority should reflect the substantive preferences of the OC over any issues that cannot be entrusted to the RC. If this is true, we should see evidence in the debates that they wish to put into the realm of constitutional governance those agenda items that they cannot – for historical reasons, or because they do not know who will be in government – trust the government to pursue. We should see both allusions to the failure of past governments to respond to particular demands, and predictions as to the likelihood that future governments will do, or not do, what is being constitutionalized.

The alternative view is that the constitution has more of an expressive than a constitutional governance function. If the point is the expressive, symbolic, function of the constitution – if the goal is that the constitution should proclaim those values that the coalition finds most important, regardless of whether they are threatened – then the point of the discussion should be not whether those values are in peril, but whether they truly represent what the OC believes. Similarly, the discussion should examine the instructive effect of proclaiming those values. The OC's ideological commitments, which in this model are what the OC wishes to trumpet in the constitutional text, matter in our account as well. However, these commitments should be placed in the realm of constitutional governance only if they cannot safely be pursued in ordinary politics.

Similarly, the degree of autonomy – the result of the nature and composition of the CGC – of the system of constitutional justice should be a function of the dominance (or not) of the expected RC within the OC. We expect the OC to fashion a more inclusive, less purely majoritarian, CGC when the expected RC is a smaller percentage of the OC. The OC should seek to allocate control over, and access to, the system of constitutional justice to those it can imagine as its successors. The OC's successors could include, for example, opposition parties, if the OC represents a minoritarian party, or the professions and civil society, if the OC members are political outsiders.

We have argued that designers, implicitly or explicitly, imagine constitutional courts as part of a system for the ongoing production of constitutional meaning, and for the dynamic governance of a series of issues entrusted to the realm of constitutional justice. If this is so, we should see some reference to the need to ensure that control rests in the right hands. The alternative view is that they see constitutional commitments as fixed, and law and courts – at least when they are functioning properly – as a technology divorced from politics that can protect those fixed commitments against later politics only to the extent that the courts are fully insulated from the political process.

We will also look for alternative explanations. The borrowing of foreign models, sometimes called diffusion or transplantation, is often asserted to be an important determinant of the content of a constitution. We do not deny that diffusion plays an important role in providing the raw materials out of which constitutions are crafted, but in Chapter 3 we argued that, in our view, designers would borrow those foreign elements *à la carte* to get the combination of attributes that best suits their particular goals, or, failing that, tweak borrowed elements to the same end. Similarly, we know that a country's prior models are also influential (Elkins et al. 2009), but we argued that these prior models would also be selectively deployed and tweaked to better fit the logic of constitutional governance, rather than blindly incorporated for the sake of continuity or tradition. In what follows, we will also discuss the use of historical or contemporary comparative models, to see the extent to which even the process of borrowing and copying follows a logic of constitutional governance.

5.3.1. *The Originating Coalition and the Construction of the CGC*

The eighty-eight members of the 1985 National Constituent Assembly (the NCA) were elected on July 1, 1984 in elections that were widely viewed as free and fair. Nearly 80 percent of registered voters cast a ballot – an exceptionally high participation rate by Guatemalan standards, according to one of the representatives[15] – although a very high number of null and blank votes suggests some dissatisfaction with the alternatives on offer. Still, no fewer than seventeen political parties presented candidates, and ten different political parties were represented within the Assembly. García Laguardia (2001: 96), a contemporary of the NCA and a constitutional scholar whose work was influential in the debates, describes the mood this way: "Participation [in the election] was massive and enthusiastic, much greater than in previous elections. [But] the campaign took place in an atmosphere charged with uncertainty . . ." The constituents took their seats in an atmosphere of great expectation, but also great tension, as the fighting continued within Guatemala.

Catalina Soberanis, also a member of the Constituent Assembly, recalls that the Assembly began its deliberations in the context of the Cold War, with the United States and the Soviet Union disputing their hegemony in Central America. The Sandinistas had won the revolution in Nicaragua, the FMLN guerrillas in El Salvador looked quite strong and controlled important portions of that

---

[15] Author interview Catalina Soberanis, former member Constituent Assembly, Guatemala City, Guatemala, July 20, 2012.

territory, and the conflict in Guatemala was ongoing. The armed Left was certainly not present within the chamber, and it does not appear that there were informal negotiations with them either. Members of the guerrilla indicated that they initially viewed the constitution-making process as a farce.[16] Militarily, the Left was battered and on the run, and mostly focused on staying alive.[17] In fact, their connections to social movements and other organizations were at an all-time low (España Nájera 2009). Gustavo Meoño, who was in charge of relationships with social movements for the EGP, notes that he was completely removed from what was happening within the NCA. He and the remaining leadership were either in exile in Mexico or hiding in the mountains, trying to regroup. "At that moment, we were not focused on negotiations toward peace, or returning to politics. Nothing. We [and the remaining guerrilla movements] had been battered and we had to strengthen our internal unity."[18]

But the perceived need among Constituent Assembly members to set a foundation for ending the conflict and bringing the guerrillas back into the political process set them up as important implicit players in the deliberations. The guerrillas, in a sense, marked the limits at one end of what was possible, simply because without some assurance that they and their demands were included in the constitutional pact there was little likelihood the armed struggle for social justice in Guatemala would come to an end. This argument was put forth most passionately by Rep. García Bauer in the powerful drafting committee, known as the Commission of the Thirty (hereafter the C30), in its debates over the social function of property:

> What will the socialist youth of the world say, when it looks at the Constituent Assembly, at the Commission of the Thirty, and realizes that it is closed . . . to the thousands and thousands of dispossessed in our Homeland? Where is our social sensibility? . . . I say these things because if Cuba is communist today, it is because once, the majority of its private property was held by a few. Because of their selfishness, the Revolution came, backed by many, and, of course, by the Soviet Union. The same thing happened in Nicaragua, and could happen in Guatemala . . . Here, in the Constituent Assembly, the Left is not represented, only from the Center to the Right, and the voice of the people, the true people, is barely represented . . . We are here to legislate for the whole people of Guatemala, and this people is yearning for justice . . .
>
> (C30 (I) 22: 25–6)

Coupled with Guatemala's long history of social constitutionalism, in which several of the constituents had participated directly, this impulse is likely what led

---

[16] Author interviews Otto Zeissig (former member Fuerzas Armadas Revolucionarias), July 20, 2012; and Gustavo Meoño (former commander Ejército Guerrillero del Pueblo-EGP), August 8, 2013, Guatemala City, Guatemala.

[17] Author interview Meoño, August 8, 2013.

[18] Ibid.

the Assembly to craft a system of constitutional justice that is more robust and generous than our empirical model predicts.

Similarly, the military did not have a declared partisan representative in the Assembly. But it was certainly present in spirit. It was not averse, according to one informant,[19] to sending messages about what could and could not be done, particularly in the context of the debates around the social function of property. Indeed, in that context their influence was very clear, as we will see later in this chapter. In effect, this pair of outside actors, the guerrilla on one side and the military on the other (the latter with the assistance and support of economic elites), marked the limits of what was possible for the Constituent Assembly.

From Right to Left, the three largest parties in the Assembly were the coalition formed by the Movimiento de Liberación Nacional and the Central Auténtico Nacional (MLN/CAN), with 23 seats; the Unión del Centro Nacional (UCN), with 21; and the Democracia Cristiana Guatemalteca (DC), with 20. The first of these was a classic conservative, Right-wing party, although many of its members were opposed to the military regimes that had often stolen elections. The Unión del Centro was a classic Center-Right, small government, proto-neoliberal party. And the Christian Democrats were in the center on most issues, but pushed to the Left by Catholic social justice values, and by their affinity for some of the constituents who had played a role in the Arbenz "revolution" and the social constitutionalism of 1945. Maldonado Aguirre described them as a "Leftist" Christian Democratic party, in contrast to others in neighboring countries or in Europe that had a more centrist or Center-Right profile.

These three blocks, which represented nearly the full spectrum of permissible Guatemalan politics at the time, had sixty-four of the eighty-eight seats,[20] and were occasionally referred to as the "aplanadora" (the steamroller). Indeed, each of these three blocks had a copresident of the Assembly, with the presidency rotating monthly from one to another. Importantly, no two of the three had the majority needed to approve the constitutional text, so most provisions were approved by simple acclamation, with the votes of all three blocks, after negotiations had produced a consensus. The three blocks also dominated the C30, which was charged with producing the text that the General Assembly would debate and approve. Occasionally the DC would ally with one side or the other, plus some smaller interests, to win an argument for greater social rights, especially in the C30, but in general, all three major blocks had to concur to get anything done.

By most accounts, everyone that was associated with the political Left was absent from the Assembly as a result of the extensive political persecution that had been taking place for years:

[The] right won a total of 30 seats. Success for the DC meant it became the strongest political force in the country . . . However, there was severely restricted

---

[19] See, for example, author interview Otto Zeissig, July 20, 2012.
[20] Electoral results are taken from Nohlen (2005).

political debate, and the Left – through the United Revolutionary Front (FUR) –
sustained a not unsurprising defeat, due to the ongoing counterinsurgency
and the fear that the population felt for voting for the left . . . As a result, the
ANC became a body with a fair degree of representation of a variety of political
currents (not, of course, the Left) and obliged its members to carry out
permanent negotiation.

(Brett and Delgado 2005: 9–10)

Each of the three main blocks was fielding a presidential candidate in the elections
that were expected as soon as the constitution and electoral laws could be finalized.
No one knew who would succeed. Each should have anticipated that, even if they
won the presidency, they would not control the RC, since they would need allies in
the Legislature to accomplish anything. In our terms, then, the expected RC was a
relatively small percentage of the OC. Moreover, the interests represented by these
blocks did, by and large, expect to be in the Legislature – the DC and MLN/CAN
were historical parties in Guatemala, while the UCN was a new party meant to
occupy the Center.

Perhaps more important than the electoral uncertainty among the parties is the
fact that all of those present, except perhaps the very far Right, knew that they could
not trust the executive. Many of the constituents had considerable experience working from outside of politics or from exile due to the repressive recent political history
of Guatemala. Some of the Christian Democrats' most prominent leaders and hundreds of its adherents had been assassinated, presumably by government agents, in
the years running up to the convention. Members of moderate conservative parties
had seen their own presidents ousted in coups, or cheated of electoral wins. Indeed,
according to Maldonado Aguirre, even the party that had traditionally been a vehicle for military interests, the Institutional Democratic Party (PID, for its initials in
Spanish), which had secured five seats, was at that moment somewhat estranged
from the military leadership.[21] Some within the Assembly undoubtedly represented
extreme Right interests, but the bulk of the constituents were politicians and aca-
demics whose freedom of action was very much threatened by the continued dominance of economic elites, the military and the security services of the state, and the
executive in the ordinary politics of Guatemala of the 1980s.

Maldonado Aguirre made his distrust of these forces very clear in the course of the
debates within the C30. Maldonado was a prominent conservative member of the
OC and a fervent anticommunist, but overall on the moderate Right for Guatemala
and a self-described opponent of military interventions (Maldonado Aguirre 2004).
He was the principal drafter of the provisions related to the system of constitutional
justice, later was an unsuccessful presidential candidate, and eventually became
the longest-serving member of the Court of Constitutionality. In 2016, he became

---

[21] Author interview Alejandro Maldonado Aguirre, Guatemala City, July 23, 2014.

the provisional President of Guatemala, having succeeded the deposed Otto Pérez Molina. However, in 1985 he justified the proposals that gave the executive virtually no role in judicial appointments by expressing little confidence that the executive might represent an enlightened or majoritarian position:

> I have always believed that the excessive weight of presidential decision-making in our system has been the cause of stagnation and regret, because . . . unfortunately, our presidential history teaches us two things; one, that the people have not always been wise in their selection of a President; and two, that on many occasions, the President has been the product of an imposition or an electoral fraud.
>
> (C30 (I) 7:6)

According to our theory, members of an OC with these characteristics – not dominated by a clear expected RC, and distrustful of the executive and of whoever controls the State – should entrust a great part of their project (especially the protection of their physical integrity and liberty) to a CGC with similar characteristics. They should seek to create a constitutional justice system that will not respond directly to whoever occupies the presidential palace and that will work at arm's length from the executive. Rather, the fact that the dominant members of the constituent assembly also expected to be legislators should lead them to give the legislature a role in the CGC. In the transcripts of the C30, we find ample evidence that this motivation is explicitly at play in the design of the courts and their mechanisms of appointment.

In discussing the ex ante and ex post control mechanisms for Supreme Court justices, two things become apparent. The first is that they understand what we have called ex ante and ex post mechanisms pretty much in the way in which we have presented them here. For example, they understand ex ante autonomy not as a function of absolute insulation from politics, but rather as the product of a more inclusive and pluralistic coalition of control. Maldonado himself defends his choice of a selection mechanism on the grounds that it is "more balanced and representative" (C30 (IV) 87:17) than the alternative – an alternative that had been suggested by the Court and aimed at something closer to insulation. They specifically identify the elements we coded for ex post autonomy as important: they speak of the need to establish a fixed number of justices in the constitution in order to prevent court packing and allow justices to rule without undue pressure (C30 (IV) 89:80). Unsurprisingly, they speak of protections against the easy removal or discipline of judges as guarantees of independent adjudication (C30 (IV) 89:80). In short, the debates show that our coding decisions reflect the intentions of the drafters, as we have argued in Chapter 2 and Appendix.

Perhaps more importantly, the debates also reveal the intentions and goals our constitutional governance theory of design attributes to the constituents. Specifically in the case of Guatemala, and as predicted by the theory, the designers make explicit their intention to deny the distrusted Executive undue influence, and give themselves – or more precisely, their successors – the dominant role in both the ex ante and ex post coalitions of control. Independence in the first instance is framed in terms of freedom from Executive influence:

> How can we hope to have democracy some day in Guatemala if we do not have independence between the branches? How can we hope that the Judiciary will not be subject to the orders of the Executive, as it has been in all previous periods, committing barbaric acts that are known around the world, if we do not give them independence? . . . No, gentlemen, here justice does not matter. What matters is the imperative voice of the Executive. There, the Prosecutors' Office does not matter, or the Supreme Court, nothing matters but the benevolence of the Executive. If that is how we will continue, we will end badly . . . [We must protect the Judiciary] so that there will be peace and tranquility in this blessed country. If not, we are lost.

Rep. Cordón Schwank (defending a minimum
guaranteed budget to the courts) (C30 (IV) 89:56)

As president of the Commission of Constitutionality, Alejandro Maldonado Aguirre presented the provisions related to the organization of the judiciary to the C30 and the Plenary. Those for the ordinary judiciary he collated from a proposal by the Supreme Court and a proposal by a Coordinating Committee. Those for the Constitutional Court, Amparo, and Habeas Corpus were prepared by a Committee over which he presided. In presenting the project, he argued that judges need to be protected by secure tenure and by an appointment mechanism that excludes the Executive (C30 (IV) 87:18). The President of the C30, at that time Ramiro De León Carpio, reinforced this argument, saying judges cannot work with a "sword of Damocles" hanging over their heads, but that they must ensure "at the same time . . . that there be the proper mechanisms to control the abuses that judges may commit" (C30 (IV) 87:17, 21). So to whom would they entrust this control?

As described above, in terms of ex ante control, they located final control over approval of Supreme Court appointments in the Congress, with a simple majority. But they gave the power to nominate a majority of the candidates to a nomination committee made up entirely of unelected actors coming from civil society and the legal profession: one representative of the rectors of the public universities, the deans of all the national law schools, and an equivalent number of representatives elected half by the Bar Association and half by the courts established in the constitution. They offered a twofold justification for the existence of a nominating committee: first, that this would prevent the executive from controlling appointments, and second, that this would prevent any one faction in the Legislature from naming pet justices. González Quesada argued that this arrangement would "completely break the traditional, historical, constitutional framework in Guatemala [because] for the first time, the executive will have absolutely no role in recommending these appointments, because before they were named by the Legislature, but they were ordered from the National Palace" (C30 (IV) 90:49). Ramiro De León Carpio reinforced this sentiment, saying, "I believe we have arrived at something that is of historical importance for the country, because in this way we will be eliminating the pressures and abuse of power that has always existed on the part of the Executive Branch" (C30 (IV) 90:50–1). This is a remarkable statement by someone who was a close ally of the first runner-up in the very next presidential elections and president himself a mere eight years later.

In terms of ex post control, the initiative resides firmly in the legislature. Justices' tenure is very limited – they only keep their seats for five years – and subject to reappointment by the legislature. Their criminal prosecution and discipline is similarly subject to preapproval by the legislature. In discussing these provisions, the cautionary comments all relate to the Executive. The discussion of the Congress's power to control proceedings against sitting Justices (the *antejuicio*) is clearly framed as protection against trumped up charges by the security forces and the Executive (see, e.g., C30 (IV) 90:11, et seq.). The representatives never discuss the possibility that a legislative majority might seek to improperly pressure a sitting justice. On the contrary, the members of the constituent assembly argue that they – it is clear that they imagine themselves as future legislators – should have the ability to curb judicial abuses through legislative action.

In Chapter 1, we hypothesized that a history of violence would highlight the need for autonomy as well as greater authority for the system of constitutional justice. However, in the statistical analysis in Chapter 2 we found evidence only for an effect of past violence on the scope of the court's authority, but no evidence that such a history affected autonomy. The qualitative evidence from Guatemala corroborates this finding. In the transcripts of the debates, there are constant references to Guatemala's violent past and the need to build constitutional protections that can withstand the pressures of violent state actors. The word "violence" appears in more than one-third of all the transcripts – sixty out of about 160 – and references to "blood" appear in nearly as many – forty-five sessions. Rep. Acuña Alvarado offers an especially vivid example of this. In arguing in favor of stronger judicial protections against arbitrary detentions, he recalls how, just four years earlier, he and his fellow party members suffered an assassination attempt, and, after resisting, were "disappeared" for twelve hours by the police. The assembly needs to ensure, he says, that this important provision in the constitution does not remain a "lyrical" provision only. "Lyrical" was the pejorative adjective of choice for provisions that may remain purely formal, and also appears in forty-five sessions, most often in the context of arguing for particular and more robust protections against the State and the security forces. As the statistical analysis suggests, and as we will see in more detail in the next section, however, the constituents deployed this argument in favor of particular substantive provisions and the means of making them effective – the system's scope of authority – but not in the context of debates around the provisions that construct the CGC and determine the court's autonomy.

In sum, a review of the transcripts supports the notion that the members of the Constituent Assembly seek to locate control over the courts in the institutional and social spaces they and their successors are most likely to control in the future. They are clearly aware of the need to establish the mechanisms of ex ante and ex post control that will allow them to influence judicial decision-making going forward. Perhaps most interestingly, the transcripts also provide evidence that – for some of the constituents at least – the space of constitutional justice is a political space for dynamic governance, where the meaning of the constitution will be worked out over time, and which must therefore remain subject to the consent of a wide coalition of control. Rep. Larios Ochaíta – the author of a draft that served as the starting point for the Commission on Constitutionality, a member of that Commission, and much later a President of the Court of Constitutionality – noted the difference between constitutional and ordinary justice this way:

> When one talks of the Court of Constitutionality, for example, . . . its function and attributes, while they are juridical in some respects, they also are politico-juridical, and from this comes the manner of staffing this type of tribunal, which requires the consent and representation of all the highest institutions of the State . . .
>   . . . [W]hen it is ruling on a bill, or a . . . treaty . . . it might be serving a judicial function, but of constitutional justice, that is, we should not be confused, con-stitutional justice is that: constitutional justice. In any given moment, it's almost political justice, in contrast to the justice of legality that the [ordinary courts] would apply and carry out.
>
> (PS (IV) 71:98–9)

Note that the argument is not for full insulation, in order to freeze the meaning of the text, or in order to trust that the professional norms of insulated justices will pro-duce meaning that is faithful to the original pact, but rather that constitutional adju-dication is, by its very nature, a political enterprise, and thus needs to be entrusted to an organization that responds to the proper authorities.

5.3.2. *The Originating Coalition and the Scope of Constitutional Justice*

In this section, we look for evidence of the logic of constitutional governance through the *conditional* effect of ideology, as opposed to a more expressive, symbolic goal on the part of the constitutional designers to simply proclaim their basic values. As we might expect, participants[22] and observers (see, e.g., Brett and Delgado 2005) alike remark on how strongly the three-way tie among disparate political blocks

---

[22] Author interviews with Soberanis, Maldonado, and Zelaya. See also the speech by Maldonado, toward the end of the Assembly, in which he describes how this process – in contrast to prior ones in Guatemala – was marked by the need to reconcile the often conflicting values and goals of all the political forces of Guatemala (PS (IV) 57: 18–20).

marked the discussions, requiring extensive negotiation and compromise. However, the question is whether they sought to trumpet the values they all had in common, which would be the least threatened by any subsequent government, or whether each sought most vigorously to protect those values that it thought might be least likely to be advanced in the context of ordinary politics. If the latter is true, then much of what we would find in the constitution is related to what they all, collectively, found threatened (e.g., because someone else might be making the relevant decision), or to what any one of them considered threatened (e.g., because one of the other members of the CGC might be making the decision as the RC).

As expected, the discussions reveal that the need for a robust system of constitutional protections was felt all the more keenly because of the history of violence to which the members themselves had been exposed. As noted earlier, the Christian Democrats had experienced the killing of hundreds of their members and leaders. The identification and listing of rights was taken to be a fairly mechanical matter of making sure that none were left out: "We told all the members of the Commission on Human Rights to prepare lists, taking all the Constitutions they might have available or any they might secure, so that by next week all these lists can be collated, . . . so that we do not miss any rights, of the ones we already know or the ones that might exist in International and Comparative Law . . ." (C30 (I) 4:35). Taken on its own, this hyperinclusive enumeration of rights could be interpreted as responding to the expressive function of a constitution, working in conjunction with a diffusion process, in which any right ever listed anywhere is at least considered for inclusion in the new constitutional text. And yet, in the course of the discussions, it becomes clear that they consider this elaborate enumeration of rights necessary because these rights have traditionally been – and remain – threatened in Guatemala:

> De León Carpio: If this were not Guatemala, . . . a country where human rights have been so tremendously violated . . . it would be enough, honestly, to simply declare . . . that the State will guarantee the rights contained in [the various international instruments to which Guatemala is a party], and period.
>
> The forty plus articles that follow [i.e., the enumeration of individual rights in section 1 of the Constitution] would be superfluous if we lived in a different country, but, as in this case "unfortunately" we live in a country where, in spite of defining human rights, they are violated, and even if they are perfectly enshrined in Constitutions that are "democratically developed," in spite of this, we have to develop them further.
>
> (C30 (I) 14:66)

The right to free association is a more specific example. As discussed earlier, the 1956 and 1965 constitutions had proscribed first the Communist Party, and later anything that might have some affinity with an "internationalist" movement. The government and security forces had used the freedom these provisions implicitly allowed to go after a wide range of organizations on the Left. When the article guaranteeing freedom of association was first proposed, it too had an exception for "secret and illegal organizations," which was defended, initially, by the Right. But opposition to this phrase was almost immediate. The argument, as Rep. Téllez García framed it, was that:

> The majority of the social and political problems of this country [that is, the fact that the Left was pushed into an armed opposition] are a result of not permitting the free organization of all political parties . . . For that reason, I think we should fix this, not including any norm that at some future date could be used to prevent free association, and that it be possible in Guatemala, from this Constitution of 1984 onward, that everyone has the freedom of participation to belong to whatever party they want, of the right, the left, social democrats, etcetera.
>
> (C30 (I) 20:27)

In the end, that argument prevailed and the prohibition on "secret organizations" was eliminated.

Similarly, the strengthening of the habeas corpus regime was expressly grounded in the abuses of prior regimes, and the fear that similar events might take place. Víctor Hugo Godoy, a former member of the Constituent Assembly, and a known scholar of human rights, explained why they sought to strengthen the habeas regime, by relating his personal story.[23] In 1970, when he was twenty-two and his middle brother was twenty-one, they were detained by the security forces under suspicion of being communists. Their family presented a habeas corpus petition to a friend on the Supreme Court, who was permitted to see the young men, even though their family was not. Eventually, they were released. Nine years later, in 1979, his youngest brother was disappeared, presumably by the security forces, and Godoy himself went to a friend on the Supreme Court to present a habeas petition. This time, as Godoy recalls it, the justice responded very differently: "But my friend, how can you put me in this difficult position? You cannot ask me to do this." He never saw his brother alive again. In January of 1982, three years later, his middle brother was also taken, and twenty-four hours later, his body was found thrown into the street.

"That's why [Guatemala needed] a Solicitor for Human Rights. That's why [the Constituent Assembly created] a Court of Constitutionality," he said. They were responding to the need to create a "scaffolding," an institutional framework that would protect them from this. "For example, we knew that if we gave them 48 hours to respond to a habeas petition, that was too late," Godoy explained. "You were already dead. So we said six hours. It was a desperation measure, in some ways . . . This is what I was trying to do in the Constituent Assembly, and what I have tried to do with all my work, ever since: to make sure that this never happened again."[24] Clearly, both the enumeration of individual rights and the creation

---

[23] Author interview Víctor Hugo Godoy, Guatemala City, August 1, 2013.
[24] Ibid.

of robust, efficient, and effective mechanisms for their protection are responses to the perception that these rights may be threatened by future governments.

If anything, there was much more concern and consensus over the need to create the proper institutional scaffolding than over the specific list of rights that might be included:

> De León Carpio: I would like to call your attention to this . . . The mechanisms, the institutions we must create, that requires more work and has more content. I, frankly, if I were a member of the Commission on Constitutional Guarantees, would rather dedicate myself to this, which is what will have more importance in the Constitution, the mechanisms to make the respect for human rights prevail, to make it effective. The list of human rights, I don't think it has major importance, because it is a list, that is, we're not going to invent anything new. On the other hand, the mechanisms and the institutions we must create, that indeed has true importance and requires much study and much work because it is something innovative. I'm thinking about a tribunal, a solicitor of the people, like the one that is in Spain, for example, but it's not just a matter of throwing it into the Constitution.
>
> (C30 (I) 4:36–7)

Moreover, the participants were clearly worried about the effect that a separate system of military justice might have on constraining the space of constitutional justice and worked hard to limit this separate forum to purely disciplinary matters. "On this issue we must be very clear, very precise, that the military tribunals will handle military matters, infractions of military rules, not civilian matters . . ." (C30 (IV) 90:57). Interestingly, in the long discussion that surrounded this question, and that ended with a relatively restricted military jurisdiction, no one expressed (openly, at least) any concern that the military might not permit such a restriction. The goal was to ensure that encounters between the military and civilians were subjected to constitutional oversight, so that military justice could not be used to undermine the careful scaffolding of individual rights protections they had constructed. This was a direct response to Guatemala 1982, then in force, which subordinated all constitutional rights to national security concerns at the discretion of the military leadership.

But perhaps it seems obvious that this concern with rights would respond to prior abuses and the danger of future ones – these are individual rights of personal integrity, after all, and Guatemala was a place where these rights were being notoriously violated, even at the very time of the Constituent Assembly, so it is logical that we would find discussions of the country's violent history. Is there evidence that the same logic – of putting into constitutional space not everything that is important, but primarily those things that are threatened and unlikely to be accomplished through the RC – applies to social and economic rights as well? The discussion of the social function of property shows clearly how this worked in Guatemala.

5.3.3. *Social Constitutionalism and the Boundaries of*
Constitutional Justice for Private Property

Rep. Pivaral y Pivaral: For the tranquility of the people of Guatemala, I vote in favor [of this amendment].
   Rep. Mauricio Quixtán: Even if it costs me my life to be with my people, I vote against.

(PS (I) 29:255–6)

What manner of amendment might risk the peace and tranquility of the people of Guatemala, or cost a representative his life? The so-called "social function of property" has a long history in Latin American constitutionalism, and a very particular history in Guatemalan constitutionalism. What was at stake in the debate in the Plenary was an amendment to the clause that had been drafted by the C30, defining constitutional protections for private property. The debate in the C30 was already quite contentious, with the Right (the MLN/CAN) accusing the Left (the DC) of demagoguery, causing one DC representative to huff that he would not allow this "mediocre" person to accuse him of being a demagogue. The argument on the one side was that some degree of redistribution was necessary, at a minimum "to combat totalitarian doctrines" (C30 (I) 22:19), but also as a matter of basic justice in a country so deeply marked by inequality, as noted earlier. Rep. García Bauer argued that, "If Cuba is communist today, this is because once the majority of its private property was held by a few" (C30 (I) 22:26). He argued that the violence in Guatemala was due, not to the failed modest attempt to redistribute land that led to the US-backed coup against President Arbenz three decades earlier, but rather to the refusal to carry out serious social reform: "We have 100,000 orphans, indigenous orphan children . . . because of the shortsightedness of not wanting to carry out social reforms, because of the shortsightedness of wanting to hoard all the land, because of the shortsightedness of not having a social function" (C30 (I) 22:27).
   Eventually, this argument carried the day in the C30, and a coalition of the DC and UCN managed to report out a private property rights clause permitting – indeed, requiring – the government to enact laws that would ensure that private property fulfilled its social function. As it came out of the C30, all but the final clause sounds quite like a fairly uncompromising vindication of the right to property. However, in the end it ambiguously opens the door to the RC to ensure that property is fulfilling its "social function," rather than leaving that decision to the owners themselves: "Private property is guaranteed as a right inherent to all people. The State will guarantee all citizens its exercise, will pass laws and create the conditions to ensure that property holders may use their goods in an efficient and useful manner, so that private property may fulfill a social function" (C30 (I) 22:59, et seq.). This clause was approved by the C30 on November 27, 1984, and was scheduled for discussion in the Plenary Session in mid-January 1985. When it finally came up for debate on

January 16, the debate over these two words ran for twelve hours, until nearly 3:30 a.m., on the morning of January 17.

Between November and January, the fact that the C30 had dared to write a "social function" property rights clause very nearly brought the entire constitutional project to an end. There were petitions to dissolve the Assembly, threatening editorials in the newspapers, and protests from members of the business class. On January 14, the balcony of the room where the Plenary Sessions were held was filled with people, primarily there to protest against the social function clause. On January 15, they were back, with constant commentary on the discussion. Upon opening the discussion, the President of the Assembly could not even finish reading the article. He was forced to stop and threaten to evacuate the precinct before he even got to the phrase "social function." The record reflects shouts, catcalls (*"bulla"*), and clapping from the audience during that initial reading.

In both the C30 and the Plenary Sessions, this clause was understood – perhaps appropriately in light of Guatemalan and Latin American constitutional history – to place the question of the redistribution of land squarely in the territory of ordinary politics. The point of it was, in fact, to allow future RCs to decide when someone's private property was not fulfilling its social function and could therefore be taken and put to a more "social" use. People like Luis Cabrera Hidalgo and Catalina Soberanis Reyes, of the Christian Democrats, made eloquent arguments, asserting that this was not a Marxist idea, and tracing the lineage of the social function doctrine back to Catholic social teaching (PS (II) 29:46–62). They tried to demystify the phrase, arguing that, by its terms, it merely recognized what has always been true – that private property is often subordinated to social interests, through taxation, regulation, and eminent domain, for example. They argued that "this great killing [that has happened in Guatemala] was the product not of the social function of property, but because of the way certain property owners sought to exercise [their property] right over the rights of the community" (Soberanis, PS (II) 29:62). The social function advocates were repeatedly interrupted by the audience with shouting and catcalls, to such an extent that the President of the Assembly gave up trying to stop it, and simply advised speakers that they should wait silently through the shouting and speak when they could again be heard.

The opposition, in turn, attributed every possible ill to these few words. They referred to the history of attempted land reform in Guatemala, and the use of the phrase in the 1945 Constitution: "These words bathed our country in blood" (PS (II) 28:87); "The words social function are dangerous . . . blood stained our country . . . because of that demagogic formula" (PS (II) 29:100). In a reference to the Iron Curtain, they argued these words would convert Guatemala from a country with fences on the border to keep people out, to a country with dogs at the border to keep people in (PS (II) 29:14). Speaking on behalf of the Right wing of the Assembly – the MLN, the CAN, and the PID – Rep. Villeda Moscoso cautioned explicitly against putting the question of property rights protection in the sphere of ordinary politics, for fear of what a future RC might do. The applause lines followed one after the other:

> The property that belongs to private citizens, which we call private property, is acquired by individuals personally with the sweat of their brow, with the sweat of the brow of their families and it is not just . . .
>
> (Constant shouting)
>
> . . . that we should leave it as a social function, because that would be not to leave one door open, but to leave one hundred doors open so that a government with leftist leanings, socialist or communist can come . . .
>
> (Intense shouting from the balcony, clapping)
>
> . . . I was saying, it would be to leave open one hundred doors, so that a government with, I repeat, leftist, socialist or communist, inclinations, might come and strip the legitimate owners of their goods that have cost them so much . . .
>
> (Intense shouts and clapping)
>
> . . . and, what will happen is that they will create in Guatemala a political, economic, and social chaos, as is happening with the socialist government of Napoleón Duarte[25] . . .
>
> (Constant shouting)
>
> . . .
>
> . . . what I can guarantee you and I give you my word, is that what is happening in El Salvador will not happen in Guatemala, because the Movement of National Liberation will not permit it, here . . .
>
> (Intense shouting, hurrahs, and clapping)
>
> . . . here, in Guatemala, we will defend with tooth and nail the right to private property
>
> (Intense shouting and hurrahs)
>
> . . . that is why, honorable Representatives, I beg you to think very carefully about what we are going to do, let us not compromise in any way the social, political and economic future of Guatemala . . .
>
> (Whistling, shouting and clapping from the balcony).
>
> (PS (II) 29:64–6)

Jorge Skinner Klée, at that time a member of the UCN, who had served in the Government of Castillo Armas (the government that replaced Arbenz after the coup), reminded those present that, even with this clause, the boundaries of the right to property would be placed in the hands of justices, in the sphere of constitutional justice: "If there were a discussion regarding the reach of the right to property in the Republic of Guatemala, it would be aired out in the courts of justice, and it would be judges, men of the law, who would have to interpret the reach of the

---

[25] Napoleón Duarte had been elected president of El Salvador in 1984. Although many abuses by security forces occurred during his leadership, he was a Christian Democrat who sought to provide a middle ground between Right and Left in his country, began negotiations with the guerrillas, and was in opposition to ARENA, the party of the far Right in El Salvador.

constitutional text" (PS (II) 29:86). And yet he judged that, in light of Guatemala's constitutional history – specifically, the reliance by the Arbenz government on the social function to justify land reform and redistribution – the inclusion of a reference to a social function would make that task too uncertain. As he explained, "I put myself in the shoes of a judge trying to do exegesis, trying to interpret this article of the Constitution and he will be left empty handed, there is no way to reach a clear interpretation [of the texts proposed by the DC and Revolutionary Party] but it appears as though private property must, as a condition *sine qua non* of its existence, fulfill a social function" (PS (II) 29:87).

We have argued that designers constitutionalize those issues that seem especially at risk in a country. Offering "smoking gun" evidence for this claim, in the course of his speech on the need in Guatemala for unambiguous property rights protection, Skinner Klée explicitly makes our argument through an analogy to efforts to restrict inheritance rights in Spain: "For that reason, the Spanish Constitution recognizes the right to inherit. Precisely, to guarantee what in that country was seen as threatened; we have no need, because we do not see our right to inheritance threatened, so we have no need to say that" (PS (II) 29:91).[26] By implication, he went on to argue, a "social function" property rights clause was unacceptable in Guatemala because it would likely be interpreted to permit the RC to expropriate and redistribute land. For this reason, then, the constitution must unambiguously place unqualified property rights under the aegis of constitutional justice.

Villeda Moscoso's speech on the perils of ordinary politics for property rights, delivered with such passion and to such approval from certain sectors of society, and Skinner Klée's references to constitutional justice, exemplify exactly what the more quantitative analysis shows. Not everything that is important needs constitutional protection – in other countries the long list of individual rights might not be needed. In other countries, an unqualified property rights clause might not be so crucial. In other countries with other threats to property, other protections – such as inheritance rights – may be more important. But here, the particular interests of large landowners are too threatened to be left in the realm of ordinary politics, for fear of what a future RC might do. And, given the politics of the Constituent Assembly, it was necessary to protect them, or the entire constitutional project would fail.

Had the Right been more confident of its electoral future, and had the Left in Guatemala (and elsewhere in Latin America) not threatened expropriation and redistribution of land, this clause would not have been so vitally important. After all, the clause in question at best "opened the door," as Villeda Moscoso put it, for a future RC to engage in some redistribution. To have any effect, it required, as they saw it, the future collaboration of a willing congress and executive, and the approval,

---

[26] "Por eso, la Constitución Española reconoce el derecho de herencia. Precisamente, para garantizar lo que allá se dio como una amenaza, nosotros no tenemos necesidad, porque no nos sentimos amenazados, el derecho de herencia, no tenemos necesidad entonces de decir eso."

as Skinner Klée argued, of the courts of justice. And yet it became the most fiercely debated, most publicly fought over, and most contentious article in the entire constitution. In the end, the DC and the UCN abandoned their original position and joined with the MLN/CAN bloc to pass a property rights clause that was stripped of the offensive language, and remains in the constitution to this day:

> **Article 39. Private Property.** Private property is guaranteed as a right inherent to all people. All persons can freely dispose of their goods in accordance with the law.
> The State guarantees the exercise of this right and must create the conditions that enable property owners to use and enjoy their goods, in order to achieve individual progress and national development for the benefit of all Guatemalans.[27]

Were this apparent triumph of the Right over social constitutionalism the end of the story, Guatemala 1985 would have defined a much thinner system of constitutional justice. It would have continued to robustly protect individual rights, which were uniformly seen as threatened, but failed to include much in the way of social and economic rights.

However, after losing this battle, the Social Democrats and those further to the Left fought successfully to scatter their concerns for social justice throughout the rest of the constitution. Víctor Hugo Godoy Morales, of the Revolutionary Party, insisted toward the end of that passionate debate that the social function language was necessary, in light of Guatemala's constitutional history, and voted to include it in the constitution. But while agreeing that the constituents were much more focused on the protection of personal integrity, he recently confided that once they lost the fight for the social function, they worked to include the same concern for basic social justice in many other parts of the constitution.[28] Soberanis, who was forced to vote against her own proposal in the Plenary Session, insisted at the time that the reference to "the benefit of all Guatemalans" in the final proposal actually created

---

[27] To appreciate just how little language separates the initial, vilified proposal, from the final one, we must put the two clauses side by side, in the original Spanish. The key difference is that the use of "social function" was code for redistribution, while the new provision only requires/empowers the state to take such actions as might support property owners in the use and enjoyment of their property:

> *C30 proposal*: Artículo 39. Se garantiza la propiedad privada como un derecho inherente a la persona. El Estado garantizará su ejercicio a todos los ciudadanos, emitirá las leyes y creará las condiciones que aseguren que el propietario se sirva de sus bienes en forma eficiente y útil, de manera que la propiedad privada cumpla una función social.
> *Final clause*: Artículo 39. Propiedad privada. Se garantiza la propiedad privada como un derecho inherente a la persona humana. Toda persona puede disponer libremente de sus bienes de acuerdo con la ley.
> El Estado garantiza el ejercicio de este derecho y deberá crear las condiciones que faciliten al propietario el uso y disfrute de sus bienes, de manera que se alcance el progreso individual y el desarrollo nacional en beneficio de todos los guatemaltecos.

[28] Author interview Godoy Morales, Guatemala City, August 1, 2013.

even more room for social justice than her original proposal. And she too recently recounted how they had worked hard to create an *"estado social de derecho"* – a state under the rule of law, but with a concern for social rights.[29] In the end, even Alejandro Maldonado, a member of the Right-wing bloc that scuttled the social function clause, recognizes that the moderate Left managed to carve out some space for social rights constitutionalism, especially in the area of indigenous rights, though perhaps not as much as they had hoped.[30]

In sum, both in terms of individual civil and political rights and in terms of the boundaries of social constitutionalism, the representatives' perceptions of what was at stake – what was threatened and what was not – drove the decisions about what merited protection in the sphere of constitutional justice. The Left looked at the long history of state violence and social exclusion and concluded that a robust system of constitutional justice was needed to advance both the state's social mission and individuals' personal freedom and security. The Right agreed that the State was the primary threat to individual rights. In his biography Maldonado Aguirre (2004: 456–7) recounted the various parties' positions in the lead-up to the Constituent Assembly, and noted that "this brutal repression touched any political movement that interfered with [the Government's] plans," targeting leaders of the Christian Democrats as well as of the Right. Parties from across the spectrum were in accord on the desperate need to construct an institutional framework to protect civil and political rights.

As to social rights, the Right recalled the brief reformist period three decades earlier and blamed it for the subsequent violence and bloodshed. It saw the strength of the Christian Democrats and, looking around Central America, concluded that an unconditional property rights clause was a necessary bulwark against a socialist or communist future. Two-thirds of the Assembly were, in fact, either of the far, conservative Right (the MLN/CAN), or of the essentially neoliberal Center-Right (the UCN), with the result that they chose to privilege an unconditional right to private property. In the end, the influence of the Christian Democrats within the OC, and the need to bring the revolutionary Left into the political arena, meant this strong right to property had to coexist with a series of commitments to particular social rights – such as education, health, and workers' protections. As a result, both sides could expect to pursue and protect some of their core threatened interests through constitutional means, but land itself was protected from expropriation in the pursuit of a more egalitarian Guatemala.

For Alejandro Maldonado, a conservative, the principal architect of the system of constitutional justice, and later on a justice on the Court of Constitutionality, the constitution was too generous.[31] Just as we argued with respect to the Right generally

[29] Author interview Soberanis, July 20, 2012.
[30] Author interview Maldonado, July 23, 2014.
[31] Ibid.

(see Chapter 1), he believed then, and believes now, that the constitution should have a limited agenda, and leave governing to the RC. In particular, he now argues that the courts ought not to push a social agenda, and calls some of the more activist courts in Latin America "populist."[32] But even Maldonado approvingly concedes that the Court has become an important space for developing some of the social pretensions of that original document, especially for developing the indigenous rights that were included in the constitutional text in 1985.[33] The logic of constitutional governance is clearly at work in the final conformation of Guatemala 1985.

5.3.4. *Other Logics at Work*

While it appears that the logic of constitutional governance was uppermost in the considerations of the constituents, at the same time other logics appear in the debates from time to time. In particular, the transcripts shed considerable light on the ways in which other models exert their influence – on the process that underlies the diffusion of constitutional models. Maldonado says they began thinking about the Court of Constitutionality with the German Constitutional Court model in mind, but were also strongly influenced by the Spanish Constitutional Court. But they immediately had to make changes, he says. For example, the Constituent Assembly made Guatemala's constitutional court more easily accessible and open to more people.[34] In the course of the debates, dozens of foreign texts were mentioned as models. The Christian Democrats, for instance, acknowledged a plethora of sources in the creation of their proposed draft: "We have used the Constitutions of 1945, 1956, and 1965; some parts of the Constitution of Bayonne, and all the text of the Constitutional Digest, provided by the Bar Association. The Central American Constitutions of Honduras, El Salvador, Costa Rica and Panama; the Constitutions of Peru and Ecuador; the Spanish Constitution and the Constitution of the Republic of China [Taiwan]" (C30 (I) 12:121). The constitution of Taiwan was an important referent, as a fellow traveler in the anti-communist crusades of the Cold War, especially in relation to institutions of control (C30 (I) 9:66–72). As noted earlier, the Commission of Individual Guarantees noted that they looked at prior constitutions and many sources in identifying the list of rights they wished to include. Clearly, borrowing was frequent and openly acknowledged.

However, as the Commission of Individual Guarantees said, "We believed that, in response to the needs of our country, we had to enact . . . advances that respond to our reality" (C30 (I) 13:7). Many of the innovations that most clearly respond to Guatemalan domestic imperatives go to the core of the construction of the sphere of constitutional justice, and, in particular, to configuring the CGC. One of the

[32] Ibid.
[33] Ibid.
[34] Ibid.

sui generis provisions was the protection against the notorious Civil Patrols that the government had used as a sort of conscripted paramilitary force to combat the guerrillas. Similarly, the denial of any role for the executive in the appointment of justices is quite unusual, and does not reflect the design of either the German or the Spanish courts. The choice of extremely short tenures for both Supreme Court and Constitutional Court justices responds to a perception that, in Guatemala, the coalition of control needed to keep a shorter rein than either Spain (where Constitutional Court justices serve nine years) or Germany (where they serve for twelve) on people in positions of power, as recounted above. In general, especially when it comes to the conformation of the coalition of control and other important aspects of the system of constitutional justice, it seems quite clear that foreign models are often used as inspiration. But far from being models to be copied wholesale based on their prestige or their popularity, they are disaggregated into their components and then used as a source vocabulary for expressing and addressing local fears and aspirations.

Although vote-seeking is often portrayed as the dominant rationale for legislators, the electoral ambitions of individuals and parties are not often credited with an important role in constitutional design, and yet they seem to have played a significant role in shaping Guatemala 1985. By many accounts, the fact that the members anticipated the first national elections of a new democratic period, and that many were expecting to run, introduced a populist impulse into the Assembly. On the one hand, participants say, the representatives saw the Constituent Assembly as a means to gain adherents by granting favors. On the other hand, debates were occasionally marked by allusions to the effect that taking one position or another might have on a party's presidential ambitions: "The only thing I want to say to these friends from UCN . . . is that if they continue to oppose these things, they may be signing the epitaph of a party that could have reached . . . the Presidency of the Republic" (Rep. García Bauer, in the context of debates on protecting life since conception, C30 (I) 14:55). Indeed, nearly all the members of Assembly we interviewed argued that the constitution became more generous because those representatives who expected to run for the legislature did not want to alienate potential voters.[35] This sensitivity to upcoming elections is something that is not in our model and the nearness of elections to the work of the Assembly could partly explain why the resulting levels of authority are higher than we predicted.

5.4. OTHER CONSTITUTIONS WITH SIMILAR FEATURES

The process that produced Guatemala 1985 was marked by a history of violence and a Right-leaning OC in which the expected RC was a clear minority. Roughly two-thirds of the members of the Assembly favored a more free market approach to

---

[35] Author interview Soberanis, July 20, 2012; Maldonado, July 23, 2014; Godoy, August 1, 2013.

development and the economy, and practically all of them had reason to fear the security forces. Moreover, the unexpected strength of the Christian Democrats in the election made them the favored party to win the upcoming presidential elections. Thus the most likely RC was an influential but at best a minority interest in the OC. This creates a nice contrast to the Right-dominant OC that crafted Chile 1980, Pinochet's constitution. Chile 1980 is interesting in no small part because it illustrates some of the more counterintuitive implications of the logic of constitutional governance. In this case, a dictator who expected to rule for some time, but eventually to return to a more democratic system, built a system of constitutional justice that is, by most standards, a model of constitutionalism.[36] The sphere of constitutional justice is restrained, in line with the recommendations of many experts in constitutional law, and the Constitutional Court has impressive autonomy from the RC. Why might Pinochet, a dictator, have granted the court so much "independence"?

Other accounts (e.g., Barros 2003) attribute the autonomous behavior of the post-1980 Court to splits within the ruling junta, which responded to the three branches of the armed forces. And, indeed, this may explain how the Court found the political space to act with some autonomy on such issues as the 1988 plebiscite on Pinochet's continued rule. But if we focus on the Court's design, and look more closely at the coalition of constitutional control defined in the Constitution, we can see evidence of the logic of constitutional governance. Rather than seeking to insulate the Court from all pressures, the design establishes a coalition of ex ante control that clearly responds to members of the junta's coalition of support, and a coalition of ex post control that is similarly weighted toward the regime's allies. Moreover, the overall system is designed in such a way that this Right-wing coalition might continue to have disproportional weight in the sphere of constitutional justice, even in the event that Chile returned to a democratically elected government.

Chile did not have a Constitutional Tribunal until 1970, when a constitutional amendment declared, "There shall be a Constitutional Tribunal, composed of five Justices who will last four years in their functions, and can be reelected. Three will be designated by the President of the Republic with the approval of the Senate, and two by the Supreme Court from among its members" (Art. 78 (a) Chilean Constitution of 1925, as amended in 1970). Justices of the Supreme Court were appointed by the President from a list of five nominees submitted by the Supreme Court itself. Some have written that this system, coupled with an informal norm of deference to the Supreme Court's nominees, created a Supreme Court that was very

---

[36] We speak here of the system of constitutional justice, not the democratically questionable authoritarian enclaves included in Chile 1980, such as the senators for life. Still, even those elements of the Chilean constitution are consistent with the basic countermajoritarian logic of classical constitutionalism – we might feel less poorly disposed to them if they were meant to protect, say, a minority ethnic group, rather than a minority political and economic interest associated with the dictatorship.

much insulated from politics, but that nevertheless developed a passive, formalistic culture (see, e.g., Hilbink 2003, 2007; Couso and Hilbink 2011). It seems at least plausible that the decision by the executive not to interfere in judicial affairs was in turn attributable to a conscious or unconscious decision on the part of the justices not to interfere in the executive's affairs. The executive's preeminent role in their appointment and replacement may well have prompted a strategic decision on the part of the Court to remain passive.

Setting aside the question of whether an informal norm of presidential non-interference could trump the constitutional arrangement, this amendment, in 1970, configured a fairly pro-majoritarian Constitutional Tribunal: a majority of its members (three) were appointed by a majoritarian actor (the President) with the approval of another majoritarian actor (the Senate), and the remaining members (two) were appointed by other presidential appointees (the Supreme Court). Their short terms, which coincided with the electoral cycle, and the potential to be reelected, further exposed them to the politics of the RC. By our measure, this court has low autonomy, so that its low profile is not at all unexpected.

Similarly, the Tribunal's scope of authority was designed to serve the interests of this relatively majoritarian coalition. The Tribunal had the power of abstract (a priori) review,[37] but access was limited to the President, the leadership of each chamber of the Legislature, and a group of at least a third of legislators. Moreover, the President could request a ruling that a certain law was constitutional, and if he were successful, then no other court, including the Supreme Court, could refuse to apply the law on grounds of unconstitutionality. This device centralized control over the constitutionality of laws and restricted the questions that might be raised to those that were of concern to either the RC or, at best, a dissident one-third of the Legislature. In substantive terms, as might be expected, the 1970 amendments had a Left flavor: they added labor rights – including the right to strike, protections for unions, and wage protections – and expanded guarantees of free expression and a few other rights.

This outcome is quite consistent with our theory of constitutional governance. In 1970, the RC in Chile was quite far to the left, and relatively weak. Salvador Allende, a Marxist, was elected President with only 35 percent of the vote. This accounts for a desire to constitutionalize a Left project.

However, in 1973, Pinochet ended not only this experiment in Left politics, but also the experiment with new systems of constitutional justice: "In light of the fact that . . . the existence of the . . . Constitutional Tribunal is unnecessary . . . the Constitutional Tribunal is hereby dissolved . . ." (Decree Law [Decreto ley] no. 119

---

[37] That is, it could review laws before they went into effect, to determine whether they passed constitutional muster. Its powers were similar to those of the Conseil Constitutionnel established in 1958 in France, as amended in 1974 to allow a minority of legislators to challenge laws (see, e.g., Stone Sweet 1999).

of 1973). Eventually, the Junta turned to the creation of a new constitutional order, and assigned a group of civilian lawyers the task of drafting the 1980 Constitution, which was to be submitted to a referendum.

Although the 1980 Constitution is closely identified with Pinochet, it is clear that there was a (very) slightly more diverse OC than just the General himself. Barros (2003) details the divisions within the Junta that led to the drafting of the constitution – what divided the coalition was primarily the institutional interest of each of the branches of the armed forces. In any event, it was a coalition that was devoted to perpetuating the regime's social and economic agenda, even beyond a return to democracy. The goal of the coup, after all, had been to establish a new social, economic, and political order that would prevent a return to the politics that had triggered the intervention. What did this OC put into the document then? In particular, where did it locate control over the system of constitutional justice it created?

The 1980 Constitution defined a new Constitutional Tribunal whose governance coalition was almost the opposite of the previous, pro-majoritarian one. Actors who responded to Pinochet and came from outside electoral politics dominated the coalition of ex ante control. Three of the seven justices were appointed by the Supreme Court, which had already established itself as a close ally of the regime (Hilbink 2007). Two were appointed by the National Security Council, which was composed of representatives of the armed forces plus the President. Thus, five of the seven came from outside partisan politics and could be counted on to be reliable allies of the Right. One more was appointed directly by the President. The last one was named by the Senate, which the same constitution packed with representatives of the Right, through its senators for life and its binomial election laws (Siavelis 2000: 33, et seq.). Until he lost an election, Pinochet essentially controlled three appointments (his own and two from the National Security Council), plus the three coming from the Supreme Court.

Even after a transition to democracy, and in the event it (predictably) lost legislative and presidential elections, the Right could count on appointing, directly or indirectly, five of the seven members of the Tribunal. In fact, until 2006, seventeen years after the transition to democracy, the Right controlled the Senate, despite losing general elections (Siavelis 2000: 40). Thus, even after the transition, it controlled all the appointments to the Constitutional Court except for the lone presidential appointment. The design is congruent with Pinochet's deep distrust of democratic, electoral politics, and especially of the more populist, more representative lower chamber. It privileges actors associated with the Right wing of the political spectrum, such as the Court, the Security Council, and the Senate. The logic of hegemonic preservation (Hirschl 2004) fairly leaps off the pages of the constitution, protected by close attention to the logic of constitutional governance.

In terms of its scope of authority, the constitution was also quite clear. The principal goal was the unqualified protection of property rights, less tinged with a social democratic impulse than the one we saw in Guatemala (Coddou and Contesse 2014). The constitution also eliminated some of the protections for public sector (and other) workers, and defined a list of rights that is, by Latin American standards today, quite abbreviated. As a whole, the constitution promotes a neoliberal, market-based economic model and restricts the RC from deviating from this model (Boylan 2001). The system of constitutional justice is, in substantive terms, in service to this project. Moreover, the Tribunal remains closed to ordinary citizens but open to the President, the presidents of the two legislative chambers, and any fourth of the members of each chamber. Even this last provision, which opens the court to minority interests, is quite clearly designed to favor the Right. It was expected, and in fact it turned out, that the Right would be a perpetual minority in the Chilean Legislature (Siavelis 2000), and this final provision simply makes it easier for the Right to challenge the actions of the inevitable Left-leaning RC.[38] In short, the system of constitutional justice constructed in Chile 1980, upon close examination, reveals itself as a mechanism designed to constrain majoritarian electoral politics, in the event of a return to democracy, in the service of a CGC that is dominated by the successors to Pinochet's design coalition.

The story, of course, does not end there. Despite the deep layers of protection for Pinochet's CGC – including designated Senators-for-Life, plus electoral rules that favored the Right, and high thresholds for making constitutional changes – the constitutional governance arrangement was too incongruent with Chilean democratic outcomes to last. Eventually, even the post-transition Right found itself chafing under some of the restrictions in the constitution, and a broad multilateral accord emerged that would permit extensive amendments to the Constitution to eliminate what were known as the "authoritarian enclaves."

The 2005 amendments, done in democracy by a Left-oriented but pluralistic OC, changed the Constitutional Tribunal's coalition of ex ante control significantly, as our theory would predict. The Tribunal grew from seven to ten members – in no small part to speed up the process of reconstituting the court with fresh faces. Of the ten justices, the president now names three, the Senate names two, and the Chamber of Deputies names another two with the consent of the Senate. Both the Senate and the Chamber of Deputies must act by a two-thirds vote. The Supreme Court selects the remaining three in a secret vote. In other words, the President now has three appointments rather than one; the Congress has four (including two by the more representative lower house) rather than two; and the Court still has three, but their influence is diluted in a more numerous court. The Security Council no longer has any appointments.

---

[38] The Supreme Court may hear the petitions of ordinary citizens, under what is called the "recourse of inapplicability in individual cases" (*recurso de inaplicabilidad para casos particulares*). But any ruling in such a case is expressly limited to *inter partes* effects.

The changes mean that the appointment process is much more weighted toward democratically elected actors, while configuring a coalition of control that still significantly exceeds the RC. Seven of the ten justices come from the representative branches of government, but opposition parties still have influence over the appointment of four members, by virtue of the supermajority rule. Moreover, the Court might be counted on (for now) to appoint relatively more conservative justices. The Right, through the Senate, can still veto four of the ten appointments, and retains indirect influence through the Supreme Court's three appointments. As a result, the Court remains a space that is designed to be countermajoritarian and leaning to the Right.

And yet, for all that, the Court is clearly more integrated into the democratic politics of the country. Given that the Right was a necessary player in a plural OC that was located squarely in partisan, representative spaces, this result aligns well with our predictions. Given institutional inertia – and the century-old tradition of relatively conservative, formalistic legalism in Chile – we should not expect the change in coalitions of control to have an immediate impact on the Court's behavior, but there are signs that the post-2005 Constitutional Tribunal is significantly different from its more authoritarian predecessor (Couso and Hilbink 2011).

5.5. CONCLUSION

In sum, in the lower quadrant of Table 2.1, we find courts that were forged in the crucible of the Cold War or following the dictates of the Washington Consensus. But they all bear the marks of the logic of constitutional governance. In Guatemala, where the constituent assembly was less dominated by the outgoing military regime, the designers sought to locate control over the system of constitutional justice where the executive could not reach it. Similarly, in Chile, Pinochet's designers crafted a CGC that could protect the interests of the regime even after it turned control over to a democratically elected government. In both cases, the goal was to ensure that the constitutional justice system would protect property rights and a market-oriented system. The Guatemalan system nevertheless secured greater authority because the designers concluded that they needed to include some concessions to the excluded Left in the document, if they were ever going to put an end to the conflict.

6

Argentina (1994)

Negotiating a Plural Space of Constitutional Justice

[We have chosen to require the consent of two thirds of the Senate] out of the understanding that, if the constitution is what the justices say it is, each time we name a judge of the Court we initiate a partial and everyday process of reform of the Tribunal and, in the final analysis, of the National Constitution. For that reason, it should only be possible to occupy that position by means of a consensus that has some equivalence to what would be needed for a formal constitutional reform.

Rep. Enrique Paixao, of the Unión Cívica Radical (UCR).
Transcript of Debates in the plenary sessions of the National
Constitutional Convention, July 27, 1994, p. 2210.[1]

After several years of single-party dominance over constitutional interpretation, 1994 offered Argentina's opposition parties a unique opportunity to negotiate for a more plural, more inclusive space of constitutional justice. Democracy had been reestablished a little more than ten years earlier, and the Peronist party, formally called the Partido Justicialista (PJ), was in power. President Menem wanted to amend the constitution to permit his reelection, and was threatening to do so unilaterally, through a plebiscite, although he did not quite have the requisite legislative majorities. To forestall that possibility and to advance his own longstanding project to reform the constitution, Raúl Alfonsín, the previous president and leader of the main opposition party, the Unión Cívica Radical or UCR, negotiated an accord to reform certain aspects of Argentina's 1853 constitution. This agreement, known as the Pacto de Olivos, in effect traded presidential reelection for a reduction in the ability of the

---

[1] "Con relación a los jueces de la Corte Suprema de Justicia de la Nación . . . se eleva el nivel de consenso senatorial requerido para ser miembro de ese tribunal en la inteligencia de que, si la Constitución es lo que los jueces dicen que es, cada acto de nombramiento de un juez de la Corte implica la puesta en marcha de un proceso parcial y cotidiano de reforma del tribunal, y en definitiva de la Constitución Nacional. Por ello, solamente resulta posible ocupar esa magistratura a través de un consenso que tenga alguna equivalencia con el que se requiere para la reforma constitucional propiamente dicha."

executive to control all the political spaces in Argentine governance. Along the way, it also opened up a process that led to the most significant enduring reforms to the 150-year-old constitution.

These reforms to the oldest living constitution in Latin America made that country's system of constitutional justice more ambitious and subjected it to a more inclusive coalition of control. The Constitutional Governance Coalition (CGC) it defines has significant representation of opposition parties, although it remains dominated by elected officials, in contrast to Guatemala 1985, where control was partially outsourced to unelected social actors. Meanwhile, the scope of constitutional justice was significantly expanded, mostly through the efforts of a coalition of minoritarian, Center-Left actors, who gained more prominence in the Constitutional Convention than they ever had, or would have, in legislative politics. These actors, marginal in the neoliberal politics of the Menem era and initially opposed to a constitutional convention, insisted not only on the inclusion of social, economic, and cultural rights – accomplished by the wholesale incorporation of international human rights treaties into the Argentine constitutional framework – but also on the explicit constitutional protection of mechanisms to enforce these rights. The newly reformed constitution creates procedural mechanisms that have proven quite important in the ensuing politics of constitutional meaning. The collective amparo, in particular, coupled with the judicial protection of diffuse and collective rights, and the reliance on international instruments and interpretations, has fundamentally transformed the politics of environmental and health regulation, of housing and social provision, and most of all, of accountability for past human rights violations.

This chapter chronicles the way that the logic of constitutional governance led to these ultimately very consequential changes. It was the desire on the part of minoritarian actors to configure a space within which to push back against the concentration of power, and against the then-dominant neoliberal model, that led to these design choices. And it was the driving ambition to be reelected, coupled with the need to secure the approval of at least the first minority, and preferably even smaller factions within the Constitutional Convention, that led the dominant party to concede this much power. The Peronists, to be sure, had a dominant position in the Convention, and managed to weaken many of the key aspects of this system of constitutional justice, as our theory predicts the expected Ruling Coalition (RC) would seek to do. But there was enough diversity within the Originating Coalition (OC) to produce a significant expansion in the scope of constitutional justice and the CGC. The result is a system with moderately high levels of both autonomy and authority, well predicted by our statistical model.

6.1. THE HISTORY OF ARGENTINA'S CONSTITUTIONAL JUSTICE SYSTEM

Argentina's first long-lasting, fully effective constitution was adopted in 1853, and this remains the basic constitutional text, albeit with important amendments and one relatively brief interregnum in which a different constitution was in effect. The initial constitutional imperative in Argentina was simply to establish control over a vast, sparsely occupied territory. As we might expect from a narrowly elitist, exclusionary political system, nineteenth-century constitutionalism in Argentina configured a limited sphere of constitutional justice, closely tied to a narrow RC of elites. Constitutional debates, such as they were, rotated around federalism and center–periphery conflict. By the twentieth century, however, as in Guatemala, much of the debate was over social constitutionalism and the scope of constitutional justice. Once the political system became more inclusive, demands to increase the scope of constitutional justice drove constitutional change. However, in terms of its autonomy, the system remained tied to the RC, with a dominant role for the executive, either in the form of more unilateral populist rulers or in cooperation with copartisans in the Senate.

The official declaration of independence in 1816 was succeeded by proposed constitutions in 1819 and 1826. The 1819 Constitution was drafted by the same assembly that declared independence. It centralized control in an indirectly elected executive who was given the title of "Director" (Constitution of Argentina 1819, Art. LVI and ch. II). The judicial function was entrusted to a "High Court of Justice" (Art. XCII), which was comprised of seven justices and two prosecutors. As in the US Constitution, the members of the court would be designated by the "Director" with the consent of the Senate, and would serve for life "during good behavior," as the US Constitution says. Also mirroring Art. III of the US Constitution, the remaining details of the judicial structure were left to ordinary legislation. In short, compared to Guatemala's original court, this constitution contemplated a similarly majoritarian mechanism for ex ante control, although justices were selected by elected officials, thus concentrating power more in existing office holders. It did, however, have considerably more ex post autonomy. This basic pattern would persist throughout all of Argentina's early constitutions.

With regard to the scope of constitutional justice, Argentina 1819 framed a narrow sphere of concern, and is remarkably similar to the first Guatemalan Constitution, its contemporary. In its very first clause, the constitution establishes the Catholic faith as the state religion, and declares that all inhabitants owe this religion "all respect, whatever may be their private opinions" (Art. I). In its final section, entitled "Declaration of Rights," the constitution claims to protect the rights of all "members of the State" to "life, reputation, liberty, security and property" (Art. CIX), and declares that these rights cannot be suspended (Art. CXXI). Specified rights included standard due process protections and, remarkably, the right to a jury trial.[2]

---

[2]   In an oft-remarked oddity of Argentine constitutional history, the right to a jury has been present in its constitutions from the beginning, with the exception of Argentina 1949, but actual jury trials were only used (since 1987) in the provincial courts of Córdoba, and never actually implemented in other provinces, or at the federal level, until the last few years.

Practically every one of the provisions, however, explicitly allows the RC to regulate
the scope of the right in question – freedom of the press is declared to be essential but is subject to existing and future legislation (Art. CXI). There is protection
against arbitrary search and seizure of papers and effects, but "the law will determine
in what cases and with what justification" they can be seized (Art. CXV). Private
property is afforded more robust protection – "property is a sacred and inviolable
right," although it can be taken pursuant to law or after a trial, subject to just compensation (Art. CXXIV). There is no explicit mention of the power of judicial review
or procedural devices, such as amparo or habeas corpus. All in all, the court's scope
of authority, as defined in the text, is quite limited.

As Gargarella (2013: 48–9) notes, Argentina 1819 was drafted by a tiny elite with
the goal of allocating power within that elite, so it is not surprising that it configures
such a narrow and tightly controlled space of constitutional justice. It clearly was
never imagined as a space in which true outsiders could contest dominant visions
of the public good. In any event, whatever might have been its advantages or disad-
vantages, this document was never fully implemented. Written without the participation of most of the Argentine provinces, and celebrated only by the province of
Buenos Aires, it was immediately rejected by the other provinces for concentrating
too much power in the federal government. In fact, it made no mention at all of
provincial authorities and powers, and created an exceptionally strong central executive. A period of civil war followed, with the provinces ultimately securing their
autonomy from the national government on the battlefield. None of the national
institutions proposed in Argentina 1819 ever came into being, although in many
respects their design set the pattern that would mark the Argentine constitutional
justice system until the middle of the twentieth century.

The civil conflict between Buenos Aires at the center and the provinces at the
periphery led to a new constitution only seven years later. Argentina 1826 was
drafted with greater participation by the outlying provinces but remained a centralizing document. The new text is only slightly more federalist in nature, and configures a sphere of constitutional justice and mechanisms of constitutional control that
reflect the first document in virtually all respects. The High Court of Justice would
have nine justices rather than seven, but they would still be named by the President
(as the executive was now called) with the consent of the Senate. As before, they
enjoy life terms during good behavior. This institutional arrangement continues to
give the executive the dominant voice in staffing the constitutional justice system,
but it preserves the right of the provinces, through the Senate, to check the process
by giving or withholding consent.

The scope of constitutional justice remains essentially unchanged. There is still
no explicit mention of judicial review (although it is likely that this was considered
implicit, since the US model was one of the key references in this period). There
is no explicit provision for habeas corpus, and no reference to an amparo or similar
device for protecting individual rights. The list of rights is copied verbatim from

Argentina 1819, under the more innocuous title "General Dispositions." The only real change is a slight strengthening of property rights in Art. 177, which prohibits the confiscation of property as a penalty for crime. Given the expansion of the OC, we might have expected the scope and autonomy of the system to increase slightly in relation to Argentina 1819. But it seems the provincial elites who were added to the OC, like the Right in the twentieth century, were more interested in limiting the powers of the federal government than in assigning it an expansive project. As a result – consistent with our argument and the findings of the quantitative analysis in Chapter 4 – to the extent they had any influence, they entrenched their preference for a narrow scope of constitutional justice. The system remains limited and closely tied to the RC, even as the center of gravity of that RC shifted slightly toward the provinces.

However, the document was so widely understood as a centralizing pact that it triggered a second round of rejections by provincial governors, leading to yet more civil war and decades marked by the near absence of a central government. During most of that time, the governor of Buenos Aires, Juan Manuel de Rosas, exercised a loose de facto national rule over a confederation of provinces, each with its own governor. It was only after the end of his rule, in 1853, that the leaders of the provinces of the interior adopted a new constitution. This constitution was initially rejected by Buenos Aires, until that province joined the confederation and signed on to the constitution in 1860. The addition of Buenos Aires to the national pact marks the true beginning of constitutional government over the entire Argentine territory, and is important enough that the constitution is sometimes referred to as the Constitution of 1853/1860. For convenience, however, and given the most common usage, we refer to this document simply as Argentina 1853.

By most accounts, this is the constitution that is still in place in Argentina today, although this claim requires some qualification. In 1949, then-President Juan Perón crafted and put in place a new constitution, which was in effect until 1955, when Perón was overthrown by the military and exiled. Two years later, the military regime reinstated Argentina 1853 with some amendments, by means of a constituent assembly – the legitimacy of which is still questioned today – convened by military decree. In 1994, another constituent assembly amended the 1853 document to such an extent that some refer to "the 1994 Constitution." But by its terms, the constitution currently in force in Argentina claims to be the one "sanctioned by the General Constituent Congress on May 1st, 1853, reformed and collated by the ad hoc national convention on September 25, 1860, and with the reforms of the conventions of 1866, 1898, 1957 and 1994."[3] By this account, then, Argentina has only had two effective constitutions: Argentina 1949, Perón's constitution, which was in effect for only six or eight years, depending on whether one counts to the

---

[3]   See official text of the Preamble to the Argentine Constitution, e.g., at www.senado.gov.ar/deInteres.

coup or to the new constituent assembly; and Argentina 1853, which came into effect in most of the territory on that date, and over all the territory of the nation in 1860, and which was the formally effective constitution before 1949 and again after 1957. The most important reforms to this document are the 1860 reforms that incorporated Buenos Aires into the confederation and the 1994 reforms, but it remains the same document, claiming a lineage that goes back to the country's foundational moments.

As García Lema, one of the key participants in the 1994 Constitutional Convention, puts it, "In 1853 the ideals were of liberty and spontaneous [i.e., laissez faire] progress" (García Lema 1994: 107). As he describes it, the document was a frankly elitist and exclusionary document. The main challenge was to populate a vast territory, and the idea was to do so with immigrants who would have economic freedom but lack a real voice in governing (ibid.: 269–70). The government would be quite clearly "representative" in the sense that a small self-appointed elite would paternalistically care for the needs of "the people." The most explicit representation of this idea is in Art. 22 of the constitution: "The people neither deliberates nor governs, except by means of its representatives and the authorities created in this Constitution." Notably, even the Preamble, for the most part, copied word for word from the US Constitution, begins with, "We *the representatives of* the people," rather than with the (less accurate but more inclusive) "We the people."

At the inception of constitutionalism in Argentina, then, "representation" is set up to be more like a tutelary regime. Some of the members of that generation went so far as to say, "universal suffrage is absurd" (García Lema 270, quoting Esteban Echeverría, one of the members of the so-called "generation of 1837"). As a result, Art. 20 guarantees some civil rights to foreigners but does not include in that enumeration the rights to free speech or assembly, and accords them no political rights. Gargarella (2013: 35–6) gives an excellent account of the ideological currents that converged in the 1852 Constitutional Convention and, ultimately, in the 1853 Constitution. For our purposes, what matters most is the commitment to a limited role for the state, and restricted political participation by a narrow, exclusivist, and *laissez faire*-oriented OC.

These commitments required an equally restricted view of constitutional justice. In principle, Argentina's 1853 constitution guaranteed a relatively full set of civil rights, but restricted political participation to a small number of established elites. The rights included in Argentina 1819 and 1826 are all present, but they are constrained by "laws that regulate their exercise" (Art. 14). These guarantees include the rights to work and pursue any legal occupation; petition the authorities; publish ideas without prior censorship; use and dispose of property; associate "for useful purposes;" and profess a religion (Art. 14). Due process rights are somewhat strengthened, with guarantees of due process and promises (that remain unkept to this day) of dignified and humane treatment in prisons. The right to property is singled out for special protection, as mentioned in Art. 14, then spelled out in greater detail in

Art. 17, where it is declared inviolable. The specification and protection of voting rights is relegated to ordinary law – and therefore entrusted to the RC (Art. 37). This regulation is first done on a state-by-state basis and later by the National Congress.

Perhaps the greatest weakness of the authority of the constitutional justice system is not so much the list of rights, but the mechanisms to make them effective. All the rights enumerated in Art. 14 are expressly made subject to regulation by law. There continues to be no mention of habeas corpus or any other procedural device to enforce the laws. The Supreme Court of Justice of the Nation is not expressly given the power of judicial review. Both the executive and the legislature have the power to declare a state of siege, suspending all guarantees (Arts. 23, 49, 64(26), and 83(19–20, 23). And the national government has the right to intervene in the provinces, suspending their rights and putting them under receivership (Art. 6). The list of rights is consistent with liberal constitutions of the period, if not overly generous, but their enforcement is subject to a great deal of discretion on the part of the RC.

The CGC defined in Argentina 1853 is also congruent with this restrictive model of political inclusion. In an arrangement that will seem completely familiar to those who know the system in the United States, appointments to the Supreme Court and all inferior federal courts are entrusted to the President, with the consent of a simple majority of the Senate. The constitution does not impose any qualifications for judges, or any special decision rules or procedural mechanisms for nominations or approvals, and does not contemplate any input from interests that are not represented among those who hold the executive and a majority of the Senate. The justices did, however, enjoy reasonably high ex post autonomy – slightly more than in the United States – with appointments for life and an impeachment process that required first an accusation by a two-thirds vote of the Chamber of Deputies, and then conviction by another two-thirds vote of the Senate.[4] The weak link in ex post protections that would later emerge – the ability to pack the court by changing the number of justices – was in 1853 placed out of reach by specifying that the court would have nine justices (Art. 91). In short, the system contemplated tying appointments closely to the RC, and then leaving these justices free to decide according to their preferences.

Given this design and a narrowly restricted elite RC, the justices could be counted on to support the basic elite ruling project. But this did not necessarily mean that a court that was unable to preside impartially over the key disputes of the time. Divisions within this elite were all too clear in the aftermath of decades of civil war and political assassinations. Temporary majorities could control appointments, but given the justices' life terms, reasonable political competition, and some alternation in power among elites, the system could reasonably be expected

---

[4] In the US Constitution, the impeachment process is initiated by a simple majority of the House of Representatives, although a conviction requires two-thirds of the Senate (Art. I, Sections 2 and 3, Art. II, Section 4).

to produce a court that reflected the core values of the entire dominant coalition. To the extent that disagreements arose within that elite, then, the Supreme Court could be viewed as a reasonably impartial third-party dispute resolver – but it should not be seen as an instrument for the protection of politically subordinate interests, or even ordinary citizens. Domingo Faustino Sarmiento, one of the principal political thinkers of this generation and the second president under this constitution, put it this way: "A Constitution is not the rule for public conduct for all men. The Constitution of the popular classes is made up of the ordinary laws, the judges that apply them, and the security police. It is the educated classes that need a Constitution that assures the press, the rostrum, property, etc." (quoted in García Lema 1994: 271). In short, constitutional justice was, as our theory would predict, primarily meant to advance and protect the interests of the narrow elite that constituted the OC.

The reforms adopted in 1860, when Buenos Aires joined the confederation of Argentine provinces, introduced some changes to the system of constitutional justice, including one that would prove momentous at key points in Argentine history. The Argentine Confederation became the Argentine Nation, some of the language was cleaned up, and there were some adjustments to incorporate Buenos Aires into the union, but these changes, which are the ones most often noted, are not the ones that affected the scope and governance of the system of constitutional justice. Rather, the scope of constitutional justice is, at least in theory, slightly expanded in Articles 32 and 33. The first of these protects freedom of the press from federal (though not provincial) interference, by adopting language similar to that of the First Amendment to the US Constitution, but more explicitly limited to the national legislature: "The Federal Congress shall not enact laws that restrict the freedom of the press or establish federal jurisdiction over it" (Argentina 1853, Art. 32). And the second reserves unenumerated rights: "the declarations, rights and guarantees enumerated in the Constitution shall not be construed as the negation of other rights and guarantees, not enumerated, but that spring from the principle of popular sovereignty and the republican form of government" (Argentina 1853, Art. 33).

This expansion, however, was accompanied by a weakening of the ex post autonomy of the Court. Article 91, which established a nine-member Supreme Court, was replaced by a new provision that does not specify a number. This seemingly inconsequential change was much used and abused in the twentieth century to expand and contract the court in order to produce a judicial majority that was more congenial to the interests of the RC – an RC, moreover, that under this design had relatively unrestricted appointment power until 1994. The combination of the power to create vacancies nearly at will, combined with the power to fill them by a simple majority, proved noxious over the long run for the court's autonomy from the RC (see, e.g., Kapiszewski 2012). This system – with a relatively well-developed set of rights for the period, but without strong mechanisms to make them effective, and with a CGC that closely tracked the RC – would persist until Perón's 1949 attempt to refound Argentina's constitutional justice system.[5]

Argentina 1949, Perón's constitution, is the Argentine equivalent of Guatemala 1945, the "Revolutionary Constitution," but shows an even greater concentration of power in the executive than Guatemala's text did. As Gargarella (2013: 121) notes, and following the pattern of other mid-century social constitutions, as we have seen, it combined "a novel commitment to social rights with a more traditional commitment to centralized political authority." The new text simultaneously expands the scope of the system of constitutional justice, while continuing to restrict participation in the CGC – more authority, but less autonomy. It creates a new, more powerful system subjected to tight control by the RC. This new system is very much cut from the same cloth as the other social constitutions that appeared in the region at this time and met with the same early, violent fate.

Stylistically, Argentina 1949 preserves much of the original constitution, but it adds a thick layer of social constitutionalism and economic nationalism. It maintains the original preamble, for example, but adds an "irrevocable decision to constitute a socially just, economically free, and politically sovereign nation" (Constitution of 1949, Preamble). The most visible changes are the incorporation of Chapter III, on the "[r]ights of workers, the family, of old age, and education and culture," and Chapter IV on "[t]he social function of property, capital and economic activity."

Chapter III is remarkably expansive, going far beyond Mexico 1917 or Guatemala 1945. The state has an express obligation to "provide an occupation to anyone who needs it" (Art. 37 (I)(1)). Workers have the right to just remuneration, to training, to dignified working conditions and health care, to overall welfare and social security, to join in unions, and even to the protection of their families (Art. 37 (I)(2–10)). People in their old age have extensive rights, including not only basic subsistence rights, such as the right to housing, food, clothing, and health, but also the rights to care for their "moral health," to recreation and entertainment (*esparcimiento* and *entretenimiento*), to peace and quiet (*tranquilidad*), and to respect and consideration (Art. 37 (III)(1–10)). This chapter includes an express guarantee of free primary education, and a plan for regional universities that would teach not only their normal subjects, but also the unique traditions of each region. Perhaps more troubling, these universities would teach "obligatory and uniform courses . . . for the political formation of the students of all disciplines." Additionally, Chapter III obligates the state to provide grants and family assistance, so that the more capable students can pursue the highest levels of instruction, and it protects the artistic and historical patrimony of the country (Art. 37 (IV)(1–7)).

---

[5] Later reforms, while consequential for other reasons – an 1866 reform to consolidate central control over finances, and an 1898 reform to adjust political representation to changing population size – did not affect the system of constitutional justice.

Still, commentators argue that Chapter IV, on the social function of property and capital, was much more developed than Chapter III on social rights (Herrera 2014: 391–414). Chapter IV includes only three articles, but in the hands of a willing RC, they have potentially breathtaking reach. In keeping with many other Latin American constitutions of that era, the first article of this chapter makes private property subject to the obligation to fulfill a social function, and thus "subject to the obligations the law might establish for purposes of the common good" (Art. 38). The second one extends the social function to capital: "Capital must . . . have as its principal object social welfare. Its various forms of exploitation cannot contradict the goal of common benefit for the Argentine people" (Art. 39). The final article in the trilogy (Art. 40) sets the foundation for a firmly statist, interventionist development approach. Wealth and its exploitation must seek the wellbeing of the people, within an economic order that "conforms to the principles of social justice." The state "may enact laws to intervene in the economy and monopolize a certain activity," and private enterprise cannot seek to "increase its profits in a usurious way."

If only they had been paired with a robust set of mechanisms to enforce these rights, these three articles, with the others in Chapter III, might have offered a blueprint to a truly ambitious system of constitutional justice. As they stand, they vastly expand the powers of the RC, while doing little to expand the powers of the court to monitor their implementation. In only one respect does Argentina 1949 strengthen the procedural powers of the court – Art. 95 makes explicit what had been more or less a practice in Argentina, albeit one that continues to generate some discussion today: "The interpretations of the constitution by the Supreme Court of Justice . . . shall be binding on national and provincial judges and tribunals." However, the authority of the court is undermined by the continued absence of explicit mechanisms to enforce constitutional rights. Under these conditions, the expansive list of social and economic rights must be seen more as enabling the RC to intervene widely in society and the economy, rather than as constituting a separate sphere of constitutional justice in which the full meaning and implementation of these rights could be developed under judicial oversight.

Perhaps more crippling is the new system of constitutional justice's lack of autonomy. The constitution continues the practice of giving the President the power to appoint justices with the consent of the Senate. In a context in which the President had the unconditional support of exactly 100 percent of the Senate, that external check on executive power was unlikely to be very effective. The provisions for ex post autonomy were also left unchanged, and thus continued to be fairly strong, at least on paper. The fact that Perón had sufficient political support to impeach all the incumbent justices, however, suggests that even these ex post protections were likely to be ineffective, at least for the foreseeable future. Especially given its political context, the new system clearly lacked ex ante autonomy by design, and was likely to lack ex post autonomy as well, simply as a consequence of the actual distribution of power, giving the opposition little reassurance that there would be an impartial arbiter to adjudicate differences.

It seems likely that this is exactly what Perón's framers intended. Even the principal ideologue behind the text, Arturo Sampay, put the onus for moving social rights forward directly on the RC, rather than exporting the constitutional task to a separate sphere, responsive to a different control coalition. According to Herrera (2014: 404), Sampay understood that the principal social norms in the constitution would have to be made concrete by means of ordinary legislation. As a result, the new Argentine Constitution "authorizes interventionist legislation to compensate for the contractual inferiority . . . of the poor within the modern capitalist system" (Herrera 2014: 404), but it does not do much to empower groups to act separately from the RC. Indeed, conspicuously missing from among the workers' rights is the right to strike. In short, observers concluded that this constitution, far from being a constraint on power, was meant as a governance tool for the RC. As Herrera (2014: 413) remarks, "In reality, as Gino Germani points out, the promotion of social rights within a populist framework was meant to have not so much a judicial-constitutional efficacy but rather a political one."

In the end, the combination of a socially oriented text giving the RC an expansive agenda for social and economic transformation, on the one hand, with a virtually authoritarian concentration of power, on the other (see Negretto 2013, ch. 4, showing that the 1949 Constitution sought to consolidate power) was the undoing of the scheme. The combination led to the self-exclusion of both the Left and the Right from the constitutional process. The Socialist Party abstained from the reform process and called for a boycott of the election for representatives to the constitutional convention. The second largest party, the Radical Party (known as the Radicals, or the UCR for the initials, in Spanish, of its full name, "Radical Civic Union"), walked out of the convention shortly after it began. As a result, the constitution was written unilaterally – and the resulting lack of a strong and autonomous sphere of constitutional justice is exactly what our theory would predict under those conditions. As we have already anticipated, and not coincidentally, Perón's government, like that of nearly every other mid-twentieth century president with a social constitutionalist project, ended badly. Perón was overthrown in a military coup in 1955, and in 1957 his social charter was replaced by a slightly modified version of the liberal 1853 Constitution.

According to our theory of constitutional governance, two factors explain the simultaneous limitation of autonomy and the (qualified) expansion of the sphere of constitutional justice found in Argentina 1949. First, for all his authoritarian style, Perón's populism responded to interests – the formal working class and the poor – that had been excluded from Argentine politics before (Negretto 2013: 117). The new rights represented by his social constitutionalist project respond to this new constituency. Secondly, Perón dominated both the OC and the expected RC. He was not a member of the traditional elite, and did not come from either the traditional parties or the more recent Radical party; his party was a personalist vehicle responding directly to him. His dominance of ordinary politics was, moreover, nearly complete. He held every seat in the Senate and had 69 percent (in other words, more than two thirds) of the Chamber of Representatives, allowing him to remove the existing justices, who otherwise stood in the way of his populist, redistributive policies, and his constitutional project. Like Guatemala 1945, and in keeping with other mid-century social constitutionalist models, this constitution failed to create an autonomous sphere of constitutional justice.

Given his dominance, it might seem puzzling that he constitutionalized so much of his social and economic project. As we showed in Chapter 3, a party that is confident in its ability to govern will not feel the need to place its entire agenda in the sphere of constitutional politics, where it might be subject to vetoes and interference by additional actors. Perón was certainly able to rule unconstrained, so why bother with a social constitution? Why not just carry out the project? The problem was that the existing constitution imposed constraints on his ability to pursue his agenda. Like Venezuela's Hugo Chávez many years later, Perón needed the help of the system of constitutional justice to dismantle the existing normative framework and impose a new one. As Negretto (2013: 121) points out, Perón's primary argument for the need to reform the constitution was that he had to remove aspects of Argentina 1853 that stood in the way of the necessary social transformation. More importantly, as we saw above, the changes primarily empowered the RC to act, rather than creating juridico-constitutional constraints on it. Finally, to the extent that some issues are entrusted to constitutional justice, the sphere of constitutional justice remained closely tied to the RC. As with Guatemala 1945, the social constitutionalism of Argentina 1949 was more about clearing the way for pursuing a political project than about constraining the choices of the RC and subjecting it to oversight.

Continuing the Argentine tradition of monologic constitutional texts, the military government that deposed and exiled Perón derogated his constitution and called for a convention from which the Peronists were excluded. It then orchestrated a text that won the approval of only 51 percent of the members of the Constituent Convention (Thury Cornejo 2005: 35). As already mentioned, the text that emerged was essentially a republishing of the 1853 Constitution, with the significant addition of a new article containing workers' rights, titled "Article 14 bis."[6] Gone from the constitution were the social function of property and capital, the expansive rights afforded to the aged and the family, and the role of the state in crafting a more just social order. What remained, through Article 14 bis, was the incorporation of much of the country's existing labor legislation into the constitution. This article mirrors Art. 123 of Mexico 1917, requiring labor laws to guarantee dignified conditions of labor, limited work days, paid vacations, a minimum salary, protections against

[6] "Bis" is Latin for "twice" and was used in order to add an article after the existing Art. 14, without having to renumber the following articles.

arbitrary dismissals, and so on. Unlike Argentina 1949, it also guarantees the right to strike. Beyond workers' rights, the article requires the state to create systems of social security and pensions, to ensure minimum family compensation, and to guarantee access to dignified housing.

Article 14 bis was the project of the Radical and Socialist parties, not the military rulers who called for the convention.[7] Nor was it the plan to make only this one reform. The delegates had only managed to vote on this one change before so many members withdrew from the Assembly that it lost a quorum and was unable to proceed. Rather than declare the entire event a failure and reinstate the 1853 Constitution by military fiat, whatever happened before the dissolution of the Assembly was accepted as accomplished, so that the regime could claim some legitimacy for the newly amended constitution.

The rights included in Article 14 bis are not trivial, but in the end remain mostly hortatory. The increase in the scope of authority of the system is not paired with any mechanisms for enforcing rights and continues to rely on a system that has little ex ante autonomy. The presence of labor rights in the constitution since 1957, however, highlights the difficulty of making a complete about-face once social constitutionalism has made its first inroads in a country's constitutional framework. The dominant political actors of 1957 embodied a nearly absolute rejection of the Peronist economic and political model. And yet, they embraced the idea that the constitution needed to contain social rights – in particular, some protection for workers, even (or especially) within a capitalist economic system.

From 1853 until 1994, in short, we can identify three models of constitutional justice in Argentina. The 1853 model, like its 1819 and 1826 predecessors, follows the classic Latin American models of its time: it has a narrowly circumscribed scope, embraced a laissez faire economic model, and was concerned (in all respects but the religious) more with individual autonomy than with social provision. Moreover, it defined a CGC that was essentially coterminous with the RC (in all respects but ex post control, which potentially includes the congressional opposition through a two-thirds majority requirement for impeachment). The 1949 Constitution, in contrast, sought to impose a model – like Guatemala 1945 or Venezuela 1999 – in which a much more ambitious sphere of constitutional justice was tied closely to an RC that responded directly to the executive. As in Guatemala, when this model was violently rejected, the return to the 1853 document marked only a partial retreat from this expansion of constitutional justice. The amendments that accompanied the reinstatement of Argentina 1853 included a series of social (primarily labor)

---

[7] In an interview, Elva Roulet, a 1994 Constituent Assembly member, indignantly denied that this article was somehow a concession to Peronists, as implicit compensation for ending the Peronist regime, exiling their leader, and proscribing their party. Social constitutionalism, she claimed, had long been part of the Radical constitutionalist project (author interview with Elva Roulet, Buenos Aires, June 17, 2014).

rights partially replicating those found in Argentina 1949. For the next forty years –
saving periods when the constitution was suspended – Argentina would have a system of constitutional justice that at least nodded toward a notion of justice that went
beyond nineteenth-century liberal protections of individual autonomy.

The historical progression is strikingly similar to Guatemala's (compare
Figure 4.1 to Figure 5.1), although throughout most of its constitutional history,
Argentina's system shows somewhat more autonomy than Guatemala's does. Still,
the one constant in all this history is the failure to separate governance of the
sphere of constitutional justice from the RC. Each of the reforms emerges from
a monolithic OC, sometimes (as in the sequence from Argentina 1853 to 1949 to
1957) in a set of tit-for-tat responses to the opposition. As Alfonsín (2004: 197) himself would later put it, a broad consensus was especially important in 1994, because
the previous Argentine constitutions (1819, 1826, 1949, and 1957) had all been
unilaterally imposed. As Marcelo Alegre, a well-known Argentine constitutional
scholar, puts it, "In this case [1994] no one was left out. There is no comparison
to the constitution of 1957. The opposition didn't even get their salary. The one in
'49, Perón's, was partisan and excluded the opposition. The one in '57 was done
with Peronism outlawed. When you compare all these reforms, this one [1994] was
very inclusive."[8]

The reliance on constitutional imposition, rather than participatory and inclusive
negotiation, led to systems of constitutional justice that were meant to advance the
dominant project, whatever it was. The constitutional justice system did not provide
a space where competing visions of the common good – between, say, Peronists
and their opponents, in the second half of the twentieth century – could be contested and decided. Certainly that was not the intended point of either the 1949
or the 1957 Constitutions. Sampay, the theorist behind Perón's constitution, held
that countries should have a single unifying "dogma, that is, an incontrovertible
doctrinal content . . . that all components of the State would know and accept without reservations" (quoted in Segovia 2007: 187). The military regime that followed
Perón was no more interested in a pluralistic constitutional space than the Peronists
had been. Nor were the coalitions that dominated most of Argentina's constitutional
history looking for a broad commitment to social rights. Throughout Argentina's
constitutional history, with the partial exception of Argentina 1949, and the inclusion of Article 14 (bis) in Argentina 1957, the scope of constitutional justice was
tightly restricted.

A system with few rights that is closely tied to the RC works reasonably well as a
neutral dispute resolver when that coalition is divided on some issue, as in the early
period, when the elite was working out the balance between center and periphery.
But it does not work on behalf of groups that are excluded from the RC altogether.

---

[8] Author interview Marcelo Alegre, June 12, 2014, Buenos Aires, Argentina.

It was not until Argentina 1994 that a truly new model of constitutional justice would emerge, placing Argentina near the middle of the upper right-hand quadrant in Figure 2.4. It is this change that finally configures constitutional justice as a major political field for substantive policy debates.

6.2. KEY FEATURES OF THE 1994 SYSTEM OF CONSTITUTIONAL JUSTICE

The system that emerged in 1994 was, for the first time in Argentine history, less subject to control by the RC in general, and by the executive in particular, and more expansive than the preexisting classically liberal model. Although it was not as disruptive of existing property relationships as the 1949 version, it pushed into many different areas that Perón's constitution did not touch at all, and clearly entrusted them to a separate sphere of constitutional justice. The new amendments include a long list of issues – the environment, consumer rights, health, education, indigenous rights – that go well beyond the traditional class- and labor-based concerns of social constitutionalism. In addition, the new text incorporates all the international human rights treaties into the constitution, giving them constitutional rank, although they cannot modify the individual rights laid out in Part I of the constitution. The judicial appointments process was quite intentionally modified to require the consent of a congressional minority and – implicitly – of the public at large, and the strong formal ex post protections were maintained intact. At the formal level, as Figure 6.1 shows, the changes produced an increase in ex ante autonomy and scope of authority and do not modify the already high levels of ex post autonomy.

Although many at the time denigrated the reform process as merely a vehicle to ensure the sitting president's reelection, the seemingly small changes fundamentally reshaped the CGC and, by all accounts, have deeply affected the Court's behavior. Before the amendment, the court was unambiguously tied to the executive. "The median justice's degree of political opposition to the sitting president exceeded 0.5 on a 0–1 scale on only five occasions from 1935 to 1997 and never for more than two years in a row. The degree of political opposition of the median justice was exactly zero forty-six out of those sixty-three years (73% of the time)" (Brinks 2005: 607, citing Iaryczower et al. 2002). In contrast, since the first appointments affected by the amendment, most observers would agree that the Court has established itself as a relatively reliable check on executive and ruling party overreach. It has, at minimum, emerged as a consistently distinct political actor, rather than one that routinely legitimizes the official project. Moreover, the Court has placed itself at the center of a great many debates that had never been part of its jurisprudence before (CELS 2008; Sigal et al. forthcoming). By all accounts, the institutional changes have, both formally and de facto, increased the Court's autonomy and authority.

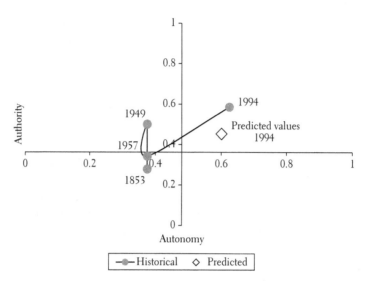

FIGURE 6.1. Ex ante autonomy and authority in Argentina's constitutions

When we look more closely at the details we find that the Court's scope of authority expanded both because of the rights specified in the constitution and because of the tools the court was given to enforce those rights. First, as to rights, it was clear from the beginning that there could be no retreat from the status quo. As detailed in the next section, the terms of the amendment process precluded any changes to Part I of the constitution, which contained the full recitation of rights detailed in the first section of this chapter. This included not only the classic negative rights – like freedom of expression, the free exercise of religion, the right to publish without prior censorship, the right against unwarranted search and seizure, and due process protections – but also the rights contained in Article 14 bis, discussed above. What had already been a relatively well-stocked quiver of individual rights would remain intact.

To this, the Constituent Assembly added what was called Chapter Two, New Rights and Guarantees (*Capítulo Segundo, Nuevos Derechos y Garantías*). The chapter opens with a clause that is clearly inspired by the recent history of coups and repression, declaring that the constitution shall remain in force, even if its "observance is interrupted by forceful acts against the institutional order and the democratic system" (Art. 36). The first set of clauses deals with political rights. These articles constitutionalize rights that had long been part of ordinary Argentine legislation – such as universal, equal, and secret suffrage, and the right to form and join political parties – in effect shifting those issues from the sphere of ordinary politics into the space of constitutional justice. It guarantees equality of political rights for men and women, and requires affirmative actions to ensure "real equality of opportunities between men and women" (Art. 37). It adds a series of direct democracy mechanisms (Art. 40). Chapter 2 of the constitution also incorporates second- and third-generation rights. All inhabitants have the right to a healthy, balanced environment, and productive activities must balance current needs against the needs of future generations (Art. 41). New consumer protections are also created (Art. 42). These political rights and more generous social rights transformed the prior constitution from an elitist document, evidently distrustful of the people, into a more politically inclusive governing document.

The reforms recognize indigenous rights and indigenous groups, but are ambivalent about including them in constitutional justice. These rights are mentioned only in the listing of the attributes of Congress. Congress has the power (but not explicitly the duty) to "recognize the cultural and ethnic preexistence of Argentine indigenous peoples," and to "guarantee respect for their identity," as well as a series of other rights (Art. 75 (17)). Notably, by requiring Congress to do so, the members of the Constitutional Assembly themselves avoided recognizing indigenous peoples and their rights. The inclusion of indigenous rights was in large part the result of the strong presence and lobby of indigenous groups during the convention, even though none of the members or parties were identified as indigenous.[9] One can perhaps read too much into this drafting choice, but it seems unlikely that, if there had been a strong indigenous presence within the Constituent Assembly, the Assembly could have avoided a more straightforward declaration and recognition of indigenous rights.

The most important expansions in the scope of constitutional justice, however, are due to the incorporation of a series of human rights treaties into the constitution, and the explicit constitutional recognition of the amparo with generous standing requirements. Article 42 articulates a right to bring an amparo claim any time a constitutional right is violated or threatened, and no other more suitable cause of action exists to protect the right. Not only those directly affected, but also the national ombudsman (the "*Defensor del Pueblo*") and any associations organized to protect these rights, are empowered to file such a claim. Moreover, the constitutional rights in question are not only the ones described above, which are explicitly enumerated in the constitution. Article 75 (22) also lists all the human rights treaties to which Argentina was party at the time and accords them constitutional status.[10] The listed treaties can lose constitutional status, and future human rights treaties can secure

---

9   Author interview Marcelo Alegre, Buenos Aires, June 12, 2014.

10   Explicitly listed in paragraph 22 are the following treaties: "The American Declaration on the Rights and Duties of Man; the Universal Declaration on Human Rights; the International Covenant on Economic, Social and Cultural Rights; the International Covenant on Civil and Political Rights, and its Optional Protocol; the Convention on the Prevention and Punishment of Genocide; the International Convention on the Elimination of all Forms of Racial Discrimination; the Convention on the Elimination of all Forms of Discrimination Against Women; the Convention Against Torture and Other Cruel, Inhuman or Degrading Punishments; [and] the Convention on the Rights of the Child."

it, only upon the vote of two-thirds of the members of each legislative chamber. Together, the collective and individual amparo, and the references to international human rights law, have exercised a profound influence on Argentine constitutional justice and politics. Although the text is not the most generous in Latin America, collectively these provisions produce a justifiably high authority score for Argentina's system of constitutional justice, after 1994.

6.3. THE EMERGENCE OF A SOCIAL DEMOCRATIC SYSTEM OF CONSTITUTIONAL JUSTICE IN ARGENTINA IN 1994

What are the politics that turned Argentina's constitutional justice system from its 130-year-old tradition of a stripped down, elitist liberalism to a more generous and inclusive, moderately rights-rich constitutionalism in 1994? Reviewing the politics of the Constituent Assembly and the transcripts of the debates, in this section we trace the changes in the scope of constitutional justice to a governance logic, driven by the substantive preferences of the OC in light of its relationship to the expected RC. We can show that the influence of expressive goals or global trends on what would be included was secondary. Moreover, it is clear that the desire for a more autonomous court with a broader agenda is less aptly described by an insurance logic than by a governance logic. What emerges is a picture of designers crafting a separate sphere of constitutional justice and politics, with the full expectation of continuing to participate in governing within that sphere as part of a diverse coalition of interests.

The end of the Cold War and a decade of democratic history since the end of the last military regime meant the 1994 Constituent Assembly took place in an atmosphere far less charged with violence than Guatemala's. Hope dominates fear in these debates. Rather than fearing for the continued existence of their economic and political system, the delegates here were fighting over questions of executive power, the balance across the branches, the generosity of the welfare state, and the inclusiveness of the system of constitutional justice, all within the context of a relatively stable democracy. Only a few on the far right invoked the familiar specters that haunted Guatemala's Cold War-era debates.

And yet there are important similarities between the concerns expressed by constitution-makers in both countries. As in Guatemala, the discussion of rights was colored by a "never again" mindset, in which all sides of the drafting coalition were deeply interested in setting forth rights that would protect political freedoms and personal integrity. Here, as there, the parties that were less certain of dominating the RC (the first minority (the UCR), and even more so the smaller parties on the Left) were more interested than the dominant party (the PJ) in strengthening the system of constitutional justice and expanding its governance coalition. In contrast to Guatemala, where the principal power player to be feared, the military, was outside the convention, here the threatening hegemon – the Peronist party and especially the Menemist faction within it – was an important part of the OC. These differences led to different design choices, particularly in the conformation of the CGC, which here is firmly located within partisan politics, albeit with a role for opposition parties. In both places, however, the debates show that the delegates were aware of the crucial impact that the gears and levers of constitutional justice would have on their hopes and fears.

The reform project had long antecedents, starting with former president Raúl Alfonsín in 1985, who created the Council for the Consolidation of Democracy as a think tank for developing new constitutional ideas in hopes of producing a more current and more democratic constitution. He abandoned the project shortly after a catastrophic electoral defeat in 1987, but Menem and the Peronist party picked up the idea of constitutional reform in the early 1990s. Interestingly for our purposes, the chronology belies an "insurance" (Ginsburg 2003) account of constitution-making. It is always the party in power leading the charge for reform, and the loss of power derails the project. The prehistory of the Constituent Assembly has been fully developed elsewhere, including by its protagonists (García Lema 1994; Alfonsín 2004; Gargarella 2010, 2013; Negretto 2013). Here we will simply highlight the elements of that history that are most pertinent to the development of the more robust system of constitutional justice that emerged after 1994.

6.3.1. *The Originating Coalition*

Perhaps fearing the potential for constituent assemblies to exceed the purposes of their initial call, the Argentine Constitution details a rigid and constrained procedure for constitutional reform. Article 30 allows a full or partial reform of the constitution under very limited conditions: "The necessity for reform must be declared by the Congress with the vote of no less than two thirds of its members; but it shall not be carried out except by a Convention convened for that purpose." In the case of the 1994 Constitutional Convention, there was a prior step that further limited the possibilities of reform. Former president Raúl Alfonsín and then-current president Carlos Menem met at the presidential residence in Olivos, a suburb of Buenos Aires, to negotiate and sign a pact often referred to as the "Pacto de Olivos." The agreement was penned by Ricardo Gil Lavedra (for Alfonsín) and Alberto García Lema (for Menem), and detailed a "Nucleus of Basic Agreements" (*Núcleo de Coincidencias Básicas*) laying out the core elements that would be included in any constitutional reform (García Lema 1994: 144–5; Feijoó 1995; Alfonsín 2004). This "Nucleus" was presented to the Legislature and, once approved by the requisite two-thirds of each chamber, was understood to constrain the work of the Convention.

To ensure that an impartial arbiter would be standing by to police the process, Menem and Alfonsín agreed that three justices who were overly identified with the governing party would step down from the Supreme Court, to be replaced by candidates acceptable to both (García Lema 1994: 145). Thus, the Convention was

meant to proceed under the watchful eye of a mutually acceptable, specially constituted Supreme Court, and within the bounds of a preexisting agreement that
laid out the parameters for the reform. The preliminary agreement even specified
a core set of provisions that would have to be included. In yet another echo of
the debates around the right to property that roiled the Guatemalan Constituent
Assembly, this agreement contained a clause explicitly prohibiting any changes
to the rights included in chapter I of the constitution – a clause that was in part
designed to protect the right to property from any suggestion of a "social function."[11]
As in Guatemala, the designers avoided this inflammatory language, while carrying
out what is essentially an end run around it through the inclusion of extensive social
and economic rights in the constitution.

The election for the Constitutional Convention was an intensely partisan
affair. The Peronists pushed strongly for the reform as a vehicle for Menem's
reelection. The opposition, on the other hand, was deeply divided – some supported
Alfonsín's bid to reform the constitution and others rejected it altogether, precisely
because they viewed the reform as no more than a vehicle for Menem's reelection. Many who wanted deeper constitutional reform saw the Nucleus of Basic
Agreements as overly constraining, reducing the Constituent Convention to a mere
rubberstamp for an agreement already reached by Alfonsín and Menem – one in
which Alfonsín, moreover, had given up too much. For Alfonsín, however, "presidential reelection was a secondary consideration. The accord needed to be a pact with
guarantees that would avoid hegemony and perpetuation, that would facilitate the
discussion of alternative projects and models" (García Lema 1994: 133). Alfonsín's
language clearly evokes the way we have described systems of constitutional justice
that have high autonomy and high authority (see Table 2.1 in Chapter 2), exactly
like the one that resulted from the 1994 reform. Whatever he may have given up
in other respects, in this sense, at least, Alfonsín got what he was looking for –
the 1994 reforms configure a system in which alternative visions of constitutional
justice can be disputed.

On December 29, 1983, the Senate approved the law, declaring the necessity
of a constitutional amendment and calling for a constitutional convention. The
Convention had to begin within 60 days of the election of its delegates, and had
only 90 days to complete all its work. It was empowered to vote up or down on the
Nucleus of Basic Agreements as a whole, and it could deliberate and vote individually on the matters identified in Art. 3 of the law. Presidential reelection (after a
shortened four-year term), of course, was in the Nucleus. But, more importantly
for this project, so were the provisions for a Judicial Council that would govern the
lower federal courts, and the provisions for appointment and removal of federal
judges, including Supreme Court justices.

---

[11] Author interview Néstor Pedro Sagüés, Buenos Aires, June 16, 2014.

As the quote from Alfonsín suggests, the Nucleus itself already contemplated more autonomy for the system of constitutional justice in exchange for presidential reelection. Whatever the failings of the Judicial Council in the long run – many of which can be attributed to design deficiencies – it is clearly an attempt to pluralize the politics of appointment and removal for lower court judges. And the changes to Supreme Court appointments and removals similarly expand the CGC to at least the first legislative minority, if not to additional small parties, given the expected structure of party competition. Article 3 of the enabling law, in turn, empowered the Convention members to negotiate more freely on some of the crucial elements of the new system of constitutional justice, such as the status of international treaties, political rights, environmental protections, economic and social rights, indigenous rights, and consumer rights. The Nucleus, in short, mandates an expansion of the CGC to the first minority, while Art. 3 opens the door to all the elements that would appear in Chapter Two of the constitution, expanding the scope of authority of the system of constitutional justice in Argentina.

We have argued that constitutional designers are, consciously or unconsciously, designing a system of constitutional governance that will ensure they can continue to participate in governing areas in which they feel their interests are threatened by the likely future RC. In the case of Argentina, one possible objection to this argument is that the constitutional designers basically had their hands tied by a prior elite agreement. In fact, this prior agreement supports our claim, for two reasons. First, that elite agreement reflects our logic. In the Pacto de Olivos, the expected RC (represented by Menem) is a strong actor but cannot act unilaterally, and the UCR, which expects to be the first party in opposition, negotiates for a voice in the appointment of justices to the Supreme Court (among other things), thus securing a role in the future CGC, just as we predict. If the basic power relationship had changed dramatically in the Convention, we might have expected the proposal to be defeated, but the shift that took place was not enough to derail that basic agreement – the UCR and the Menemists were strong enough to win that argument. Second, the OC did, as we will see, become more inclusive at the Convention stage than at the Pacto de Olivos stage. It was that greater inclusiveness, driven in part by the UCR and Peronist desire for broad support of the new constitution, that led to a more substantial expansion of the constitutional justice system's scope of authority than the Pacto de Olivos contemplated. Far from challenging the logic of constitutional governance, this within-case variation from one stage of constitutional negotiations to the next strongly confirms it.

Menem's party, the Justicialist Party (PJ, for its initials in Spanish), fell remarkably short of its expectations in the elections for the Constitutional Convention. This drop was mirrored by a surprising win by the most vocal critics of the Pacto de Olivos, a coalition of Center-Left parties known as the Frente Grande (Feijoó 1995: 83). The Frente Grande amply exceeded expectations and established itself as a key power broker in the convention. The PJ and UCR won 37.7 percent and

19.9 percent of the votes, respectively, while the Frente Grande won nearly 13 percent, and a far-Right party, MODIN, took 9 percent. About 5 percent was left for three smaller parties, mostly of the Center-Left. The largest party in the OC was the Menemist wing of the PJ, which preferred neoliberal reforms and strong presidential powers. The PJ was joined by the UCR, a more classically liberal party promoting core civil and political rights and strong checks and balances against what it perceived to be a likely PJ-controlled RC. To a lesser extent, it was interested in the issues pushed more vigorously by the Frente Grande. The Frente Grande (the third-largest party), in turn, was further to the left, and unlikely ever to govern on its own. As a result, the Frente Grande was much more interested in expanding the space of constitutional justice to include social guarantees and international human rights, including social, economic, and cultural rights.

Given the simple majority requirement for agreement by the Convention, the PJ and UCR could have acted alone, but both parties wanted the widest coalition possible. Alfonsín, the leader of the UCR in the Assembly, argues in his memoir (with ample justification, as we have seen) that all the previous Argentine constitutions lacked legitimacy because they were unilaterally imposed (Alfonsín 2004: 197). Similarly, Gil Lavedra, a member of the UCR, in a foreword to García Lema's account of the reforms, argues that the only way to secure institutional stability in Argentina was through an inclusive, elite pact: "The political stability of a system is directly proportional to the degree of accord reached by its political and social forces" (García Lema 1994: 21). Indeed, this drive for a broad consensus is reflected in the final vote of the Constitutional Convention: the final text of the reform was approved unanimously, despite the many disagreements that had marked the debates to that point.

The shift in the two main parties' positions, as their power positions shifted, also demonstrates that the logic of governance trumps ideology when it comes to designing the system of constitutional justice. The UCR, when Alfonsín was president and working through the Council for the Consolidation of Democracy, argued against expanding the Bill of Rights to include more social guarantees (García Lema 1994: 240). The PJ criticized the project, arguing that Argentina needed more social constitutionalism. By 1994, however, with the PJ in power, the positions had reversed. Alfonsín would argue that it was their "duty to construct a progressive response . . ., promoting a social democracy that could be an alternative to the neoliberal model that was sweeping the world, and that would rescue an idea of justice that ran through our history and was rooted in fundamental ethical issues" (Alfonsín 2004: 159). This was something that he, presumably, thought he could do without constitutional assistance in 1985. The PJ, meanwhile, argued against the further expansion of rights in 1994, saying a simple allusion to international rights would suffice, which García Lema (1994: 241–2) considered to be more closely subject to congressional control, through ratification and nullification, and thus subject to closer control by the RC.

Thus was the stage set for the Constitutional Convention. The UCR and the PJ were united in their defense of the Nucleus and had a bare majority with which to impose it if necessary. But the Frente Grande, which was ideologically close but to the left of the UCR (they would later form a coalition to compete in national elections), would push hard for more social constitutionalism. The PJ – except insofar as it might be a bargaining chip to trade for presidential reelection – was clearly not interested in establishing a more autonomous judiciary. That was the main project of the UCR. The debates that took place in the various subcommittees and on the floor of the Convention reflect these differences and show remarkably clearly how well the delegates understood the role of constitutional justice in future governance. In the following section, we again use the delegates' statements as evidence of their motives and intent in designing the system of constitutional justice that emerged from the reform.

Citations to the plenary sessions follow the format "(PS, p. xxxx)," where xxxx refers to the specific page numbers of the transcript. References to the debates in the various specialized drafting committees are similarly noted as follows: the transcripts of the Commission on the Basic Agreement, known in Spanish as the Comisión de Coincidencias Básicas are cited as "(CCB, p. xxxx)" (the transcripts of debates in this commission can be found at pp. 3247–304); the Commission on New Rights and Guarantees – Comisión de Nuevos Derechos y Garantías – as "(CND, p. xxxx)" (they can be found at pp. 3522–32); the Commission on Systems of Control – Comisión de Sistemas de Control – as "(CSC, p. xxxx)" (pp. 3532–75); and the Commission on Regional Integration and International Treaties or Comisión de Integración y Tratados Internacionales as "(CTI, p. xxxx)" (pp. 3590–640).[12]

6.3.2. *The Construction of Constitutional Governance*

We have insisted throughout that the close attention designers pay to the composition of the coalition that will eventually control the courts is, at least in part, a function of a not-always-explicit understanding of the nature of constitutionalism and its connection to post-constituent politics. Specifically, we argue that designers understand that a system of constitutional governance is a system designed to influence the evolving meaning of a foundational pact, rather than a way to lock away gains entrenched in the original text. In Argentina, Enrique Paixao, a member of

---

[12]   The transcripts of the plenary debates can be found in the library of the Argentine Congress, in the Diario de Sesiones de la Convención Nacional Constituyente de 1994. They can also be downloaded, as zipped files of each day's transcript, from here: www1.diputados.gov.ar/dependencias/dip/Debate-constituyente.htm. This page includes a fairly comprehensive topical index, indicating which topics were being treated on a given date. The transcripts of the commission debates are only available in hard copy, in the full transcripts of the Constitutional Convention, compiled by the Ministry of Justice of Argentina and published in 1995 as Obra de la Convención Nacional Constituyente 1994 (Buenos Aires: La Ley).

the UCR and one of the leading constitutionalist scholars in the Assembly, makes this understanding explicit:

> [We have chosen to require the consent of two-thirds of the Senate] out of the understanding that, if the constitution is what the justices say it is, each time we name a judge of the Court we initiate a partial and quotidian process of reform of the Tribunal and, in the final analysis, of the National Constitution. For that reason, it should only be possible to occupy that position by means of a consensus that has some equivalence to what would be needed for a formal constitutional reform.
>
> (PS, July 27, p. 2210)

The members of the convention were preoccupied with specifying the actors who would have to be part of that consensus – exactly the process we have called the construction of the CGC.

Even the far Right, which might be expected to espouse a more traditional view of the law as inflexible and formalistic, understood that constitutional adjudication is crucially shaped by post-constitutional politics. Alejandro Vásquez of MODIN said, "there can never be in a republic a branch that is isolated in a sort of bell jar, far from the aspirations of the people . . . Of course, partisan politics must remain outside the Judicial Branch, . . . [and] selfish and momentary interests, but not the great strands of Argentine politics" (PS, p. 3274). This is simply another way of saying what we have argued throughout: constitutional justice is subject to post-constituent politics, but it can be (when properly designed) a politics that is more inclusive than ordinary politics. How to secure the right kind of politics for shaping the courts, then? As Raúl Zaffaroni, who represented the Frente Grande in the Convention (and later served as a member of the Supreme Court), makes clear – and as we too have argued throughout – we cannot secure impartiality by somehow isolating the Court from politics, but rather through pluralism and inclusiveness. He best expressed this understanding in a quote we have used already: "You cannot secure impartiality by putting someone above what is human. If someone thinks he is above human frailty, more than a candidate for judge he is a candidate for therapy. Impartiality in a democracy is secured through a guarantee of institutional pluralism" (PS, p. 3254, authors' translation).

That institutional pluralism, as Paixao articulated, is expressed in the mechanisms of ex ante and ex post control that constitute the CGC. When the OC is itself pluralistic, it will seek to define a CGC that is pluralistic and that includes institutional spaces for the successors to the members of the OC. As we saw in Chapter 2 and the opening pages of this chapter, in Argentina as in much of Latin America, the status quo was a justice system that was closely tied to the RC. In Argentina, this was primarily a function of low ex ante autonomy – majoritarian appointments, tied especially close to the president by a party system that gave the executive a great deal of control over its legislative delegation, at least during times when the Peronists were in power. The formal institutions provided for high ex post autonomy, however, so that future governments were frequently saddled with courts that were ideologically closely identified with their predecessor, unless they could find a way around those formal institutions.

The resulting tension led to the appearance of what some have termed an informal institution of insecure tenure (Helmke 2005) – the routine firing with every change of government of all or most justices because they were seen as hostile to the new administration or regime. This practice began with Perón's replacement of justices in 1947 and continued through the Menem administration in the late 1980s and early 1990s (Kapiszewski 2012). As we saw, it was partially replicated in the run-up to the Constituent Convention, when the opposition demanded the resignation of some justices as a condition of proceeding with the amendment. In other words, since Perón's presidency, the Argentine Supreme Court had low ex ante and low ex post autonomy, and was at all times closely identified with the RC. As a historical matter, at least, Menem was clearly justified in asking, "Why should I be the only president in fifty years who has not had his own court?" (quoted in Larkins 1998: 428). This is the situation that the 1994 reforms were meant to rectify, as the Convention debates make clear. The goal of the Convention was to constitute a CGC that was more expansive and pluralistic than the RC.

6.3.2.1. Ex Ante Autonomy

The focus during the reform process was largely on ex ante autonomy, apparently based on the sense that political leaders had always been able to select close allies to serve on the Court, and that this arrangement had served to maintain the Court too closely tied to the RC in general, and to the executive in particular. As former President Raúl Alfonsín noted in the debates, "The members of the Supreme Court of Justice will be named by the President with the consent of two-thirds of the Senate, in a public session called for that purpose . . . In our understanding, this is one of the most transcending reforms, since, unless we have a situation of an overwhelming majority in favor of a given political party, it will require a wide consensus in order to secure the appointments" (PS, p. 2729). Clearly he, as one of the two signatories to the original reformist pact, and the other members of the constituent assembly understood that this seemingly small change – from a simple majority to a two-thirds requirement for senatorial consent – would have the effect of broadening the Court's coalition of ex ante control, with potentially dramatic effects for the Court.

The supermajority threshold virtually assured the UCR, typically not a party that controlled the legislature, but for years the second largest legislative party, a role in the control coalition. It is no surprise, then, that this was one of the central planks that Alfonsín and his people negotiated in the Nucleus of Basic Agreements. As reflected in the epigraph to this chapter, it is clear that this is exactly how the members of the Convention understood the two-thirds requirement for consent to a nominee: "the new system of appointing . . . the members of the Supreme Court of Justice of the Nation – through the two-thirds vote of the Senate . . . – will . . . further increase the independence of the judiciary" (PS, August 1, 1994, p. 2576). Similarly, in the debates in the Commission on Basic Agreements (which was charged with drafting the provisions that would give effect to that pact), the representatives presented the two-thirds' requirement and a provision requiring public hearings as a way to limit the power of the executive to unilaterally appoint justices: "Through this reform, we have . . . established a procedure for appointment that must be made by the Senate with two-thirds of the members present and moreover, in a public session, which represents a way to moderate the discretion of the executive branch when nominating judges of the Supreme Court" (CCB, July 11, 1994, p. 3250).[13]

But it was not simply a matter of limiting the discretion of the executive by insulating the court from politics – an idea that would fit better with an insurance metaphor for judicial empowerment. In fact, the discussions show an awareness that the change would empower a new CGC, one that reflected the OC. There is no question that the reforms were meant to bring in at least the first minority in Congress, and possibly one or more of the smaller parties as well. Soon-to-be-President Fernando de la Rúa made this explicit: "beginning with the new Constitution, the justices of the Supreme Court will be appointed with the agreement of two thirds of members present of the Senate. I am proud to have suggested that majority . . . This two-thirds requirement, together with the addition of the third senator,[14] means that no political party will have the unilateral ability to appoint members of the Supreme Court of Justice" (PS, pp. 2444–5).[15] Others said much the same thing: "This [supermajority] clause, which we later used repeatedly . . . allows the incorporation of the minority in Congress . . ." (Miguel Angel Ortiz Pellegrini, UCR, PS, August 1, p. 2790). See also statements by Juan Carlos Maqueda (PJ) (PS, p. 2618).

As our theory predicts, the PJ was largely happy with the status quo, but conceded some control over constitutional justice in exchange for the reforms it really wanted, while keeping the executive and the major parties at the center of the CGC. Meanwhile, the UCR, as the largest opposition party in the Convention, as the second component of the OC (and second signatory to the Pacto de Olivos),

---

[13] "A través de esta reforma, se ha planteado diferenciar la designación de los miembros de la Suprema Corte y se ha establecido el procedimiento de su designación en cuanto a que debe ser hecha por el Senado de la Nación con los dos tercios de los miembros presentes y, además, en sesiones públicas, lo que significa un modo de morigerar el discrecionalismo del Poder Ejecutivo a la hora de nominar a los jueces de la Suprema Corte de Justicia."

[14] The new constitutional text granted each province a third Senator, who would represent the first minority party in that province.

[15] "a partir de la nueva Constitución los jueces de la Corte Suprema serán designados con el acuerdo de los dos tercios de los miembros presentes del Senado. Tengo el orgullo de haber sugerido esa mayoría . . . Estos dos tercios para el acuerdo en el Senado, unido a la introducción del tercer senador significa que ningún partido político tendrá exclusividad en la designación de los miembros de la Corte Suprema de Justicia."

and as the party most likely to be the first opposition party in future Senates, sought an arrangement that would include it in the CGC once the constitutional moment was past. The PJ and the UCR together, as the core of the CGC, wanted to establish themselves as the key members of the coalition of control in post constituent politics, and largely succeeded.

Indeed, some saw this new bipartisan coalition as too exclusive. As a result, De la Rúa, of the UCR, was at pains to suggest that the further fragmentation of the Senate might make room for smaller parties. The new "pluripartisan profile of the Senate," he argued, "assured a greater margin of debate and consensus" for all the decisions that required a supermajority (PS, p. 2768). But several representatives of the smaller parties were skeptical. Nancy Avelín de Ginestar, of the small provincial party Cruzada Renovadora (San Juan) argued that the new arrangement was simply set up so that "each of the Pacting parties [meaning the PJ and UCR] might have their men in the ranks of the Judicial Branch" (PS, August 1, p. 2738). In contrast to what happened in Guatemala, and as befits a pact originally negotiated between two presidents, the executive continued to have a very strong role in the appointments of Supreme Court justices, but the appointment would have to meet with the approval of at least the two largest parties in the Senate.

Some smaller parties, as a governance logic would predict, argued for a true outsider appointment process. Roberto Cornet, of the provincial party Union for a Democratic Center, explained how in crafting a constitution for the Province of Córdoba he had tried to persuade the PJ and the UCR to agree to an external appointment mechanism and argued for a similar arrangement here (CCB, p. 3263–4). To support his argument, he alluded to courts that he believed had acted on behalf of true outsiders to the political process – African-Americans in the United States and Palestinians in Israel. He proposed a strong and effective nominating committee, made up of six people coming from the legal profession, half judges and half practicing attorneys, plus five from electoral politics, three senators, and two from the executive. This, he argued, would ensure that the residents of Argentina could trust in the law. Horacio Conesa Monez Ruiz, of Fuerza Republicana, another small party, echoed that sentiment, calling for Supreme Court nominations to be placed under the Judicial Council that was being designed for the lower courts (CCB, p. 3268). If the smaller parties had had more influence in the Convention, it seems likely that the resulting arrangement might have looked more like Guatemala's, relying more heavily on actors external to electoral politics.

Thus, we see the positions on the conformation of the ex ante control coalition line up perfectly with each party's expected position in post-constituent politics. Given the dominant position of the UCR and the PJ in the OC, the ultimate result was an arrangement that gave the first- and second-largest parties, who can be expected to control the executive and the Senate, the dominant role in determining the expected preferences and philosophies of the members of the Supreme Court. In further keeping with the political dynamics of the Convention, the expected fragmentation of the Senate tempered this otherwise strictly two-party arrangement somewhat, giving smaller parties some expectation that their interests will also be considered in the process of appointment, although they will be largely dependent on their association with the other two.

6.3.2.2. Ex Post Autonomy

In contrast to the extensive debate on ex ante autonomy, ex post control of the Supreme Court received less attention during the debates. In part this is, as noted at the beginning of this section, because the goal was to produce an autonomous court, and the existing arrangement for life tenure and removal by impeachment on the vote of two-thirds of each chamber of the legislature already provided for a highly pluralistic coalition of ex post control. On impeachment, the problem had been the practices and informal norms, not the formal arrangement, so the removal procedures did not need to be strengthened. The logic of ex post control, on the other hand, was fully debated in connection with removal of lower court judges and to a lesser degree in connection with two other proposals: one to constitutionally specify the number of justices on the Supreme Court, and another which called for the retirement of Supreme Court justices at age 75, both elements in our scoring of a court's ex post autonomy. In what follows, we show that the members of the Convention understood that their decisions on these issues affected the extent to which ex post control of constitutional justice would be exposed to ordinary politics.

In the discussion of the design of a system of control for lower court judges, the Assembly members noted that the goal was actually to ease the difficulty of removal, but without subjecting judges to the whims of the RC. Paixao (UCR) was careful to note that the impeachment process for members of the Supreme Court would not be affected by any of the changes. It remains subject to a two-thirds vote by the Senate (Argentina 1994, Art. 59). But he noted, in connection with lower court judges, that, "Argentine society wants greater transparency in the appointment of its judges, and greater efficiency in the removal of judges who have committed acts of misconduct . . ." (PS, p. 2210). To produce this without affecting their independence, he said, "we have procured an intermediate solution in which the democratically elected branches retain an important role in the appointment of judges, but in which simultaneously – through the participation of judges themselves . . . and lawyers and others – the system might be governed with pluralism" (PS, p. 2210). Similarly, in the committee debates, the proponents of the new arrangement argued that it would subject judges to greater control, but by a more pluralistic coalition (CCB, pp. 3251 et seq.).

Not all agreed with this new arrangement. In keeping with our expectations, a few members of smaller parties argued for maintaining the existing impeachment arrangement for lower court judges, because they thought the new Council would be controlled by the RC (Vásquez, representing MODIN, CCB, p. 3271). On the other hand, Cornet, of the Unión del Centro Democrático, agreed with the proposal to shift from impeachment to trial before the Council, but justified his position with a countermajoritarian logic. He considered that the greater vice of the existing impeachment process was the penchant for the large parties to block any attempt to discipline lower court judges who were friendly to them, no matter how much they misbehaved (PS, p. 2269). He then argued for greater safeguards to prevent the RC from controlling the Council – a failed but prescient demand, given the history of this body over the last two or three decades.

In keeping with yet another of the claims we have made regarding institutional design, this discussion of governance for the lower courts included multiple references to a possible beneficial trade-off between ex ante and ex post autonomy. For example, Zaffaroni of the Frente Grande argued that the way to guarantee "democratic judges" would be to seek qualified ones in the selection process without imposing a political filter, but then create a "more flexible" mechanism for ensuring judges' political responsibility (CCB, p. 3261).

Perhaps more revealing of the Convention's attention to a governance logic is the objection to a provision that was ultimately adopted. This provision requires Supreme Court justices who reach the age of 75 to be reappointed for successive five-year terms [Argentina 1994, Art. 99(4)]. "The only thing this is going to do is tie the Judicial Branch to the political powers, destroying its real and authentic independence, which is what all we Argentines desire" (Nancy Avelín de Ginestar of Cruzada Renovadora, PS, pp. 4642–3). Although perhaps indulging in some hyperbole, given that this provision would only affect justices who reach 75 years of age while on the bench, Representative Avelín de Ginestar's comments reflect the intuition we used to score ex post autonomy: justices subject to reappointment are exposed to political pressures, especially if their terms are short. Their need to please all the members of the coalition of ex ante control, any one of whom can veto a reappointment bid, reduces their autonomy. This is not to say there are no good reasons to require reappointment for justices of such an advanced age, but this is clearly a provision that allows for closer oversight of sitting justices by the coalition of control.

Many members of small parties also called for specifying the number of justices on the Supreme Court in the constitutional text, or at a minimum for making the number hard to change, to avoid court-packing efforts by the RC. The strongest plea was made by Germán Kammerath, of the Unión del Centro Democrático: "We believe that, in order to strengthen the independence of the Judicial Branch, the Constitution should specify the number of members of the Court, in order to put a permanent limit on what has been a grave problem in all the countries of the world, including the United States of America . . . If this is not established, . . . then we should require a qualified majority to expand the number of members of the Supreme Court . . . The modification of the number of members of the Court should require, in our opinion, at least two-thirds of the Chambers of the National Congress" (PS, p. 2323–4). Interestingly, Kammerath continued the theme that

Paixao had established, that changing the composition of the court is tantamount to amending the constitution. His demand went beyond the requirement for appointment (executive plus two-thirds of the Senate), to the requirement for amendment of the constitution (two-thirds of each chamber, plus the assent of the executive). For reasons that are never explained, however, and despite a recent history of court packing, the UCR did not insist on this safeguard, and the court remains subject to expansion and contraction by ordinary legislation.

On a similar theme, members of the smaller parties complained that the Judicial Council, which would control appointment and removal of lower court judges, was insufficiently specified in the constitution and would remain vulnerable to tinkering by the RC. Cornet, of Córdoba's Unión del Centro Democrático, says it is crucial to specify its composition, so that "a matter of such importance" will not be subject to "occasional parliamentary majorities" (CCB, pp. 3264–5). Along the same lines, the MODIN argued that the composition of the Council should be specified in the constitution, so it would not simply be packed with representatives of the RC. "We don't know who will name [the members of the Council]. The consequence will be a grave politicization of its composition, as it leaves it in the hands of the political powers of the government, which will produce a resulting unease in the judges with respect to their stability . . ." (Alejandro Vásquez, MODIN, PS, p. 2228). The ex post coalition of control, these members of minority parties felt, should not too closely resemble the RC.

In summary, the removal provisions for members of the Supreme Court remained strongly weighted in favor of autonomy, requiring the participation of the two pacting parties, at minimum, and possibly more in light of the anticipated fragmentation of the Senate. The designers could have increased protections for the Court by specifying the number of justices or requiring a supermajority to expand the court, but they did not do so. They slightly decreased ex post autonomy by adding a quasi-retirement provision, requiring justices who pass 75 years of age to go through a reappointment process every five years, but they seem to have been fully aware of the potential tradeoffs of this move, since they passed it despite objections by the smaller parties.

The discussion, whether in relation to the Supreme Court or the lower courts, is sophisticated and cognizant of the ways in which politics affects judicial behavior. The positions taken by the various parties align well with our theoretical expectations regarding their preferences, and the justifications expressed reflect an awareness of the logic of constitutional governance as we have laid it out. The result is more or less what we would expect of an OC with these characteristics: the resulting CGC is largely controlled by the dominant political factions of Argentine politics, but control cannot be exercised unilaterally by any of them. If greater safeguards were not approved, the demands for them on the part of small parties suggests it was not an oversight, but rather a product of the political dynamics of the Convention.

6.3.2.3. Scope of Authority

The Convention's political dynamics also had the expected effect on the content and scope of constitutional justice in Argentina: the constitution was rewritten by a pluralistic but Left-leaning OC that crafted an expansive constitutional bargain. In Chapter 3, we presented quantitative evidence for the notion that an OC will place within the sphere of constitutional justice those matters that it wishes to subject to shared governance by its successors, rather than leaving them in the realm of ordinary politics. Not all of the OC's ideological goals should go into the constitution, but only those it feels might be threatened, or simply not pursued, by a future RC. Other goals can be entrusted to ordinary politics. We should see evidence that the designers understood that they were laying a foundation so that they and others who shared their goals could continue to affect policy on issues they placed within the constitutional justice sphere.

In the case of Argentina, we have an OC that leans substantially to the left of the party in power. It was pushed in that direction by the vigorous participation of the Frente Grande, which could find some common ground with both the PJ and the UCR in pursuing a social democratic agenda. Moreover, neither the Frente Grande nor the UCR had any assurance that they would be able to pursue that agenda through ordinary politics, given the dominance of the PJ and the neoliberal policies it was then pursuing. We expect, then, that these more minoritarian parties would push for inclusion of much of their agenda in the sphere of constitutional justice. Conversely, we would expect parties on the Right, like the MODIN, to resist expanding that sphere, despite their minoritarian status – they should certainly seek to constitutionalize property rights protections and basic civil and political rights, but no more. Alternative explanations – such as simple imitation of international models, or using the constitutional text as a political manifesto – should find less support in the record of the debates.

The debate surrounding which rights to include in the constitution generated the largest number of proposals, more than 100 from members of the Constituent Assembly and members of the public (PS, p. 2854). It is clear from the debates that the drafters understood that all the new rights, including social and economic ones, would be justiciable. Elisa Carrió, now a prominent politician and then a member of the UCR bloc, said, "We must be very clear – we will be very emphatic in this regard – that although [second and third-generation rights] might be programmatic norms, no measures taken by state power can affect or restrict these programmatic norms" (PS, p. 2864). Similarly, Carlos Corach, in many ways the leader of the Peronist delegation, argued:

> Other [rights] are programmatic, they incorporate a strong political will in which the State makes itself responsible before the individual and the international community to develop that program . . . and if it does not do so, it incurs in a sort of constitutional omission for which compliance can be demanded. The fact that

they might be programmatic matters does not mean they have lesser rank than the operative ones. The State is the obligee that recognizes and can be held liable for complying with all these rights.

(PS, p. 2832)

According to Socialist Guillermo Estevez Boero, the value of incorporating these more programmatic rights is that, even if they do not have the same "imperative force" of other elements found in the reform, including them "creates a juridical obligation not to work against these rights . . . It may not represent a concrete construction forward, but it is a limit behind . . ." (PS, p. 2915). Horacio Rosatti, of the PJ, also remarked that giving these rights constitutional rank makes them subject to constitutional claims in the courts (PS, August 2, p. 2999).

Importantly, they did not expect litigation to be the only mechanism for transformation through constitutional law. Elisa Carrió, at least, invoked Michel Foucault to argue that she hoped the new rights-rich constitution would have an internally transformative effect on the reproduction of power through knowledge, opening up opportunities for "emancipatory projects" (PS, pp. 2865–6). In one way or another, the members of this OC expected that what they were doing would transform the politics of social justice in Argentina, from labor to indigenous rights, from health and education to basic social provision, regardless of the neoliberal turn the country was taking under then-President Menem.

No one, of course, expected that these rights would have some sort of magical properties, causing injustice and suffering to instantly disappear. "Our work [of realizing these rights] will not end when we swear in the Constitution, it will only begin" (Blanca Roque, UCR, PS, p. 4079). The members of the OC did, however, expect that introducing these social and economic rights and adding procedural mechanisms for enforcing them would transform politics and create an alternative space for post-constituent politics on affected issues.

> With the introduction of these new rights . . . we are strengthening no more and no less than citizenship itself, and we are giving the old concept of citizenship a new dimension . . . [After the transition to democracy] it seemed, at moments, as if the only thing a citizen would keep for himself in the final analysis was the capacity to decide freely with the vote. What we are doing now is, in addition to the vote, putting at citizens' disposal spaces and tools for participation that will transform the relationship between the State and citizens, in a two way street.
>
> (Francisco Delich, UCR, PS, p. 4108)

Supportive statements like these belie suggestions that the subsequent legalization and judicialization of policies touched off by these rights were a surprise, as do the frequent warnings from opponents that this is what would happen. They emphasize a continuing role for citizens and participation, directly contradicting a notion of constitutionalism that depends on the technology of law and the technocracy of courts to preserve foundational commitments set in stone at the constitutional moment.

Humberto Quiroga Lavié, one of the most prominent UCR constitutionalists, extols the importance of judicial interventions on behalf of rights in discussing the innovations in the amparo:

> By incorporating the institution of the amparo into the text of our basic law, this Constituent Convention is constitutionalizing the third great system within this constitutional reform [along with re-balancing the three branches and renewing federalism] . . . The third system is that of judicial actions, which, as the keystone of the judicial system, is the one that directly matters to society and mobilizes it in defense of its rights.
>
> (PS, p. 4120)

This is important, in large part, because "the law is what judges say it is" (PS, p. 4120). "The protection of individual human rights norms includes the programmatic norms in the Constitution . . . If we are not clear on this, if we continue to say the programmatic norms in the Constitution are not juridical, we will be misunderstanding the function of the Constitution" (PS, p. 4120). He then made it clear that he believes it is the welfare state itself that is protected by these norms (PS, p. 4120), and that, when necessary, judges will step in to create positive obligations: "Faced with the omission of the legislature . . . it is possible that the judiciary may substitute the legislature to ensure the supremacy of the Constitution" (PS, p. 4121).

Even those on the Right who opposed the move, like the MODIN, understood that the new rights were creating a new constitutional politics of provision. Dina Rovagnati, of the MODIN, complained that creating a cause of action for the protection of collective rights would mean putting public policy in the hands of litigants and courts (PS, p. 4058). She worried that this would shift decision-making power away from the realm of ordinary politics. "In practice giving [NGOs] standing in defense of collective interests means relocating political representation . . . Without any doubt, it also presupposes a political utilization of the Judiciary that is offensive to our republican system" (PS, pp. 4059–60).

Of course, we have argued that this is precisely the point of the expansion of the constitutional justice sphere: to create new "spaces and tools for participation," in the words of Delich, for all those issues that were included in that sphere. We have already shown how the constituents understood that the selection of justices to sit on the court opened the door to a "quotidian" amendment of the constitution through interpretation. In the discussions of social and economic rights, and of the mechanisms for their enforcement, we see the substantive counterpart of this process. The OC is giving certain issues a place, and certain parties standing to participate, in a post-constituent politics of constitutional meaning. The goal is not merely to set up the courts as a veto player with special concern for the fairness of the democratic process, as the insurance model suggests. In this social democratic model it is, rather, to create a robust, constitutionally inflected politics of social provision that gives organized civil society and the courts an important, though not exclusive, role.

The new constitution, they understood, would give all of law a distinctly new orientation. The Convention was creating a new legality, Esteban Llamosas (PJ) said,
"a legality understood as translating and modifying social injustice in Argentina" (PS,
p. 2923). These rights were expected to be operative and not merely ornamental.

> There is an unsatisfied social demand with respect to second generation human
> rights, that is rights to work, to housing, to health and education; and with respect
> to those of the third generation, such as the rights to the environment and ethics
> in public life . . . People want to return to faith in law, which requires that it be
> transformed and become an effective instrument that permits the modification of
> social injustice.
>
> (Jorge Busti, PJ, PS, pp. 2992–3)

Clearly, they understood that the social and economic rights would constrain the
RC. As Angel Pardo (PJ) noted, "Those who complain about this reform do so
because they realize that it will mean a significant harm to the establishment to
which they belong, especially those liberals who defend private property over and
above the rights of society" (PS, p. 2907).

This call for a social justice-oriented sphere of constitutional justice is consistent
with an OC that was uncertain of realizing its desired social welfare goals through
ordinary politics. It resonated with the traditional ideology of the Peronist party,
despite its neoliberal orientation at the time of the Convention, and with its Left
wing. It perfectly reflected the social democratic impulses of the Frente Grande,
the third largest block in the OC. And it was not entirely inconsistent with the goals
of many in the UCR, like Alfonsín, who had followed a less orthodox economic
approach and at times espoused a more social democratic ideology. Indeed, the
original social democratic element in the Argentine Constitution, Article 14 (bis),
was put there by the UCR in 1957.[16] Given Menem's strength and neoliberal orientation at the time of the Convention, the Left wing of the PJ and the other parties
all had good reason to put their progressive policies into the constitution, in the
hopes that they could pursue these goals in the sphere of constitutional justice. As
Carrió noted, the hope was that even the more "programmatic" rights would allow
organized groups to challenge any actions by the RC that might negatively affect
social provision.

In addition to the desire for a space in which to pursue social welfare in an
increasingly neoliberal political context, Argentina's painful political history
comes up again and again as the reason the sphere of constitutional justice must
be especially robust. The new constitutional text "will serve citizens as a weapon
for protection of their rights . . . This has to do with our realities and suffering, with our burdens and our contemporary political history, because it is no

---

[16] Author interview Marcelo Alegre, Buenos Aires, June 12, 2014. Author interview Elva Roulet, Buenos
Aires, June 17, 2014.

coincidence that we have remembered here . . . the relationship between habeas corpus and enforced disappearances of people in Argentina" (Rodolfo Parente, UCR, PS, p. 4134). In strong echoes of what we heard in Guatemala, Horacio Rosatti of the PJ argues that his party's history is what compels him to seek an expansive set of rights:

> The greatest number of political prisoners kept at the discretion of the Executive Power of the Nation during the black night of Argentina, during the greatest genocide of its history, belong to the Justicialist national movement. The greatest part of its disappeared also; and many of those who suffered from that persecution, who were detained by the executive power, today . . . occupy seats in this Convention.
>
> (PS, p. 2926)

Elisa Carrió echoed this sentiment and expressed the hope that the inclusion of human rights treaties in the constitution will change the mindset of judges, who had notoriously legitimized de facto governments and their actions in prior decades. She enumerated events in which Argentine judges collaborated in repression, and then concluded:

> In light of these experiences, and others even more near to us . . . regarding the conduct of magistrates and functionaries, we consider that the incorporation of human rights treaties with constitutional rank, and the mention of these treaties in the text will produce an advantage we still have not weighed, that is, the opening up of a more rights-oriented [*"garantista"*] sphere of knowledge among magistrates and functionaries charged with respecting and guaranteeing rights . . .
>
> (PS, pp. 2865–6)

In short, in light of the repeated failure of the whole of Argentine politics to secure respect for basic human rights, it is clear that these constituents seek to ground normative authority and some enforcement capacity in the international community. In this respect, the move toward wholesale inclusion of international human rights treaties, rather than merely listing the rights themselves, is yet another attempt to expand the CGC beyond the sphere of ordinary politics. The logic of this move goes well beyond short-term pure power politics, in the sense that even the largest party is interested in crafting a strong and effective space in which to challenge the actions of the state. The move has strong elements of an insurance logic in that it remains grounded in a fundamental uncertainty about the future. And yet it is clear that the designers see constitutional justice as more active and contested than an insurance metaphor would suggest. As we have argued throughout, the careful attention to who will be acting within the sphere of constitutional justice to support the court, challenge the executive, exercise the tools of constitutional justice, and enforce the limitations written into the constitution makes constitutional governance a better description of what is expected to happen long after the constitutional moment is over.

6.3.3. *Other Logics at Work*

Although the previous discussion shows the ways in which the logic of constitutional governance structured the discussions of autonomy and authority provisions, the designers in Argentina were also animated by other logics. On substantive provisions, there is a strong modernist and internationalist argumentative thread running through the debates, elements of which we saw in the previous section. Marcelo Alegre, a prominent Argentine constitutional scholar who was close to Alfonsín and his team, suggests we should not discount the influence of constitutional scholars, whose expertise included a sort of "checklist for modern constitutions" that influenced the final text beyond the immediate calculations and ideologies of the politicians involved.[17]

These less obviously political logics are clearly reflected in the debates. In particular, the discussion of the incorporation of international treaties into the constitution is replete with allusions to a new conventional wisdom regarding the increasing importance of international law, and in particular international human rights law, in the domestic sphere. To incorporate international human rights law into the constitution, in this view, is to craft a truly modern constitution, as Juan Pablo Cafiero put it when he opened the first meeting of the Commission on International Treaties (CIT, p. 3590). Similarly, there is a strong sense that any modern democracy must rest on a strong foundation of international human rights. If divorced from the perceived governance needs of the polity itself, these more universal arguments for expanding the scope of authority of constitutional justice go beyond the logic of governance we have laid out, which is more specific to the political interests and substantive concerns of local politics.

As noted earlier, many of the constituents – all but those on the far Right, as the quantitative results in Chapter 4 also suggest – apparently felt that an appeal to international human rights was the proper technology for ensuring that Argentina's future did not include the sorts of massive human rights violations it had so recently experienced. Even here, however, the need to establish an expansive constitutional human rights sphere is made especially pointed by Argentina's relatively recent history. "The constituent, in this transcendent moment we are living, is taking decisions and chances, we could almost say gambles, because he or she looks at the past – seeing the good and bad experiences – and looks to the future to change that reality" (PS, p. 2446). The universalism of human rights was especially attractive to parties like the Frente Grande that did not come from the core of the bipartisan pact, but these provisions also had to be included in the constitution precisely because of Argentina's particular history. Eduardo Barcesat, of the Frente Grande, put it this way:

> There is not an Argentine human rights or an Argentine amparo. There are human rights for Argentines and there shall also be an amparo cause of action for those

---

[17] Author interview Marcelo Alegre, Buenos Aires, June 12, 2014.

human rights. But these causes of action, like the rights they protect, are imprinted with the stamp of universality and "for everyone"; there is no way we can purport to present them as if they were particular to us, or borne out of our individuality. In any case, it has been the tragedy of our individual history that has called for the incorporation of these texts in the National Constitution.

(PS, p. 4051)

Similarly, the incorporation of other national models is, of course, as much at work in Argentina as it was in Guatemala. This is clearest in the debates surrounding the creation of the Defensor del Pueblo, an institution patterned after the Swedish ombudsman.[18] All the discussions of the Defensor del Pueblo are marked by references to the experiences of various countries, and the lessons that can be taken from those experiences. Along the same lines, in the debates on which rights to include in the Argentine Constitution there are multiple references to the constitutions of Brazil, Peru, Guatemala, Nicaragua, Chile, Colombia, Spain, Portugal, France, Greece, Germany, Sweden, Denmark, the European Union, the Inter-American human rights system, Eastern Europe as a whole, and others. Sometimes these experiences are used as cautionary tales – "... introducing these 'Megatherium' treaties takes us in the direction of the Brazilian or Colombian model ... Obviously that is completely unenforceable" (PS, August 3, p. 2965) – and sometimes they are used as positive examples. The European Union, for instance, is held up as a positive example of how, in the future, countries will rely less on domestic and more on international norms.

But the model of diffusion that emerges is not slavish copying, nor is it wholesale adoption in hopes of achieving the results that other countries have achieved. The members of the Assembly acknowledge the need to adapt the borrowed institutions to the perceived needs of Argentine society. The debates show the constituents casting about for international models that can be adapted to the needs of Argentina, and using foreign examples in their efforts to persuade each other of the benefits of this or that preferred arrangement:

> In 1853 ... the constituents also created institutions borrowing partly from French legislation, a lot from American, partly from Spanish, on other topics that we have already discussed, but no one thought they were doing something very strange because they were expressing what they understood to be the best of different institutions that were in different political and geographic situations in that moment. We here are also bringing in parts of some institutions, adapting them to our reality, and doing so with the greatest goodwill and good faith.
>
> (CCB, p. 3294)

---

[18] The Swedish legislative ombudsman was an early example of an institution that now appears in many modern constitutions. The office is meant to field complaints from citizens about state misconduct and to mediate solutions.

The specific examples illustrate an approach to borrowing that is modular and adaptive to local political needs. Appointment power for the ombudsman, for example, was located within the legislature. The same spirit also led the Constituent Assembly to curtail executive authority in a dozen other ways, such as through the mechanisms of constitutional justice and in the realm of constitutional governance. In response to the same impulses that led to the expanded scope of constitutional justice, the Defensor was explicitly given authority to bring legal claims on behalf of collective rights. In the end, as one of the critics put it, "In relation to the ombudsman, if we are going to give it standing to file legal claims, it's no longer the Swedish or Danish ombudsman; it's Argentine, different, so let's not call it ombudsman, let's call it defender of the people . . ." (CSC, p. 3571, Héctor Masnatta, PJ). A long debate on the wisdom of adding labor treaties to the list of included treaties was all premised on the history of labor rights and labor relations in Argentina. In short, the debates were peppered with references to other countries' experiences, but these references did not detract from the influence of domestic politics. Rather, they expanded the repertoire available to the designers as they pursued their political interests and ideological commitments.

6.4. OTHER CONSTITUTIONS WITH SIMILAR FEATURES

As a system with moderately high autonomy and high authority, Argentina 1994 falls in the middle of the northeast quadrant of Figure 2.4, in Chapter 2. According to our conceptual map, these are courts with a broad social democratic agenda. They are designed to be important spaces for policy contestation rather than the imposition of outcomes. Moreover, they are enabled by their relative insulation from political pressure, their accessibility, and a broad toolkit to exert their influence across many domains, and occasionally to act against the interests of dominant political actors. This upper right quadrant, which contains what we have called Major Policy Player courts, includes effectively no courts from the 1975 period (Brazil's pre-1988 Supreme Court is just barely above the mean on authority), but several by the first decade of the new millennium. In addition to Argentina 1994, by 2009 this quadrant includes Colombia 1991, Costa Rica after the 1990 amendments, Mexico as amended after 2000, and Brazil 1988. All these courts have by all accounts become significant players in the major policy disputes of each country. Also included is Ecuador 2008, which has a different trajectory. Our argument and quantitative findings suggest that the courts in this quadrant will have been designed by pluralistic, Left-leaning coalitions, perhaps marked by a history of recent political violence. Here we discuss only a few of these new courts, to provide some suggestive evidence that our argument holds for them as well.

Most observers consider Colombia the country with the most active and consequential court in the entire region, and it scores as the system with the highest degree of authority among this group, so we will examine whether its origins fit well with the logic of constitutional governance. Much has been written about the origins of Colombia's current system of constitutional justice (Nielson and Shugart 1999; Cepeda Espinosa 2004, 2007; Schor 2008; Nunes 2010a). Our goal is not to repeat this, but to draw on it. Fortunately, there is strong consensus on the points that concern us most. The Constituent Assembly that produced Colombia 1991 was triggered by mass mobilization and the suggestion by some guerrilla groups that they would be willing to lay down their guns in exchange for meaningful participation. Just as in Argentina, Manuel José Cepeda Espinosa, an active participant as a member of the President's team, called the resulting process "by far the most inclusive in the country's recent history; even active guerrilla groups took part in the discussion" (Cepeda Espinosa 2004: 545). In addition to active and recently demobilized guerrillas, the Assembly included candidates who represented not only political parties, but also indigenous groups, evangelicals, unions, community movements, students, the press, and more (Cepeda Espinosa 2007: 348).

The resulting distribution of forces within the Assembly was balanced across the entire political spectrum. The government's party, representing a Center-Right, modernist party with a neoliberal agenda, won only 31 percent of the vote. The M-19, a guerrilla movement representing the far Left, was the second-largest block, after winning nearly 27 percent of the vote. And the third largest block was the Movimiento de Salvación Nacional (MSN), a conservative, Right-wing nationalist party, which won a little more than 15 percent of the vote. With their respective alliances, each of these led roughly one-third of the delegates. Proposals had to be approved in two successive votes by a simple majority vote, although if anyone wanted revisions to the main proposal on the second vote, the revisions would have to be approved by two-thirds. Most of the time, a stable coalition composed of the President's supporters in the Liberal Party coalition and the supporters of the M-19 formed the winning coalition on any contested vote (Cepeda Espinosa 2007: 361). The MSN and its supporters lost more votes than any other block.

In short, Colombia 1991 was written by a broadly inclusive, Left-leaning OC, as we would expect. Moreover, more than in nearly any other Assembly, both the centrist but free-market Liberals and the recently demobilized Left had special reason to fear they would not be able to carry out their agenda in ordinary politics. Similarly to Argentina, the M-19 had just laid down its weapons and secured a stunning victory in the special circumstances – and under the special rules – of the Constituent Assembly elections, but the actual government was in the hands of a popular, neoliberal president. The Liberals had thus suffered a surprising reversal, and could reasonably have feared that they might lose power in subsequent elections. Both parties, then, had good reason to constitutionalize important parts of their agenda, and to place themselves within a broadly inclusive CGC to direct the sphere of

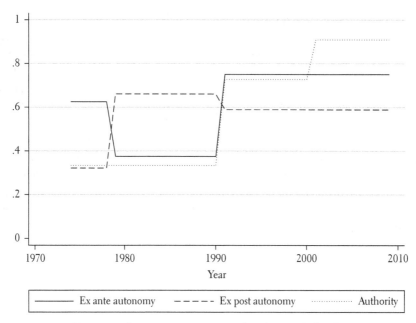

FIGURE 6.2. Ex ante and ex post autonomy, and authority, Colombia 1975–2009

constitutional justice in postconstituent politics. Without going into great detail on the institutional arrangements, suffice it to say that they earn high scores across all three dimensions of design, scoring second highest in the region on authority, and among the highest on ex ante autonomy, as depicted in Figure 6.2.

Descriptions of the designers' goals and of the resulting system are remarkably consistent with the argument we have presented here. Manuel José Cepeda, who was perhaps the key member of the President's constitutional design team on these issues, makes this point. He criticizes the old system of judicial review by the Supreme Court because it was not connected to elected, democratic institutions (the justices were named by the Supreme Court itself), and therefore, constitutional meaning could not evolve (Cepeda Espinosa 2004: 541). According to Rodrigo Nunes,

> Gaviria wanted a Constitutional Court not to constrain his opponents, but to facilitate the accomplishment of a programmatic goal . . . [The] government was conscious of the potential for judicial activism from a Constitutional Court, but it believed that such an institution would be able to adapt its decisions to the 'requirements of the moment' . . . As Gaviria would later explain, the creation of the Constitutional Court was designed to develop the rule of law in accordance with the demands of globalization
>
> (Nunes 2010a: 78, citations omitted)

The Left, meanwhile, meant the Constitutional Court to be a space where social and economic rights could be enforced, protecting the welfare state from the hazards of the market (Nunes 2010a). Both negotiated to incorporate their core values into the space of constitutional justice, and both partly succeeded in doing so (Rodríguez Garavito 2010).

In following years, constitutional justice would live up to this ambivalence. The ensuing clash of neoliberal and social welfarist values in the space of constitutional justice, and the leading role that the Constitutional Court has taken in defining the meaning and reach of these rights, is no more than a reflection of this ambivalence within the OC, with the consequent "disharmony" (Jacobsohn 2010) and construction of an equally pluralistic CGC. Consistently with the Constitutional Governance model, given this background, the space of constitutional justice has become the place where the tension between a more market-oriented economic model and a social welfare state gets worked out, with extensive intervention and participation by civil society, government actors, and courts (Cepeda Espinosa 2004, 2009, 2011; Schor 2008; Rodríguez Garavito 2009; Wilson 2009; Rodríguez Garavito and Rodríguez Franco 2010; Brinks and Forbath 2011, 2014; Yamin et al. 2011; Urueña 2012; Bonilla Maldonado 2013).

The formal design of Nicaragua, the one Central American country where the Left won the violent struggles of the 1980s, and which has had a consistently strong Leftist party, is within this quadrant as well. The current constitution is the product of an initial, more or less unilateral constitutional process that took place under Sandinista control in 1987 (which replaced a decree by the revolutionary de facto government), and a second, much more contested and pluralistic process of major reform in 1994. The former can be seen as an embodiment of a Sandinista – that is, revolutionary Left – constitutional project, and thus of an RC-dominant OC (albeit one that was under pressure from US-sponsored counterrevolutionary forces). The latter, on the other hand, required negotiations between an embattled Sandinista opposition and a relatively weak Center-Right government. Predictably, from a constitutional governance perspective, the first one produced a system with low authority and low autonomy, despite the ideology of the dominant party, while the second one kept authority low (reflecting the ideology of the new RC) while dramatically increasing ex ante autonomy, as shown in the following graph. Ex post autonomy appears much less responsive to these political changes in Nicaragua, as the quantitative results suggest (Figure 6.3).

The Mexican Constitution, long recognized as one of the first to incorporate social and economic rights, also brought its constitutional justice mechanisms more into line with this impulse. With a series of reforms, including the ability to strike down a law in the abstract for unconstitutionality, the addition of indigenous rights, stronger nondiscrimination provisions and so on, the Mexican Court moved up in authority while preserving a design that seemed intended to insulate it from the

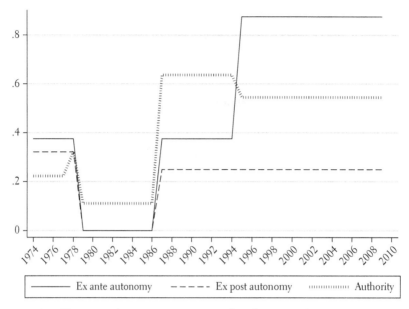

FIGURE 6.3. Ex ante and ex post autonomy, and authority in Nicaragua, 1975–2009

political realm.[19] As expected, the movement coincided with the increasing plural-ism of the Mexican Legislature, which approved the constitutional amendments that produced this change. Increased activism by indigenous groups led to their inclusion within constitutional justice. Increasing diversity in the political sphere led to a stronger, more streamlined amparo process. Lastly, pressure from the oppo-sition led to a more pluralistic judicial appointment process. In general, the move-ment fits well with the expectations of the constitutional governance model.

6.5. CONCLUSION

Despite the many differences in the constitutional processes that moved all the cases discussed in this chapter into the upper left quadrant of our conceptual map, some of the dynamics are constant. The constitutional changes result from processes that are more inclusive and pluralistic than any experienced previously in the history of these countries. The OC always includes a strong representation by the Left, but not to such an extent that the Left is dominant and can confidently expect to achieve its goals in ordinary politics. A history of political violence pushes designers to enact greater protections and to craft stronger legal tools for the enforcement of rights.

---

[19] Of course, Mexico was dominated by a hegemonic party that responded quite directly to the President for many years, so the executive had considerable authority, in spite of its formal weakness. By the same token, institutional protections had limited consequence in a context in which one party dominated the executive, the national legislature, and all state legislatures.

The resulting constitutional texts ward against the fears rooted in a country's recent political history, but also provide a platform to pursue the hopes of the members of the OC, in a way that is much more open-ended than a strict insurance metaphor would suggest.

This openness is clearly a function of the broad and ambitious agenda entrusted to constitutional justice, which goes far beyond procedural rights. But it is also the result of the understanding that constitutional meaning will evolve over time, under the guidance of newly empowered judges who are responsive to a supermajoritarian CGC. In all these cases, we see procedural mechanisms like amparo and tutela, habeas data and habeas corpus, and collective causes of action in support of pro-grammatic, affirmative rights that will permit opposition actors to efficiently and effectively challenge the actions of the government and the state. The systems of constitutional justice go well beyond protecting the political process, and appear to be designed explicitly to permit non-majoritarian actors – and the government as well – to pursue their policy goals. But what distinguishes these cases is the plu-ralism of the OC, and the ensuing pluralism of the CGC, which ensures that the space of constitutional justice remains open to contestation and debate. In cases like Argentina and Colombia we see the results of this pluralism. The debates involve a great diversity of actors, from the traditionally marginalized indigenous and Afro-descendant groups to the government itself. The outcome of these debates around constitutional meaning are never a foregone conclusion, but they keep constitu-tional language and processes at the center of the country's politics.

7

Bolivia (2009)

Governance Logic in the New Constitutionalism

They said, 'since we're the majority in the country, we will end up choosing the candidates.'
. . . The aspirations of the people to not have a justice that is at the service of those on top
dovetailed with the desire of those at the top to have direct control over justice, without being
accused of controlling the judges.

> Jorge Lazarte, Bolivian Constituent Assembly member,
> on why the majority in the Assembly opted for the popular
> election of Constitutional Court Justices (author interview,
> June 27, 2014, La Paz, Bolivia).

Bolivia's most recent constitution is often highlighted as an example of Latin America's
new constitutionalism. It identifies the country as "plurinational," rather than posit-
ing a more monistic view of the nation; it allows for alternative sources of legitimate
authority by recognizing customary laws and governments at the local level; and it
proposes a participatory model of democracy, rather than a more purely representative
one (Uprimny 2011). Others suggest that these apparent differences are mere rhetorical
flourishes that mask a return by the populist Left to the traditional hyper-presidentialist
modes of governance that long prevailed in Latin America (Couso 2013).

However, the question for us here is what these differences mean for the logic
of constitutional governance and the construction of the system of constitutional
justice. Is the new constitutionalism of Latin America, seen most clearly in the constitutions of Bolivia and Ecuador, driven primarily by ideology, so that it escapes
the logic of constitutional governance? Similarly, does the constitutionalism of the
populist Left, which in addition to Bolivia and Ecuador influenced constitutions in
Venezuela, Nicaragua, and elsewhere, escape that logic? In this chapter, we will take
up primarily the 2009 constitution of Bolivia for an in-depth look at the most recent
expressions of this purportedly new strain of Latin American constitutionalism. In
addition, we will much more summarily discuss the process that led to Venezuela's
1999 constitution and the resulting system of constitutional justice. Like Bolivia,
Venezuela is likely the purest expression of populist Left constitutionalism, since the

constitution was written essentially unilaterally by President Hugo Chávez's supporters, with no check from an opposition party at all. We find that these constitutional
designers also follow the logic of a constitutional governance model of institutional
design, albeit with some differences in the case of Venezuela.

As in our examination of Guatemala and Argentina, we first examine the constitutional history of Bolivia to see the extent to which it tracks with the logic of constitutional governance and the extent to which that history informs current constitutional
choices. In Bolivia, we find something that breaks in some respects from the regional
patterns we have seen so far, without, however, breaking from the logic of constitutional governance. Predictably, for a political system that is less than fully democratic, the Originating Coalitions (OCs) for the many constitutions Bolivia has seen
are not very inclusive. As a result, as we would expect, these coalitions crafted systems
of constitutional justice with quite restricted autonomy and scope of authority. The
difference is that, as we will see, for long periods formal ex ante control of the courts
was located in the legislature, rather than, as was the norm, in the executive. And
the expansion of constitutional politics implied by the social constitutionalism of the
mid-twentieth century was never rolled back – Bolivia came nearly to the end of that
century with its social constitution intact. In these two respects, at least, Bolivia departs
from the pattern we saw in Argentina, Guatemala, and other countries of the region.

The big break in this constitutional pattern came in 1994, with Bolivia's first constitution written under democracy. Ex post autonomy had long been quite strong,
and did not change. On the other hand, as expected, a more pluralistic OC led to
a text marking a strong expansion of the scope of constitutional justice and a somewhat less significant improvement in ex ante autonomy. But the 1994 Constitution
did not survive the political upheaval that marked the arrival of Evo Morales and his
party, the Movimiento al Socialismo (MAS), on the political scene. Shortly after he
was elected, he led the push for a new constitution.

The primary focus of this chapter is on the chaotic Constituent Assembly that
followed, and on the subsequent pact that produced Bolivia's 2009 Constitution.
Throughout that process, the opposition was weak, but retained some veto power, as
we will see. As a result, it managed to secure some concessions, raising the system's
scope of authority and ex ante autonomy from what it might have been by securing
for itself some rights protections and some participation in the appointment of justices. But ex post autonomy was reduced, and overall, the current system is weaker
than we would have expected if it simply expressed the ideology of the leading party
and the period in which it was crafted. The difference, we will show, results from
the logic of constitutional governance, lending additional support to our theory.
A Ruling Coalition (RC) with strong electoral support sought to expand the scope of
constitutionally inflected ordinary politics, but not necessarily the scope of authority
or autonomy of the system of constitutional justice. Whatever its ideological differences, the "new constitutionalism" of Bolivia continues to follow the logic of
constitutional governance.

7.1. BOLIVIA'S CONSTITUTIONAL HISTORY

Bolivia has had at least eighteen constitutions (depending how one counts), including the original 1826 text written by the Liberator Simón Bolívar. While the early constitutions do not appear to have had much purchase on the politics of the country, we can see a gradual strengthening of constitutional justice over time – at least in formal institutional terms. The technology of institutional design was more limited early in the country's history, but the movements we see toward or away from greater autonomy, or greater authority, roughly correspond to moments of greater or lesser political inclusion even very early in the country's history. Until 1994, none of Bolivia's constitutions were written in a truly democratic moment by an inclusive OC, but relative inclusiveness led to relatively more judicial autonomy and some additional authority, while more authoritarian moments led to a centralization of control over the judiciary and weaker courts. The successive constitutions slowly added more rights and then stronger powers of judicial review, while the appointment process saw the most changes as the executive was successively given and denied a role in that process. Given the complexity of this constitutional history, we have summarized and presented a very succinct version of the key changes in Table 7.1. The constitutions with years labeled in bold are those that mark a significant (positive) change in the conformation of the system of constitutional justice.

Simón Bolívar drafted the country's first constitution and simply sent it to the Constituent Assembly for approval. In that text, Bolívar set himself up as president for life with considerable authority, but, perhaps to balance his projected life tenure, he created a tricameral legislature and gave control over judicial appointments entirely to the other branches. The Senate was to propose a list of three nominees for each vacancy, from which the Chamber of Censors would pick the justices for the Supreme Court (Bolivia 1826, Arts. 47(6), 60(1)). The Chamber of Censors was made up of twenty lifetime appointees who were meant to watch over compliance with the constitution. Indeed, this Chamber can almost be seen as a sort of protoconstitutional court.[1] The same two chambers had the dominant role in initiating the impeachment of public officials: the Censors would accuse before the Senate, triggering a complicated process that eventually involved all three legislative chambers and the Supreme Court. The constitution contains no explicit reference to a separate impeachment process for Supreme Court justices, so it seems they would be subject to the same process. The process is convoluted, but not necessarily counter- or supermajoritarian – all decisions are taken by legislative majorities or the court.

---

[1] The Chamber of Censors had few formal powers, the most important of which was probably to accuse other governmental actors of having violated the constitution (Bolivia 1826, Arts. 50–61). They were the third chamber of the Legislature, in addition to a Chamber of Tribunes and a Senate.

TABLE 7.1. *Key changes to system of constitutional justice in Bolivia – 1826–2009*

Year	Nomination	Approval	Powers
1826	Senate	Chamber of Censors	Very weak – Court can only interpret laws – ultimate constitutional authority lies with legislature (censors).
1831	Senate	Executive	Very weak – Court can only interpret laws.
1834	Senate	Executive	Very weak – Court can only interpret laws – loses authority to try President.
1839	Municipal Councils	Senate	Very weak – Court can only interpret laws – legislature wins right to authoritatively interpret constitution, weakening courts further
1843	Senate	Executive	Very weak – Court can only interpret laws – ultimate constitutional interpretation authority granted to executive
1851	House of Reps.	Senate	Populist insurrection leads to new constitution that includes explicit grant of diffuse judicial review, more rights (Salamanca 2005: 363–67).
1861	Executive	Assembly	A step back for judicial power: Supreme Court (renamed Corte de Casación) can apply constitution over laws, but set of rights is more limited and now legislature issues advisory opinions on constitutionality.
1868	Executive	Senate	Another step back: "Only Congress can resolve any doubts that might arise regarding the interpretation of the constitution." But still requires courts to apply constitution before laws.
1871	Council of State	Assembly	Keeps "Only Congress . . ." language and provision requiring courts to apply constitution before laws.
1878	Senate	House of Reps.	No change
1880	Senate	House of Reps.	Constituent Assembly with two balanced parties grants increased authority - explicit centralized judicial review - in exchange for more limited (ex post) autonomy: terms limited to 10 years, renewable. Model lasts 60 years.
1938	Senate	House of Reps.	Bolivia's first "social constitution." Habeas corpus had been added through decree/referendum in 1931.
1945	Senate	House of Reps.	No real change – more social constitutionalism.
1947	Senate	House of Reps.	No change
1961	Senate	House of Reps.	No change
1967	Senate	House of Reps.	Keeps habeas corpus and amparo and adds concentrated abstract review.

(continued)

TABLE 7.1 *(continued)*

Year	Nomination	Approval	Powers
1994	Joint Session elects members of Constitutional Tribunal by 2/3		First democratic constitution. Creates new Constitutional Tribunal with more powers and more accessibility, adds justiciable rights, and retains amparo and habeas corpus. Justices continue to have 10-year renewable terms.
2009	Assembly preselects by 2/3	General Election	All-new Bolivarian Constitution: Increase in enumerated rights, but not a dramatic change in court powers; weakens ex post autonomy.

In our terms, this gave the Supreme Court moderate ex ante and ex post autonomy, with control over the Court located firmly in the legislative branch (albeit in the lifetime-appointed Censors), which was a relative oddity for the period. The life-tenured Censors might have even generated some distance between judicial appointments and current majorities. The president had no direct role in appointments or removals.

In terms of its scope of authority, however, Bolivia's Supreme Court was exceptionally weak. It had no explicit powers of judicial review. It had the power to hear "the doubts of the remaining courts regarding the interpretation of any law," in which case it was to "consult with the Executive so that it might promote the required declaration in the Chambers" (Bolivia 1826, Art. 110(8)), thus giving the legislature the final word even in statutory interpretation. The constitution makes no reference to habeas corpus or similar emergency causes of action for violations of constitutional rights. It also includes only the bare minimum rights. Under Art. 149, "the Constitution guarantees to all Bolivians their civil liberty, individual security, property, and equality before the law, whether it rewards or punishes." Art. 150 guarantees freedom of speech, and Art. 152 protects against arbitrary searches of homes. The constitution further abolishes hereditary titles (Art. 154) and allows all manner of work, so long as it does not violate public customs or harm security and safety (Art. 155).

Although it only lasted two years – primarily because of its proposal of a president-for-life – this constitution looms large in the imagination of Bolivian constitutionalists. Salamanca Trujillo (2005), in a detailed history of eighteen Bolivian constitutions, devotes nearly 200 pages to this one ephemeral document. Indeed, he argues that its structure informs all subsequent constitutions (2005: 308). This may well be true in some respects, at least until 2009, but two of its most unique features quickly disappeared: the tricameral legislature and the presidency-for-life did not last beyond those two years. What appears to endure, in a break with the patterns of the day, which nearly always placed the executive at the center of judicial appointments, is an ambivalence over giving the president too much influence over the courts. As importantly, despite abolishing the Chamber of Censors, for the following almost four decades the succeeding texts understood constitutional control as a purely political, not a judicial, function (Santiváñez 2009).

This earliest text appears to have set a precedent for an appointment process that did not involve the executive. What we see in subsequent constitutions, from 1831 to 1880, is a tug of war between an appointment process that gives the Senate the power to name, and the lower house the power to approve, justices, and one in which the Senate names justices subject to the executive's approval, as shown in Table 7.1. Five of the nine constitutions that were in place during these fifty years placed appointments exclusively in the hands of the legislature, with one chamber naming and the other approving the nominations.

In 1831, as noted, the Chamber of Censors disappeared, and the right to approve the Senate's judicial nominees (still a list of three for each vacancy) went to the executive (Bolivia 1831, Arts. 45 and 72(28)). The impeachment process was simplified, but the threshold for a conviction rose to a two-thirds vote of the Senate, on accusation by the lower chamber (Bolivia 1831, Arts. 37 and 43), thus giving the Supreme Court some additional ex post autonomy. The similarity in the language of the 1826 and 1831 Constitutions suggests that this reallocation of authority was accomplished by essentially parceling out the various attributes of the Censors among the remaining branches, without modifying anything more than was necessary. This may well account for the relatively unusual arrangement in which nominees originate in the legislature for the approval of the executive, rather than vice versa. The power to nominate was already located in the Senate, so they simply shifted the Censors' approval powers to the executive. The "Guarantees" chapter was expanded very slightly to protect the secrecy of personal mail and forbid the seizure of effects; however, the same chapter also punishes as sedition any attempt by a person or group to make a petition "in the name of the people" without their authorization (Art. 162). Generally, the constitutional justice system remained weak.

Only three years later, President Andrés de Santa Cruz amended his own constitution, making a single consequential change – eliminating the President's criminal responsibility for various forms of misconduct while in office. According to Salamanca (2005: 329, 331), de Santa Cruz did this in anticipation of doing certain things that he expected might trigger criminal responsibility. Salamanca blames this incident for setting a precedent in which powerful presidents use constitutions to advance purely personal agendas. While this change technically did not affect the sphere of constitutional justice, it did eliminate the Court's authority to oversee the president's conduct using the tools of criminal law, weakening the Court even further.

In 1839, a war that pitted the advocates of a union between Peru and Bolivia against those who wanted continued Bolivian independence, ended with a new constitution written, in its own words, "Against the so-called Peru-Bolivian Confederation" (Bolivia 1839, Preamble). Although the primary focus was, of course, reestablishing the Bolivian Republic, this text continued experimenting with ex ante autonomy, setting up a Supreme Court with territorial representation. The new Supreme Court would have seven justices, each nominated by a municipal council (by a simple majority) and approved by the Senate (Bolivia 1839, Art. 37(6)). The municipal council was the main legislative authority for each department, the main geographic subdivision of Bolivia. As before, the Supreme Court would have the authority to interpret laws, but the legislature was now explicitly empowered to issue authoritative constitutional interpretations by a two-thirds vote of both chambers, essentially denying the Court the power of judicial review (Art. 147). A mere four years later, a new constitution once again returned nominating power to the Senate and final appointment power to the executive (Bolivia 1843, Art. 26(3)).

Neither of these constitutions gave the Court the power of judicial review, now assigning that ultimate constitutional authority to the executive itself:

> The Constitution of 1839 did not establish any mechanism of [constitutional] self-protection, and the subsequent fundamental norm of 1843 reestablished the Council of State under the new name of National Council, albeit with a different composition (two senators, two representatives, two ministers of state, two ministers of the Supreme Court of Justice, an army general, an ecclesiastic of dignity and a head of one of the offices of Treasury), entrusting it with the function of watching over the observance of the Constitution, transferring to the Executive Power the appropriate reports in cases of an infraction
>
> (Segado 2001)

The next constitution, in 1851, came out of the first inclusive moment in Bolivia's constitutional history. It was written explicitly as a tool to build bridges between a new president who had led a populist insurrection and his opponents (Salamanca Trujillo 2005: 363, 365, 367). Consistently with our theory, this more inclusive moment led to more authority and more autonomy for the Supreme Court. First, and most importantly, the courts secured the power of judicial review for the first time (Bolivia 1851, Art. 82 ("the judicial power has exclusive authority to . . . apply this Constitution in preference to other laws")). According to Francisco Segado, an 1857 organic law formalized this article further recognizing the Supreme Court's (exclusive) power of abstract constitutional control (Segado 2001). Appointments rested in the hands of the two chambers of the legislature, and the powers of the Court were increased, with a more robust set of rights to go with the explicit grant of the powers of judicial review. However, as did so many of these early experiments, this constitutional period ended in a coup ten years later, and was replaced by a new constitution in 1861 that was simply meant to legitimize the new government (Salamanca Trujillo 2005: 367).

Again in keeping with our theory, the more restrictive process in 1861 led to a loss of autonomy and authority for the system of constitutional justice – appointment power returned to the executive and the set of rights was more limited than before. The new constitution authorized the courts to apply the constitution over any inconsistent laws, but immediately undermined this apparent strengthening of the Court's authority with a clause giving the Congress the power to interpret the constitution. Seven years later, an amendment took this a step further, including a modified clause saying, "*Only* Congress can resolve any doubts that might arise regarding the interpretation of the constitution" (Art. 85). In the end, it is clear that this dictatorial moment produced an exceptionally weak system of constitutional justice.

Indeed, an anecdote from the time recounts the dictator Melgarejo's disdain for either of these constitutional texts. As the story goes, the president was at a function with a number of legislators when one of them praised the new 1868 Constitution as an improvement over the 1861 text. The president is said to have replied, "The learned gentleman who just spoke, and all the honorable deputies here present, should know that I put the Constitution of 1861, which was very good, in this pocket (pointing to his left pants pocket), and I have already placed the law of 1868, which is better still according to these doctors, in my other pocket (pointing to his right pocket), and that no one governs in Bolivia but me!" (Alcides Argüedas, Obras Completas, pp. 943–4, cited in Salamanca Trujillo 2005: 377). Clearly, the formal weakness of the institutional arrangement for constitutional justice was matched by contempt for constitutionalism in practice.

The executive remained the dominant actor in the appointment process until ten years later, in 1871, when the dictator was overthrown and a more participatory political moment again led to a new text. As our constitutional governance theory would suggest, this new constitution expanded the coalition of control by giving the executive's nominating powers to the Council of State (itself named by two-thirds of the unicameral legislature) and approval powers to the Legislative Assembly. The newly empowered legislature, however, retained the exclusive power to interpret the constitution, thus limiting the Court's authority.

This model of ex ante control lasted only seven years, until Bolivia adopted the model it would follow for the next sixty years. In 1878, another coup led to a new constitution. The return to a bicameral legislature in 1878 provided the opportunity to give the Senate nominating authority and the House of Representatives approval powers (Arts. 60, 64, and 110). This appointment mechanism was ultimately replicated in the constitutions of 1880, 1938, 1945, 1947, 1961, and 1967. But the 1878 Constitution was the child of General Daza, who was blamed for the calamitous failure of the War of the Pacific, in which Bolivia lost access to the sea to Chile. Two years later, after Daza's removal from power, a constituent assembly with two dominant parties – Conservatives and Liberals – more preoccupied with limiting dictatorial power and enacting liberal values, crafted a new constitution (Salamanca Trujillo 2005, 395–422).

The 1880 text was based on the 1878 Constitution but included some significant changes to align it more with the liberal inclinations of newly empowered mining elites. It would last fifty-eight years, a record for Bolivia. Finally, in this text, the legislature abandoned its power of constitutional interpretation and explicitly gave the Court concentrated powers of judicial review. In addition, the 1880 Constitution expanded freedom of religion to permit other religions beyond Catholicism (Art. 2). In exchange, the newly empowered justices were to be kept under some control of the legislature by relatively short – ten-year – renewable terms (Art. 119). Although Salamanca (2005) claims that it is a sham to call this a new constitution, given how much it borrowed from the previous text, it enacted some noteworthy changes to the scope of authority of the system of constitutional justice. This expansion of judicial power responded to a more balanced distribution of power between Conservatives and Liberals within the OC, in the aftermath of a disastrous war and the overthrow of the dictator who led the country into war. The more inclusive OC set up the text for its noteworthy endurance over the succeeding fifty-eight years (cf., Elkins et al. 2009, finding that more inclusive constitutional moments lead to longer lasting constitutions).

After a long respite from constitution-making, another disastrous war led to the 1938 Constitution, which marked the arrival of social constitutionalism in Bolivia. As we saw in Guatemala and Argentina, the early mid-twentieth century was the moment for social constitutionalism in all these countries, albeit under often less than democratic circumstances. Similarly, in Bolivia, the 1938 Constitution is the product of a military regime. In this case, however, although in the context of a dictatorship, the Constituent Assembly included "interesting elements as much from the Right as from the Left, but above all from the Center" (Salamanca Trujillo 2005: 442), suggesting far greater pluralism than what we described in Guatemala or Argentina for the same period. In fact, Gargarella notes that this Convention, "for the first time, included representatives from the working class" (Gargarella 2013: 113). Consequently, the new text is marked by an increase in social provisions and the maintenance of a fairly high degree of judicial autonomy – the mechanisms of judicial control, unchanged from the preceding nineteenth-century constitution, exclude the executive.

The question is whether the new social rights were – as in Argentina 1949 and Guatemala 1945 – more a green light for the RC to intervene widely and deeply in society and the economy, or whether they marked the construction of a separate and more capacious sphere of constitutional justice. The greater pluralism and inclusiveness of the OC would suggest the latter, although the authoritarian context should temper this impulse.

The 1938 Constitution is clearly inspired by Mexico 1917. The new text nationalizes natural resources (Art. 107) and declares that the economy must respond primarily to social justice principles (Art. 106). It declares that all corporations operating within Bolivian territory are nationals of Bolivia and are subject to its laws and authorities (Art. 110). It sets up the state as the protector of capital and labor (Art. 121), providing for basic social protections (Arts. 122, 124, 130) and making it the basic mediator between workers and their employers (Art. 128). These provisions are roughly equivalent to the ones we saw in Perón's 1949 Constitution or Guatemala's 1945 Revolutionary Constitution.

Compared to earlier Bolivian constitutions, some greater scope for constitutional justice was apparent. For one thing, the Constitution maintains explicit provisions for judicial review and provides for direct and open access to the Supreme Court in cases alleging constitutional violations. Art. 143(10) preserves the Supreme Court's original jurisdiction over claims against "the resolutions of the Legislative Branch or one of its Chambers, when such resolutions affect one or more concrete rights . . ." Moreover, for the first time in the history of this majority indigenous country, the constitution acknowledges and gives explicit rights to indigenous communities (Arts. 165–7). We can find the rights to education (Art. 154) and health (at least for workers and children) in this document (Arts. 124, 134). Also, unlike in Argentina 1949, the rights to unionize and to strike are protected (Arts. 12–6). Some expansion of the scope of constitutional justice is, therefore, evident in the text, although we still do not see some of the features that truly popularize constitutional justice, such as the amparo or tutela.

The significance of this text was marred by the almost immediate self-anointing of Germán Busch as sole dictator of Bolivia, and his suicide two years later. But in contrast to the other experiments in social constitutionalism that we have seen, this one lasted for decades, with a relatively minor deepening of the model in 1945, and some essentially irrelevant (for purposes of constitutional justice) changes in the texts of 1946 and 1961. This social constitution was ample enough to accommodate even the nationalist socialism of the National Revolutionary Movement (MNR for its initials in Spanish), which took power in 1952. Even in Bolivia, with its history of replacing constitutions every few years, this revolutionary government did not feel the need to draft a new national compact, although it formalized some of its nationalist policies in the 1961 Constitution.

The revolutionary period ended with the 1967 Constitution, which was crafted by an inclusive Assembly with the goal of easing a transition back to democracy. The increasingly democratic nature of the 1967 Assembly, in comparison to previous ones, explains the strengthening of authority in the sphere of constitutional justice in 1967. The new constitution included an expanded habeas corpus provision (Art. 18) and an article adding a robust version of the amparo to the Bolivian constitutional repertoire (Art. 19), while preserving the Court's centralized powers of abstract review (Art. 127 (5), (10)).

But the most significant increase in the autonomy of the constitutional justice system happened in 1994 under Gonzalo Sánchez de Lozada. Bolivia 1994 is technically not a new constitution but rather an extensive amendment to the 1967 Constitution. This text, however, produced the first system of constitutional justice designed in a democratic moment in the history of Bolivia. As we would expect

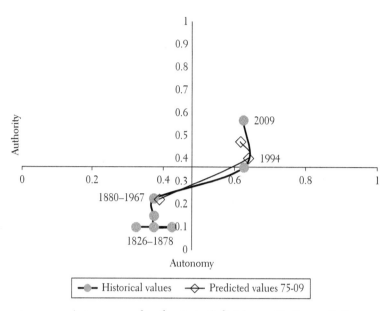

FIGURE 7.1. Autonomy and authority in Bolivia's constitutions, 1826–2009

with a more inclusive design coalition, the new text maintained the already high level of ex post autonomy, and added considerable ex ante autonomy. At the same time, Bolivia 1994, drafted in the midst of a neoliberal reform effort, described a system of constitutional justice with a quite narrowly circumscribed scope of authority for the time and the country. This is especially true in comparison to others that were being drafted at this time, such as Brazil 1988, Colombia 1991, or Argentina 1994, and even more so in light of Bolivia's long and uninterrupted history of social constitutions.

The pattern matches the results of our quantitative analysis – a more inclusive OC leads to high levels of autonomy, but if it leans to the Right, it will maintain a preference for low levels of authority, even if fragmented. In fact, as those results suggest, on the authority dimension the preferences of this inclusive but Right-leaning OC match almost perfectly those of the less inclusive Left-leaning OC that designed Bolivia 1967, with a slight bump upward for the passage of time. On autonomy, on the other hand, the more inclusive design coalition expressed a preference for a great deal more ex ante autonomy, while keeping ex post autonomy high. Figure 7.1 shows the design of the various systems of constitutional justice observed in Bolivia from its independence to 2009, and the predicted values from our analysis in Chapter 3 from 1975 forward.

The institutional vehicle for these important changes in constitutional justice was a new standalone Constitutional Tribunal. The new Tribunal would sit in Sucre and be composed of five justices. Justices were appointed by both houses of

Congress in a joint session, by two-thirds of the members present, from lists of nom-inees prepared by a Judicial Council. Once again, the executive was excluded from the appointment process, but now an outside body intervened in the selection and legislative minorities had a voice in the appointment. The justices served ten-year terms, and could be reappointed, but only after another ten years had passed from the expiration of their last appointment. The impeachment process remained very stringent, requiring a two-thirds vote in the Senate to convict, upon an accusation by the lower house.

At the same time, the court's scope of authority was expanded, but not dra-matically for the period. The constitution explicitly prescribes that a declaration that a law is unconstitutional is binding on everyone, and will render the law inapplicable (Art. 121). As in Brazil 1988 or Colombia 1991, the designers gave the Court both abstract and concrete powers of review. However, the Bolivian designers gave only the president, a senator, a deputy, the attorney general, or the national Ombudsman standing to bring abstract claims (Art. 120). Amparo, for expedited concrete claims, and the rights provisions that underpinned amparo, were essentially unchanged, although they had the potential to become more effective, as they were paired with a stronger court. As we might expect from a Right-leaning OC, the constitution did not include the full panoply of justicia-ble economic, social, and cultural rights, although it did have a complete set of civil and political rights. As one observer notes, "without doubt, the creation of the Constitutional Tribunal was one of the most positive aspects of the [1994] Bolivian constitutional reform . . . as proven by the subsequent practice of the new Bolivian constitutional organ" (Prado 2001: 339).

The 1994 Constitutional Tribunal, however, ended its existence as a crippled institution, unable to decide anything for lack of a quorum, when outgoing justices were not replaced. Nor did it lack critics. For supporters of the MAS, the problem was that appointing justices by a two-thirds vote of the legislature gave too much power to the political parties in the legislature, which were collectively perceived as being too neoliberal. Sergio Paz, an indigenous lawyer who was instrumental in the design of the electoral regime for the 2009 Constitutional Tribunal, argued, "That tribunal that was selected by two thirds of the legislature . . . in reality did not protect the interests of the state because it came out of a neoliberal model . . . That Tribunal only represented the neoliberal class."[2] Note, of course, that his comments implic-itly acknowledge our claim that the Court, in an important sense, "represents" and responds to its Constitutional Governance Coalition.

In a return to nineteenth-century patterns of instability, new amendments followed only ten years later, in 2004, in response to significant mobilization

---

[2] Author interview Sergio Paz, June 26, 2014, La Paz, Bolivia.

and unrest among the highland indigenous population. On the one hand, these amendments made very slight modifications to the system of constitutional justice. Bolivia retained its Constitutional Tribunal essentially unchanged. It added a provision for habeas data (Art. 23), giving citizens the right to secure access to information about them, added gender-neutral language in certain provisions (e.g., Art. 38, on acquisition of citizenship by marriage), and in the most significant concessions to the protesters, included political rights for indigenous groups (e.g., Arts. 61 and 223) and added mechanisms of direct democracy (Mayorga Ugarte 2006). On the other hand, the main goal of the reform was to require a Constituent Assembly for a complete rewrite of the constitution (Art. 232), to complement the existing partial reform provisions. This provision laid the foundation for the process that would take Bolivia to its current constitution and created some of the conditions that would give the opposition some leverage in the constitution drafting process.

The inclusion of Arts. 231 and 232 in Bolivia 2004 was driven by the expectation that, one way or another, the country would be drafting a new constitution, under pressure from the movement Evo Morales was leading (see, e.g., the discussion in Salamanca Trujillo 2005: 618–27). At the time, the well-known political scientist and constitutional scholar Jorge Lazarte wrote in an editorial, "Today all roads lead to a Constituent Assembly . . . this is an already inevitable process in light of October's events" (Salamanca 2005: 626 [quoting Jorge Lazarte editorial dated April 1, 2004]). Article 232 was an attempt to impose some constraints on the making of a new constitution, in order to make the expected constituent process less purely majoritarian. It gave exclusive authority to draft a new constitution to a Constituent Assembly, which had to be summoned in a "Special Law," which would also detail the electoral process for the Assembly. Crucially, this law had to be approved by two-thirds of the members of Congress present at the time of the vote, and was not subject to a presidential veto. In effect, this amendment – passed even as Evo Morales and his party, the MAS, gained in strength – was meant to allow the opposition to set conditions in exchange for summoning a constituent assembly, setting the stage for the construction of the current system of constitutional justice in Bolivia.

7.2. CONSTITUTIONAL GOVERNANCE AND
THE DESIGN OF BOLIVIA 2009

7.2.1. *The Originating Coalition*

As expected, Morales was elected president in 2005, and, again as expected, made a new constitution one of his first priorities once he took office in 2006. Following the path blazed by Chávez in Venezuela, as we will see in final section of this chapter, the summoning law, Act 3364,[3] was passed in March, a scant two months after Morales' inauguration. In contrast to Venezuela, where the electoral arrangement was meant to maximize the RC's influence, this enabling law reflected the opposition's self-protective impulse. Indeed, the political process leading to the Constituent Assembly, with its roots in the constitutional amendment of 2004, perfectly tracks with the logic we have laid out for constitutions in this text. We argue that design coalitions will seek to create the conditions that will give them influence in future constitutional decision-making instances. That is effectively what happened here: the drafters of the 2004 amendments required a two-thirds majority to pass a law calling for the Assembly, to ensure that they would have some say in the process. Then they used that supermajoritarian rule to require a two-thirds decision rule within the Assembly, so that they would be assured of a voice in the drafting of the new constitution.

The special law summoning the Assembly called for a large number of members – 255 – and went to great lengths to ensure extensive representation for the opposition. Two hundred and ten constituents would be elected from the existing electoral districts, three per district, two for the majority and one for the first minority. The forty-five remaining constituents would be elected at the departmental level, five for each department, with two seats going to the first majority, and one each to the second through fourth parties. In effect, no more than 158 members – roughly 62 percent, nearly five points short of a two-thirds majority, not coincidentally – could belong to the majority party, even in the unlikely event that that party won a straight majority in all the districts and departments of the country. To complement the electoral arrangement, the law provided that the new constitutional text had to be approved by two-thirds of the Constituent Assembly.[4] Between this decision rule

---

[3]   In pertinent part, the law provided as follows:

> Artículo 14°.- (Elección de Constituyentes)
>   210 Constituyentes serán elegidos en las 70 suscripciones aprobadas por la Corte Nacional Electoral para la última elección nacional. Tres de cada una de las circunscripciones, dos por primera mayoría y uno por segunda mayoría.
>   45 Constituyentes serán elegidos cinco por cada circunscripción plurinominal departamental e la siguiente forma:
>
> – Dos constituyentes para la mayoría,
> – Un Constituyente para la segunda fuerza,
> – Un Constituyente para la tercera fuerza y
> – Un Constituyente para la cuarta fuerza
>
> En caso de que la tercera y/o cuarta fuerza no obtengan un porcentaje igual o mayor al 5% de los votos validos los Constituyentes restantes se repartirán entre las dos primeras fuerzas de acuerdo al residuo mayor que éstas obtengan.
>   Bolivia, Ley especial de convocatoria a la Asamblea Constituyente, 6 de marzo de 2006, Acto 3364.

[4]   Bolivia, Ley especial de convocatoria a la Asamblea Constituyente, 6 de marzo de 2006, Act 3364, "Artículo 25°.- (Aprobación del Texto Constitucional) La Asamblea Constituyente aprobará el texto

and the electoral design, the summoning law effectively guaranteed the opposition a veto over any resulting text.

At least at the outset, the law had its intended effect. The members of the Assembly represented a wide variety of both political parties and nontraditional *campesino* and indigenous organizations and social movements[5] (Buitrago 2007). The MAS had a majority, with 137 delegates (plus four members who were elected on the Movimiento Bolivia Libre list, as an electoral strategy) (Gamboa Rocabado 2009: 494; Schavelzon 2012: 147–8), but far short of the supermajority needed to work unilaterally. The largest opposition party, and the second largest force in the Assembly, was PODEMOS, with sixty seats (Gamboa Rocabado 2009: 494). Although some complained that the process ultimately excluded the social movements that had pushed for a new constitution to begin with (Schavelzon 2012: 145–6), the MAS legitimated this proceeding through a survey that showed that many constituents self-identified as indigenous (see also de la Fuente Jeria 2010). The OC for Bolivia 2009, therefore, was meant to be quite inclusive, although with the very strong presence of the MAS, which would dominate procedural decisions and committee appointments (Gamboa Rocabado 2009: 496).

In Argentina 1994 and Guatemala 1985, this combination of pluralism and minority vetoes led to a cooperative, deliberative environment and a consensual document. In Bolivia, on the other hand, the combination soon led to dramatic polarization and deadlock within the Assembly and astonishing levels of social conflict around it.

The MAS and PODEMOS, its main opposition, lost the first half year to endless debates about the two-thirds decision rule, which was supposed to be settled already, as the MAS claimed that PODEMOS's obstructionism justified moving to a simple majoritarian decision rule (see, e.g., de la Fuente Jeria 2010: 19, alluding to the "blackmail of the two-thirds"). Ultimately, the Assembly allowed for two ways to secure approval of the final text.[6] The initial proposal would be approved in principle

---

de la nueva Constitución con dos tercios de votos de los miembros presentes de la Asamblea, en concordancia con lo establecido por Título II de la Parte IV de la actual Constitución Política del Estado."

[5] The traditional parties represented within the Assembly were the following: (1) Movimiento de Izquierda Revolucionario (MIR-NM), (2) el Movimiento Bolivia Libre (MBL), (3) La Alianza Poder Democrático (PODEMOS), (4) Unidad Nacional (UN), (5) Movimiento Nacionalista Revolucionario (MNR, MNR-A3 y MNR-FRI). Among non-traditional political parties we find (6) Movimiento al Socialismo (MAS), (6) Concertación Nacional (CN), and (7) Movimiento Originario Popular (MOP). Furthermore, other organizations from civil society were (8) Alianza Andrés Ibáñez (AAI), (9) Autonomía Para Bolivia (APB), (10) Alianza Socialista (AS), (11) Alianza Social Patriótica (ASP), (12) Movimiento AYRA, and (13) Movimiento Campesino San Felipe de Austria (MCSFA).

[6] It is unclear, in our view, whether the process described here is actually what the rule required, or whether this was a forced interpretation, adopted a year later by a Constituent Assembly crippled by polarization and deadlock. It is also unclear whether this procedure complies with the requirements of the special law summoning the Assembly. But this is the process that the Assembly ultimately followed.

(literally *"en grande"*) by two-thirds of those present – a sort of approval of the overall agenda and structure of the document. Then the wording of the final text had to be approved, clause-by-clause, *"en detalle,"* by two-thirds of those present. If all the clauses were approved by two-thirds of those present, then the entire text would go to an up-or-down vote for approval by two-thirds of the whole number. If, however, some of the initial clauses failed to reach two-thirds approval, then, at least according the interpretation finally adopted by the Assembly, the proposed alternatives would go to the people in a "deciding referendum," rather than back to the Constituent Assembly. In theory, then, the Assembly's internal rules mostly preserved the minority veto contemplated in the enabling law, despite often strenuous arguments by the majority that the Assembly was sovereign, not derivative of prior legislatures or constitutions, and could set its own rules. The rules did, however, contemplate the possibility of going to the people for a final decision if the Assembly failed to agree.

Outside the hall, the entire process, which lasted over a year, was marked by violence and social upheaval. Indigenous people suffered public beatings in cities controlled by the opposition, and large crowds of MAS supporters periodically forced the members of the Assembly to move under heavy guard, and even to flee on foot under cover of darkness from angry mobs that were breaking into the deliberative chamber. As the time neared to approve the text, the situation seemed more like a barely contained civil war than a constitutional debate. On the first day of the final debate, 180 people were wounded, two people died, and forty were arrested in clashes surrounding the Assembly (Schavelzon 2012: 336). On November 25, 2007, the day the Assembly members voted to approve the text *"en grande,"* they simply read the titles of the various sections out loud and voted to approve them en masse. The Assembly was literally under siege. The transcript of the reading and voting is dramatically punctuated by the delegates' expressions of concern that protesters had surrounded the Assembly, were about to invade it, were breaching the outside wall, and calls that it was not safe to remain even until nightfall (see also, Schavelzon 2012: 341, for a first-person account of the events). In the end, the protesters burned down the local police station and captured (and even physically abused) some members of the Assembly, while other members spoke of emigrating to other countries because they felt they could not safely return home (Schavelzon 2012: 345–6).

Inside the hall, the problem began with the fight over procedural rules, but it did not end there. Nearly all the Commissions issued majority and minority reports, rather than approving consensus proposals, and many were not even able to finalize their work, turning in either incomplete reports or nothing at all (Gamboa Rocabado 2009: 504). Further controversies erupted around such issues as the location of the capital and departmental autonomy. The debates were full of acrimony and name-calling. Jorge Lazarte, one of the members of the Constituent Assembly, recounted the difficult situation. First, he said, there was no plenary debate – ever, over any part of the constitution. Second, he went on, in the commissions "passion took the place of reason . . . We mistook arguing for insults and wronging each other."[7] In some commissions, he claimed, the MAS split into two groups so they could control both the majority and the minority report.

The Assembly failed to finish its work within the allotted time, was granted an extension, and ultimately rushed into a vote on a final text as time ran out. Here is where the difference between two-thirds of those present and two-thirds of the whole came dramatically into play. As the process wound down in Oruro, where the Assembly was gathered, the opposition boycotted the proceedings – or was prevented by physical threats from participating in them (Schavelzon 2012: 362) –, so the majority forged ahead without it. The text was approved in principle with the votes of all the MAS-aligned constituents, thus easily reaching two-thirds of those attending, over the opposition of the four sole remaining opposition members (Schavelzon 2012: 362–71).

When it came time to approve the text "in detail," it was obvious that the MAS would not be able to muster a two-thirds majority of the full number of members. In order to bypass that requirement, the leadership quite openly manufactured a disagreement over an innocuous provision, so that all the provisions but one were approved by two-thirds of those present. Then it invoked its interpretation of the rules of procedure to argue, with a strange backward logic, that only if all the clauses were approved by two-thirds of those present would it be necessary to go to two-thirds of the whole for approval of the entire text. If one or more of the clauses failed to meet that threshold, they argued, the text could be sent directly to a popular referendum for approval by a simple majority of the population:

> Paragraph 1) of Article One of Law No.3728 of August 4, 2007, provides that "in the event that all the Articles are approved in detail by the vote of two-thirds of the members present, the final text of the new Political Constitution of the State shall be approved by the vote of two thirds of the total of all the members of the Constituent Assembly," a situation that is not applicable in this case because we have one article that was approved at the detail stage by less than two thirds of the members present at the Plenary, *therefore the approval of the final text of the new Political Constitution of the State does not require the approval of two-thirds of the total members of the Constituent Assembly.*
>
> Plenary Resolution of the Constituent Assembly, Oruro, December 9, 2007
> (quoted in Schavelzon 2012: 329; emphasis added)

René Mayorga, a well-known Bolivian political scientist who is a critic of the government, wrote at the time:

> Burning bridges, the MAS government has approved in principle, in an illegal and aberrant manner, its constitutional project. Locked inside a military installation, against a background of violent confrontation provoked by the government,

---

[7] Author interview Jorge Lazarte, June 27, 2014, La Paz, Bolivia.

with several dead and hundreds of wounded, without having read what they were approving, violating the rules of the constituent assembly itself, and transgressing constitutional principles, the MAS constituents played a sad hand-raising charade, submitting to the government's strategy of authoritarian imposition of a constitutional reform.

(Mayorga 2007)

Supporters, of course, received the news of final approval quite differently: "The rest was a celebration more from relief than happiness, since we knew in any event that the final word had not been spoken" (de la Fuente Jeria 2010: 26).

Outside observers suggest that the text finally approved by the remaining members of the Assembly was not even the one prepared in the committees but one prepared under cover of darkness by the MAS: "The constitutional text published between the end of December of 2007 and February of 2008 is in the end an apocryphal document, if compared with the original majority and minority reports prepared by the 21 commissions through July 2007" (Gamboa Rocabado 2009: 505–6). The extent to which this is true is virtually impossible to verify, since the only official record of the Constituent Assembly, the "Enciclopedia Constitucional" put together by the government after the Assembly concluded its work, does not include the copies of the various committee proposals.

Whether or not the MAS's conduct inside and outside the Assembly was quite as reprehensible – and whether the opposition was quite as blameless – as these observers might suggest, what is clear is that the text that came out of this Constituent Assembly did not reflect the debates and negotiations of the various opposing forces within it. In theory, the text had to be approved by two-thirds, and the opposition was a necessary member of the OC. In reality, however, the RC and its sympathizers unilaterally drafted the text that came out of the Assembly. According to our argument, *ceteris paribus*, such a process should produce a system of constitutional justice with limited authority, regardless of the ideology of the RC, and with sharply limited autonomy. The extremely low levels of ex post autonomy fit perfectly with this account. On ex ante autonomy and authority, however, as can be seen from Figure 7.1, the system that ultimately emerged is closer to the middle of the distribution. How did this happen?

As de la Fuente noted, the Constituent Assembly did not have the final word, and its design is not the one ultimately reflected in Bolivia 2009. Although she blames the opposition, Raquel Yrigoyen Fajardo argues that the final text was fundamentally negotiated outside the Assembly. The Bolivian constitutional process, she says, was "ensnared, . . . forcing [the government] to pact a text outside the assembly" (Santos 2010: 13). Before moving to set up the final plebiscite, the legislature approved an "interpretive" law giving itself the authority to modify the text approved in December, by a vote of two-thirds of the Congress, thus restoring the role of the minority in crafting the text. The government countered by bringing pressure to bear with massive demonstrations surrounding the Legislature, at times preventing the entry of opposition legislators altogether. Evo Morales personally led a march on the capital. Meanwhile, the opposition vowed to resist and prevent the plebiscite from taking place (Schavelzon 2012: 420–32).

In the end, a bargain between the government and the opposition permitted the Congress to approve amendments to 180 articles, nearly half of the 411 articles in the original text. Crucially for our argument, some of those amendments affected the design of the system of constitutional justice in exactly the way our theory would predict. The new text explicitly adds the full exercise of individual and collective rights and equality before the law to the definition of citizenship. It also adds the rights to housing, work, health, and education, and it strengthens the system of constitutional justice by restricting the role of indigenous justice in favor of constitutional principles, among other things (Schavelzon 2012: 486–92). As Lazarte somewhat begrudgingly put it, "The original constitution didn't have anything we wanted . . . [But in the aftermath,] the pact reincorporated some liberalism – they improved the constitutional text, although within the MAS's model."[8]

What does this late reincorporation of the opposition mean for the effective composition of the OC of Bolivia 2009? In Guatemala 1985 and Argentina 1994, the looming threat and recent memory of military intervention had led to a search for a broad-based elite pact that had given minority groups perhaps more influence than was warranted by their size and popular base. In Bolivia, in contrast, the mass mobilization outside the halls where the constitution was being negotiated minimized the influence of the minority. The dominant rhetorical call in Bolivia was not to build consensus, but to purge the foundational text of elite influence, and to turn it into an expression of the collective wisdom and demands of the people. This call was backed with often-violent mobilization to block the opposition from access to the deliberative spaces in which the new text might be discussed and a consensus built. The opposition was literally, physically, excluded from the debate at key moments; consequently, the initial text was drafted and approved without the participation of the opposition. And yet the final text, with the Congressional amendments, was negotiated with the opposition, and drafted and approved with minority participation.

Does this second step mean we should consider the opposition a full-fledged junior member of the OC? In the end, the opposition played a minor moderating role, but one that is less important than what their size, coupled with a two-thirds decision rule, would suggest. What gave the legislative contingent of the opposition some leverage was that the new text had to go to a plebiscite under a law approved by two-thirds of the Congress – although in this case, two-thirds of those voting would suffice. A series of strategies employed by the majority stole some of their leverage.

---

[8] Ibid.

The majority faction initially tried to exclude the opposition from this approval process altogether. As participants tell it, Álvaro García Linera, Morales' vice president, called the members of the opposition to a meeting in his offices in February, ostensibly to discuss the details of the law. At one point, he excused himself from the meeting, insisting that the rest carry on without him. García promptly went from the meeting to the floor of the Legislature, where he called for a vote on the referendum, easily securing the vote of two-thirds of those present for its approval, while the crowds that had declared a siege of the Congress prevented the opposition from re-entering the chamber (Schavelzon 2012: 386–7). Only the Electoral Court prevented this stratagem from working, forcing the matter back to the Congress and setting the stage for a more negotiated solution. Its intervention eventually led to the multiple amendments to the Assembly's text detailed above (Schavelzon 2012: 387).

However, at least according to Morales, García Linera, and their advisors, this was essentially what they had expected and planned for all along (Schavelzon 2012: 432). It is worth quoting García Linera's description of the process and its outcome in full:

> Faced with the need sooner or later to secure the approval of two-thirds of the mid-sectors of the Right, the Unity Pact designed a strategy that consisted in incorporating into the draft of the Constitution articles that were more radical than what was either necessary or historically sustainable, so we could later straighten out the drafting as far as the social movement might require and could sustain, securing that way the necessary agreements to unlock the approval by two thirds of the votes, whether in the Constituent or in the Congress.
>
> (quoted in Schavelzon 2012: 432)

He went on to say they made the necessary modifications to the text seated at the table under the watchful gaze of multiple international institutions, including the Organization of American States (OAS) and the United Nations (UN):

> As the hours wore on, the "enveloping strategy" produced its results. We were changing the text precisely where we had bent the rod in an intentionally exaggerated manner, so that we could "straighten" it in the negotiations as a concession that would add social and electoral support. *In the end the Constitutional text incorporated visions and minimal rights of other sectors of society, but we did it in such a way that they were articulated around a solid guiding constitutional framework, dominant, made up of the interests, rights and state project of the indigenous peasant worker and popular organizations.*
>
> (quoted in Schavelzon 2012: 432, n.367, emphasis added)

Save the triumphalist tone, this is exactly what Lazarte said in the interview quoted earlier: the post-Assembly pact incorporated concessions to the opposition's liberal preferences, but within the MAS's model. Santos (2010: 75) agrees that the final negotiations incorporated the concerns of the opposition, although he is less sanguine about this than García Linera, complaining that all the changes are in a "conservative" direction.

Precisely as we expect, then, adding new actors to the OC adds more interests and rights to the system of constitutional justice, expanding its scope of authority. This was true even in Bolivia, with its conflictual, intensely polarized, and nondeliberative Assembly process. In this case, however, the opposition – outplayed, weak, and under siege – likely managed to secure less than we might have expected from the formal rules and the de jure distribution of authority alone.

7.2.2. *The New System of Constitutional Justice*

Ultimately, the system of constitutional justice that was crafted by this fractious OC follows the logic of constitutional governance. In Chapters 5 and 6, we showed how the constituents in Guatemala and Argentina articulated core elements of the logic of constitutional governance in explaining and justifying the features of their constitutional proposals. In Bolivia, as well, the outcome largely reflects the predictions of our theoretical model, and key actors articulate the logic we have laid out: the system of constitutional justice is meant to protect threatened elements valued by members of the OC, and to be subjected to a dynamic system of governance under the influence of the successors to that coalition. However, as we have seen, the crucial architects of this system were not the constituents speaking in open debates, but rather the government's strategists and ideologues working behind the scenes. At best, the opposition was able to participate in closed negotiations leading toward the final text approved in the Congress.

Still, we can glean some clues from the record, revealing a vision of constitutional justice that matches our expectations, given the power dynamics of the founding moment. In this section, we analyze the features of the system to see whether they match our theoretical expectations given the power relations of the design process. On the scope of authority, we show that opponents retain the tools to constitutionalize the production of public policy on crucial issues, but that the majority's key goals are left to the discretion of the RC. On the autonomy dimensions, we see a system of constitutional justice that responds to popular majorities – justified by its proponents by the need to have constitutional justice reflect the wisdom of the people – tempered by the participation of legislative supermajorities in the vetting of candidates to the Constitutional Tribunal, and in an impeachment process with fairly low thresholds. Very short terms further allow majorities to keep the court close to its preferences.

The overall picture supports the notion that this system of constitutional justice was designed to serve the governance needs of the majority party, since that party played the dominant role in the bargaining process, as we have seen. At the same time, the opposition's veto power in the constitutional process (threatened by mass mobilization though it was), allowed it to negotiate a veto role in the appointment and removal of justices, and some basic security in the form of rights and robust mechanisms for rights protection, so that it too could participate in constitutional governance.

Scope of Authority. Based on its length, the number of clauses, and the number of new and uncommon topics covered, the conventional wisdom is that Bolivia 2009 is a vastly inflated constitutional text. The text is, in fact, remarkably prolix, with many declarations and statements regarding the nature of the state, society, and history, and multiple, individualized recognitions of the subordinate groups and interests that made up the majority coalition. As Fabián Yaksic (2010: 17), a Bolivian politician, said, "Our hearts [were] committed to the need to consolidate and deepen democratically this process of political, social, economic and cultural transformations that are required to build [the new] constitutional democracy." The constitutional task was seen as a transformative one, on all these multiple dimensions, and one that had to reach deep into the fabric of Bolivian society.

As a simple example, the article that specifies the official languages of Bolivia would, in an ordinary constitution, be quite short if it existed at all. Here, in contrast, it includes two subclauses and 134 words (in Spanish), as it runs through each of the language groups in the country and lays out five considerations to take into account in selecting a second departmental official language:

ARTICLE 5
I. The official languages of the State are Spanish and all the languages of the rural native indigenous nations and peoples, which are Aymara, Araona, Baure, Bésiro, Canichana, Cavineño, Cayubaba, Chácobo, Chimán, Ese Ejja, Guaraní, Guarasu'we, Guarayu, Itonama, Leco, Machajuyai-kallawaya, Machineri, Maropa, Mojeñotrinitario, Mojeño-ignaciano, Moré, Mosetén, Movima, Pacawara, Puquina, Quechua, Sirionó, Tacana, Tapiete, Toromona, Uruchipaya, Weenhayek, Yaminawa, Yuki, Yuracaré and Zamuco.

II. The Pluri-National Government and the departmental governments must use at least two official languages. One of them must be Spanish, and the other shall be determined taking into account the use, convenience, circumstances, necessities and preferences of the population as a whole or of the territory in question. The other autonomous governments must use the languages characteristic of their territory, and one of them must be Spanish.

Many of the provisions that make the constitution so long are oriented toward establishing mechanisms of participatory politics and separate governance regimes for indigenous communities. Others establish separate judicial regimes for agricultural and electoral matters, and several governance and monitoring institutions that are not present in most constitutions of the world. As a result, large portions of the text are devoted to allocating authority across multiple actors at different levels of government. It is entirely possible that this complex and detailed document will, in time, give rise to considerable constitutional litigation over the meaning and reach of its provisions. Still, despite the length of the document, the provisions that do constitute the system of constitutional justice are not, in the end, all that exceptional.

As noted in Chapter 2, the scope of authority of a system of constitutional justice depends on four different parameters: the number and type of issues that are entrusted to the court's jurisdiction; the ease and openness of access to the court; the ease with which the court can reach authoritative decisions; and its ability to issue broadly binding decisions. Read carefully, Bolivia 2009 marked increases on the first dimension – the most visible aspect of the new constitution – and perhaps a slight diminution on the second of our authority parameters over Bolivia 1994, while the other two parameters remain essentially unchanged from the previous text.

On access, authoritativeness, and decisiveness, most characteristics simply carried over intact or with slight curtailments from Bolivia 1994. Perhaps the most significant expansion of constitutional justice is the new Popular Action (*Acción Popular*, see Arts. 135–6), which protects collective rights and can be brought by individuals, civil society actors, or the national Ombuds office. In Argentina, as we saw, this protection of collective claims has led to some of the most significant assertions of authority by the courts over matters of broad public import. It seems an indication that the drafters intended to give collective actors – indigenous communities, popular and worker organizations, and NGOs – easy access to constitutional justice for their claims. As noted in the majority report for the commission that worked on this clause, "The popular action is a statement that in order to advance in the decolonization of justice, it is necessary to build a social and communitarian justice . . . and gives strength to . . . social organizations in the event judges engage in corruption or fail to carry out their work" (Enciclopedia Constituyente, Tomo III, Vol.1, p. 373).

With this exception, and the addition of a provision for privacy protections (Arts. 130–1), Bolivia 2009 mostly continues the pattern set in 1994. The court retains the ability to declare laws unconstitutional in concrete cases, with effects *erga omnes* (Art. 133); it also keeps the power of abstract review, both of which are broad powers. And yet access on abstract claims is more limited than before. In the new constitution, the Attorney General and the Ombudsman lose the ability to file abstract cases, so access is now limited to elected officials at different levels of government (the president, legislators, and the leaders of autonomous territories; Art. 202). Amparo remains the basic mechanism for vindicating concrete rights violations, but the new constitution limits the action by requiring any amparo claim to be filed within six months of the alleged violation (Art. 129, II). Habeas corpus remains prompt and easily filed with only a name change (to "Liberty Claim" – *Acción de Libertad*; Art. 125), but of course, habeas corpus actions are purely vehicles for the protection of personal freedom.

There is a new cause of action against government officials for failure to comply with constitutional or legal requirements (*Acción de Cumplimiento*; Art. 134), but if a failure to comply led to a constitutional violation, the same ends likely could have been reached under the authority specified in Bolivia 1994. In short, with the exception of the protection of collective rights, the changes, at best, produce no change in the system's scope of authority and, at worst, restrict access to the system to more majoritarian actors.

Where the constitution innovates is in the enumeration of rights beyond the standard canon. Here too, however, it is unique not because it includes elements that no other country has included, but because it includes more of them than most and describes them at greater length. It incorporates international human rights (Arts. 13, 14(3), 29(I)) but, as we have seen, so do several other constitutions in Latin America at this time. It incorporates basic civil and political rights, but so do all of the region's constitutions by this point. The set of social, economic, and cultural rights is more detailed, but only slightly more extensive than the norm. Basic social services like water and sanitation are declared "fundamental rights." Labor rights and collective bargaining rights are protected. People with disabilities have specific education and health rights. In a concession to the middle class, as in Argentina, consumers have strong protections. The constitution guarantees the rights to a healthy environment, health care, and education. Indeed, the provisions dealing with education alone run nearly 2,000 words long (in Spanish). For all their specificity and verbosity, these provisions likely do no more to empower constitutional oversight than similar, though more succinct, ones in Argentina 1994, as their similar scores on our scope of authority measure suggest. Finally, the Constitutional Tribunal lacks any of the ancillary powers that other courts in the region have been accruing.

In sum, the final score on scope of authority – well above the regional mean for the entire period but not at the very top of the scale – seems justified, even though the word count of the overall text might suggest an even more expansive scope. There are lots of rights, but the provisions for access and decisiveness are similar to – or more restricted than – those in, for example, Argentina.

There may be one way, however, in which our coding fails to capture some of the relevant features of this "new constitutionalist" system of constitutional justice. The politics of Bolivia in the aftermath of the 2009 Constitution are powerfully marked by the idea of "decolonization," a concept that is also found in the constitution, as we saw in the context of the Popular Action. Like the "social function" of property in the past, decolonization is a highly visible rhetorical signifier for the extent to which this new constitutional pact was meant to upset the existing legal and political order, and to unseat former elites. The question is whether this constitutional imperative should be coded to give Bolivia 2009 a higher score for the scope of authority, or whether we should treat this imperative as we treated the social function of property in the last social constitutionalism, as something that is more aimed at empowering the RC than at structuring constitutional justice. Does such an open-ended concept increase the scope of authority of constitutional justice, or does it limit it, by giving the RC ample leeway to act without effective constitutional oversight?

It seems clear that, in the hands of an ambitious court, the constitutional mandate to "decolonize" could easily become part of the sphere of constitutional justice. According to Jorge Lazarte, the concept gives the RC strong tools with very few inherent limitations: "Decolonization means everything and nothing. It's a political weapon. If it means anything, it is to tear down everything that comes from the past."[9] But the current Constitutional Tribunal states that its mission is "to ensure respect for and observance of constitutional rights and guarantees, within a framework of plural and decolonizing justice . . ."[10] Given the current politics of constitutional governance, and as we would expect from a court that acts as a regime ally, the Constitutional Tribunal could very well use decolonization as a powerful constitutional tool to legitimize the government's actions, as the latter dismantles many elements of the existing legal order. With a different politics of constitutional governance, of course, it is not inconceivable that the Tribunal might also begin to find limits to what can be done in the name of decolonization.

In the end we decided, with some misgivings, to treat decolonization as a principle that is more relevant to ordinary politics than to constitutional justice. On the one hand, the impetus for decolonization will have to come from the RC, not litigants or the court. It has emerged powerfully in debates about educational reforms and curricula, for instance. And on the other hand, any limits the court may eventually find will have to come from elements of the constitution we have already included in our coding: due process, property rights protections, and so on. Whether we are right or wrong will be revealed in coming years as the court either actively incorporates this idea into its interpretive principles, or simply steps aside, giving the RC freedom to follow decolonization wherever it might lead. While it is hard to know exactly how this concept should affect the scope of authority of the system of constitutional justice, it serves as a useful reminder that rights are not the only constitutional weapons in a court's or a government's arsenal.

As with decolonization, Bolivia 2009's reputation for expansive constitutionalism is likely due more to the multiplication of spaces for ordinary politics than to the expansion of the sphere of constitutional justice. Schilling-Vacaflor (2011: 4), for instance, highlights the "new spaces for participation and social control at all state levels in Bolivia," as much as the inclusion of social and economic rights in the new constitution. For its supporters, the innovation in Bolivia 2009 resides not in a more expansive Western-style constitutional or human rights justice system, but rather in its embrace of plurinationalism and direct, participatory democracy, in the recognition and inclusion of previously marginalized indigenous populations, and in the postliberal, postcapitalist, anticolonial impulse the new constitution

---

[9] Ibid.
[10] www.tcpbolivia.bo/tcp/content/misi%C3%B3n-y-visi%C3%B3n-del-tribunal-constitucional-plurinacional.

embodies (Santos 2010). These results, tending more toward an unfettered RC than to a strongly countermajoritarian constitutional justice system, are entirely consistent with the power dynamics of the constitutional design process we have described in this chapter.

Ex ante autonomy. The guiding principle in designing the system of ex ante control was to wrest control over the court from the old elites and return it to the people. In a clear break with global and regional patterns, under the new constitution the justices of the Constitutional Court (as well as the Supreme Court and various other lower courts) are selected in a nationwide popular vote (Arts. 198, 182). This is unique, as far as we know, in the civil law world today – although as we saw, the first high court judges in Guatemala were also elected. The idea to elect judges originated with the government, and close observers indicated well before the beginning of the chaotic constitution-making process that this, and presidential reelection, would be the two government proposals that would survive any compromise with the opposition (Schavelzon 2012: 152, quoting Samuel Doria Medina, one of the leaders of the Unidad Nacional Party and a prominent presidential candidate). Clearly, selecting justices by means of a popular election favors the electorally popular MAS faction over the more elite-based opposition, giving it control over the ultimate selection of justices for as long as it can maintain its electoral advantage, and shifting power indefinitely away from the urban elites the MAS opposed.

As noted above, this purely majoritarian system is tempered by the requirement that candidates for the positions must secure the two-thirds approval of the legislature in order to get on the ballot. In fact, the preapproval provision gives the legislature a voice in the process, while (formally) the President does not participate directly at all, at any stage. Most importantly, however, it gives the opposition a veto over the slate of potential candidates, although not control over the initial identification of candidates. This arrangement, as we would expect, mirrors the power relationship between the majority and the opposition in the negotiations toward the final constitution – the opposition had little power of initiative, but it did retain a veto of sorts over the process.

Ex post autonomy. To further tie the court to contemporary politics, the justices serve only single, six-year nonrenewable terms. Impeachment – by accusation of the lower house and conviction upon a two-thirds vote of the Senate – would almost necessarily require the assent of the opposition. But impeachment is a costly and unnecessary process when justices are unlikely ever to be far from stepping down by the time they come under fire. Changes in the preferences of the majority, or displeasure with an overly contestatory court, could fairly quickly be reflected in the election of new justices. In fact, presidents, who are allowed two consecutive five-year terms, are likely to serve longer than their constitutional court judges. This court, consequently, has one of the lowest scores on ex post autonomy of any court crafted recently.

7.2.3. *Bolivia 2009's Design and the Logic of Constitutional Governance*

The choice of a radically different appointment mechanism, such as the election of judges, might challenge the two central prongs of our argument, which assumes these choices spring from a more or less universal logic of constitutional governance. If we are right, we must find two things, regardless of ideology. First, we must find that designers understand that constitutional justice is a mechanism for the dynamic, ongoing production of constitutional meaning, and that one of the ways to participate in the production of constitutional meaning is through the appointment of justices. Second, as a result, we must find that actors who have a veto over the production of the original design will also insist on having some influence over the production of constitutional meaning by securing a role in the mechanisms of control, including appointments.

The evidence, in fact, suggests that this governance logic was at work in Bolivia as well. In explaining why the Constitutional Tribunal magistrates should be elected, Sergio Paz, a government lawyer who worked on the court's electoral law, articulated a version of our dynamic constitutional governance logic: "The demand was that the magistrates must be appointed by the people, so they would respond to the people, because they ought to protect the interests of the state."[11] The point was not to lock in constitutional meaning and then insulate the court from any pressures but to devise a mechanism that gave the people the preeminent voice in the ongoing production of constitutional meaning.

In particular, it was important to prevent the court from representing the interests of the region known as the crescent moon (*medialuna*), which had been a hotbed of opposition to Morales and the MAS: "If we did [the election of justices] by department we ran a risk. We are nine departments, and the *medialuna* are four. What happens if we end up with five magistrates against four? We lose already ... The election had to be in a single national jurisdiction."[12] Although they considered a series of different electoral systems that would have allowed for the representation of oppositional minorities on the court – justices could be chosen by circumscription, by region, by department, and so on – they concluded, in the end, that the magistrates should reflect "the census," so that the "interests [of the neoliberal *medialuna*] may not enter again, as it happened with the justice before, with the Constitutional Tribunal [that began work in] 1998." As opposition Constituent Assembly member Jorge Lazarte put it, "The central idea was that justice had to be at the service of the people, not the oligarchy. So much so that the saying was, 'Justice springs from the people and is at the service of the people'."[13] In this view, constitutional justice had to be majoritarian.

---

[11] Author interview Sergio Paz, June 26, La Paz, Bolivia.
[12] Ibid.
[13] Author interview Jorge Lazarte, June 27, 2014, La Paz, Bolivia. "Pero la idea central era que la justicia tenía que estar al servicio del pueblo y no al servicio de las oligarquías. Tanto que se decía 'la justicia emana del pueblo y está al servicio del pueblo'."

This close identification of constitutional justice with the people's wisdom and interests goes hand in hand with the logic of governance. Lazarte, for example, argues that, on the one hand, the people thought this crucial mechanism would produce a court that served its interests and not those of the elites. On the other hand, he goes on to say, the government understood that it could count on elections to produce friendly justices: "They [the majority in the Constituent Assembly] said, 'since we're the majority in the country, we will end up choosing the candidates.' . . . The aspirations of the people to not have a justice that is at the service of those on top dovetailed with the desire of those at the top to have direct control over justice, without being accused of controlling the judges."[14] In short, the election of Constitutional Tribunal magistrates was meant to ensure that these justices would respond to and articulate the wishes of the majority, as understood by the ruling party and its elected representatives, while preserving their democratic legitimacy.

These – and arguments for giving the court more authority – were exactly the issues that divided the Commission that worked on justice system issues. The Commission had ten members, only three of whom belonged to the opposition (two to PODEMOS and one to MNR); six belonged to the MAS and one to the MBL. The opposition wanted a method like the one already in place – selection by two-thirds of the legislature – while the government faction wanted elections, which could produce majoritarian justice (Enciclopedia Constituyente, Tomo III, Vol. 1, p. 744). Elections ultimately prevailed.

The purpose of such a system of constitutional justice – one that principally reflects the will of the majority in the production of constitutional meaning – is not obvious. Why have a Constitutional Tribunal at all, if it is going to do no more than reflect what the RC might have done on its own? The existing one had been allowed by the government to languish into virtual extinction, by failing to appoint replacement justices until the court was down to a single member, without a quorum to decide anything. The MAS and Morales could have simply decided to continue doing without the Tribunal altogether. The existence of a separate constitutional court was, in part, simply a continuation of the existing arrangement in response to what Lazarte calls the "international cooperation" (the various international donors and experts) who pushed for it. As Lazarte recounts, the international experts said, "You need a Constitutional Tribunal because otherwise you can't call what you're doing there in Bolivia a democracy."[15] As noted earlier, international actors were present during this new constitutional process, so it is likely that the Tribunal survived, as a marker to outside audiences, to symbolize the commitment to democracy.

But of course the devil is in the details – and the details of the Tribunal respond to the logic of constitutional governance. According to Lazarte, the current system, which has power but no autonomy, is helpful to the government because it can

---

[14] Author interview Jorge Lazarte, June 27, 2014, La Paz, Bolivia.
[15] Ibid.

legitimize the decisions that the majority takes and can modify the law in its favor, eliminating legal-constitutional obstacles to the government's agenda.[16] Moreover, Lazarte finds the behavior of the new court sharply undemocratic: "I think this idea of a system of justice that is at the service of the people is a populist idea, that in the end is connected to a despotic vision of power. It appeals to the people, . . . and it ends up being an instrument of power."[17] The judiciary is sufficiently at the service of the RC, he says, that rather than using physical force, in Bolivia the government now represses the opposition using the judiciary as a tool.[18] Far from a check on the majority, this court, in its actual behavior, acts as a Regime Ally, one of the possible outcomes of a system for ongoing constitutional governance identified in Chapter 2. It is an instrument for legitimating and advancing the project of the dominant majority. As we will see shortly, the court designed in Venezuela in 1999, which has fewer constraints, carries this impulse to the extreme.

Does this strongly majoritarian system of appointments and moderately high level of authority contradict our expectations for the politics of design, given the opposition's veto power in Bolivia's constituent process? Or does the two-thirds vote in the preselection of candidates restore some balance, as we would expect from our theory?

Our relatively high autonomy score for the system, which we have just described in fairly negative terms, is based on the intervention of two collective actors that go beyond legislative majorities – a two-thirds vote giving the opposition veto power over the pre-selection of candidates and a final, decisive intervention by an outside actor (the electorate, in this case). As an institutional arrangement, this seems like a fairly robust way of ensuring that no single actor or interest, like the executive or a legislative majority, can capture the court. It is certainly more robust than the system in the United States, which is controlled by the executive and a simple majority of the Senate. Critics like Lazarte, however, charge that the checks do not work. The government – President Evo Morales, to be precise – controls the legislature and thus the preselection process. The electorate is merely a stand-in for the government, which can win elections with some ease. If this is true, then our coding counts nonexistent veto players and overstates the court's ex ante autonomy.

In fact, while this is partly true, it is not a contradiction of either our coding or our argument about the politics of constitutional design. First, it is only partly true because, in spite of the many criticisms it has earned, the system does introduce a series of intermediaries between what the executive wants and what it gets, making it somewhat harder for the president to closely control the preferences

---

[16] Lest we think this is a particular pathology of the Bolivian system, this argument finds clear echoes in the political science literature on the United States, which has a similarly majoritarian system of judicial appointments (see, e.g., Dahl 1957; Graber 1993; Whittington 2005).

[17] Author interview Jorge Lazarte, June 27, 2014, La Paz, Bolivia.

[18] Ibid.

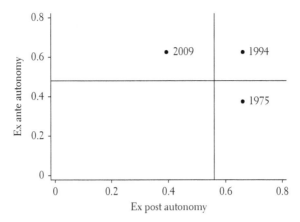

FIGURE 7.2. Ex ante and ex post autonomy of constitutional justice in Bolivia since 1975

of the justices on the tribunal. In fact, even Lazarte acknowledges that the government has had some trouble with the initial set of justices on the Plurinational Constitutional Tribunal, who have defied it on occasion.[19] Supporters of the Government also note that the Tribunal issued some rulings that ran against what "the people" wanted on issues that were important parts of the government's anti-corruption agenda.[20] And an organized and aware opposition should be able to negotiate some concessions in exchange for approving the slate of candidates. In sum, the process introduces some distance between the RC's preferences and the resulting composition of the Tribunal.

Moreover, we have argued for a three dimensional analysis of the system of constitutional justice and, as we have seen in this case, the very low level of ex post autonomy ties the court closely to the politics of the day. To put this in context, according to our measure, political control over the court in Bolivia since 1975 (actually, since 1967, when the constitution in force at the beginning of our coding was drafted) has shifted across three quadrants – from a court with vulnerable appointments but strong ex post protections, to a court that was insulated both ex ante and ex post in 1994, to the current court, with high ex ante autonomy and very low ex post autonomy (Figure 7.2). Only Bolivia 1994 scores high for both ex ante and ex post autonomy. Before and after the 1994 Constitution, the court is vulnerable, either ex ante or ex post. The low levels of ex post autonomy in Bolivia 2009 clearly reflect the weakness of the opposition in the design process.

Finally, on a more conceptual level, we have emphasized throughout that this project is not about judicial behavior but about the design choices that constitutional designers make. It may be that the minority veto is currently too weak to give the

[19] Ibid.
[20] Author interview Sergio Paz, June 26, 2014, La Paz, Bolivia.

opposition a meaningful voice in the politics of judicial selection, but this is, to some extent, beside the point. Our theory predicts that the minority voices in the OC will seek a voice in ex ante control, not that they will secure a dominant voice, or even that the role they have negotiated will prove effective. And we have seen that, for a number of reasons, the Bolivian opposition in 2008 and 2009 had a weak veto at best, given the mass mobilization and conflict that surrounded the Constituent Assembly and its aftermath. As a result, it should not surprise us that they secured a weak veto, at best, in the process of judicial selection – a veto that may nevertheless prove sufficient to improve the court's autonomy, once their electoral fortunes improve.

We have argued that the actual outcome matches what we would expect from a governance logic. The remaining, secondary, question is whether the weaknesses we have discussed match the opposition's real weakness in the constituent process better than they match our relatively high score for ex ante autonomy, so that our coding scheme is not up to the task of accurately scoring Bolivia's unusual design. The fact that the government can capture the process is no objection to our scoring; it is, of course, true that no institutional arrangement is immune from its political context. It seems likely, for instance, that the current system would produce greater autonomy if the opposition gained some electoral support. Again, our coding scheme simply measures the veto points that are introduced into the process. More veto points should make it harder for any one party to control the court, but if one party can capture all those veto points, the result will be a controlled court.

In summary, the design of the system of ex ante control seems moderately strong, but has to some extent failed because of the current political context in Bolivia. The opposition's formal veto power in the process of design is reflected in a formal veto of the candidates to the court. Their influence was, however, weakened by the political context of the constituent moment, and that weakness is reflected both in the relatively majoritarian process of selection and in the low levels of ex post autonomy. The court's scope of authority is moderately high, partly in response to the opposition's increased leverage in the final moments of the constituent process, but remains underexercised, given the court's current lack of effective autonomy. Overall, our autonomy and authority scores seem warranted, and both the unusually conflict-ridden process and the unorthodox design continue to reflect the logic of constitutional governance.

7.3. OTHER CONSTITUTIONS WITH SIMILAR FEATURES

The Bolivian Constitution is often mentioned in the same breath with the Venezuelan and Ecuadorean Constitutions, which are assumed to be driven by a similar Bolivarian socialist ideology (Couso 2013). As a result, it may be useful at the conclusion of this chapter to see whether the similarities (and differences) among them are driven by ideology, or by something more like the governance logic that we defend in this book.

Venezuela, more than Ecuador, presents an extreme case of a design moment controlled by the RC.[21] Whereas in Bolivia, the very decision to call for a Constituent Assembly required compromise and allowed the opposition ultimately to set some of the terms of the debate, in Venezuela, the process was unilateral from the very beginning. After Hugo Chávez was elected president in 1998, he made a new constitution one of his first priorities. Famously, in his oath of office he vowed "upon this dying constitution"[22] to replace it with a new constitution. According to *The New York Times*, Chávez said, "The Constitution, and with it the ill-fated political system to which it gave birth 40 years ago, has to die. It is going to die, Sirs! Accept it!"[23]

True to his word, only a couple of weeks after taking office he issued Decree No. 3 calling for a constituent assembly.[24] As Martínez Dalmau (2004: 31), a Chávez supporter who was himself involved in drafting the new constitution (Couso 2013), describes it, this extraordinary measure was needed precisely because the new RC did not have the requisite majority in the legislature to pursue the avenues to reform expressly contemplated in the existing constitution. The call sought to bypass explicit constitutional requirements for amendment by relying on two existing mechanisms: a referendum that was legally premised on Art. 4 of the 1961 constitution, which declares that "sovereignty resides in the people;" and the 1988 Law of Suffrage and Political Participation,[25] which allowed the President to call a popular referendum on matters "of special national transcendence" (Art. 181). Although the way in which the Assembly was called remains controversial, the Supreme Court at that time effectively validated the approach, albeit with some modifications (Martínez Dalmau 2004: 33; Brewer-Carías 2009: 480).

On April 25, 1999, Venezuela's people voted to approve the reform, and in July of that year, the members of the Assembly were elected. Using a seat allocation mechanism that was harshly criticized by the opposition, Chávez's supporters managed to secure more than 95 percent of the seats (125 out of 131), even though they won a bare majority of the popular vote. In contrast to Bolivia once again, the Constituent Assembly was free to declare its own rule of procedure ("*Estatuto de Funcionamiento*"), which it did on August 13, only ten days after the delegates were

---

[21] Ecuador follows a pattern quite similar to Venezuela's, but somewhat attenuated. The government faction won 70 percent of the seats in the Assembly in the former and 95 percent in the latter, for instance.

[22] "Juro delante de mi pueblo y sobre esta moribunda constitución . . ." El Tiempo, "Chávez Juró sobre Constitución Moribunda," February 3, 1999 (available at www.eltiempo.com/archivo/documento/MAM-875563).

[23] Krause, Clifford, "New President in Venezuela Proposes to Rewrite the Constitution" (February 4, 1999) www.nytimes.com/1999/02/04/world/new-president-in-venezuela-proposes-to-rewrite-the-constitution.html.

[24] Gaceta Oficial de la República de Venezuela, No. 36,634, February 2, 1999.

[25] Gaceta Oficial, 5233 Extraordinario, May 29, 1998.

sworn in.[26] Brewer Carías (2009: 485) identifies this moment as the "breakdown of constitutional order" as the Assembly declared itself the "depositary of the popular will and the expression of sovereignty with original [and therefore unconstrained, as opposed to derivative and thus regulated] power to transform the Venezuelan state." This was precisely the debate that the government lost in Bolivia. As a result, both the process and the results are significantly more unbalanced and unilateral than what took place in Bolivia, although as we have seen, the Bolivian opposition was gradually stripped of its influence during the constituent process itself.

The role of the courts in supervising the process also stands in sharp contrast to what happened in Bolivia and Argentina. In Bolivia, the courts were invoked with some frequency to protect the process – the rulings of the Electoral Tribunal were crucial in protecting the opposition's veto in the final steps in the process, and some of the constituents relied on amparo rulings to maintain their ability to participate. Jorge Lazarte, for instance, secured an amparo protecting his right to vote in the Assembly. In Argentina, the impartiality of the court was so much a prerequisite for entering into the process of reform that the negotiating elites even agreed to replace some of the justices, as described in that chapter. In Venezuela, on the other hand, the Constituent Assembly created a Commission of Judicial Emergency to control the judiciary, and promptly dissolved the Supreme Court, destroying whatever semblance of autonomous judicial oversight there might have been.[27] Chavez's supporters were essentially free to write whatever constitution they desired, subject to the relatively weak (for an electorally popular president) constraint of a referendum for approval.

It took four months from the time the delegates were elected until the text was approved. The entire process, from a plebiscite calling for the Assembly in April, to a plebiscite approving the final text in December, took a little less than eight months.

What system of constitutional justice did this unilateral process produce? From a constitutional governance perspective as we have laid it out, the outcome is surprising in terms of its scope of authority. Venezuela 1999 scores higher than any other constitution in terms of authority. This is contrary to our expectation that, when the RC dominates design, it will keep the sphere of constitutional justice spare, in order to rule unconstrained thereafter. The outcome in terms of autonomy is more predictable, since, as we would have expected, the system is well below the mean in ex ante autonomy, and scores relatively low in ex post autonomy. Combined, the results argue strongly for a multidimensional analysis of courts and judicial design. As we will see, we feel the decisions on scope of authority were strongly conditioned on prior decisions on autonomy.

---

[26]   Gaceta Oficial N° 36,764, August 13, 1999. The decree can be found here: www.juancandelario.com/
      archivo1999/1999/09/proceso-constituyente-decreto-que-regula-las-funciones-del-poder-legislativo.
[27]   In fact, the Assembly even dissolved the Legislature and assumed legislative functions itself (Brewer
      Carías 2009: 487–90).

More concretely, the system's scope of authority is inflated by a series of rights-friendly provisions. The text grants constitutional hierarchy to human rights treaties.[28] It creates a strong amparo mechanism, authorizing both diffuse (Art. 334) and concentrated (Art. 335) review of constitutionality, and giving the court's decisions binding authority over other authorities, including the other chambers of the Supreme Court (Art. 335). In fact, the Constitutional Chamber even has the power to emit advisory opinions upon the request of the President (Art. 214). Access is wide open, and amparo is strong.

In terms of autonomy, the court is fairly well insulated from ex post pressures – at least formally, although these rules have been extensively violated in practice (Inter-American Commission on Human Rights 2009). However, it has exceptionally low ex ante autonomy. It is composed of seven magistrates and their substitutes (Casal 2009: 507) for a term of twelve years (Art. 264). The appointment process is purely majoritarian and gives the executive strong agenda-setting power. A Committee of Judicial Nominations appointed by the legislature does a first selection of candidates. The candidates are then submitted to the Citizen Power, which is composed of executive appointees: the Ombudsman, the Attorney General, and the Controller (Art. 273). The Citizen Power chooses the final nominees and submits them to the National Assembly, which makes the final selection by a simple majority. The process gives the president and the legislative majority – which in 1999 was fully expected to be the Chavista movement for the indefinite future – tight vetting authority and the ability to appoint justices essentially at will. The system has been much criticized for producing a subservient court and contributing to the erosion of democracy in Venezuela (see, e.g., Brewer-Carías 2010, and his many other writings on this subject).

In short, our constitutional governance theory predicts quite well the low degree of autonomy we actually see in the Venezuelan case, but not the expansive scope of authority that the court was given in 1999. Why the anomaly? Our theory that dominant RCs will invest less in constitutional justice is premised on the idea that putting an issue into the sphere of constitutional justice exposes it to some constraints, however minimal, so RCs will avoid doing so if they can. It seems clear that in the Venezuelan case, Chávez was quite willing to invest his new court with considerable authority. At first blush, the result seems more consistent with a "manifesto" theory of constitution writing than with our constitutional governance theory. It may be that, because Chávez was unconstrained, he loaded up his text with all his rhetorical goals and made them fully part of the system of constitutional justice as a way to demonstrate his commitment to a new model of state and society.

---

[28] Human rights treaties "have a constitutional rank, and prevail over internal legislation, insofar as they contain provisions concerning the enjoyment and exercise of such rights that are more favorable than those established by this Constitution and the laws of the Republic, and shall be immediately and directly applied by the courts . . ." (Art. 23).

Although our explanation is somewhat tentative and post hoc, we disagree with this interpretation. We feel Chávez's design decisions might have been driven by a governance logic, albeit one that serves a slightly different governance purpose – as with "decolonization" in Bolivia, and as we have suggested in our description of a Regime Ally court, his goal may have been to craft an ally that would help him upend the existing legal order, which he felt was overly constraining.

The combination of low autonomy and high authority for the system of constitutional justice in the 1999 Constitution is perfectly suited if the goal is a radical reordering of existing legal arrangements. First, the court's low autonomy ensures that the court will be closely subject to government control, so that any constraint upon the RC issuing from the sphere of constitutional justice is likely to be slight at best. As designed, the court could be counted on to be friendly to the *chavista* revolutionary project. Second, and relatedly, a powerful court with jurisdiction to intervene broadly in many different arrangements could help dismantle the existing legal order and reshape it to his specifications in order to carry out his agenda. Chávez was about to upend existing property rights, restrict traditionally well-protected freedoms for the press and others, and disrupt longstanding institutional arrangements, such as the protections for the national oil company, civil service careers, and more. For that, a constitutional court that would not only not stand in his way, but actually promote his goals and clear away legal obstacles, would be very useful. As he swore when he took his oath of office, he needed a charter "adequate to the times," and he got exactly that: a charter that would assist in his revolutionary project (Brewer-Carías 2009).

Indeed, the fruits of this design decision are abundantly clear now that the *chavista* movement has lost the legislature. By the time this was written, the Constitutional Chamber had stripped the opposition of legislative powers and blocked their efforts to remove Chávez's successor, Nicolás Maduro, from office.[29] Especially in the eyes of the regime's critics, far from being an impartial arbiter of competing constitutional visions, the court has simply become an ally in the *chavista* governance project (Brewer-Carías 2007). In practice, then, the Bolivian and Venezuelan courts have ended up in roughly the same place – they are regime allies, primarily dedicated to advancing the government's projects through the mechanisms of constitutional justice. But the opposition's stronger role in the design of the former allows for some hope that, if the opposition should strengthen in Bolivia, the court might be pulled away from the government and begin to offer an alternative space to contest the meaning of constitutional justice.

---

[29] See, e.g., Venezuela's Supreme Court Suspends the Opposition-Dominated Parliament, Foreign Policy, January 13, 2016 (http://foreignpolicy.com/2016/01/13/venezuelas-supreme-court-suspends-the-opposition-dominated-parliament/); Venezuela Supreme Court overrides impeachment of President Maduro, The Jurist, January 10, 2017 (www.jurist.org/paperchase/2017/01/venezuela-supreme-court-overrides-impeachment-of-president-maduro.php).

7.4. CONCLUSION

In the end, the logic of constitutional governance is at work in both of these countries in recognizable ways. Ideology plays an important role in determining the goals to which the system of constitutional justice will be put. In both cases, the RC had an ambitious agenda for the state and that agenda is reflected in the constitutional text. In Bolivia, in a move that is more reminiscent of the social constitutionalism of the middle of the last century, that agenda was entrusted to ordinary politics. The court was kept moderately weak so it would not get in the way, but the opposition had enough strength to retain a minor role. In Venezuela, in contrast, Chávez appears to have counted on the court to do some of the work of clearing the way for his Bolivarian revolution. In both cases, it is the power dynamics of the design process, coupled with the governance goals of the dominant actor in that process – rather than ideology or imitation or a desire to freeze constitutional commitments – that determines the extent to which the system will be at the service of the RC, or serve as a space to contest majoritarian decision-making. In its response to the power dynamics of governing, the "new constitutionalism" of Venezuela, Bolivia, and Ecuador, is not so new at all.

8

Conclusion

The Politics of Constitutional Justice

Our work will not end when we swear in the Constitution, it will only begin.

Blanca Roque, Member of the Argentine Constituent Convention for the UCR[1]

At the outset, we made the claim that designers crafting a constitutional justice system will follow a logic of constitutional governance. At its core, the logic of constitutional governance holds that constitutional justice is not, as some models of constitutionalism would suggest, about locking certain values or rules away from politics and entrusting them to apolitical, technocratic lawyers, and judges. Rather, constitutional justice seeks to ensure the dynamic governance of a particular set of issues, through the mechanisms, language, and procedures of constitutional justice. This occurs on behalf, and under the loose tutelage, of a Constitutional Governance Coalition (CGC). Under this system, governance is dynamic because it responds to contemporary politics, and both the originators and the operators of the system understand that the point is to evolve – or defend – constitutional meaning over time. The composition of this CGC depends on the power dynamics of the constitutional moment. Every Originating Coalition (OC) will seek to secure a seat at the table of constitutional governance for its successors in interest. The extent to which the ensuing CGC is designed to overlap with the Ruling Coalition (RC) will largely depend on the extent to which the OC overlaps with the RC.

Constitutional justice systems, in short, set up a sphere of constitutional justice for shared governance of the issues that are included in that sphere. Although it is possible that the original preferences of the designers will be protected, it is equally likely that the designers' successors will choose to evolve the meaning of constitutional principles in ways that are unanticipated at the moment of creation.

Both the quantitative analysis and the case studies bear out the influence of the logic of constitutional governance on constitutional design. Moreover, the language

---

[1]   Transcript of Debates in the plenary sessions of the National Constitutional Convention, p. 4079.

the delegates used in the constitutional debates that gave rise to these systems of constitutional justice demonstrates that the patterns uncovered by the statistical analysis were not happenstance. Our analyses of the various constituent assemblies include a remarkable abundance of quotes from delegates who were explicitly articulating many of the key elements of constitutional governance – from the central tenets to the more tangential, but still direct, implications of this logic. Enrique Paixao, a prominent constitutionalist and a representative in the 1994 Argentine Constitutional Convention, offers perhaps the clearest statement of the logic of dynamic governance: "[We have chosen to require the consent of two-thirds of the Senate for judicial nominations] out of the understanding that . . . each time we name a judge of the Court we initiate a partial and mundane process of reform . . . of the National Constitution."[2] As Paixao continues, he makes it clear that the designers fully understood the role of the CGC in controlling the mechanism that produces that meaning: "For that reason, it should only be possible to occupy that position by means of a consensus that has some equivalence to what would be needed for a formal constitutional reform."[3]

The idea that constitutional justice has close ties to contemporary politics, and not just to its founding, is pervasive. Rep. Larios Ochaíta – who was a Guatemalan Constituent Assembly member, the author of a draft that served as the starting point for the Commission on Constitutionality, a member of that Commission, and, much later, a President of the Court of Constitutionality, described this paradox of constitutional justice this way:

> When one talks of the Court of Constitutionality, for example, . . . its function and attributes, while they are juridical in some respects, they also are politico-juridical, and from this comes the manner of staffing this type of tribunal, which requires the consent and representation of all the highest institutions of the State . . . [W]hen it is ruling on a bill, or a . . . treaty . . . it might be serving a judicial function, but of constitutional justice, that is, we should not be confused, constitutional justice . . . [i]n any given moment, it's almost political justice, in contrast to the justice of legality that the [ordinary courts] would apply and carry out.
>
> (PS (IV) 71:98–9)

In other words, even in Guatemala in 1985 – before the advent of rights constitutionalism, in a very conservative legal environment, and in a country with a strong civil law tradition – it was clear to the representatives that constitutional justice should not be understood as something foreign to politics. It is political and it is justice. What we have tried to articulate in this volume is exactly the way in which it remains justice, even as it is political, and remains political, even as it is justice,

---

[2]   Rep. Enrique Paixao, of the Unión Cívica Radical (UCR). Transcript of Debates in the plenary
      sessions of the National Constitutional Convention, July 27, 1994, p. 2210.
[3]   *Ibid.*

by identifying a CGC that is conceptually distinct from ordinary politics but still political.

How does this square with the basic assumption that the role of constitutions was to put certain issues, or more accurately, certain outcomes, beyond the reach of contemporary politics? For those who care about democracy and about the protection of rights and freedoms, that is simultaneously the promise and the peril of constitutionalism. And yet, when we look more carefully at the logic that drives the design of actual systems of constitutional justice, we find that the designers, by and large, expect those systems to be spaces for a continuing politics of constitutional meaning – subject to contemporary politics through the gears and levers that connect constitutional justice systems to their political context. We thus have two ideas in tension. On the one hand, it is clear that designers often intend constitutionalism to protect certain values and interests from majoritarian politics in a democracy. On the other hand, it is equally clear that they understand that this protection is a function of our own politics and not some automatic byproduct of a constitutional text and judges who are both wiser than the rest of us and insulated from our folly.

We can begin to resolve that tension if we acknowledge – as the designers we have seen clearly do – that our ordinary politics and our politics of constitutional meaning, while both contemporary, can nevertheless be quite different. Depending on the system, the two kinds of politics might respond to partially, but not completely, overlapping sets of actors; they might take place in only partially overlapping sets of arenas; and they might use only partially overlapping concepts and logics. In the best of cases – and depending in part on their design – constitutional justice systems can be more inclusive than our ordinary politics, and thus serve to raise issues and protect interests that might otherwise get short shrift in an ordinary politics driven by a more clearly electoral logic. Many of the interventions by the Colombian Constitutional Court or the Argentine Supreme Court, among several others, seem to fit this description. The issues and interests included are those that each political community has decided, in its constitutional moment, are worth some special solicitude beyond the space of elections and lobbying.

But the lesson of this book is that, depending on the design and the context, the system of constitutional justice might do something altogether different from providing a more inclusive arena in which to debate fundamental questions of constitutional meaning. In some cases, the system empowers actors who are deeply at odds with contemporary politics to put a check on widely consensual policies. This is arguably what happened in Chile over the first two decades after its redemocratization – at least on social issues like reproductive rights, Chile's Constitutional Court represented the interests of a conservative Right, even as the country's ordinary politics moved into the Center-Left. As we saw in Chapter 5, we can trace this outcome directly back to design choices made by Pinochet, which were only partly undone in later, more democratic, constitutional moments. In other cases, the system might simply act as a tool of majorities – or of the executive alone – to impose their vision on those who would oppose the regime. Here, Venezuela is a classic example. Ever since the opposition gained control of Congress, the Supreme Court has been President Maduro's iron fist in a quite threadbare velvet glove, stripping the Congress of much of its power, until it virtually shut it down altogether, and authorizing a new constitutional process in apparent violation of the express terms of the constitution. As described in Chapter 7, this outcome is congruent with design choices made by a Chávez-controlled Constituent Assembly.

US federal judge Learned Hand famously suggested that constitutions and courts cannot save us from ourselves: "I often wonder whether we do not rest our hopes too much upon constitutions, upon laws and upon courts. These are false hopes; believe me, these are false hopes. Liberty lies in the hearts of men and women; when it dies there, no constitution, no law, no court can even do much to help it."[4] Hand's intuition lines up well with the model of constitutionalism we have defended in this book. Constitutionalism and constitutional courts are not alien to our politics. Rather, constitutional governance is dependent on a coalition of actors who exercise continued, dynamic influence over a country from the space of constitutional justice. If that coalition does not embrace and defend the values enshrined in the constitution, then no court can or will do much to defend those values. And if the CGC is coterminous with the coalition that makes the key decisions in ordinary politics, then no constitution, no law, and no court is likely to protect alternative visions of what those values might require against the depredations of a tyrannical majority. Such a system is unlikely to be a credible space in which to have those debates.

But Hand also expressed a deeper skepticism, suggesting that constitutions and courts may not be very useful in the best of cases: "While [liberty lies in the hearts of men and women,] it needs no constitution, no law, no court to save it." The constitutional designers of Latin America, while not naïvely trusting in the power of parchment barriers, are far from holding that skeptical view. In fact, they embrace the idea that the constitution, the law, and the courts can strengthen the hand of certain members of a polity who feel that they might otherwise lose their liberties. They recognize that liberty does not live or die in the hearts of every member of a society at once. To put it less dramatically, different members of a political community place different weights on different constitutional values, and understand those values to apply differently in various concrete instances; a well-designed system of constitutional justice will help in resolving the tensions that this creates. Consider the following groups: the first congressional minority, after the 1994 reform in Argentina; the Center-Left, after the 1985 Guatemalan Constitution; and the conservative Right in Chile, even after the transition to democracy. All these groups had a stronger voice in the space of constitutional justice than they did in ordinary

---

[4] Learned Hand, "The Spirit of Liberty," speech at an "I Am an American Day" ceremony, Central Park, New York City, May 21, 1944. Hand, *The Spirit of Liberty*, 3d ed., enl. ed. Irving Dilliard, p. 190 (1960).

politics, precisely because their values and their roles in the system were part of the DNA of constitutional justice in those countries. The system of constitutional justice – properly constructed – can be the space in which disagreements about how to live out constitutional values are debated and eventually decided. But no decision is final. The Coalition of Constitutional Governance can reshape, influence, and ultimately even overrule a judicial decision. In this sense, the system of constitutional justice is not alien to our politics, but it can enrich our political debates by considering alternative views and values that may not find full expression in ordinary electoral politics.

The logic of constitutional governance allows us to square notions of a politically embedded judiciary and contested constitutional meaning with the idea that constitutions actually serve to protect certain interests that would otherwise be flattened by purely majoritarian democratic politics. It recognizes both that constitutional law is distinctive from ordinary politics and that it is not apolitical. It is congruent with Jacobsohn's (2010) description of a constitution, the meaning of which evolves as the key actors (including, but not limited to, the courts) work out the disharmonies embedded in the text and the contradictions between the text and the social order, the aspects of their political society that people want to preserve and those they want to change. The DNA of constitutional justice includes not primarily those matters on which we all agree, but rather those matters we understand to be both important and challenging to achieve or protect. Chapter 6 presents perhaps the best cases in which the OC was sufficiently diverse and pluralistic to produce important and interesting disharmonies. Moreover, it shows that such a design moment can produce a system in which the CGC cannot easily be captured by one or another political faction. The combination gives the constitutional justice system both the raw material and the autonomy to work out those disharmonies in ways that are most consistent with the ideals of constitutionalism.

Understood this way, constitutionalism need not be inescapably unrepresentative or conservative. It may well be countermajoritarian, if by majoritarian we mean the set of actors who have decisive authority in ordinary politics. Of course, as Dahl (1957) warned us, the national lawmaking coalition is not necessarily majoritarian in a strong sense. A constitutional justice system may put undue weight on the values, interests, and views of certain minorities if those are built into the DNA of constitutional justice. However, if constitutional justice responds to a more inclusive coalition than ordinary politics, as it is more likely to do when the OC is broadly inclusive, it can also represent an evolving supermajoritarian social and political consensus. And if it is the product of a dynamic and contemporaneous system of constitutional governance, we need not "reconsider the tradition of strong entrenchment of constitutions" in order to avoid its perceived "inescapable conservatism" (King 2013a: 95).

This means that constitutionalism can still be a source of stability, which is one of its principal selling points. In our model, however, stability is a function of the difficulties of building a broad current consensus for more radical change, not (necessarily) a sign that we are inevitably in the grip of the dead hand of long-vanished majorities. It is a function of having relatively centrist judges, and of adding veto points to the decision structure for certain issues. And although we have not belabored that issue in this book, it can be a function of the discipline of law, which requires justices to ground new decisions firmly in the existing normative framework, as suggested by Stone Sweet (1999).

Subjecting every decision to such a broad coalition would almost inevitably lead to deadlock, which is why ordinary politics is properly a generally more efficient majoritarian process. By delegating decision-making to broadly consensual judges who are legitimized by a pluralistic and inclusive CGC, however, we may be able to retain the legitimacy of broad consensus and yet avoid deadlock and even make boldly progressive decisions that nevertheless fall within that consensus. Occasionally (perhaps not often), the values and interests we have entrusted to the sphere of constitutional justice, and the discipline and logic of the law, may lead judges to the conclusions that our expressed values require, even if short-term or self-interested calculations in our ordinary politics prevent us from getting there otherwise.

It is true that, if all that matters are the politics we highlight here, the system of constitutional justice is unlikely to protect true outsiders – groups whose interests are not built into the DNA of constitutional justice and who are not assigned a role in the CGC. But to the extent that their values and interests are congruent with those of the CGC, it is entirely possible that outsiders, too, will find some leverage within the system. And because the system is dynamic, former outsiders might well gain entry to the CGC, and begin to bend the arc of justice in their direction, as African Americans did in the United States.

Thus, the logic of constitutional governance suggests that constitutionalism is both less separate from politics, and more likely to evolve to protect contemporary notions of justice, than a naïvely legalistic model of constitutionalism would suggest. Moreover, a constitutional governance model with an inclusive CGC may offer more hope for constitutionalism that protects unpopular groups than, for example, Ackerman's (1991) more majoritarian vision of popular constitutionalism. Furthermore, it can do so without requiring supermajorities to rise above self-interest. We do not deny that the logic and discipline of constitutional law can sometimes lead thoughtful and bold justices to outcomes that are inconsistent with the preferences of those who integrate the coalitions of ex ante and ex post control, and even inconsistent with their own interests. But our model of constitutionalism does not depend on heroics, on the absence of politics from law, or on herculean justices. It works simply by acknowledging that the constitutional justice system might be representative of a somewhat different coalition of interests than the system of ordinary politics, just as the upper and lower chambers of a legislature might represent different interests.

The logic of constitutional governance also requires us to think differently about the idea of judicial independence. While judicial impartiality is a core requirement for a system of constitutional justice to work well, that impartiality need not – indeed cannot – be the product of courts that are isolated and insulated from their context. Certainly, as we have seen, that is not how designers understand courts to work, and their understanding is generally congruent with what our theories of judicial behavior suggest. It is clear – from the debates, from the care and concern put into the different aspects of judicial design, and from the clear patterns that emerge from the quantitative analysis – that constitutional designers are aware of the influence of politics on judicial behavior. And it is clear from the debates, and from the patterns in the data, that the designers also understand that, in real politics, impartiality is best produced through a balance of partialities, as Holmes (2003: 50) argues.

In other words, impartiality is best achieved through the inclusion of many different voices, not by a futile attempt to strip the politics out of constitutional justice. If the goal of independence – what we have called autonomy – is impartiality (see, e.g., Brinks 2005) then the way to secure it is by pluralistic mechanisms of control, not by trying to craft autarchic systems, which are both unlikely to persist and likely to lead to stale, self-referential, and corporatist judicial bodies, as we argue in the opening chapters.

It seems fairly clear from our findings that designers put more faith in ex ante than in ex post controls, while scholars, by and large, do the opposite (see, e.g., Epstein et al. 2002; Helmke and Ríos Figueroa 2011). Scholars appear to embrace a more rationalist version of judges and perceive them as actors who calculate the odds that they will be able to enact their preferences over the objections of outside actors. Designers, on the other hand, appear to assume that judges will largely follow their preferences and training, so that the most important consideration is to be able to influence judicial appointments. While designers do worry about insulating justices once they are seated, they are more likely to fight over who will get to name them in the first place. This may be because the designers feel they have already granted judges the basic minimum of ex post protection needed in order for the judges to follow their preferences. Or it may be because the designers feel it is often politically too costly to openly discipline justices using ex post mechanisms. If either of these suppositions is true, then our more strategic models should work less well than a more straightforward preference-based model of judicial behavior.

The care and thought that constitutional designers put into their task also belies some of the models of constitutional borrowing that we sometimes find in the literature (Goderis and Versteeg 2013). Elkins and Simmons (2005) ask "whether diffusion is responsible for nations squeezing into ill-fitting but fashionable institutions or whether it leads them to the most functional and efficient ones available." As applied to courts, the question is premised on the idea that designers adopt the normative goal – strong courts – and then either blindly imitate fashionable judicial institutions in hopes of achieving that goal, or learn how to craft functional, powerful judiciaries adapted to local conditions that will actually achieve the goal. We argue that, while designers might cast about for institutional models from around the world, they pursue their own political interests through relatively fine-tuned institutional design. As a result, once we get past the broadest outlines of the institutions in question, our data tell a story of differentiation, rather than of convergence. It is true that the countries we look at are adopting new constitutional courts and new rights. But there are more differences than similarities among them when it comes to the specifics. This becomes especially true once we focus on the mechanisms that allow for continued influence over the system of constitutional justice.

The process of borrowing that emerges from the debates in constituent assemblies can better be described as adaptation (Elkins and Simmons 2005) than as copying. It is the rational – if not always perfectly prescient – adoption of new knowledge about policy solutions (sometimes in reluctant response to pressures by external actors), though not necessarily normative ends. Other countries' policy solutions are modified to fit local conditions and interests. The constitutional debates in Guatemala and Argentina, in particular, make it clear that the designers were using the set of global constitutional models in a way perhaps best captured by Günter Frankenberg (2010) in his essay revisiting what he calls "IKEA constitutionalism." They repeatedly returned to their own prior constitutional forms and to a global repository of "ideas, norms, institutions, and opinions" (Frankenberg 2010: 570), and drew on those that seemed best to suit their purposes. A model of diffusion that assumes something more like blind imitation is inconsistent not only with the discussions that we have highlighted in the case studies, but also with the patterns we see in the quantitative analysis. If court designers had simply caught the constitutional court bug and were blindly adopting foreign models, we would not have seen such systematic variation in autonomy and authority in response to local conditions.

This systematic variation says a great deal about the concrete preferences of constitutional designers. It contravenes any assertion that "founding fathers," or what Ackerman (1991) calls "constitutional moments," are somehow above self-interest. For example, we find that designers, when they can act more unilaterally, prefer a friendly judge to help them develop constitutional meaning in line with their preferences. Only if they cannot get a friendly judge will they settle for an impartial one. The logic seems to be that an impartial judge is a wonderful thing to have, but one that is actually on your side is better. In sum, designers clearly seek to advance their interests until the need to build consensus pushes them to consider the interests of others.

But not everything is a function of pure self-interest. In Guatemala and Argentina, participants were unanimous in claiming (and many observers agreed) that the constitutional design process matters quite a lot, and can elevate the final result above the prior preferences and narrow interests of the various factions. One of the Argentine constituents, for example, related how the constant presence of indigenous groups in the halls and outside the building forced the consideration of the rights of indigenous peoples and the ultimate inclusion of a provision, however weak and tentative, recognizing their rights, even though indigenous peoples were not actually directly represented among the members of the Assembly. In Guatemala, several constituents remarked that civil society groups came into the chamber at different times, and managed to secure protection for interests that would otherwise have been ignored – again leading to the inclusion of the rights of indigenous peoples. In both countries, despite the deep divisions that existed among the members of the OC, delegates felt that the Constitutional Assembly forced them into real deliberation and more compromise than would be expected from a purely rationalist, self-interested model. These experiences support a view of constitutional moments as marked by a (qualified) "higher politics" (Ackerman 1991).

In Bolivia, in contrast, as Jorge Lazarte put it, "passion took the place of reason," and the delegates "mistook arguing for insults and wronging each other."[5] The two-thirds decision rule led to stalemate, stalemate to acrimony, and acrimony to violence – both inside and outside the Assembly. What seemed to be at stake for the majoritarian Movimiento al Socialismo (MAS) party and its supporters was the very nature of the incoming regime. The goal for the majority was to decolonize the state and to craft a new model of participatory, multinational democracy. To bend in the direction of liberal democracy, as the liberal minority wanted, seemed a violation of basic principles more than an accommodation. But for many in Guatemala – with perhaps even more justification in light of the forty-year history of domestic civil war and the global Cold War – what was at stake was an equally existential choice, and yet the constituents sought consensus. An important and difficult question remains unanswered: What aspects of the process and the country's political history led to a more deliberative dialogue in the case of Guatemala 1985 and Argentina 1994, but led to a battle of monologues inside the hall, and a paroxysm of social conflict outside, in the run-up to Bolivia 2009?

So what did this strange mix – of passion and reason, of imposition and deliberation, of ideology and power-seeking, and of ideals and self-interest – produce in Latin America? We have described the patterns and variation quite extensively in Chapter 3, so here we limit ourselves to a brief summary. Our three-dimensional description of these courts gives us a relatively fine-grained map of the constitutional changes, supporting our decision to disaggregate our measure of court power. Our descriptive measure suggests that, over the last four decades or so, courts have become significantly more autonomous from the RC. Moreover, to the extent it remains, control over courts has shifted from the executive (through appointments) to the legislature (through less burdensome removal processes and greater oversight). A significant part of courts' increased accountability comes from a move toward shorter tenure for justices, especially on special-purpose constitutional courts, where justices tend to have delimited terms of five to ten years. This puts control back in the hands of

---

5   Author interview Jorge Lazarte, June 27, 2014, La Paz, Bolivia.

whoever controls appointments. Overall, though with notable exceptions, the resulting courts are not so much insulated from politics as they are subject to control by
supermajoritarian coalitions. These coalitions typically overlap with the RCs produced by the latest election, but they also include important minoritarian interests.

In addition, constitutional designers have dramatically increased these courts' scope
of authority. This has occurred through the creation of expanded rosters of rights, low-
cost, effective mechanisms for rights enforcement, generous standing rules, a combination of concrete and abstract review, and the ability of courts to make broadly
binding rulings. It is, therefore, not surprising that the literature on courts in Latin
America is no longer dominated by jeremiads about the inconsequence of courts,
but rather by descriptions of the increased role of constitutional courts in the politics
of the region, punctuated by warnings of the perils of the *"gouvernement de juges."*
But the change is not uniform, as shown in Figure 2.6. The courts of the region did,
in fact, almost universally shift out of the lower left quadrant of the table, so that the
region is no longer dominated by the Sidelined Courts we described in Table 2.1.
They did not, however, converge on any one other quadrant, but rather spread out
across the other three quadrants, becoming Procedural Arbiters, Major Policy Players,
and Regime Allies, depending on the politics of the constitutional moment.

The key force behind the increased autonomy of Latin America's constitutional
courts, as both the quantitative analysis and the longer history of the case studies
demonstrates, is the increasing degree of political inclusion in Latin America, and
the consequently more pluralistic coalitions that give rise to new constitutional
arrangements. In the last forty years, as much as in the previous 150 years, when one
party dominates the constitutional moment the courts are closely subordinated to
the RC. Moreover, we find this to hold regardless of the ideological orientation of
the OC. That is, the question is not so much whether the system of constitutional
justice was designed by the Left or the Right – or by the "bad" Left or the "good"
Left, as described in the literature on the recent turn to the left in Latin America
(Weyland et al. 2010; Levitsky and Roberts 2011) – but whether it was designed
under circumstances in which it became important to share power.

Interestingly, there is one somewhat unexpected connection between the ideology of the designers and the ensuing autonomy of the system of constitutional
justice. Early in the period, as our quantitative analysis suggests, the Right did in fact
build in more ex post autonomy than a pure power analysis would predict, relative to
the Left. By the end, however, it was building in less autonomy and more accountability than the Left in similar circumstances. We can read this pattern to suggest that
the Right initially subscribed to the Washington Consensus ideal of independent
courts as unconditional guardians of civil and political rights, property rights, and
the market. By the 1990s, however, it had become clear that the most visible courts
in Latin America were distinguishing themselves as much for their protection and
expansion of the social welfare state under the aegis of social and economic rights
as for an approach based on negative rights, individual autonomy, and promotion

of the free market. This appears to have led the Right to prefer more accountable constitutional courts by the 2000s, as we see in Figure 4.6. Learning is clearly compatible with a governance logic in which attentive designers who are trying to craft a system of constitutional justice to protect their interests look at courts' track records and tweak their design choices.

The story behind the growing scope of authority of these courts is complex and involves the interplay between political inclusion and an ambitious, social-democratic constitutional agenda, both of which are features of Latin America's constitutional moments after the 1970s. We argued that the Left, which has a more ambitious statist agenda, will constitutionalize more of that agenda when it is less certain that it can accomplish its goals through ordinary politics. The Right, by contrast, will typically craft a more restrictive constitutional agenda, regardless of its ability to govern in post-constituent politics, simply because it has fewer issues and fewer groups it wishes to include in the constitutional sphere. Our findings are consistent with this argument. Pluralistic OCs that include strong factions with a social welfarist agenda craft more expansive spheres of constitutional justice, in order to pursue their goals even when ordinary politics are less conducive to their ends. Meanwhile, OCs that tend more toward the right construct a relatively spare, market-oriented sphere of constitutional justice, regardless of the extent to which the future RC controls the design.

We have, in the course of this book, undoubtedly expressed strong sympathy toward systems of constitutional justice that are more pluralistic and inclusive. This stems from our view that such systems provide otherwise marginalized groups one more place to bring their demands and can construct important spaces within which to work out the meaning of constitutional commitments. But we are also aware of the constraints that strong constitutionalism places on ordinary politics. We recognize that there are times when the consequences of this can be somewhat troubling from a democratic perspective. When the constitutional justice system ends up being considerably to the left of ordinary politics, as in Colombia after 1991, the politics of social welfare and distribution end up running as much through constitutional justice as they do through ordinary politics, often to the great frustration of democratically elected presidents, whatever we might think of their neoliberal policies. When the constitutional justice system ends up quite far to the right of ordinary politics, as in democratic Chile under the 1981 Constitution, constitutional features can constrain the RC from pursuing more distributive policies. Any movement from the status quo on a long list of issues requires a supermajoritarian consensus or judicial leave.

The potential for, and implications of, this stability varies considerably depending on the model of constitutional justice that emerges. We began our theoretical discussion with a figure depicting the relationship between the OC and the RC. The same figure could serve to depict the various potential relationships between the resulting CGC and the post-constituent RC, as shown in Figure 8.1.

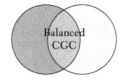 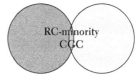

FIGURE 8.1. Relationship of the Constitutional Governance Coalition to the Ruling Coalition

We have tried to make it clear that we believe the precise composition of the CGC can only be imperfectly predicted and engineered by the OC. But it is abundantly clear that institutional design can profoundly affect the extent to which the system of constitutional justice becomes more or less majoritarian, as we have seen in the extreme cases of Venezuela 1999 and Chile 1981. And, although this was not the goal of our book, it has become clear in the course of reviewing historical and contemporary cases that the models at either extreme are less stable than the more balanced models at the center of the figure.

When the RC retains an important but not overwhelming role in the CGC, constitutional justice does not feel like a mere extension of ordinary politics – but neither does it feel like an external imposition. In Venezuela, it seems likely that the end of Chavismo will also spell the end of Chávez's constitution – if it lasts that long – just as the end of Perón's rule marked the end of his constitution. Similarly, the Chilean Constitution has been vulnerable to critiques and the subject of repeated attempts to profoundly amend or replace it – precisely because it is seen as an intertemporal imposition of preferences by the Pinochet regime, as well as a shackle on ordinary politics. The Venezuelan model of Regime Allies, in which the constitutional justice system advances the interests of the RC, is democratic in that it responds to whoever wins elections, but it suppresses what O'Donnell (2010) described as the liberal and republican components of contemporary democracy. The Chilean model, with its lack of any participation by the contemporary RC, is too countermajoritarian and far more vulnerable to the Bickelian critique (Bickel 1962). In both cases, the constitution can all too easily be associated with a particular political project, rather than with the task of crafting a common project. When that occurs, constitutional justice becomes the place where a particular political vision is advanced and defended, rather than a place where competing visions of constitutional ends can be worked out.

This book, and the systematic evidence we have presented, has focused on the logic that animates the design of courts. We do not mean to suggest either that the designers are clairvoyant, or that an institution's future is cast in stone at the moment of creation. On the one hand, the examples we have provided demonstrate that, in many cases, the resulting courts behave in the way that our logic of constitutional justice predicts, and therefore roughly in the way that their designers intended. This is clear in Venezuela, where the system of constitutional justice was unilaterally designed by the Chavista majority, and has ever since been a frequent weapon in the hands of the RC. In fact, the court continued to back the executive against an empowered opposition even in the face of strong social conflict and dissent. Similarly, it is clear in Argentina that the court has truly become a space in which to pursue alternative politics in the face of a dominant governing party, as the minoritarian designers had hoped.

On the other hand, it is clear that the outcomes in various countries do not, at times, match the preferences of the designers. Bolivia is one such example. There, the experiment in judicial elections has, by most accounts, left both the government and opposition unhappy – to the point where it is entirely possible that the process will be amended in the near future. More generally, it seems likely, as the change in preferences over ex post autonomy suggests, that the Right underestimated the power of the courts to enforce social and economic rights, and thus ended up with more protection for the welfare state than it intended to provide. In Colombia, the outcome seems likely to be close to what the Left would have hoped for, but clearly the party in power there has found some cause to regret the presence of such a strong constitutional court. This has led to various efforts to bring back "accountability" for judges in that country – such as the successful attempt to add a principle of "fiscal sustainability"[6] and a more effective oversight mechanism for judges in the "amendment to balance the three branches of government."[7] A similar impetus led the Workers' Party in Brazil, which had long benefited from a strong system of constitutional justice, to pass amendments increasing oversight over the courts and centralizing control over them (Brinks 2005).

Whether these instances of buyer's remorse are part of a broad impending backlash against the strong rights constitutionalism of the region, or simply minor adjustments in a region that is experimenting with a major shift in constitutional models, remains to be seen. But it is undeniable that the more pluralistic recent politics of many of the region's constitutional moments have strongly marked the DNA of the region's systems of constitutional justice with the concerns of many groups that had long been excluded from ordinary politics. The Left in many countries; the Right in a few; indigenous groups and Afro-descendants; women and environmentalists; and consumers and civil rights advocates all often find a more congenial space for their politics in the sphere of constitutional justice. The resulting systems have proven remarkably open to the claims of these various groups, transforming the politics of social provision, identity, health care, autonomy, territorial control, and many other issues. This new, more robust and encompassing constitutionalism seems

---

[6] See Legislative Act No. 3 of 2011 (July 1, 2011), available at http://constitucioncolombia.com/reforma/33. This "principle" was first billed as a right to fiscal sustainability.

[7] See Legislative Act No. 2 of 2015 (July 1, 2015), available at http://wp.presidencia.gov.co/sitios/normativa/actoslegislativos/ACTO%20LEGISLATIVO%2002%20DEL%2001%20JULIO%20DE%202015.pdf.

more likely to enhance than to detract from democracy by tempering pure majoritarianism and giving a stronger voice – without necessarily a veto – to traditionally marginalized groups and interests. In contrast, more monopolistic constitutional moments have led to constitutional systems that dismantle existing legal protections and enhance the power of the RC at the expense of robust democratic political competition. Whatever the occasional excesses of some constitutional courts, the experience of the last couple of decades does not suggest that a less autonomous constitutional justice system is good for democracy.

The fundamental point of our analysis, however, is that these systems are not designed to be alien to the contemporary politics of each country. Rather, they respond to the power dynamics of the constitutional moment, and are meant to be systems of constitutional governance that respond to a particular constellation of interests – what we have called the CGC. The extent to which a system of constitutional governance enhances or detracts from the quality of the resulting democracy is in part a function of its DNA and in part a function of the contemporary politics of constitutional meaning. In this volume, we have explored in great detail what that constitutional DNA looks like and what its political origins are. What remains to be done, in future work, is to explore how nurture affects nature in the context of constitutional justice. Paying closer attention to the character and composition of the CGC, and the levers by which it controls and guides the system of constitutional justice, should prove to be a fruitful way to approach that task.

APPENDIX A

Judicial Power: Concepts and Measures

As we have noted earlier, since approximately the 1990s we have seen a burgeoning literature on the comparative study of courts, contributing greatly to our understanding. And yet, some of the most basic concepts – like judicial power or independence – remain undertheorized. We have seen a dizzying array of definitions and measures for judicial power, but very little agreement on the concept or measurement of judicial power (Ginsburg 2003: 94). Power is a subtle and slippery concept to measure, to be sure, and yet we feel it is both possible and necessary to have a measure that helps us understand its origins and effects. In this appendix we explain our approach to the crucial first step in evaluating de jure judicial empowerment: crafting a conceptually sound, theoretically informed, comprehensive, and systematic mapping of the diversity of judicial institutional arrangements that formally structure the way in which courts influence, and are influenced by, their political environments.

Whether or not we ultimately conclude that institutional variables are important to behavioral outcomes, we can understand neither the causes nor the consequences of institutional design without such a map. A good understanding of the relevant dimensions of judicial institutional design is the starting point for any study of the political forces that shape particularly consequential (or inconsequential) courts. Moreover, without a good measure of institutional design we cannot examine the ways in which formal institutional features shape judicial behavior. Our own attempt to offer such a measure has required that we rethink what we mean by "judicial independence" and "judicial power."

As shown in Chapter 2, we organize our analysis of judicial power along three dimensions: ex ante autonomy, ex post autonomy, and scope of authority. In this appendix, we explain how we translated these three concepts into concrete numerical indicators. We will address the specifics of each dimension in more detail below. In a brief first section, we lay out three basic principles that inform the creation of our institutional measure, just as they should inform efforts to create other measures. First, our measures – especially the de jure, institutional indices – should be explicitly informed by our theories. Institutional measures, in particular, always have causal assumptions built into them, and we can better evaluate the measures and the assumptions if we make those theories explicit. Second, the way we build the indices should be explicitly informed by the question we seek to answer. Third, once we settle on a set of indicators, we need to be explicit, thoughtful, and theory-guided in our choice of aggregation schemes. None of these principles are particularly novel, but they seem worth recalling, as we set out to create our own indicators.

The second section presents our operationalization of the concept we want to capture with our index – de jure judicial power. In that section, we also explore how that concept connects to particular theories of judicial behavior. In the third section, we compare our measure to existing efforts to systematically characterize judicial institutional design. We conclude with individual country graphs that show the trends in each country from 1975 to 2009.

A.1. GENERAL OBSERVATIONS ABOUT CREATING INSTITUTIONAL INDICES

A.1.1. *Our Measures Should Be Explicitly Informed by Our Theories*

The observation that an implicit causal theory informs the scoring of institutional arrangements should be relatively obvious. Yet it is by no means the norm to be explicit about the theory that connects a particular indicator of judicial independence, for example, with the expected outcome. Nor is it always obvious which theory should connect an observed institutional feature with a particular outcome. Ishiyama Smithey and Ishiyama (2000) score courts higher if they have abstract review than if they have concrete (which they call "incidental") review. By contrast, Couso and Hilbink (2011) argue that it was the granting of concrete review to the Chilean Constitutional Court that finally empowered a body that had, until then, largely failed to use its powers of abstract review. Ishiyama and Ishiyama do not make their causal theory explicit, but their coding appears to be based implicitly on the theory that courts are more powerful when they hear cases that come closer in time to the legislative process, and can have more universal effects, as abstract cases do. Couso and Hilbink, in contrast, argue that cases that bring real people with real problems into the courtroom motivate and empower justices to intervene more than when they are presented with a relatively antiseptic, abstract claim by political elites. Both theories are plausible and tend in opposite directions. An index that seeks to rank the power of courts that have either abstract or concrete review must choose and defend one theory or the other.

Other examples abound. Many of the institutional measures include the simple declaration of judicial independence in the constitutional text as a positive factor for independence. However, it is not clear what theory would connect such a declaration with more independent behavior by the judges. In a recent article, Ginsburg and Melton (2014) suggest that such a declaration might prompt more disclosure of information about threats to the judiciary and might serve to coordinate a defense of the courts. As they acknowledge, that seems like a rather tenuous foundation for behavioral judicial independence, and after testing for the effects of such declarations, they conclude it is not, in fact, likely to be a significant factor. Making the theory explicit at the moment of creating the institutional measure – and, where, possible, testing it after – should help create more persuasive indices.

A.1.2. *Different Research Questions May Need Different Indices, Even for the Same Institutions*

Making the theory explicit will also help us ensure that our measures are appropriate to the research question. There are at least two different goals we could be pursuing with a de jure measure of institutional design – whether it relates to judicial independence, power, autonomy, or actors and institutions that have nothing to do with courts. The first research goal might be to test whether elements of institutional design actually have interesting effects – here, institutions are the independent variable. We could use such a variable to test whether institutional design affects levels of judicial activism or any other behavioral outcome of interest. The measure we need would identify those elements of judicial design that we have theoretical reason to believe might produce those effects. A project like ours, on the other hand, which seeks to identify the actors who are more inclined to empower courts and the circumstances under which they will wish to do so, requires something subtly different. For a project of this nature, with design as the dependent variable, the measure should identify those elements of judicial design that were intended by the designers to give their courts more power. These designers could be completely wrong about what will happen, but the political dynamics of design and the bargaining over this or that feature will be based on the assumption that they are not wrong, and that they are designing more (or less) powerful institutions.

   If the designers are sophisticated scholars of judicial structures, there might be a great deal of overlap between these two measures of institutional power, but we should not lose sight of the distinction. Many projects that use institutions as dependent variables use measures that were designed to be independent variables and vice versa – or at least, they use institutional measures without stopping to think of how they were conceived and how they relate to the research question. Each of these institutional measures implicitly includes a causal theory of the relationship between institutional arrangements and behavior. The difference is that for the former, we should deploy our best theories, even if novel and counterintuitive. For the latter, on the other hand, we need to identify the conventional wisdom among designers, or at least the most intuitive and self-evident arrangements that tend to produce outcomes in the designers' desired direction – even if they later turn out to be ill-advised, counterproductive, or simply useless. If designers sincerely believe that declaring judicial independence as a constitutional value will make it so, then that should be included in our dependent variable measure. But if we do not believe it will do so, then it should not be included in our independent variable measure. Explicitly acknowledging the purpose of the measure can help us decide what elements to include, how to aggregate them, and how much to weight various elements.

One more example will suffice to make this point. Since the time of the Federalist Papers, designers have understood life terms as essential devices for producing judicial independence. The implicit theory is, in part, that judges who need not worry about losing their jobs, or about securing work after their tenures expire, will be less likely to yield to the influence of outside actors, and thus more likely to rule according to their own view of what the law requires – one of the definitions of behavioral judicial independence. But Helmke and Staton (2011) cast doubt on this intuition, showing that judges should value longer terms more highly, and should thus worry more about losing a life-tenured job than about losing a short-term appointment, perhaps making them more sensitive to pressures. The argument is plausible, theoretically and empirically. Evidence that short-term, tenure-insecure judges can be very activist can be found on the Indian Supreme Court, the Colombian Constitutional Court, Ecuadorean courts, and elsewhere. No matter how counterintuitive or iconoclastic the claim, if our goal is to identify the institutional determinants of judicial behavior, we should follow our theory (or, better, test both the conventional wisdom and our cleverer intuitions). But if our goal is to understand the motivations of judicial designers, an overly theoretically sophisticated measure may well be too clever by half.

A.1.3. *Weighting and Aggregation Rules Should Also Follow Basic Theoretical Principles*

The vast majority of existing institutional measures of judicial power or independence follow the simplest possible aggregation rule – a simple addition of equally weighted components. For example, one early index used by Ishiyama Smithey and Ishiyama (2000) adds one point for each of six dimensions of judicial power, implicitly assuming both that all features contribute equally to judicial power, and that every feature has a cumulative effect, rather than a conditional one. But that, on its face, seems implausible. Their index captures features that range from the nature of the court's jurisdiction, to the length of justices' tenure, to the identity of the body that decides the court's procedural rules. Surely some of these features are more important than others. In the creation of an index, we must be sensitive to the possibility that some institutional features only have meaning in the presence of other features – requiring a multiplicative aggregation scheme – and that some institutional features should be weighted more than others.

To take the simplest example, in our measure of a court's scope of authority, we include a value for the nature and number of rights the court is given to enforce, and another value for the court's legal authority to issue a broadly binding ruling. These two elements both contribute to a court's authority, but the effect of one is almost certainly conditional on the other. Having the ability to issue *erga omnes* declarations of constitutional meaning means little if the court has few or no rights to enforce, and a great deal if the court is given a broad charter of justiciable rights. Similarly, lofty declarations of guaranteed rights take on different meaning when the court has the ability to use them to create new universal rules at the stroke of a pen, as compared to when the court can only issue rulings that are binding on the actual parties to the case, or when those rights are explicitly said to be nonjusticiable, or when access to the court is very restricted. The same is true for our measure of judicial autonomy. An easy process to remove justices from their seats has very different meaning when the judges sit for a maximum of five years than when they are appointed for life.

A.2. FROM CONCEPT TO MEASURE: OPERATIONALIZATION

A.2.1. *Ex Ante Autonomy*

We make ex ante autonomy a function of the number of institutional veto players required for appointment – capped at 3 – plus 0.5 if one of the veto players is a collective actor (e.g., a legislature as opposed to the executive),[1] plus another 0.5 if one of the veto players is a true outside actor, plus 1 if there is a supermajority requirement at any stage that affects a majority of the court.[2]

Recall that what we are looking for is not complete isolation from the political context, but instead the involvement of an inclusive, diverse coalition of interests in the appointment process, as this prevents capture by any single outside interest. By definition, adding institutional veto players adds institutional actors to the process and thus creates representation of institutional interests. A court that is named jointly by the executive and legislature is more likely to adequately police the separation of powers than one that is named by only one or the other branch. We cap

---

[1] This requirement only makes a difference in a few cases, since in Latin America nearly all the appointment mechanisms require the approval of two actors, and the second is almost necessarily a collective one. In practice, then, this requirement only distinguishes between those judges who are named unilaterally by the executive – as happens in a few cases – and those who are named unilaterally by the legislature – as happens in a tiny number of cases.

[2] Some courts are populated through a representative rather than a cooperative system. In these courts, each subset of judges is appointed, more or less unilaterally, by a given actor. In Chile today, only those appointed by the Congress are subject to a supermajority requirement, so that a majority of the justices is not subject to supermajority approval. As a result, we do not consider this to be a supermajoritarian appointment process.

the number of institutional veto players at three for several reasons. First, it is rare for an appointment system to involve four actors. This only happens if, for instance, there is a nominating commission that proposes a short list to the executive, who then must gain the approval of both chambers of the legislature for the chosen nominee. The only other instances in which we have seen four or more actors are in cooperative systems, where a number of different actors each nominate a subset of the justices (e.g., the Constitutional Court in Ecuador before 2008). It seems likely that adding up to three veto players can add distinct interests to the process. The involvement of both executive and legislature, for example, ensures that the appointed judges will not be outright cronies of the executive and may have some regard for the interests of the legislature, and thus the separation of powers. It may not, however, add much ideological diversity in places where presidents consistently count with – or can cobble together – ruling majorities. Adding a third actor – the upper house, for instance, which may be elected using a different system or at a different time – makes it slightly more likely that a minoritarian interest will become crucial in the process, and much more likely that the executive will be checked. But adding more actors after that, without more,[3] is unlikely to add significantly to the mix of interests represented.

Having a "true" outside actor, on the other hand, adds a significant social interest to the mix, whether it is the third or the fourth actor in the process. A moderate number of Latin American countries have adopted nominating commissions for the initial selection of judicial candidates. We code as "true" outside actors those groups that are composed of actors who have, or who represent, a defined social function distinct from simply nominating judges. Examples in our data include commissions made up of people who represent the Bar Association, the judiciary, the deans of the national law schools, labor unions, employer associations, and so on. We do not count as outside actors those nominating committees that are simply composed for that purpose by existing political actors. In our data, we have nominating committees that are appointed by the executive, the legislature, or a combination of the executive and legislature. In such cases, we consider the committee to be simply an efficient way to ensure that the interests of the appointer are represented, not a way to add a distinct social interest to the process. A true outside actor adds at least one player who has some interests in addition to those represented by elected officials and the representative branches.

A supermajority requirement warrants a full additional point since it should (in most polities) produce a more inclusive appointment coalition. By definition,

---

[3]   That is, it is hard to imagine that simply adding another institutional veto point would add another politically significant interest, unless it is expressly designed to do so. We can imagine, though none occur in Latin America, consociational systems that seek to include, say, additional minority ethnic groups to the Constitutional Governance Coalition (CGC) by giving them a voice in appointments, but simply adding another institutional actor is unlikely to diversify the CGC in the same way. Typically, in fact, we are simply looking for the inclusion of the majority and the opposition.

it will require the participation of a collective actor – usually the legislature – and unless there is a truly hegemonic party, it will require the majority to negotiate with the minority in order to reach the typical two-thirds requirement. Anecdotal evidence suggests that the supermajority requirement, especially in two-party systems, is one of the most important elements in ensuring a judiciary that is not closely linked to the ruling party or the executive. In Argentina, for example, this simple change turned a Supreme Court that was congenitally predisposed to favor the executive into one that has become a (relatively) formidable opposition force. It is the reason that the Argentine Supreme Court was short one member by the end of the Cristina Fernández de Kirchner Administration. The main opposition parties refused to approve the candidate that the President had recommended, who was widely regarded as a likely ally of the government. Similarly, in Mexico, a 1994 reform added the supermajority requirement, transforming appointments from a PRI-controlled process to one that required the assent of at least one of the two main opposition parties.

After adding all these elements, we have a measure that, both conceptually and empirically, runs from 1 to 5. We subtract one and divide by four to transform it to a variable with a 0–1 range, a mean of 0.48, and a standard deviation of 0.25.

A.2.2. *Ex Post Autonomy*

Our measure of ex post autonomy is conceptually related, as noted above, but considerably more complex in terms of institutional design. It is conceptually close because we are checking the institutional configuration to see whether the coalition of control is likely to significantly exceed the Ruling Coalition (RC) through the inclusion of additional interests. It is more complex because the mechanisms for putting pressure on sitting judges are numerous, ranging from the often-illegitimate court-packing scheme, to the routine nonrenewal of a sitting justice's appointment at the expiration of a term, to impeachment, to manipulating salaries.

Our measure is made up of the following elements. We give a court 0–4 points for the length of judicial terms (0 if at will; 1 if <5 years; 2 if 5–7 years; 3 if 8–10 years; 4 if >10 years, including life). The score for term length is cut in half if judges are subject to reappointment, based on the logic that judges will have to start thinking about the security of their tenure at least halfway through their terms, if not from the very first day on the job. We give the court a bonus ranging from 0 to 2 for difficulty of removal, which is a function of both ease of impeachment and length of term. We will explore this in more detail in the next paragraph. Essentially, the idea is that impeachment of a justice is always a public and costly event, even if the procedure is fairly efficient, and a very short term makes the possibility of impeachment somewhat superfluous. As a result, tightening procedures for removal of justices will matter more when justices have longer terms. To put it differently, difficult impeachment procedures add more security to longer terms than to shorter ones. We give a court a 0.5 point bonus for each of two pressure points if they are protected

TABLE A.1. Bonus for difficulty of removal

Difficulty of removal	Length of term				
	0 (at will)	1 (<5)	2 (5–7)	3 (8–10)	4 (>10, inc. life)
0	0	0	0	0	0
0.125	n/a	0.125	0.25	0.375	0.5
0.25	n/a	0.25	0.5	0.75	1
0.375	n/a	0.375	0.75	1.125	1.5
0.5	n/a	0.5	1	1.5	2

in the constitution: (1) number of judges (making court packing more difficult) and (2) salary (protecting judges from direct financial pressures).

We calculate the bonus for difficulty of removal by multiplying the measure of the coalition needed to remove a justice by the length of the justice's term. Just as with appointments, difficulty of removal is equal to the total number of actors required to impeach, on a scale from 0 to 3. We assign a 0 to the few cases in which the justices are explicitly said to serve at the will of the executive. We add 1 if there is a super-majority requirement (because this adds a veto player), producing a four-point scale. We rescale the four-point scale to run from 0 to 0.5, and interact that with the length of the term, so that the actual bonus runs from 0 to 2, as depicted in Table A.1. We restrict the range to 0–2 rather than 0–4 in order to limit the weight of this component in the overall index, precisely because we feel that removing a justice is usually a public and relatively costly event.

In short, ex post autonomy is a function of term length, which can range from 0 to 4, with a bonus of up to two points if removal is difficult, plus one point if the number of justices or their salaries are protected. This gives us a measure with a theoretical and empirical range of 0–7, which we divide by 7 to rescale to 0–1. The regional mean for the resulting variable is 0.56 (standard deviation = 0.24), just above the midpoint of the scale.

One could argue about the relative weight to be given to each element in the calculation, which at times can seem somewhat arbitrary, but we believe the weights assigned are justifiable. Almost 60 percent of the scale can be determined by the term length, while ease of impeachment accounts for up to 30 percent, and other protections just over 10 percent. This seems plausibly reflective of how most design-ers would intuitively think of design (and how they might think of disciplining the court), and of the factors that might be imagined as influencing judges' behavior on the resulting court. The first of these factors is how long justices should hold their seats. The second is how hard they will be to remove. The third consideration, if justices cannot be outlasted or removed, is whether the door is left open to permit the executive or legislature to punish or outflank them through salary manipulation and court packing.

Although we believe the complexity of the calculation is justified conceptually – indeed, it illustrates a basic point we want to make, which is that aggregation rules should be theoretically informed – we also calculated a simpler version to ensure that our results were not due to overly clever coding. In this second version of ex post autonomy, we took each of the four elements that contribute to ex post autonomy, re-scaled them so they run from 0 to 0.25, and summed them to come up with a scale that runs from 0 to 1, both in theory and in fact. The mean for this variable is higher (0.62), but the correlation between the two is 0.97. The different modes of calculating ex post autonomy lead to essentially the same results, so we use the more conceptually satisfying version, which is also empirically centered closer to the middle of the theoretical range and has slightly more variance.

A.2.3. *Authority*

As noted, the court's scope of authority is a function of four components: (1) the kinds of issues that are entrusted to the court's jurisdiction, (2) its openness and accessibility for taking on those issues, (3) the ease with which it can reach an authoritative decision, and (4) its ability to produce broadly binding decisions. We consider that the latter three components modify the first. The first component lays out the potential field for judicial intervention, but the latter ones determine whether the court will hear the cases, whether it will reach a binding decision on those cases, and what the effect of that decision will be.

To see what disputes are placed under the court's authority, we first count the number of civil and political rights (CPR) included in the constitution, as well as the number of economic, social, and cultural rights (ESCR) included. We also code whether the constitution incorporates international human rights treaties. We use the counts of CPR and ESCR to divide the cases into three ordinal categories that run from 1 to 3, with cutpoints that, for each class of rights, divide our sample into three groups of approximately equal numbers. We rescale the CPR measure so that it runs from 0.33 to 1, and the ESCR measure so it runs from 0.5 to 1.5, in order to weight ESCR 1.5 times as much as CPR. We overweight ESCR because they give willing courts much more latitude to address questions of public policy and a broader platform to intervene in a broad range of substantive disputes. We add one point if the constitution incorporates international human rights treaties because these provide a source of jurisprudence and authority that is external to domestic politics. The empirical range for this subcomponent is 0.83–3.5. In theory, it could range from 0 to 3.5, but no constitution is completely devoid of rights.

Next, we add one point for each of a court's most typical ancillary powers – impeachment of the president and supervision of elections – since these bring important additional issues into the sphere of constitutional governance. Finally, we impose a 0.5 penalty for the presence of military courts that are not under the jurisdiction of the Constitutional Court. Given the subcomponents, out of a maximum score of 5.5, a court's jurisdictional reach is comprised of up to 70 percent rights (with ESCR overweighted by 1.5) and 30 percent ancillary powers, with a possible 10 percent penalty for the presence of a military court system.

But that is only the first component. The court's ability to deploy these rights effectively is a function of who can bring claims (standing or access) and with what effect (effect). We find that, in practice, the formal effect of a court's decision is often conditional on who can bring that class of cases. Thus, abstract review cases always have *erga omnes* effects, but are frequently limited to political elites. Concrete cases, on the other hand, are generally open to anyone, but often have only *inter partes* effects. To capture the diversity of arrangements in this regard, we created an ordinal variable, *"standeffect"* (running from 1 to 5). This component denotes the effect of decisions of unconstitutionality, with an extra bump if the broadest effects can be produced in the context of actions that can be brought by anyone, instead of only in the context of actions that can be brought by elite political actors (like the president). The variable is coded as shown in Table A.2.

The court is penalized (by demoting it one level in *standeffect*) if it has the nominal capacity to emit a particular category of decision, but has internal decision rules that limit its ability to make those decisions. In Latin America, this is manifested primarily in the requirement of a supermajority vote to produce a binding decision in certain classes of cases.

After calculating these subcomponents, authority is simply a function of the court's jurisdictional scope multiplied by its decision-making capacity: *authority = jurscope*standeffect multiplier* (the multiplier can be found in Table A.2). As with the other two dimensions, we rescale the variable so that it runs from 0 to 1 (in practice it runs from 0.04 to 1, since no court has zero authority), with a regional mean of 0.36 (standard deviation 0.19).

While the calculations are made complex by the notable variety of designs that can be found, conceptually they are relatively straightforward, and appear justified by the empirical record. Note how this plays out in the Mexican case. The Mexican Constitution specifies only *inter partes* effects for amparo, but with open standing until 1994, putting the court in Category 2. The rules for producing binding jurisprudence through an action of amparo are byzantine and cumbersome, so individual decisions typically have very little generalized impact. Indeed, people often remark on the traditional weakness of the Mexican amparo, attributing it precisely to these rules (see, e.g., Pou Giménez 2012).

In 1994, an amendment added an action of unconstitutionality that can only be brought by no less than one-third of either chamber of the legislature and other elite actors (potentially bumping the court up to Category 4). This new power could have given the court the ability to intervene in disputes between congressional majorities and minorities – converting it, like the French Conseil

TABLE A.2. Calculating the multiplier for ease of access and decision-making capacity

	Definition	Examples	Multiplier
1	Courts with no ability to declare laws or executive actions unconstitutional	Guatemala and Nicaragua, during periods of exception	0.5
2	Courts for which (a) the text explicitly specifies that decisions have only *inter partes* effects or (b) where the text gives the courts an "action of inapplicability" only, with no *erga omnes* effects specified (this action traditionally has only *inter partes* effects)	(a) Many early courts, including Mexico; (b) Chile's Supreme Court	0.85
3	Courts with no abstract review, but that have either (a) amparo or (b) the general power of concrete review, and nothing is specified regarding the effect of a decision	(a) Brazil, pre-1964; (b) Argentina, pre-1994	1
4	Courts with some version of abstract review, in addition to amparo or concrete review, but access to abstract review is closed (either only for the president to refer a bill for unconstitutionality or enumerated majoritarian actors, like a subset of the legislature)	Peru, Panama until 2009, Bolivia 1994, Brazil through 1988	1.15
5	Courts for which the text specifies that decisions of unconstitutionality have a binding effect on all public authorities, or that have abstract review or its equivalent (as when the text specifies that the result of a decision is the nullity of the law found unconstitutional); and the actions that produce these effects are open to the general population	Colombia after 1945, Ecuador 2008	1.5

Constitutionnel, into an important policy player. But the amendment also stipulated that, to strike a law, the court must rule by a majority of eight of the eleven justices. The supermajority requirement made it extremely unlikely the court could favor the minority with a broadly binding decision in any closely contested, controversial case. As a result, under our rules, it is demoted to Category 3. A vote by a simple majority of the court remains akin to a judgment of inapplicability: it applies to the parties, but does not strike the law. What the court has, then, is a set of powers that are better than a Category 2, but not as consequential as a Category 4. This potentially powerful court ends up limited by the rules that restrict the effect of its amparo decisions, and that hamstring its ability to efficiently reach a binding decision in abstract cases.

TABLE A.3. Descriptive statistics for key variables

Variable	N	Mean	Std. Dev.	Min	Max
Ex ante autonomy	665	0.48	0.25	0	1
Ex post autonomy	665	0.56	0.24	0	1
Scope of authority	665	0.37	0.19	0.04	1

This sequence of events – especially the granting of additional authority conditional on limited standing and a supermajority decision – is by no means unique to Mexico. It suggests that drafters used to governing unchecked, like the Mexican Legislature, are especially wary of judicial decisions that have *erga omnes* effects, since they are akin to legislation. In response to the threat, they craft special rules to either limit the impact of these decisions or make it unlikely that the court would reach such a decision unless there is a broad consensus that a constitutional violation has taken place (or both). In Mexico, the drafters did this even as they remained willing to freely grant access to amparo claims, for which they assumed (or specified) a purely *inter partes* effect.

A.2.4. *The Results*

To apply this measurement framework, we applied our coding scheme to all constitutional events (all new constitutions and all constitutional amendments) in force in Latin America from 1975 to 2009 to secure thirty-five years of data. Wherever possible, we used variables identical to those developed by the Comparative Constitutions Project, led by Tom Ginsburg and Zach Elkins, but we supplemented those as needed for our coding.[4] We employed research assistants to code the constitutional texts in their original language, and then checked their coding ourselves against the text of the constitutions in question. As a separate test of the validity of our coding, where the variables overlapped, we compared our data to data provided by the Comparative Constitutions Project, and resolved any discrepancies by rechecking the relevant constitutional text.

Although authority has a low mean and less variance, the resulting variables are reasonably comparable (Table A.3).

Notably, the three dimensions do not run together. The measures of authority and ex ante autonomy are positively (but very moderately) correlated. The correlation coefficient for ex post autonomy and authority is about half that. Lastly, ex ante and ex post autonomy are orthogonal to each other (Table A.4).

---

[4] For more details on this project, see www.comparativeconstitutionsproject.org.

TABLE A.4. Correlation among dimensions (significance level)

	Ex ante autonomy	Ex post autonomy
Ex post autonomy	0.02	–
	(0.59)	–
Authority	0.21	0.12
	(0.00)	(0.00)

A.3. RELATIONSHIP TO EXISTING ACCOUNTS OF JUDICIAL POWER

We now turn to other systematic and comprehensive efforts to measure judicial power or independence. Many analyses of courts aggregate de jure measures of "independence" and de facto measures of "influence," making it difficult to evaluate the contribution of formal features relative to other factors.[5] Even those that do measure them separately tend to collapse these factors in their analyses or do not analyze how different elements of judicial design might affect each other (e.g., Navia and Ríos Figueroa 2005).

All the measures discussed in this section have been advanced as quantitative, cross-national measures of judicial independence. We are grateful to Jeffrey Staton, who has made the data available on Harvard's Dataverse website[6] and to his collaborators, Julio Ríos Figueroa and Drew Linzer, for sharing their data. The excellent review of these indicators by Ríos-Figueroa and Staton (2014) demonstrates that many are meant to measure very different things.[7] Some are de facto, while others are de jure. For some, the definition of independence is tied to a notion of autonomy, while for others the definition has more to do with influence (possibly closer to what we have called authority, although it is meant to include actual compliance). Finally, some are based on expert surveys (whether in the field or performed by staff), while others are based on observed behavior. At times, the observed behavior is that of courts in salient cases. In other instances, the observed behavior is of different actors who are thought to be influenced by the quality of courts.

As Ríos Figueroa and Staton point out, none of the variables directly measure the behavioral independence of judges. The de jure measures, like ours, measure institutional arrangements that the researchers expect to produce independent courts.

---

[5] See, e.g., Ríos Figueroa and Taylor (2006), who develop a framework that includes both de jure and de facto indicators to explain variation in policy outcomes in Brazil and Mexico.

[6] Harvard University, Harvard Dataverse, https://dataverse.harvard.edu/dataset.xhtml?persistentId=doi:10.7910/DVN/L716E8.

[7] Given how exhaustive their analysis is, we will not repeat it here, but we refer readers to their paper for fuller descriptions of these variables. Here, we give only as much information as is required to evaluate their relationship to our measure. Full references and sources for these variables are given in Section A.5.

The expert surveys measure outsiders' perceptions of the behavior of judges. The ones that are based on State Department reports use observations about legal outcomes – the extent to which the population of a particular country experiences human rights violations, for example – that are understood to depend, at least in part, on judicial independence. The measure of "contract intensive money" (CIM) seeks to infer judicial independence from social confidence in the security of legal agreements, as denoted by the use of noncash forms of money. Latent Judicial Independence (LJI), the measure developed by Linzer and Staton, is meant to uncover the latent variable – judicial independence – that underlies all these other measures, and so is meant to estimate the actual judicial behavior that produces all these different perceptions and behaviors.

Our variables bear some relationship to all these other variables, but are not identical to any. They are closest in spirit, of course, to the de jure variables, but since our primary interest is exploring the politics of judicial design, ours are meant to measure the institutional arrangements that would have been expected *by constitution-makers* (implicitly or explicitly) to produce impartial/autonomous courts with a broad scope of authority (or closely controlled ones, with little authority). We are officially agnostic, at this point, as to whether and how these arrangements actually do produce such courts; unofficially, of course, we suspect that institutional arrangements do bear some relationship to judicial behavior, more or less as the designers expect. In any event, our variables and the de jure variables are meant to measure the same thing – institutional arrangements – and so any correspondence between the two is a function of whether we have chosen to count the same institutional elements, weight them similarly, and use a similar aggregation rule.

A correspondence between our variable and the de facto variables suggests something else – a correlation at least, if not a causal relationship, between institutional arrangements and actual behavior (or reputations for behavior), or a correlation between institutional arrangements and trust in the system, depending on the variable. Thus in Table A.5 we separate out the de jure measures (A) from the de facto ones (B), and among the latter, we separate the ones that aim at autonomy (B.1) from the more numerous ones that look for "influence" (B.2), according to Staton and Ríos Figueroa. Finally, among the "influence" variables, we distinguish among those meant to capture perceptions of judicial behavior directly (B.2.a) and those that capture perceptions of (or actual) societal outcomes that are thought to depend on judicial independence (B.2.b).

Ríos Figueroa and Staton (2014: 106) find that the existing de jure measures bear virtually no relationship to existing behavioral measures: "Put simply, indicators of de jure and de facto independence are at best weakly correlated – in some cases, they are negatively related." Ríos Figueroa and Staton find this is especially true in low and middle-income countries, while the correlations are higher among high-income countries. Our own sample is entirely made up of low and middle-income countries, precisely the places where existing de jure indicators seem less helpful, and yet we find some interesting correlations between our variable and actual outcomes. Using simple correlations with our disaggregated measure of judicial design,

TABLE A.5. Correlations between existing quantitative measures of judicial independence and measures of ex ante and ex post autonomy and authority

	Ex ante	Ex post	Authority	Overlapping observations
A. Institutional/**de jure** measures				
Feld & Voigt de jure	0.03	0.39	0.26	15
Keith	0.33**	0.18**	0.15**	359
La Porta, et al.	0.16	−0.24	−0.20	12
B. Behavioral measures				
1. Measure aimed at **autonomy**				
Howard & Carey (SD)	−0.16*	0.10	0.11	152
2. Measures aimed at **influence**				
(a) Reputation-based measures (expert survey or staff coding):				
Bertelsman T Index	−0.09	0.22	−0.27	38
Feld & Voigt de facto	−0.23	0.45*	0.08	15
Fraser (GCR)	−0.09	0.27**	−0.10	112
Law & Order (PRS)	0.11**	0.15**	−0.01	475
Polity (xconst2)	0.30**	0.09**	0.30**	628
Henisz	0.03	0.13**	−0.03	475
(b) Behavior-based measures and latent measure				
Tate and Keith[8] (SD)	−0.08	0.29**	0.16**	285
CIRI (SD)	−0.13**	0.08*	−0.11**	551
CIM	0.30**	0.23**	0.29**	466
LJI	0.19**	0.16**	0.21**	630

The original sources of all the variables we test here are listed at the end of this appendix.

$**p < 0.05$, $*p < 0.1$; SD indicates the measure is based on US State Department reports.

presented in the following table, we find some relationship between our de jure measures and the other de jure ones – although the results are surprisingly weak and mixed given that we are all seeking to measure the same thing. The negative correlation with La Porta et al. is strange, but based on only twelve observations. More interestingly, in a simple bivariate relationship, we find some correspondence between some of the elements of our measure and one or another of the behavioral measures – in particular, the Polity, CIM, and LJI measures. The relationship is often significant when there is a sufficient number of overlapping country-years.

The results for the comparison of de jure measures support the decision to disaggregate judicial design into three dimensions. Looking at the de jure measures

---

[8]   Tate and Keith (2007) classify judiciaries into "non-independent," "somewhat independent," and "independent." For this analysis, we converted that classification into a 1–3 scale, in that order.

suggests that the differences among them are due to a focus on different aspects of design. The La Porta, et al. de jure measures are negatively correlated with ex post autonomy and authority, and positively correlated with ex ante autonomy. The Keith measure also tracks more closely with ex ante autonomy, while the Feld & Voigt de jure measures have more in common with ex post autonomy and authority.

Staton and Ríos Figueroa note the low levels of association between extant de jure and de facto measures. The problem is even more acute for countries that fall in the middle ranges on these measures, since Linzer and Staton show that there is much more agreement among measures at the extremes of the continuum. Our own observations, which cover Latin America's more democratic period, tend to fall more in the middle of the continuum, where the correlations are expected to be lowest. Table A.6 shows the pairwise correlations among all the variables discussed here, for our sample. Thus, the correlations are different than the ones reported either in Ríos Figueroa and Staton (2014) or in Linzer and Staton (2012).

The conceptual relationships among all these variables are complicated and we do not attempt to parse them fully here. Some (such as LJI or Henisz) are derived from other variables in this table. Others attempt, at least, to include identical information, while still others are based on independent codings of the same sources, sometimes with different conceptual ends. Please refer to Ríos Figueroa and Staton's (2014) analysis for an exhaustive evaluation of all these relationships. Suffice it to say, they are justified in concluding that we have not uncovered, properly measured, or adequately tested for the institutional roots of judicial behavior.

Notably, our own measure has significant correlations with the de facto measures even for our sample, although it also has a complicated relationship with the different behavioral measures. Measures that use different sources and evaluate different behavior are associated with distinct elements in our measure. The odd differences between the results for Tate and Keith's de facto measure and CIRI, both of which rely on coding US State Department human rights reports, but appear to have the opposite associations with our measures, are mostly due to the different samples included in each paired comparison. If we restrict the sample to the cases covered by Tate and Keith, the associations are more consistent, but remain thoroughly unimpressive. Finally, the Law & Order measure from PRS, which is meant to evaluate compliance with the law by citizens and political elites alike, is significantly – though not very robustly – associated with ex ante and ex post autonomy, but not with our authority measure. This makes some sense, as Law & Order is meant to measure the extent to which the law is applied evenly and generally followed – which are behaviors we would associate with a court's autonomy more than with the scope of its authority. None of these are meant to describe the behavior of the system of constitutional justice, which is the focus of our measure.

Table A.6. Correlations among extant quantitative indicators of judicial independence for in-sample observations

	F&V (de jure)	Keith (de jure)	Laporta (de jure)	H & Carey	BTI	F&V de facto	Fraser	Law & Order PRS	Polity	Henisz	Tate & Keith	CIRI	CIM
F&V (de jure)	1												
	18												
Keith (de jure)	—	1											
		359											
Laporta (de jure)	0.15	—	1										
	12		12										
Howard & Carey	—	0.08	—	1									
		90		152									
BTI	—	—	—	—	1								
					38								
F&V (de facto)	0.42	—	−0.48	—	—	1							
	15		10			15							
Fraser	0.40	0.56	0.12	0.42	—	0.62*	1						
	18	7	12	7		15	112						
Law & Order PRS	−0.2	0.23*	0.21	−0.02	0.37*	0.16	0.22*	1					
	18	230	12	152	38	15	112	475					
Polity – xconst2	0.04	0.23*	0.40	0.38*	0.51*	0.11	0.32*	0.30*	1				
	18	345	12	151	38	15	110	468	628				

(continued)

TABLE A.6 (continued)

	F&V (de jure)	Keith (de jure)	Laporta (de jure)	H & Carey	BTI	F&V de facto	Fraser	Law & Order PRS	Polity	Henisz	Tate & Keith	CIRI	CIM
Henisz	-0.19	0.13*	0.33	0.07	0.24	-0.05	-0.02	0.80*	0.34*	1			
	18	230	12	152	38	15	112	475	468	475			
Tate & Keith	0.34	0.27*	0.41	0.57*	–	0.46	0.73*	0.18*	0.29*	0.12*	1		
	18	126	12	152		15	94	285	282	285	285		
CIRI	0.12	0.26*	0.33	0.47*	0.73*	0.45	0.68*	0.22*	0.25*	0.28*	0.59*	1	
	18	281	12	152	38	15	112	475	521	475	285	551	
CIM	–	0.21*	–	0.35*	–	–	0.19	0.47*	0.35*	0.44*	0.30*	0.19*	1
		336		144			18	304	450	304	198	358	466
LJI	0.12	0.33*	0.30	0.64*	0.84*	0.49	0.73*	0.49*	0.80*	0.45*	0.66*	0.61*	0.54*
	17	338	11	144	36	15	107	450	596	450	270	522	440

* $p < 0.05$.
"–" Variables with no temporal or geographic overlap.

Reassuringly, the relationship with LJI, the Linzer & Staton latent variable measure of de facto independence – which we trust more – is more straightforward and intuitive, and holds up if we run a regression using the three disaggregated variables to predict LJI.[9] At a minimum, these results, although very preliminary and tentative, suggest that different combinations of judicial attributes may be associated with very different outcomes – such as more protection of economic rights, more protection of human rights, greater constraints on the executive, and so on.

A.4. JUDICIAL DESIGN IN LATIN AMERICA SINCE 1975

In Chapter 2 we presented aggregate, regional results of our measure. In Figure A.1 we briefly present the individual trajectories of all the countries. When we plot the disaggregated variables by country, we see much more experimentation in the ex ante and authority dimensions than in the ex post dimension. As the correlations we show in Chapter 2 suggest, it is more common for ex ante autonomy and authority to be part of a common package of reforms, in which additional authority is accompanied by additional ex ante autonomy.

As we saw in Chapter 2, when we look at individual countries, we can often trace changes in behavior back to particular changes in institutional design. Moreover, as we note above, there is a statistically significant relationship between these variables and Linzer and Staton's measure of judicial independence. In the end, none of these de facto measures really evaluates the behavior in which we are interested – just how consequential the constitutional courts have become in representing the interests of the broad CGC versus the interests of the RC. Still, we expect that we would find a much more robust association with these measures or a more appropriate measure once we take the political context into account, since we believe the effect of institutional design is conditional on the presence of partisan veto players who can exercise the levers created by institutional design (Brinks 2011). Interacting a good measure of design with the effective number of parties, we should find that courts designed to be powerful actually become so, as the control coalition exceeds the RC. In future work, we plan to explore the actual behavioral effects of design in more detail, but that is beyond the scope of this project.

---

[9] Not reported. Results available from the authors upon request. We ran a simple regression, controlling for first-order autocorrelation and using heteroskedastic, panel-corrected standard errors. We also ran a pooled OLS analysis with fixed effects, and in both instances, found that authority and ex ante autonomy are significantly and positively associated with LJI (and CIM), while ex post autonomy is not a significant predictor.

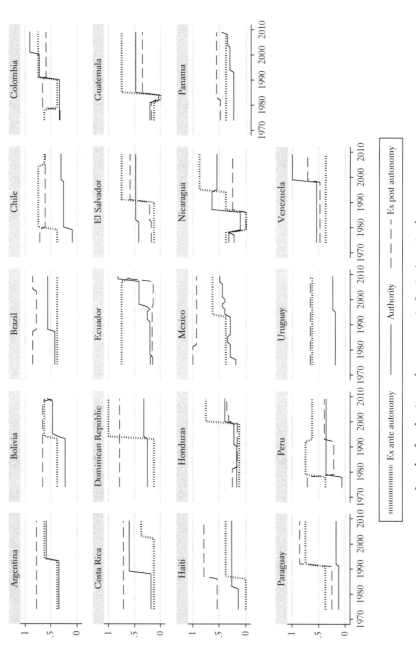

FIGURE A.1. Levels of authority and autonomy in Latin America by country, 1975–2009

A.5. SOURCES FOR VARIABLES MEASURING JUDICIAL
INDEPENDENCE AND THE RULE OF LAW

Polity IV "Constraints on the Executive" ("xconst2"): Monty G. Marshall, *Polity IV Project* (2014), www.systemicpeace.org/polity/polity4.htm.

Contract Intensive Money Measure (CIM): Christopher Clague, Philip Keefer, Stephen Knack, and Mancur Olson, Contract-Intensive Money: Contract Enforcement, Property Rights, and Economic Performance, 4(2) *J. Econ. Growth* 185 (1999).

Wittold Henisz's measure of "judicial independence" ("Henisz"): Witold J. Henisz, The Institutional Environment for Infrastructure Investment, 11(2) *Ind. Corp. Change* 355 (2002).

Political Risk Services "Law & Order" measure ("PRS"): The PRS Group, *International Country Risk Guide*, www.prsgroup.com/about-us/our-two-methodologies/icrg.

Tate & Keith measure of judicial independence ("tatekeith"): C. Neal Tate and Linda Camp Keith, Conceptualizing and Operationalizing Judicial Independence Globally, paper delivered at the 2007 *Annual Meeting of the American Political Science Association*, August 30–September 1, 2007, Chicago, IL. Available at Linda Camp Keith, Faculty Page, www.utdallas.edu/~lcko16000/APSA2006.doc.

Cingranelli & Richards measure of judicial independence ("CIRI"): David Cingranelli and David Richards, CIRI Human Rights Data Project (2014), www.humanrightsdata .com/p/data-documentation.html.

Howard & Carey measure of judicial independence ("howardcarey"): Robert M. Howard and Henry F. Carey, Is an Independent Judiciary Necessary for Democracy?, 87(6) *Judicature* 284 (2004).

Feld & Voigt de jure and de facto measures of judicial independence ("feldvoigt defacto" and "feldvoigt dejure"): Lars P. Feld and Stefan Voigt, Economic Growth and Judicial Independence: Cross-country Evidence Using a New Set of Indicators, 19(3) *Eur. J. Pol. Econ.* 497 (2003).

Global Competitiveness Report's measure of "judicial independence" ("Fraser"): World Economic Forum, *Global Competitiveness Report* (2016) http://reports.weforum.org/global-competitiveness-report-2015-2016.

Bertelsmann Transformation Index of Judicial Independence ("BTI"): Bertelsmann Stiftung, *Transformation Index BTI* (2016), www.bti-project.org/de/startseite.

Apodaca–Keith Scale of de jure judicial independence ("Keith"): Clair Apodaca, The Rule of Law and Human Rights, 87(6) *Judicature* 292 (2004); Linda Camp Keith, Judicial Independence and Human Rights Protection Around the World, 85(4) *Judicature* 195 (2002).

La Porta et al. de jure measure of judicial independence ("Laporta"): Rafael La Porta, Florencio López de Silanes, Cristian Pop-Eleches, and Andrei Shleifer, Judicial Checks and Balances, 112(2) *J. Pol. Econ.* 445 (2004).

References

Acemoglu, Daron, Simon Johnson, and James A. Robinson. 2001. "The Colonial Origins of Comparative Development: An Empirical Investigation." *American Economic Review* 91 (December):1369–401.

Ackerman, Bruce A. 1991. *We the People*. Cambridge, MA: Belknap Press of Harvard University Press.

Alfonsín, Raúl Ricardo. 2004. *Memoria política: transición a la democracia y derechos humanos*. 1. ed. Buenos Aires: Fondo de Cultura Económica de Argentina.

Alter, Karen. 2008. "Agents or Trustees? International Courts in their Political Context." *European Journal of International Relations* 14 (1):33–63.

Barros, Robert. 2003. "Dictatorship and the Rule of Law: Rules and Military Power in Pinochet's Chile." In *Democracy and the Rule of Law*, ed. J. M. Maravall and A. Przeworski. Cambridge: Cambridge University Press.

Beard, Charles. 1913. *An Economic Interpretation of the Constitution of the United States*. New York: The Macmillan Company.

Belge, Ceren. 2006. "Friends of the Court: The Republican Alliance and Selective Activism of the Constitutional Court of Turkey." *Law & Society Review* 40 (3):653–92.

Bickel, Alexander. 1962. *The Least Dangerous Branch: The Supreme Court at the Bar of Politics*. Indianapolis, IN: Bobbs-Merrill.

Bilchitz, David. 2013. "Constitutionalism, the Global South, and Economic Justice." In *Constitutionalism of the Global South: The Activist Tribunals of India, South Africa, and Colombia*, ed. D. Bonilla Maldonado. New York, NY: Cambridge University Press.

Bill Chavez, Rebecca. 2004a. "The Evolution of Judicial Autonomy in Argentina: Establishing the Rule of Law in an Ultrapresidential System." *Journal of Latin American Studies* 36:451–78.

—— 2004b. *The Rule of Law in Nascent Democracies: Judicial Politics in Argentina*. Stanford, CA: Stanford University Press.

Bonilla Maldonado, Daniel, ed. 2013. *Constitutionalism of the Global South: The Activist Tribunals of India, South Africa, and Colombia*. New York, NY: Cambridge University Press.

Botero, Sandra. 2015. "Agents of Neoliberalism? High Courts and Rights in Latin America." In *Penn Program on Democracy, Citizenship and Constitutionalism: Citizens, Constitutions and Democracy in Post-Neoliberal Latin America (May 8, 2015)*. Philadelphia, PA:

University of Pennsylvania. Available at www.sas.upenn.edu/dcc/sites/www.sas.upenn
.edu.dcc/files/uploads/Botero-Courts(PennDCCConference).pdf.

2017. "Agents of Neoliberalism? High Courts, Legal Preferences and Rights in Latin
America." In *Latin America Since the Left Turn*, ed. T. Falleti, E. Parrado and R. Smith.
Philadelphia, PA: University of Pennsylvania Press.

Boylan, Delia M. 2001. *Defusing Democracy: Central Bank Autonomy and the Transition
From Authoritarian Rule*. Ann Arbor, MI: University of Michigan Press.

Brett, Roddy, and Antonio Delgado. 2005. "The role of Constitution-Building Processes
in Democratization: Case Study Guatemala." ed. International IDEA/Democracy-
building and Conflict Management. Stockholm: International Institute for Democracy
and Electoral Assistance. Available at www.idea.int/cbp/upload/CBP-Guatemala.pdf.

Brewer-Carías, Allan R. 2005. Mecanismos nacionales de protección de los derechos humanos.
San José: Instituto Interamericano de Derechos Humanos.

2007. "Quis Custodiet ipsos Custodes: De la interpretación constitucional a la incon-
stitucionalidad de la interpretación." In *Colección Instituto de Derecho Público,
Universidad Central de Venezuelaed. U. C. d. V. Instituto de Derecho Público*. Caracas:
Editorial Jurídica Venezolana.

2009. *La demolición del Estado de derecho y la destrucción de la democracia en Venezuela
(1999–2009)*. Mexico: Biblioteca Jurídica Virtual del Instituto de Investigaciones
Jurídicas de la UNAM. Available at www.allanbrewer.com/Content/449725d9-f1cb-
474b-8ab2-41efb849fea8/Content/II, 4, 618. Demolici%C3%B3n de la democracia.
Libro Nohlen.pdf.

2010. *Dismantling Democracy in Venezuela: The Chávez Authoritarian Experiment*. New
York, NY: Cambridge University Press.

Brinks, Daniel M. 2005. "Judicial Reform and Independence in Brazil and Argentina:
The Beginning of a New Millennium?" *Texas International Law Journal* 40 (3
(Spring)):595–622.

2008. *The Judicial Response to Police Killings in Latin America: Inequality and the Rule of
Law*. New York, NY: Cambridge University Press.

2011. "'Faithful Servants of the Regime': The Brazilian Constitutional Court's Role under
the 1988 Constitution." In *Courts in Latin America*, ed. G. Helmke and J. Rios-Figueroa.
New York, NY: Cambridge University Press.

2012. "The Transformation of the Latin American State-As-Law: State Capacity and the
Rule of Law." *Revista de Ciência Política* 32 (3):561–83.

Brinks, Daniel M., and William Forbath. 2014. "The Role of Courts and Constitutions in the
New Politics of Welfare in Latin America." In *Law and Development of Middle-Income
Countries: Avoiding the Middle-Income Trap*, ed. R. Peerenboom and T. Ginsburg. New
York, NY: Cambridge University Press.

Brinks, Daniel M., and William E. Forbath. 2011. "Social and Economic Rights in Latin
America: Constitutional Courts and the Prospects for Pro-poor Interventions." *Texas
Law Review* 89 (7):1943–55.

Brinks, Daniel M., Varun Gauri, and Kyle Shen. 2015. "Social Rights Constitutionalism:
Negotiating the Tension Between the Universal and the Particular." *Annual Review of
Law and Social Science* 11:289–308.

Buitrago, Miguel. 2007. "El proceso constitucional boliviano: dos visiones." *Revista
Iberoamericana* 7 (26):189–96.

Carrubba, Clifford. 2009. "A Model of the Endogenous Development of Judicial Institutions
in Federal and International Systems." *Journal of Politics* 71 (1):55–69.

Casal, Jesús. 2009. "Sala Constitucional del Tirbunal de Justicia en Venezuela." In *Crónica de Tribunales Constitucionales en Iberoamérica* ed. E. F. MacGregor. Buenos Aires: Marcial Pons Editores.

CELS. 2008. *La Lucha por el Derecho. Litigio Estratégico y Derechos Humanos.* Buenos Aires: Siglo XXI.

Cepeda Espinosa, Manuel José. 2004. "Judicial Activism in a Violent Context: The Origin, Role and Impact of the Colombian Constitutional Court." *Washington University Global Studies Law Review* 3:529.

2007. *Polémicas Constitucionales.* Bogotá: Legis.

2009. "The Constitutional Protection of IDPs in Colombia." In *Judicial Protection of Internally Displaced Persons: The Colombian Experience*, ed. R. Arango Rivadeneira. Washington, DC: Brookings.

2011. "Transcript: Social and Economic Rights and the Colombian Constitutional Court." *Texas Law Review* 89 (7):1699–705.

Cheibub, José Antônio. 2007. *Presidentialism, Parliamentarism, and Democracy.* New York, NY: Cambridge University Press.

Cingranelli, David L., and David L. Richards. 2010. "The Cingranelli and Richards (CIRI) Human Rights Data Project." *Human Rights Quarterly* 32:395–418.

Coddou, Alberto, and Jorge Contesse. 2014. "Chile and its Property Constitution." www.academia.edu/8011834/_w_Jorge_Contesse_Chile_and_its_Property_Constitution.

Couso, Javier. 2011. "Models of Democracy and Models of Constitutionalism: The Case of Chile's Constitutional Court, 1970–2010." *Texas Law Review* 89 (7):1517–36.

2013. "Radical Democracy and the 'New Latin American Constitutionalism'." In *SELA 2013.* Cartagena: Yale Law School.

Couso, Javier, and Elisabeth C. Hilbink. 2011. "From Quietism to Incipient Activism: The Institutional and Ideational Roots of Rights Adjudication in Chile." In *Courtsin Latin America*, ed. J. Rios-Figueroa and G. Helmke. New York, NY: Cambridge University Press.

Couso, Javier, Alexandra Huneeus, and Rachel Sieder, eds. 2010. *Cultures of Legality: Judicialization and Political Activism in Latin America.* Cambridge; New York, NY: Cambridge University Press.

Cross, Frank B. 2001. "The Error of Positive Rights." *UCLA Law Review* 48:857–924.

Dahl, Robert. 1957. "Decision-Making in a Democracy: The Supreme Court as a National Policy-Maker." *Journal of Public Law VI* (2):279–95.

de la Fuente Jeria, José. 2010. "El Difícil Parto de Otra Democracia: La Asamblea Constituyente de Bolivia." *Latin American Research Review* 45 (Special Issue: Living in Actually Existing Democracies):5–26.

Domingo, Pilar, and Rachel Sieder, eds. 2001. *Rule of Law in Latin America: The International Promotion of Judicial Reform.* London: Institute of Latin American Studies.

Dworkin, Ronald. 1986. *Law's Empire.* Cambridge, MA: Belknap Press of Harvard University Press.

1999. *Taking Rights Seriously.* Delhi: Universal Law Publishing House.

Elkins, Zachary, Tom Ginsburg, and James Melton. 2009. *The Endurance of National Constitutions.* Cambridge, New York, NY: Cambridge University Press.

Elkins, Zachary, and Beth Simmons. 2005. "On Waves, Clusters and Diffusion: A Conceptual Framework." *Annals of the American Academy of Political and Social Science* 598 (Special Issue on the Rise of Regulatory Capitalism: The Global Diffusion of a New Order (March)):33–51.

Elster, Jon. 2000. *Ulysses Unbound: Studies in Rationality, Precommitment, and Constraints.* Cambridge, New York, NY: Cambridge University Press.

Epp, Charles R. 1998. *The Rights Revolution: Lawyers, Activists, and Supreme Courts in Comparative Perspective.* Chicago, IL: University of Chicago Press.

    2009. *Making Rights Real: Activists, Bureaucrats, and the Creation of the Legalistic State.* Chicago, IL: University of Chicago Press.

Epstein, Lee, and Jack Knight. 1998. *The Choices Justices Make.* Washington, DC: Congressional Quarterly Press.

Epstein, Lee, Jack Knight, and Olga Shvetsova. 2001. "The Role of Constitutional Courts in the Establishment and Maintenance of Democratic Systems of Government." *Law & Society Review* 35 (1):117–64.

    2002. "Selecting Selection Systems." In *Judicial Independence at the Crossroads: An Interdisciplinary Approach*, ed. S. B. Burbank and B. Friedman. Thousand Oaks, CA: Sage Publications.

Escaith, Hubert, and Igor Paunovic. 2004. "Structural Reforms in Latin America and the Caribbean, 1970–2000: Indexes and Methodological Notes." In *SSRN.* http://papers.ssrn.com/sol3/papers.cfm?abstract_id=1158491 or http://dx.doi.org/10.2139/ssrn.1158491.

España Nájera, Annabella. 2009. Party Systems and Democracy after the Conflicts: El Salvador, Guatemala and Nicaragua. PhD Dissertation, Department of Political Science, University of Notre Dame, Notre Dame.

Feijoó, María del Carmen. 1995. "Una Mirada sobre la Convención Nacional Constituyente." *Revista de Ciencias Sociales* 1 (1):71–98.

Ferejohn, J., and L. Sager. 2003. "Commitment and Constitutionalism." *Texas Law Review* 81 (7):1929–63.

Finkel, J. 2005. "Judicial Reform as Insurance Policy: Mexico in the 1990s." *Latin American Politics and Society* 47 (1):87–113.

Frankenberg, Günter. 2010. "Constitutional Transfer: The IKEA theory revisited." *International Journal of Constitutional Law* 8 (3):563–79.

    2013. *Order from Transfer: Comparative Constitutional Design and Legal Culture.* Cheltenham: Edward Elgar Publishing.

Galligan, Denis, and Mila Versteeg. 2013. *Social and Political Foundations of Constitutions.* New York, NY: Cambridge University Press.

Gamboa Rocabado, Franco. 2009. "La Asamblea Constituyente en Bolivia: Una evaluación de su dinámica." *Frónesis* 16 (3):487–512.

García Laguardia, Jorge Mario. 2001. "Guatemala: De la Exclusión a la Apertura." In *Transición Democrática y Reforma Constitucional en Centroamérica: Pensamiento y Acción para una nueva Centroamérica*, ed. J. M. García Laguardia et al. San José: Fundación del Servicio Exterior para la Paz y la Democracia.

García Lema, Alberto. 1994. *La Reforma por Dentro: La Difícil Construcción del Consenso Constitucional.* Buenos Aires: Editorial Planeta.

Gargarella, Roberto. 2010. *The Legal Foundations of Inequality: Constitutionalism in the Americas, 1776–1860.* Cambridge; New York, NY: Cambridge University Press.

    2013. *Latin American Constitutionalism, 1810–2010: The Engine Room of the Constitution.* New York, NY: Oxford University Press.

Gauri, Varun, and Daniel M. Brinks, eds. 2008. *Courting Social Justice: Judicial Enforcement of Social and Economic Rights in the Developing World.* New York, NY: Cambridge University Press.

Gibson, James L., Gregory A. Caldeira, and Vanessa A. Baird. 1998. "On the Legitimacy of National High Courts." *American Political Science Review* 92:348–58.

Ginsburg, Tom. 2003. *Judicial Review in New Democracies: Constitutional Courts in Asian Cases*. Cambridge: Cambridge University Press.

Ginsburg, Tom, and James Melton. 2014. "Does De Jure Independence Really Matter? A Reevaluation of Explanations for Judicial Independence." *Journal of Law and Courts* 2(2):187–217.

Ginsburg, Tom, and Tamir Moustafa. 2008. *Rule by Law: The Politics of Courts in Authoritarian Regimes*. Cambridge, UK; New York, NY: Cambridge University Press.

Ginsburg, Tom, and Mila Versteeg. 2013. "Why Do Countries Adopt Constitutional Review?" *Journal of Law, Economics and Organization* 30:587.

Goderis, Benedikt, and Mila Versteeg. 2013. "Transnational Constitutionalism: A Conceptual Framework." In *Social and Political Foundations of Constitutions*, ed. D. Galligan and M. Versteeg. New York, NY: Cambridge University Press.

Graber, M.A. 1993. "The Non-majoritarian Difficulty: Legislative Deference to the Judiciary." *Studies in American Political Development* 7:35.

Hamilton, Alexander, James Madison, and John Jay. 1961. *TheFederalist Papers*. Edited by C. Rossiter. New York, NY: Mentor (Penguin Books).

Hammergren, Linn. 1998. "Fifteen Years of Justice and Justice Reform in Latin America: Where We Are and Why We Haven't Made More Progress." ftp://pogar.org/localuser/pogarp/judiciary/linn2/latin.pdf.

Helmke, Gretchen. 2005. *Courts Under Constraints: Judges, Generals and Presidents in Argentina*. New York, NY: Cambridge University Press.

Helmke, Gretchen, and Julio Ríos Figueroa. 2011. *Courts in Latin America*. Cambridge; New York, NY: Cambridge University Press.

Helmke, Gretchen, and Jeffrey Staton. 2011. "The Puzzle of Judicial Politics in Latin America: A Theory of Litigation, Judicial Decisions, and Inter-branch Conflict." In *Courts in Latin America*, ed. G. Helmke and J. Ríos Figueroa. Cambridge; New York, NY: Cambridge University Press.

Herrera, Carlos Miguel. 2014. "En los orígenes del constitucionalismo social argentino: Discursos en torno a la Constitución de 1949." *Historia Constitucional* 15:391–414.

Hilbink, Elisabeth C. 2003. "An Exception to Chilean Exceptionalism? The Historical Role of Chile's Judiciary." In *What Justice? Whose Justice? Fighting for Fairnessin Latin America*, ed. S. E. Eckstein and T. Wickham-Crowley. Berkeley, CA: University of California Press.

2012. "The Origins of Positive Judicial Independence." *World Politics* 64 (4):587–621.

Hilbink, Lisa. 2007. *Judges Beyond Politics in Democracy and Dictatorship: Lessons from Chile*. New York, NY: Cambridge University Press.

Hirschl, Ran. 2004. *Towards Juristocracy – The Origins and Consequences of the New Constitutionalism*. Cambridge, MA: Harvard University Press.

2008. "The Judicialization of Mega-Politics and the Rise of Political Courts." *Annual Review of Political Science* 11:93–118.

Holmes, Stephen. 2003. "Lineages of the Rule of Law." In *Democracy and the Rule of Law*, ed. J. M. Maravall and A. Przeworski. Cambridge: Cambridge University Press.

Huntington, Samuel. 1991. *The Third Wave: Democratization in the Late Twentieth Century*. Norman, OK: University of Oklahoma Press.

Iaryczower, M., P. T. Spiller, and M. Tommasi. 2002. "Judicial Independence in Unstable Environments, Argentina 1935-1998." *American Journal of Political Science* 46 (4): 699–716.

Inter-American Commission on Human Rights. 2009. "Democracy and Human Rights in Venezuela." OEA/Ser.L/V/II. Doc. 54.

Ishiyama Smithey, Shannon, and John Ishiyama. 2000. "Judicious Choices: Designing Courts in Post-Communist Politics." *Communist and Post-Communist Studies* 33:163–82.

Jacobsohn, Gary J. 2010. *Constitutional Identity*. Cambridge: Harvard University Press.

Kapiszewski, Diana. 2012. *High Courts and Economic Governance in Argentina and Brazil*. New York, NY: Cambridge University Press.

Kapiszewski, Diana, Gordon Silverstein, and Robert A. Kagan. 2013. *Consequential Courts: Judicial Roles in Global Perspective*. Cambridge, UK; New York, NY: Cambridge University Press.

Keith, Linda Camp. 2002. "Judicial Independence and Human Rights Protection Around the World." *Judicature* 85 (4):195–200.

King, Jeff. 2013a. "Constitutions as Mission Statements." In *Social and Political Foundations of Constitutions*, ed. D. J. Galligan and M. Versteeg. New York, NY: Cambridge University Press.

King, Phoebe. 2013b. "Neo-Bolivarian Constitutional Design: Comparing the 1999 Venezuelan, 2008 Ecuadorian, and 2009 Bolivian Constitutions." In *Social and Political Foundations of Constitutions*, ed. D. J. Galligan and M. Versteeg. New York, NY: Cambridge University Press.

Larkins, Christopher M. 1998. "The Judiciary and Delegative Democracy in Argentina." *Comparative Politics* 31 (July, 1998):423–42.

Leonard, Thomas M. 1984. *The United States and Central America, 1944–1949: Perceptions of Political Dynamics*. Tuscaloosa, AL: The University of Alabama Press.

Levinson, Sanford. 2012. *Framed: America's Fifty-One Constitutions and the Crisis of Governance*. New York, NY: Oxford University Press.

Levitsky, Steven, and Kenneth M. Roberts, eds. 2011. *The Resurgence of the Latin American Left*. Baltimore, MD: Johns Hopkins University Press.

Lijphart, Arend. 2012. *Patterns of Democracy: Government Forms and Performance in Thirty-Six Countries*, 2nd edn. New Haven, CT: Yale University Press.

Linzer, Drew, and Jeffrey Staton. 2012. "A Measurement Model for Synthesizing Multiple Comparative Indicators: The Case of Judicial Independence." Atlanta, GA: Emory University.

Locke, Richard M., and Kathleen Thelen. 1995. "Apples and Oranges Revisited: Contextualized Comparisons and the Study of Comparative Labor Politics." *Comparative Political Studies* 23:337–67.

Loveman, Brian. 1993. *The Constitution of Tyranny: Regimes of Exception in Spanish America*. Pittsburgh, PA: University of Pittsburgh Press.

Mainwaring, Scott, Daniel M. Brinks, and Aníbal Pérez-Liñán. 2007. "The Evolution of Democracy in Latin America, 1945–2004." In *Regimes and Democracy in Latin America: Theories and Methods*, ed. G. Munck. Oxford; New York, NY: Oxford University Press.

Mainwaring, Scott, Daniel Brinks, and Anibal Pérez-Liñán. 2001. "Classifying Political Regimes in Latin America, 1945–1999." *Studies in Comparative International Development* 36 (1 (Spring)):37–65.

Mainwaring, Scott, and Matthew Soberg Shugart, eds. 1997. *Presidentialism and Democracy in Latin America*. New York, NY: Cambridge University Press.

Mainwaring, Scott, and Christopher Welna, eds. 2003. *Democratic Accountability in Latin America*. Oxford: Oxford University Press.

Maldonado Aguirre, Alejandro. 1984. *Las Constituciones de Guatemala*. Guatemala City: Editorial Piedra Santa.

2004. *Testigo de los testigos*. Guatemala City: Serviprensa.

Martínez Dalmau, Rubén. 2004. "El proceso constituyente venezolano de 1999: un ejemplo de activación democrática del poder constituyente." In *El sistema político en la*

Constitución Bolivariana de Venezuela, ed. L. Salamanca, Pastor, R. V., & Asensi, J. Caracas: Vadell Hermanos Editores.

Mayorga, René. 2007. "El autoritarismo del gobierno del MAS hunde a la Asamblea Constituyente." *Infolatam*, November 29, 2007. Available at http://www.infolatam .com/2007/11/29/el-autoritarismo-del-gobierno-del-mas-hunde-a-la-asamblea-constituyente/.

Mayorga Ugarte, Fernando. 2006. "Referéndum y Asamblea Constitutyente: Autonomías departamentales en Bolivia." *Colombia Internacional* 64 (jul–dic):50–67.

Melton, James, and Tom Ginsburg. 2014. "Does de jure Judicial Independence Really Mattter? A Reevaluation of Explanations for Judicial Independence." *Journal of Law and Courts* 2 (2):187–217.

Merryman, John Henry. 1985. *The Civil Law Tradition: An Introduction to the Legal Systems of Western Europe and Latin America*, 2nd edn. Stanford, CA: Stanford University Press.

Moustafa, Tamir. 2003. "Law Versus the State: The Judicialization of Politics in Egypt." *Law & Social Inquiry* 28 (4):883–930.

Navia, Patricio, and Julio Ríos Figueroa. 2005. "The Constitutional Adjudication Mosaic of Latin America." *Comparative Political Studies* 38 (2):189–217.

Negretto, Gabriel L. 2013. *Making Constitutions: Presidents, Parties, and Institutional Choice in Latin America*. Cambridge; New York, NY: Cambridge University Press.

Nielson, Daniel L., and Matthew Soberg Shugart. 1999. "Constitutional Change in Colombia: Policy Adjustment through Institutional Reform." *Comparative Political Studies* 32 (3):313–41.

Nohlen, Dieter. 2005. *Elections in the Americas: A Data Handbook*. 2 vols. New York, NY: Oxford University Press.

North, Douglass C., and Barry R. Weingast. 1989. "Constitutions and Commitment – the Evolution of Institutions Governing Public Choice in 17th-Century England." *Journal of Economic History* 49 (4):803–32.

Nunes, Rodrigo. 2010a. "Ideational Origins of Progressive Judicial Activism: The Colombian Constitutional Court and the Right to Health." *Latin American Politics and Society* 52 (3):67–97.

  2010b. "Politics Without Insurance: Democratic Competition and Judicial Reform in Brazil." *Comparative Politics* 42 (3):313–31.

O'Donnell, Guillermo. 1996. "Illusions about Consolidation." *Journal of Democracy* 7 (1): 34–51.

O'Donnell, Guillermo A. 2003. "Horizontal Accountability: The Legal Institutionalization of Mistrust." In *Democratic Accountability in Latin America*, ed. S. M. a. C. Welna. Oxford: Oxford University Press.

  2010. *Democracy, Agency, and the State: Theory with Comparative Intent*. Oxford: Oxford Studies in Democratization. 264 p.

Pásara, Luis. 2012. "International Support for Justice Reform in Latin America: Worthwhile or Worthless?" In *Woodrow Wilson Center Update on the Americas*, ed. Woodrow Wilson International Center for Scholars. Washington, DC: Woodrow Wilson International Center for Scholars.

Pereira, Anthony W. 2005. *Political (In)justice: Authoritarianism and the Rule of Law in Brazil, Chile, and Argentina*. Pittsburgh, PA: University of Pittsburgh Press.

Pérez Perdomo, Rogelio. 2003. "Venezuela 1958–1999: The Legal System in an Impaired Democracy." In *Latin Legal Cultures in the Age of Globalization. Latin Europe and Latin America*, ed. L. M. Friedman and R. Pérez Perdomo. Stanford, CA: Stanford University Press.

Pou Giménez, Francisca. 2012. "Judicial Review and Rights Protection in Mexico: The Limits of the2011 Amparo Reform." In *Joint ITAM-University of Texas Seminar*. Mexico City: Instituto Técnico Autónomo de Mexico. Available at SSRN: http://ssrn.com/abstract=2210959 or http://dx.doi.org/10.2139/ssrn.2210959.

Pozas-Loyo, A., and J. Rios-Figueroa. 2010. "Enacting Constitutionalism The Origins of Independent Judicial Institutions in Latin America." *Comparative Politics* 42 (4):293–311.

Prado, Carlos Vidal. 2001. "La Reforma Constitucional en Bolivia." *Revista de Derecho Político* 50:313–47.

Ríos Figueroa, Julio. 2011. "Institutions for Constitutional Justice in Latin America." In *Courts in Latin America*, ed. G. Helmke and J. Ríos Figueroa. Cambridge; New York, NY: Cambridge University Press.

Ríos Figueroa, Julio, and Jeffrey Staton. 2014. "An Evaluation of Cross-National Measures of Judicial Independence." *Journal of Law, Economics and Organization* 30 (1):104–37.

Rios-Figueroa, Julio, and Matthew M. Taylor. 2006. "Institutional Determinants of the Judicialisation of Policy in Brazil and Mexico." *Journal of Latin American Studies* 38:739–66.

Rodríguez Garavito, César. 2009. *"Assessing the Impact and Promoting the Implementation of Structural Judgments: A Comparative Case Study of ESCR Rulings in Colombia."* Bogotá, Colombia: University of the Andes and Dejusticia.

   2010. "Toward a Sociology of the Global Rule of Law Field: Neoliberalism, Neoconstitutionalism, and the Contest over Judicial Reform in Latin America." In *Lawyers and the Rule of Law in an Era of Globalization*, ed. B. Garth and Y. Dezalay. Oxon: Routledge.

Rodríguez Garavito, César, and Diana Rodríguez Franco. 2010. *Cortes y Cambio Social: Cómo la Corte Constitucional transformó el desplazamiento forzado en Colombia*. Bogotá: Dejusticia.

Rosenberg, G. N. 1992. "Judicial Independence and the Reality of Political Power." *Review of Politics* 54 (3):369–98.

Rosenberg, Gerald N. 1991. *The Hollow Hope: Can Courts Bring About Social Change?* Chicago, IL: University of Chicago Press.

   2008. *The Hollow Hope: Can Courts Bring About Social Change?* 2nd edn. Chicago, IL: University of Chicago Press.

Rosenn, Keith S. 1987. "The Protection of Judicial Independence in Latin America." *Inter-American Law Review* 19 (1):1–35.

Sager, Lawrence. 2004. "The Why of Constitutional Essentials." *Fordham Law Review* 72:1421–33.

Salamanca Trujillo, Daniel. 2005. *La entecada arquitectura de las 18 constituciones de Bolivia, 1826–2005: de la Asamblea constituyente originaria a la Asamblea constituyente constitucional*. La Paz: Daniel Salamanca T.

Salas, Luis. 2001. "From Law and Development to Rule of Law: New and Old Issues in Justice Reform in Latin America." In *Rule of Law in Latin America: The International Promotion of Judicial Reform*, ed. P. Domingo and R. Sieder. London: Institute of Latin American Studies.

Santivañez, J. A. R. 2009. "Tribunal constitucional (Bolivia)." In *Cronica de Tribunales Constitucionales en Iberoamerica*, ed. E. F. MacGregor. Buenos Aires: Marcial Pons.

Santos, Boaventura de Sousa. 2010. *Refundación del Estado en América Latina: Perspectivas desde una epistemología del Sur*. Lima: Instituto Internacional de Derecho y Sociedad.

Sarles, Margaret J. 2001. "USAID's Support of Justice Reform in Latin America." In *Rule of Law in Latin America: The International Promotion of Judicial Reform*, ed. P. Domingo and R. Sieder. London: Institute of Latin American Studies.

Scalia, Antonin, and Bryan A. Garner. 2012. Reading Law: The Interpretation of Legal Texts. St. Paul, MN: Thomson/West.

Schavelzon, Salvador. 2012. *El Nacimiento del Estado Plurinacional de Bolivia: Etnografía de una Asamblea Constituyente*. La Paz: CEJIS/Plural editores.

Schilling-Vacaflor, Almut. 2011. "Bolivia's New Constitution: Towards Participatory Democracy and Political Pluralism?" *European Review of Latin American and Caribbean Studies* 90 (April):3–22.

Schor, Miguel. 2008. "An Essay on the Emergence of Constitutional Courts: The Cases of Mexico and Colombia." *Indiana Journal of Global Legal Studies* 16 (1):173–94.

Seawright, Jason, and David Collier. 2014. "Rival Strategies of Validation: Tools for Evaluating Measures of Democracy." *Comparative Political Studies* 47 (1):111–38.

Segado, Francisco. 2001. "La Jurisdicción Constitucional en Bolivia. La Ley No. 1836 de Abril 1998 del Tribunal Constitucional (I)." *Verfassung Und Recht in Übersee/Law and Politics in Africa, Asia and Latin America* 34 (3):315–47.

Segal, Jeffrey, and Harold Spaeth. 2002. *The Supreme Court and the Attitudinal Model Revisited*. Cambridge: Cambridge University Press.

Segovia, Juan Fernando. 2007. "Aproximación Al Pensamiento Jurídico Y Político De Arturo Enrique Sampay. Catolicismo, Peronismo Y Socialismo Argentinos." In *Dialnet*: http://dialnet.unirioja.es/servlet/fichero_articulo?codigo=2860792&orden=0.

Shapiro, Martin. 1981. *Courts: A Comparative and Political Analysis*. Chicago; London: University of Chicago Press.

2001. "The European Court of Justice." In *Judicial Independence in the Age of Democracy: Critical Perspectives from Around the World*, ed. P. H. Russell and D. M. O'Brien. Charlottesville, VA: University Press of Virginia.

Shapiro, Martin, and Alec Stone Sweet. 2002. *On Law, Politics and Judicialization*. Oxford; New York, NY: Oxford University Press.

Siavelis, Peter. 2000. *The President and Congress in Postauthoritarian Chile: Institutional Constraints to Democratic Consolidation*. University Park, PA: Pennsylvania State University Press.

Sieder, Rachel, Line Schjolden, and Alan Angell, eds. 2005. *The Judicialization of Politics in Latin America*. New York, NY: Palgrave Macmillan.

Sigal, Martín, Diego Morales, and Julieta Rossi. 2016. "Argentina: The implementation of collective cases." In *Compliance with socio-economic rights judgments: making it stick*, ed. C. Rodriguez Garavito and M. Langford. New York: Cambridge University Press.

Skaar, Elin. 2011. *Judicial Independence and Human Rights in Latin America: Violations, Politics, and Prosecution*, 1st edn. New York, NY: Palgrave Macmillan.

Staton, Jeffrey. 2004. "Judicial Policy Implementation in Mexico City and Mérida." *Comparative Politics* 37 (1):41–60.

Staton, Jeffrey K. 2010. *Judicial Power and Strategic Communication in Mexico*. Cambridge, UK; New York, NY: Cambridge University Press.

Staton, Jeffrey, and Will Moore. 2011. "Judicial Power in Domestic and International Politics." *International Organization* 65 (3):553–87.

Stone Sweet, Alec. 1999. "Judicialization and the Construction of Governance." *Comparative Political Studies* 32 (2):147–84.

Tate, C. Neal, and Linda Camp Keith. 2007. "Conceptualizing and Operationalizing Judicial Independence Globally," paper delivered at the 2007 *Annual Meeting of the American Political Science Association*, August 30–September 1, 2007, Chicago, IL. Available at Linda Camp Keith, Faculty Page, www.utdallas.edu/~lck016000/APSA2006.doc.

Tate, C. Neal, and Torbjörn Vallinder. 1995a. "The Global Expansion of Judicial Power: The Judicialization of Politics." In *The Global Expansion of Judicial Power*, ed. C. N. Tate and T. Vallinder. New York, NY: New York University Press.

eds. 1995b. *The Global Expansion of Judicial Power*. New York, NY: New York University Press.

Thury Cornejo, Valentín. 2005. *Sistema Político y Aprendizaje Constitucional: A diez años de la reforma de 1994*. Buenos Aires: Universidad Católica Argentina.

Uprimny, Rodrigo. 2011. "The Recent Transformation of Constitutional Law in Latin America: Trends and Challenges." *Texas Law Review* 89:1587–609.

Urueña, René. 2012. "The Rise of the Constitutional Regulatory State in Colombia: The Case of Water Governance." *Regulation and Governance* 6 (3):282–99.

Vanberg, Georg. 2001. "Legislative-Judicial Relations: A Game-Theoretic Approach to Constitutional Review." *American Journal of Political Science* 45 (2):346–61.

Weingast, Barry R. 1997. "The Political Foundations of Democracy and the Rule of Law." *American Political Science Review* 91 (2):245–63.

2008. "Why Developing Countries Prove So Resistant to the Rule of Law." Paper presented at the University of Texas Comparative Politics Speaker Series, December 4, 2008, Austin, TX: University of Texas at Austin.

Weyland, Kurt. 2013. "The Threat from the Populist Left." *Journal of Democracy* 24 (3):18–32.

Weyland, Kurt, Raúl Madrid, and Wendy Hunter, eds. 2010. *Leftist Governments In Latin America: Successes And Shortcomings*. New York, NY: Cambridge University Press.

Whittington, Keith. 2005. "'Interpose Your Friendly Hand': Political Supports for the Exercise of Judicial Review by the United States Supreme Court." *American Political Science Review* 99 (4 (November)):583–96.

Wilson, Bruce M. 2009. "Rights Revolutions in Unlikely Places: Colombia and Costa Rica." *Journal of Politics in Latin America* 1 (2):59–85.

Wilson, Bruce M., Juan Carlos Rodríguez Cordero, and Roger Handberg. 2004. "The Best Laid Schemes . . . Gang Aft A-gley: Judicial Reform in Latin America – Evidence from Costa Rica." *Journal of Latin American Studies* 36:507–31.

Yaksic, Fabián II. 2010. Asamblea Legislativa Plurinacional. *Desafíos, organizaciones, atribuciones y agenda legislativa*. La Paz: Muela del Diablo Editores.

Yamin, Alicia Ely, and Siri Gloppen, eds. 2011. *Litigating Health Rights: Can Courts Bring More Justice to Health?* Cambridge, MA: Harvard University Press.

Yamin, Alicia Ely, Oscar Parra-Vera, and Camila Gianella. 2011. "Colombia – Judicial Protection of the Right to Health: An Elusive Promise?" In *Litigating Health Rights: Can Courts Bring More Justice to Health?*, ed. A. E. Yamin and S. Gloppen. Cambridge, MA: Harvard University Press.

Index

erga omnes effects, 98
Estevez Boero, Guillermo, 166
expressive value of law, 60

Federalist Papers, 24, 27
Fernández, Cristina, 39
Foucault, Michel, 166
France
    Conseil Constitutionnel, 28, 239

García Bauer, Carlos, 112, 122
García Bauer, José Francisco, 129
García Lema, Alberto, 140, 153
García Linera, Álvaro, 197
German Constitutional Court, 128
Gil Lavedra, Ricardo, 153
Godoy, Víctor Hugo, 120
González Quesada, Carlos, 116
Guatemala, 40
    Amparo Tribunal, 99, 100
    Comisión de Amparo, Exhibición Personal y
        Constitucionalidad, 106
    Commission of the Thirty, 106
Guatemala Court of Constitutionality, 102, 109
Guatemalan Constitutional Court, 102

habeas corpus, 97, 120, 177, 187, 200
Haiti, 40
Hamilton, Alexander, 27
hegemonic preservation, 17, 52, 54, 55, 132
Honduras, 40
human rights, 71, 79, 119, 151
human rights treaties, incorporation, 136, 151,
    169, 170

ideology, 43, 69–71, 84, 118, 213, 223
ideology, influence of, 58
impeachment, 33, 41
indigenous rights, 42, 149, 151
indigenous rights, Argentina, 151
informal institution, 131
institution, transitional, 12
institutional design, 29, 43, 44–6, 229
institutions, 46, 158
    informal, 45, 159
institutions, weak, 43
insurance, 17
insurance theory, 52, 54, 167
inter partes effects, 98

judicial authority, 17, 19, 28, 27–8, 30, 77–80, 223
    Argentina, 149
    Bolivia, 188
    Colombia, 174

Guatemala, 117
Nicaragua, 175
Venezuela, 210
judicial autonomy, 3, 17, 19, 20, 23, 30, 223
    Argentina, 141, 142, 149, 159
    Bolivia, 188, 207
    Colombia, 174
    ex ante, 25, 26, 33, 80–2, 159–62, 203
    ex post, 25, 26, 33, 82–4, 162–4, 203
    Guatemala, 115
    Nicaragua, 175
    Venezuela, 211
judicial behavior, 22, 25, 29, 45, 46, 220
judicial behavior theories, 25
Judicial Council, Argentina, 164
judicial culture, 131
judicial design. *See* constitutional design
judicial impartiality, 24, 158, 220
judicial independence. *See* judicial autonomy
judicial protagonism, 2
judicial review, 3
judicial tenure, 27
jurisdiction, 28
jurisdiction stripping, 27

Kammerath, Germán, 163

labor rights, 6, 101
labor rights, Argentina, 146
Lazarte, Jorge, 178, 190, 193, 204, 210
Learned Hand, 217
learning, 62, 83, 224
legal realist, 11
Liberty Claim, *Acción de Libertad*, 200
Life terms. *See* judicial tenure
Llamosas, Esteban, 168
López, Luis Alfonso, 95

M-19, 173
Madison, James, 24
Maduro, Nicolás, 212
Maldonado Aguirre, Alejandro, 106, 113, 114, 116,
    127
Maqueda, Juan Carlos, 160
Mayorga, René, 194
Melgarejo, Mariano, 185
Menem, Carlos, 135, 153
Meoño, Gustavo, 112
military coup, 37
military coup, Chile, 132
military junta, 104
military justice, 121
military rule, 41
Monez Ruiz, Horacio Conesa, 161

CPSIA information can be obtained
at www.ICGtesting.com
Printed in the USA
LVHW101542230821
695911LV00012B/1217

9 781316 630914